Industrial Relations in the NHS

D0227716

To my wife Anne and to my children –
Sarah, Joseph, Rachel, Adam, Hannah and Judith

Industrial Relations in the NHS

Roger Seifert

Senior Lecturer in Industrial Relations,
University of Keele, UK

CHAPMAN & HALL

London · New York · Tokyo · Melbourne · Madras

Published by Chapman & Hall, 2–6 Boundary Row, London SE1 8HN

Chapman & Hall, 2–6 Boundary Row, London SE1 8HN, UK

Blackie Academic & Professional, Wester Cleddens Road, Bishopbriggs, Glasgow G64 2NZ, UK

Chapman & Hall, 29 West 35th Street, New York NY10001, USA

Chapman & Hall Japan, Thomson Publishing Japan, Hirakawacho Nemoto Building, 6F, 1-7-11 Hirakawa-cho, Chiyoda-ku, Tokyo 102, Japan

Chapman & Hall Australia, Thomas Nelson Australia, 102 Dodds Street, South Melbourne, Victoria 3205, Australia

Chapman & Hall India, R. Seshadri, 32 Second Main Road, CIT East, Madras 600 035, India

Distributed in the USA and Canada by
Singular Publishing Group Inc.,
4284 41st Street, San Diego, California 92105

First edition 1992

© 1992 Chapman & Hall

Typeset in 10 on 12 Palatino by EXPO Holdings Sdn Bhd, Malaysia
Printed in Great Britain by St Edmundsbury Press Ltd, Bury St Edmunds, Suffolk

ISBN 0 412 31870 9   1 56593 040 1 (USA)

A catalogue record for this book is available from the British Library

Contents

Acknowledgements

I received help and support from all those I approached from within the NHS. In particular, from all staff organization representatives and managers who agreed to answer my insistent questions.

Phil Gray was involved in preparing some of the material for Chapter 4 and gave his support to the project in its early days.

Dr Audrey Jacobs prepared considerable amounts of material for Chapter 5, and also helped with several other chapters. She gave her enthusiastic support to the book and was a great friend when the going was rough.

Steve Weekes took the trouble to read through the final draft and provided some valuable comments.

Preface

This is the first book yet written on industrial relations in the NHS and it has been completed at a time of radical and rapid change. Some of the material, particularly in the final chapter, reflects first thoughts about the impact of the new system on industrial relations.

The book arose from my teaching experiences with health service practitioners from several of the NHS trade unions and professional associations. Many of these activists, as well as managers, expressed frustration that there was no single source about some of the issues which concerned them. This book is the result of their anxieties.

Throughout, I have assumed that the main thrust of government policy towards the NHS, at least since the early 1980s, has been to sell off important sections of the service to the private sector. There is, I believe, strong evidence for this proposition. My argument, however, is based not only on the evidence of government's will to 'privatize', but also on the behaviour of ministers, senior civil servants and senior NHS managers which adds up to a set of policies and practices which together allow the point that government runs the NHS *as if* it was going to sell it.

That is, therefore, the starting point and the rest of the book flows from the consequences of putting into place the relevant employer and management structures and practices. The book's scope is limited to the industrial relations aspects of the traditional and reformed NHS. These 'aspects' are mainly concerned with the institutions, relationships and results of collective bargaining.

Abbreviations

A&C	administrative and clerical
A&E	accident and emergency
ACAS	Advisory, Conciliation and Arbitration Service
ACB	Association of Clinical Biochemists
AHA	Area Health Authority
ANA	Association of Nurse Administrators
APEX	Association of Professional, Executive, Clerical and Computer Staff
AScW	Association of Scientific Workers
ASM	Association of Supervisors of Midwives
ASSET	Association of Supervisory Staffs, Executives and Technicians
ASTMS	Association of Scientific, Technical and Managerial Staffs
AUEW	Amalgamated Union of Engineering Workers
BAOT	British Association of Occupational Therapists
BDA	British Dental Association
BDA	British Dietetic Association
BHA	British Hospitals Association
BMA	British Medical Association
BMJ	*British Medical Journal*
BOS	British Orthoptic Society
COHSE	Confederation of Health Service Employees
CPSM	Council of Professions Supplementary to Medicine
CSEU	Confederation of Shipbuilding and Engineering Unions
CSP	Chartered Society of Physiotherapists
DATA	Draughtsmen and Allied Technicians Association
DDRB	Doctors' and Dentists' Review Body
DGH	district general hospital

DGM	District General Manager
DHA	District Health Authority
DHSS	Department of Health and Social Security
DMT	District Management Team
DMU	directly managed unit
DPO	District Personnel Officer
EETPU	Electrical, Electronic, Telecommunications and Plumbing Union
EOC	Equal Opportunities Commission
EOP	Equal Opportunities Policy
FPO	Federation of Professional Organizations
FPS	Family Practitioner Services
FUMPO	Federation Union of Managerial and Professional Officers
GDP	General Dental Practitioner
GMBATU	General Municipal, Boilermakers and Allied Trades Union
GMC	General Medical Council
GP	General Practitioner
GWC	General Whitley Council
HPA	Hospital Physicists Association
HSC	Health Services Committee (of TUC)
HSI	health service indicator
HVA	Health Visitors' Association
HWSU	Hospitals and Welfare Services Union
IHA	Independent Hospitals Association
IHSA	Institute of Health Service Administrators
IDS	Incomes Data Service
IMS	Institute of Manpower Studies
IRO	Industrial Relations Officer
IRS	Industrial Relations Service
IT	Industrial Tribunal
JCC	Joint Consultative Committee
JNC	Joint Negotiating Committee
JSC	Joint Staff Committee
JSSC	Joint Shop Stewards Committee
MEA	Municipal Employees' Association
MHA	Mental Hospitals Association
MHIWU	Mental Hospitals and Institutional Workers Union
MLSO	Medical Laboratory Scientific Officer
MSF	Manufacturing, Science and Finance

NALGO	National and Local Government Officers Association
NAHA	National Association of Health Authorities
NAHSPO	National Association of Health Service Personnel Officers
NAO	National Audit Office
NASA	National Ambulance Services Association
NAWU	National Asylum Workers Union
NBPI	National Board of Prices and Incomes
NES	New Earnings Survey
NHS	National Health Service
NUCO	National Union of County Officers
NUCW	National Union of Corporation Workers
NUGSAT	National Union of Gold, Silver and Allied Trades
NUPE	National Union of Public Employees
OME	Office of Manpower Economics
PAM	Professions Allied to Medicine
pbr	payment-by-results
PI	performance indicator
PLWTU	Poor Law Workers Trade Union
POWAR	Place of Work Accredited Representatives
PRB	Pay Review Body
prp	performance related pay
PT'A'	Professional and Technical Council 'A'
PT'B'	Professional and Technical Council 'B'
RAWP	Resource Allocation Working Party
RCM	Royal College of Midwives
RCN	Royal College of Nursing
RHA	Regional Health Authority
SEN	State Enrolled Nurse
SGT	self-governing trust
SMA	Socialist Medical Association
SoC	Society of Chiropodists
SoR	Society of Radiographers
SRN	State Registered Nurse
TASS	Technical, Administrative and Supervisory Section
TGWU	Transport and General Workers Union
TQM	total quality management
TUC	Trades Union Congress

Abbreviations

UCATT	Union of Construction, Allied Trades and Technicians
UGM	Unit General Manager
UKCC	United Kingdom Central Council
UPO	Unit Personnel Officer
USDAW	Union of Shop, Distributive and Allied Workers
wte	whole time equivalent

Chapter 1

Work, wages and the industrial relations tradition

INTRODUCTION

The reform of the NHS in the 1990s represents the greatest change to the provision of health care in the United Kingdom since the setting up of the NHS itself in 1948. Much of the reform programme is centred around financial systems based on limiting funds and stimulating managerial controls. The industrial relations within the NHS are a main element of this new corporate strategy, and will play a key part in the success of the new methods of allocating resources. It is the allocation of resources which is the prime mover in the current situation. The Conservative governments of the 1980s argued consistently that the real issue in the funding of the NHS was not the level of available resources, but rather the management of those resources. Within that is the question of how the resources are allocated as between regions, types of health activity, specialisms and medical procedures. This in turn raises a further question of how resources are allocated as between equipment, staffing levels and the employers' costs of employing any given mix of labour. It is this latter point which, in a labour-intensive industry, places pay determination and other industrial relations issues near the heart of the changes.

For most staff in the NHS the pay determination system can be characterized as a national level one in which a multi-employer group meets a multi-union group. Even with Pay Review Bodies (PRBs) for three-fifths of staff, this still describes the basic activity. The current reforms, with their self-governing trusts (SGTs) and directly managed units (DMUs), mean that there is a move away from multi-employer bargaining to single-employer bargaining. This has two main consequences which stem from the benefits of multi-employer bargaining: the new employers will need to form bargaining data bases and negotiating expertise which previously resided at national level. Secondly, and more important, health service employers will for the first time compete against each other for available labour and therefore face the possibility of pushing wages of some groups of staff higher and higher, of reducing the pay of others, and of cutting the numbers of staff.

These consequences are most prized by those employers and managers who have fought for their right to manage and their freedom to run the business as they want. This 'freedom' to manage is seen as freedom from restrictive Department of Health officials, from incompetent planners at regional level, from personnel managers seeking to impose constraints on line managers' ability to manage, and finally, freedom from trade union power.

It is the avowed objective of the reformers and of many managers that the service must become more productive. Higher productivity, therefore, forms the central managerial objective required to meet corporate objectives. The search for higher productivity leads to the implementation of flexible working practices and payment systems: flexible hours, flexible staffing levels, flexible skills and flexible remuneration packages containing an increasing number of individual performance related pay arrangements.

Once the new single employer has set its strategic objectives then other sub-strategic options become available. Within the new employer's business bargaining may take place at various levels: company-wide or workplace. The unit of bargaining, that is the groups into which the workforce are divided for bargaining purposes, may alter from the traditional functional and/or occupational (such as nurses and ancillary staffs) to cost centres which contain a range of staff or to clinical directorates.

Finally, there is the scope of the bargain to consider. This may vary as to level and unit depending on the issue, so that, for example, negotiations over time off for trade union duties may embrace all staff at the level of the employer, while oncall payments may be negotiated with each group at the lowest operational level. This assumes that the employer will continue to bargain with recognized trade unions for all groups of staff. Recent government policy and recommendations from senior managers within the NHS at national level suggest a mood for some limits on both the numbers of recognized unions and the extent of bargaining. All these points will be examined in greater detail in the final chapter, but they provide a starting point for a book concerned with the central aspects of collective bargaining: the parties, the nature of their relationship, and the outcome of the bargaining processes.

This chapter examines the importance of wages in the NHS industrial relations tradition, the nature of that tradition and recent changes, the powerful influence of customary bargaining on wage differences, and the current composition of NHS staff and management.

WORK AND WAGES

Work and wages form a fundamental aspect of modern society and combine to define the limits of job regulation. They are of great importance for both the individual and the community. The sort of work that people undertake is one important factor in explaining differences in 'morbidity, mortality, fertility, social outlook and political allegiance'.[1] One consequence of this is that those who follow a common occupation will tend to form together to protect and advance their common interests. One central element of industrial relations in the NHS is the existence and influence of powerful trade unions and professional associations. The level of union membership among all NHS occupations is currently very high although that was not always the case. One main line of argument in this book is that when employers, directed by government policy in the broad, authorize their managers to seek to improve levels of labour productivity in order to achieve set organizational objectives, then the overwhelming concern of those managers is how to control the work effort and direction of their workforce. In this search for managerial controls through management rights comes the ever more complex and subtle task of dealing with, and through, the representative bodies of the various occupations and work groups that exist in all parts of the health service. The deal has two main aspects: the carrot in the form of reward levels and payment systems, and the stick in terms of job loss and career blockages.

The British Medical Association was established in 1832, the National Union of Teachers in 1870, and somewhere in between there grew the associations of skilled craftsmen that formed the basis of the modern trade union movement.[2]

Routh's starting point, as mine, is with the trade unions and professional associations which represent the majority of employees. His main purpose was to examine and explain differences in occupational pay, including the impact of trade unionism, from 1906 to 1979. He was in no doubt of the great importance of the issue to a wider understanding of work organizations and society in general. His concern with the role of trade unions and professional associations places him firmly in the tradition of English historians and political economists who recognize the importance of the institutions associated with collective bargaining as essential to the practical understanding of wage determination. This tradition is nowhere better represented than in the considerable works of Thorold Rogers. His history of 600 years of work and wages led him to the view, first expressed in the 1884 edition, that:

I set great store by the reparative energy of labour partnerships or trade unions in improving the material prospects of the working classes. These institutions were repressed with passionate violence and malignant watchfulness as long as it was possible to do so. When it was necessary to relax the severities of the older laws, they were still persecuted by legal chicanery whenever oppression could on any pretence be justified. As they were slowly emancipated, they have constantly been the object of alarmist calumnies and sinister predictions.[3]

Another leading commentator, Phelps Brown, has developed these themes, noting that by the 1970s, 'the question of what the rate of pay for this or that job ought to be has become at once a more open and a more insistent one'.[4] In particular he is concerned to illustrate the long-term impact on wage differences of trade union activity, government policy and the power of custom. These factors are seen as ones that alter the workings of the labour market, and hence create differences that might otherwise, in some theories, have been eliminated.

It appears that for more than 100 years commentators on the industrial relations and wage determination of English employees have been concerned with the relationship of political economy to work and wages, and that the role of 'labour partnerships' has been one major factor in the analysis. This book also places the various (more than 30) trade unions and professional associations, representing the vast majority of the million employees working in the NHS, as major determinants in the work and wages within the NHS. This chapter provides a sketch of the pay levels of the various staff with special interest in their relative real pay and some recent changes. It is one of the book's main themes that the internal relativities as between occupations in the NHS is a major source of both customary bargaining practices and worker perceptions of the fairness of the wage–effort bargain. Much of the subtext of the reforms of the 1990s deals with management's concern with achieving higher levels of productivity through controls over performance at lower labour costs. Current industrial relations in the NHS, therefore, are about the ways in which the institutions and their members react to the mixture of traditional arrangements with new reforms to effect the results of bargains within the variety of national and local collective and individual bargaining forums. As Phelps Brown concludes, where there is an effective labour market then the relative pay of occupations varies with ability, education and training, experience, responsibility and status; but customary pay differences become much more important for those occupations 'whose pay, within limits, is insulated from the forces of the market'.[5]

INDUSTRIAL RELATIONS AND THE NHS

A book on industrial relations in the NHS must address the central aspects of the subject itself. These are still based on the best elements of Flanders's version of job regulation[6] – that work and wages should be regulated, on a pluralist perspective of reality, through formal and orderly joint rule-making activity. This dominant approach must be tempered by an awareness of the limitations of liberal pluralism as an analytical device for defining the relevant issues,[7] and in particular its failure to treat the work grievances of employees as one major point of departure in the analysis of industrial relations. The central concerns of the pluralist tradition are how agreements are reached and once reached how implemented. The rule-based nature of the subject displays itself in the importance of procedural rules over substantive ones. This implies that the 'how' of making and implementing is more important than the actual levels of pay and conditions of service. On this view the single best way to achieve order and control in the pursuit of organizational objectives such as minimizing costs and maximizing patient care is through joint regulation. This, in turn, is best achieved through collective bargaining and the institutionalization of possible and actual conflict through a variety of grievance and disputes procedures operating at the level best suited to the current bargaining structure. Such a general proposition was accepted by the Donovan Commission,[8] and, with the Whitley Reports,[9] remains the most significant view in the British industrial relations tradition.

Whatever perspective is adopted (unitarist, pluralist or Marxist), the major areas of concern are located in pay determination and productivity, and for most practitioners in the NHS that means, first and foremost, collective bargaining. The unitarist perspective treats the business and/or the SGT as a 'team' with managers playing the part of team captain showing leadership qualities and motivating the other team members. Team members must work hard, be loyal to the team, and share the defined goals of the enterprise. The one source of loyalty and authority is the management, and opposition is seen as disruptive and largely unacceptable. In contrast, pluralism accepts the legitimate expression of alternative non-management interests at the place of work as long as they are confined to orderly and reasonable limits.[10] Marxists view both the other perspectives as forms of management ideology and oppose them with worker-based theory. This perspective places conflict and exploitation at the heart of the employment relationship and might well adopt Miliband's famous remark as its catchphrase: industrial relations is 'the consecrated euphemism for the permanent conflict, now acute, now subdued, between capital and labour'.[11]

The parties to any collective bargaining process must be clearly identified. For the NHS these are best described as the trade unions/professional associations being the representative organizations of the vast majority of employees, and managers as the agents and/or representatives of the employers. This approach is particularly suited to the NHS since the dominant tradition has been of national level, multi-employer, multi-union collective bargaining through the structure of Whitley Councils. One important variation from this is the major, some might argue the dominant, role of the relevant Health Department on the employers' side of national negotiations. This provides a necessary corrective to the more straightforward model outlined, and raises the general issue of the state as a 'model employer'.

Our second preliminary concern is the nature of the relationship between managers and the representatives of the staff. Managers act as a collective group claiming certain rights, including the right to manage, based on their dependency on employers invested with the rights of ownership.[12] This notion of the 'right to manage' is also expressed as the right to have the 'freedom to manage'. In this latter formulation the 'freedom' referred to is from bureaucratic health departments, oppressive regional managers, misconceived protective laws on areas such as health and safety, other functional managers such as the personnel officers, and of course, from the unions and professional bodies. In this world the line managers can get on and provide an efficient service to the benefit of all. In other words managers believe that left alone they can manage the industry to a high standard. Such is the unitarist position in which decisions are unilateral and therefore unions obsolete.

The trade unions/professional associations, on the other hand, continue to pursue the interests and defend the rights of their members. These rights are often seen as originating in part from the law (unfair dismissal), in part from the labour market through the employment relationship (rates of pay), and in part from a pool of variable human rights (the right to strike). Whatever the claims of the parties with regard to their rights to manage and the rights of those being managed, the relationship tends to be of one of three, not mutually exclusive, types: communication, consultation and negotiation.

Communicating – a success verb which contains within its own meaning the definition that when one says that one is communicating then one is so doing – is what many managers most want to do well. They want to communicate to their subordinates their decisions and the correctness of their decisions in whatever terms are appropriate. Much management training and some management strategy revolves around communication as the mechanism to gain consent, compliance, trust and loyalty. Recent management reforms in the NHS have reflected an increased emphasis on 'good' communications through techniques such as team briefing, quality circles and employee participation. It is rarely appreciated by the managers themselves that the emphasis on communication as a solution to some industrial relations problems is predicated on an underlying unitarist ideology. Conflict at work is seen, on this view, as abnormal and may often be blamed on a lack of understanding by the employees of the motives, reasons, reasonableness and rationality of the management decisions. This lack of understanding is frequently blamed on poor communications within the organization, and rejects any notion that conflict might be due to alternative versions of reality and rationality. Trade unions/professional associations may well approve of management's efforts to improve the quality and quantity of communications, but they cannot view it as the prime mechanism in their relationship with the management.

Consultation tends to be what it says it is, namely seeking out the opinion of others to suggestions without any obligation to take any notice. Some legal decisions and some governmental advice bodies, such as ACAS, prefer consultation to include a more meaningful element. In the NHS, consultative bodies have often been used as negotiating bodies, and in practice there can be overlap between consultation and negotiation. Managers and the representatives of the staff tend to view consultation as second best. The trade unions/professional associations would, however, much prefer to negotiate.

Negotiating within a collective bargaining structure is what trade unions/professional associations do best, and is largely why they were formed and continue to exist. Managers often resist a negotiated settlement since 'good faith' bargaining requires the employer, through its manager-agents, to abandon some of its rights to control the organization. One aspect of industrial relations history within the NHS and elsewhere is represented by this battle over the right to negotiate on any given issue. What is and what is not negotiable have been described as the two segments of power either side of the 'frontier of control',[13] a moving frontier which reflects changes in power relations over time and which encourages the military metaphor in industrial relations – troops, generals, offensives and entrenched positions. National level collective bargaining through Whitley has been the institutional norm within the NHS and this has set out the issues that are negotiable. From time to time both sides have complained that the negotiations were a sham and this has fed into demands for the reform and/or replacement of Whitley.

The third preliminary concern is with the outcomes of collective bargaining. These are usually divided between substantive and procedural agreements. The former typically cover pay and conditions of service, and the latter procedures on union recognition, discipline and disputes. The procedural agreements, known in the USA as 'impasse resolution mechanisms', provide the form of the institutionalization of conflict as preached by the two great reforms of UK industrial relations this century: Whitley and Donovan. They tend to cover what Fox calls 'managerial relations' rather than the 'market relations' of substantive agreements. While substantive agreements have existed in the NHS since the early 1950s, once the Whitley system started working, most procedural agreements were introduced into health authorities by the mid-1970s. These were negotiated and implemented at the level of the employer in contrast to the national agreements on pay and conditions. Some of the procedural agreements, especially the disputes procedure, involve the potential for industrial action and include the possibility of reference to third party intervention. In practice this tended to be either conciliation or arbitration with less use made of mediation.

Until recently this industrial relations structure has been characterized by multi-employer multi-union bargaining at national level. In simple terms this had the advantages, from an industrial relations perspective, of providing economies of scale in terms of industrial relations expertise and information. It also allowed wages and conditions of service to be generally removed from competition between employers. This would prevent them bidding against each other and pushing pay upwards in tight labour markets. Such cartels are common in the private sector through employers' associations, and as long ago as 1776 Adam Smith commented that:

> We rarely hear ... of the combinations of masters' though frequently of those of workmen. But whoever imagines, upon this account, that masters rarely combine, is as ignorant of the world as of the subject. Masters are always and everywhere in a sort of tacit but constant and uniform combination not to raise the wages of labour above their actual rate.[14]

The new reforms aim to stop this and develop single-employer bargainers with their own industrial relations information and experts. They do not fear wage competition on the grounds that the overall levels of unemployment will allow them to bid competitively against other employers for that section of staff subject to competition from non-NHS employers, and to be more flexible in their approach to pay for those in NHS-only employee categories.

The single-employer trusts will have to decide whether to bargain with all staff on a functional basis, as now, at the level of the company or to move to a more fragmented system of bargaining through separate units at sub-employer levels. In the private sector this would been seen in plant level agreements and separate negotiations with white-collar and manual workers.[15]

Even with the establishment of precise bargaining levels and units there is still the question of with whom to bargain and over what. So union recognition becomes a new political football for employers, and the scope of bargaining in terms of which issues are and are not negotiable looms larger. These generate a set of severe practical problems for the unions and the employers, as will be discussed more fully in Chapter 8. For now, it is worth pausing to examine the notion of flexibility,[16] which is usually divided into functional and numerical flexibility.

This comes in various packages, including hours of work. For example, this may be overtime already worked by porters, flexitime for A&C staff, and more part-time working, already a dominant feature of ancillary work. There can be flexible staffing levels. These include fixed-term and temporary contracts which will escalate, especially for some newly qualified professionals, and the extensive use of subcontracted labour. It may also involve an increase in zero-hour contracts, as already in place for bank nurses.

Next comes flexible skills. A major theme of postwar British modernization has been the removal of traditional demarcations. But job territory is often fiercely defended by occupational groups, especially those practising closed unionism through professional control over the labour supply. None the less, the generic helper, health care assistant and multi-skilled nurse have arrived.

Finally comes flexible pay. This means the make-up of pay will alter. At present most of the professions receive most pay in the basic element determined through Pay Review Bodies. This is added to with a variety of allowances, leads, oncall payments, special payments and so on. The new flexible system will add performance related pay to this and the future may well see basic pay fall to three-quarters of earnings. In such a future basic pay may still be settled by pay review and/or Whitley but the rest will be subject to agreement at employer level. This means a future with a greater variation in the pay of professionals according to region, specialism and shortages. Such a view will distort career patterns and fragment national training and supply. In addition it will put pressure on the representative organizations in terms of their ability to mount national campaigns. Bargaining structures will have to be redesigned, professional and union relationships reconstituted, and pay arguments and principles re-examined.

For the rest of the staff pay flexibility has already started, and will simply continue to be more and more important. Each employer will select different job evaluation schemes, different payment-by-results packages, and different shift and overtime loads. The A&C grades have begun to move over to a range of such schemes, while ancillary staffs may well find their overtime and shift payments becoming the dominant element in their pay package through their incorporation into locally agreed spinal points.

This then is the skeleton and the rest of the book is an attempt to put some flesh onto the bones. So far it has stressed the predominance of national level multi-employer, multi-union bargaining through the Whitley structures. This has undergone three significant changes in emphasis since the beginning of the NHS as far as most staff are concerned.

The first of these changes was the introduction of employer-level local bargaining for some ancillary workers in the late 1960s. This represented a major departure from the NHS customary pay bargaining and subsequently fuelled the increase in trade union membership, the increase in the activity level of union stewards, and heralded a variety of single-employer negotiations. It also encouraged the trade union activities of the professional associations.

The second change occurred in the mid-1980s with the introduction of Pay Review Bodies for over half of the NHS staff. Doctors and dentists had had pay review since the 1960s, but in the 1980s it covered nurses, midwives and health visitors in one report and the professions allied to medicine (PAMs) in another.

The third change has come in the 1990s with the advent of self-governing trusts and directly managed units. This is the move to single-employer bargaining and the likely reduction in the number of trade unions and professional associations recognized for bargaining purposes.

Within this apparently static national collective bargaining tradition has been a set of wider themes. These include the growth in the size and influence of health service trade unions for most of the time since 1948 (Chapter 3), and the concomitant growth in size, influence and trade union activity of the professional associations (Chapter 2). Alongside these features have been employer reorganizations and management reforms (Chapter 4). There have been significant debates and changes to national bargaining arrangements (Chapter 5), the introduction of Pay Review Bodies (Chapter 6) and the development of local bargaining (Chapter 7). Finally, there has been the priority given to the search for higher productivity and greater 'value-for-money' in the late 1980s and 1990s and this has created a pay criterion of affordability (the market) in place of the customary pay comparability as used when the state was perceived, in some theoretical forms at least, as a 'model employer' (Chapter 8).

THEMES

The main thesis of this work, within the more specific hypotheses outlined above, is that the contradictions which dominated the creation of the NHS in 1948 have persisted ever since. These take the form of the role of private medicine within a state system, the funding mechanisms, the act of socialization in a profoundly non-socialist country, the dominant power of the medical profession, and the apparently untrammelled decision-making rights of senior civil servants within the Treasury and the Department of Health. The form of the service that will be provided in the 1990s depends on the outcome of the struggles generated by these central contradictions.

The basic point is that the NHS has been the most important piece of socialist construction in postwar Britain. Its purpose and formulation, more than all the acts of nationalization, embodied fundamental principles of democracy, equality and social ownership. For such a large and pervasive institution to operate in a country dominated by inequality and private ownership and largely governed by politicians and civil servants not committed to many of the norms of democracy (such as openness and accountability), the going has been tough. The combination of economic crises with the pressures subsequently generated on public expenditure, and the constant failure to renew the ideological commitment to a public health service, has created a crisis for the NHS in the 1990s of such proportions that it might end the service. The exact form of this crisis and the proposed reforms of the government will form the subject of the final chapter of this book, but there are major implications for trade union membership and operations, management and employer structures, and the control over pay and performance at local level.

The specifics of many of these points have been dealt with elsewhere in terms of rights of patients, the dominance of certain medical practices, and the economic assumptions behind such levels of public taxation and expenditure. This book is concerned with the industrial relations of the NHS in so far as they can be demonstrated in the tensions between centrally determined pay and local delivery of service, central funding and control over local employers and managers, political appointees to critical management posts, staff structures which reflect hierarchical and undemocratic systems of practice and consultation, unitarist-minded managers with collective bargaining mechanisms to work with, variable levels of and ability to measure labour productivity, and divided and anxious employees and unions.

In general common themes appear and reappear: variable labour market conditions, changing levels of skills, the role of status and qualification as an agent of staff division, the unionization of the workforce, the democratization of the unions, the control over performance at the point of delivery of the service, the distinction between economically viable and non-viable health activities, collective bargaining as the preferred mechanism for determining pay and conditions, and the unhelpful and powerful influence of senior civil servants.

Much of this general analysis can be traced through the history of the NHS. This is not the place for such an account but reference is made to historical traditions and events in so far as they aid the current analysis. The NHS was created out of an odd mixture of municipal hospitals, health services and voluntary hospitals with a variety of other institutions thrown in. This reflected the need for such a rationalization of health care and the dreadful heritage of Victorian values and early twentieth century practice.[17] From the start the NHS was labour-intensive, and therefore the wages, conditions of service and performance of all staff were crucial. The staff, an incoherent mixture of types and skills, had mixed traditions with regard to trade unionism and collective bargaining. With the NHS came a highly centralized national form of Whitley Council for the determination of pay and conditions of employment, but also a rather complex one based on functional councils below a general council.

These wider points are made to remind us that the NHS operates within a dynamic and complex society and is subject to most of the influences of that society. None the less, this book must concentrate on the main elements of industrial relations in the NHS, which include the central debates on pay for the one million staff.

PAY DIFFERENCES

When any industrial relations structure in a labour-intensive industry, such as the NHS, is examined the determination and implementation of pay rates, levels of earnings, the make-up of pay and the bargaining structures are central issues of concern. Workers and their representative organizations are greatly interested in these questions, as are their managers and employers. In this context the government as a whole and the relevant government departments are also greatly concerned. The arguments used to prosecute pay claims are extremely important in this process since the unions require the support of their members and often of the wider community in order to put pressure on their employers and their paymasters. In these circumstances arguments provide a power source for the pay claims as well as the explanations required if groups are to receive pay awards different from those expected and found elsewhere.

Within the NHS, pay differences have taken three specific forms:
1. differences between one group and another within the industry – nurses and doctors, porters and ambulance staff;
2. differences as between a group working in the NHS and an equivalent group working outside as either self-employed private practitioners or for another employer – laboratory technicians, secretaries, managers and drivers;
3. differences within the NHS occupational group – consultants and junior hospital doctors, nursing sisters and nursing auxiliaries, managers and clerical workers.

These pay differences are often referred to as differentials (1 and 2) and internal relativities (3), but the terminology is inconsistent and the more general notion of differences will be used.

A major feature of public service industrial relations in the 1980s was the concerted efforts made by the government to remove comparability as the most favoured form of pay argument and determinant. Margaret Thatcher was said to have 'derided' comparability in a meeting in 1982 with representatives from the health service unions.[18] It was to be replaced by affordability. This was in stark contrast to the previous two decades. These questions are dealt with in greater detail in Chapters 5 and 6, but for now it can be noted that comparability remains the most powerful of the pay arguments put forward by the NHS trade unions/professional associations and the one that has the most support from health workers.[19] Comparability, whether it be with a specific group or with the average earnings index, is essentially a social and moral argument associated with fairness. This was famously expressed for state employees by the Priestly Commission:

> We believe that the State is under a categorical obligation to remunerate its employees fairly, and that any [arrangement] ... which does not explicitly recognize this is not adequate.[20]

The TUC, following Clegg's comparability exercise[21] in 1979, felt that:

> Whatever its merits as a civilized means of ensuring fair pay for NHS staff without disrupting patient care, a negotiated NHS comparability arrangement would be of no value unless both Government and unions were prepared to stand by its terms.[22]

A few general points can be made with regard to customary pay differences and the workforce position on them.

In 1989 there were 490 000 whole time equivalent (wte) nurses working for NHS employers. In that year nurses, midwives and health visitors enjoyed a new grading structure. In this structure the vast majority of staff came under the grades A to G and the spread of pay rates for full-time workers by 1990 was from £5800 to £16 195 – a range of just under three. At this time earnings were still dominated by basic pay and therefore allowances and special payments did not alter this pattern.[23]

The New Earnings Survey (NES) data for nurse managers, nurses and nursing auxiliaries in 1977 and 1990 can be compared to find a general pattern (Table 1.1). The figures in Table 1.1 represent the pay and hours for full-time adult women and cannot be taken as representative of the many part-time workers

Table 1.1 Comparison between earnings of nurse managers, nurses and nursing auxiliaries in 1977 and 1990

	Average gross weekly pay (£)	Over- time (£)	pbr	Shift (£)	Hours Total Ov't
1977					
Nurse manager	78	—	—	2	na
Nurse	52	—	—	2	39.6 0.2
Auxiliary	47	—	—	3	38.6 0.3
1990					
Nurse manager	309	3	—	12	na
Nurse	229	3	—	15	37.7 0.4
Auxiliary	159	4	—	15	37.8 0.8

Source: New Earnings Survey, 1977 and 1990.

and men. None the less, they represent the majority of nurses and therefore any comments do help understand changes in internal relativities. Indeed in 1989 grades A to G represented 80% of wte nurses with about 276 000 on grades C to G (qualified clinical) and another 115 000 on grades A and B (unqualified).[24] The point is that between 1977 and 1990 both nurses and nurse managers pulled away from the auxiliary grades in relative pay. In 1977 the ratios using auxiliary as 1 were nurse 1.1 and nurse manager 1.7, but by 1990 this had moved to nurse 1.4 and nurse manager 1.9.

Internal relativities had moved, but so had the way in which earnings were composed. So in 1977 the nurses had basic pay as 96% of earnings but in 1990 this had become 85%. The next largest pay cost fell into the category of special payments (£542 million or 9.7% of the total). Overtime, weightings, allowances and leads (for psychiatry and geriatrics), while important to the individuals who received them, were of minor import in the total. So, even in 1989/90, after the introduction of new grades and great debates on local pay, the vast majority of nurses depended on the basic wage for the bulk of earnings.

In 1987, the last year of the old structure, 90.6% of all nurses were on the grades of Nursing Auxiliary/Assistant and Nursing Sister/Charge Nurse II, District Nurse, Midwifery Sister. Their pay ranged from £4265 (bottom of Nursing Auxiliary) to £10 800 (top of Nursing Sister II):[25] a factor of 2.5. So the new grading system, whatever else it has achieved, has in its early years widened relative pay amongst the majority of nurses. This prompted large scale appeals against gradings born from the fear that the new system, when linked with the advent of the health care assistant, could mean a permanent change in relativities with higher qualified nurses pulling further away from the lower grades.

How does this compare with other NHS professions?

Doctors are harder to pin down in terms of their pay and earnings. There is a clear split between hospital doctors and GPs. The overall spread of earnings is greater than for nurses, with junior hospital doctors earning four times less than consultants. In addition, consultants earn extra payments through fees, allowances and merit and distinction awards. There is no usable NES data since the definition of medical practitioners is too wide, but the vast majority of doctors earn more than the vast majority of nurses and this accords with traditional job hierarchy, the preponderance of women in nursing, and the bargaining power of the doctors.

In 1989 there were nearly 120 000 doctors and dentists working within the NHS. The three main categories were: hospital medical staff (over 56 000), GPs (just over 30 000) and general dental practitioners (just over 17 000). Again it is worth breaking down the hospital doctors into consultants (nearly 18 000) and others (nearly 38 500).[26] In 1989 a house officer started on a basic wage of £10 280 compared with a consultant's highest increment of £39 340. In addition, however, besides outside fees, consultants are awarded distinction and merit awards. These vary in value from a low C of £6935 to a high A plus of £43 075. The numbers receiving some sort of award is recommended to be 6635, or 38% of all consultants. Three features emerge so far: the spread of hospital doctors' earnings is far greater than for nurses, the numbers receiving payments above basic pay are substantially more than among nurses, and the top basic rate for a G grade nurse (only 3.8% of nurses earn more) is £14 860 which is just above point 3 for a senior house officer (£14 550), of whom about 64% earn more.[27] In other words about 95% of nurses earn less than the lowest third of hospital doctors assuming that the latter have no significant allowances.

The third main professional grouping in the NHS are the PAMs (professions allied to medicine). By the end of 1989 the were nearly 34 000 wte PAMs working in the NHS. As an important number of these are part-time workers, the actual numbers working in the service, and hence belonging to the relevant trade union, is considerably greater.[28] This figure had been nearly 33 000 in 1988, and when helpers and technical instructors are included, the figure is above 42 000.[29] This figure covers seven groups (see Chapter 2). In general they share pay grades, with the April 1990 scale varying from £9460 for Basic grade minimum through the maximum for a Senior I of £15 385 to a Chief/Head/Superintendent III maximum of £16 720. This covers the vast majority of PAMs. Amongst the senior managers, a District Senior Chief in chiropody, for example, can earn £22 495, and a District I physiotherapist, £23 300. The scope for extra earnings is limited mainly to training allowances, oncall payments and London supplements.[30] As with nurses, the vast bulk of pay comes from basic, 90%, and the only other element of note is the near 4% of the wage bill for oncall and standby. The internal relativities for the majority (Basic grade to Superintendent III) is a factor of two.

One major concern for the PAMs is their comparison with nurses. In paper 1 of their evidence to the 1990 Pay Review, they expressed their 'very serious concern about the large gap which has opened up between the evaluation of the work and worth of nurses and that of PAMs'.[31] Customary pay differences in the context of non-market pay determination are the ones that the unions push the hardest and which their members feel the most fair.

All these professional groups make up about three-fifths of the total NHS employees and their pay is now determined through PRBs. The arguments used to support their claims are public and are of vital interest at a time when the industry is moving from multi-employer to single-employer bargaining. The professions in general share the position that their pay needs to reflect NHS comparisons within agreed pay differences They tend to emphasize arguments based on cost of living, comparability, labour market, morale and workload. These correspond with traditional concerns so well presented by Wootton in her book on wage policies. She notes that it is the trade unions that carry the burden of proof for any advance in wages and therefore they will be the more informative. In contrast, the employers have been 'under no pressure to produce any specific arguments at all for rejecting particular wage claims'[32] – a familiar experience in NHS bargaining.

This remains largely the case even under the Pay Review system, in which, on the face of it at least, argument takes preference over power. Wootton continues that, 'in the whole postwar epoch probably the most popular argument for wage advances is the failure of wages to keep pace with the cost of living'.[33] She stresses that the main element in the argument is not whether wages have kept up with prices, but 'the ethical assumption that they ought to do so'.[34]

The next most popular argument is that of comparability. The general case is based on the overall rise in wages so, 'the principle involved is simple: it is assumed that any occupation in which wages can be demonstrated not to have kept pace with the general advance as shown by this index has a *prima facie* case for an increase in pay'.[35] Comparability with specific occupations and/or industries tends to be not well founded in the facts. That is, those making the claim select comparators which have recently done better than they have without great objective heed to the nature of the work and other factors. However, as Wootton suggests, 'the selection of "comparable" occupations quoted in support of wage claims is indeed a revealing process in more ways than one. It certainly shows the powerful influence of social and conventional factors'.[36]

For those seeking pay awards when their ability to take direct industrial action is limited either by rule, law or convention and when they are subject by and large to a monopsonist purchase of their labour, these arguments are paramount. Whether the same importance can be placed on them for those NHS workers who can find alternative work and who can and do take industrial action is another issue, especially when their pay is still determined by the more closed process of bargaining through Whitley.

The pay cases put forward by the unions resemble the emphases and anxieties of the professional health workers. In January 1990, for example, NALGO submitted its pay and service conditions claim for A&C staff. Its stated objectives included an overall increase for each pay point of £18 per week or 12% whichever was the greater. Other items in the claim included abolition of the same points at the bottom of the grades, rectifying anomalies from the previous year's new pay structure, and asking for more long service leave provision. The claim was supported by arguments that the 1989 settlement had started a process of catching up of these grades that had to be continued.

Hence, 'this group remains both bottom heavy and low paid in comparison with similar groups elsewhere in the public and private sector'.[37]

This partly reflected the large numbers of young women in the lowest grades. The evidence was based on (a) the relative poor levels of pay of all public sector workers in the 1980s, and (b) the especially poor levels of pay awards to ancillary and A&C grades. In particular, reference was made to the rate of inflation, the average earnings index, the low maxima for A&C, recruitment and retention issues, and the poor level of female pay.

This encapsulates the points made above about comparisons and other pay arguments, but it also reflects political pressures within NALGO with regard to the low paid, female, young workers and the close links with NUPE and their ancillary workers' pay claims. There are about 130 000 wte workers in the A&C grades and the 1990 average male earnings were £294 per week, which contrasts with the £169 for female and £167 for male ancillary workers. These figures show a greater gap when calculated on a hourly pay basis since male ancillary workers, for example, work seven hours longer per week on average than A&C grades.[38]

The internal relativities for A&C are very great, which partly reflects the heterogeneous quality of the occupations, and also the extent to which some jobs allow greater mobility outside the NHS.

Within the ancillary grades and their representation by NUPE, COHSE, GMB and the TGWU, the situation is the same. Concern is expressed over low pay, women clustered on the bottom of the pay points, the large numbers of part-time workers, and the dependence on overtime and bonus schemes to boost earnings.[39] The variations for NUPE members in this respect are important. In the case of male porters and ambulancemen the NES shows significant differences.

In 1990 a male hospital porter's average gross weekly earnings were £167 and with a median of £161 this meant that more than half earned less than the average. In addition the porter's pay had only 67% as basic with the rest reliant on overtime (17%), bonus (8%) and shift allowances (8%). In contrast, the ambulancemen earned £234, of which 95% was basic and the rest nearly all overtime.

More details of all the settlements are contained in Chapters 2 and 3; what this illustrates is that the main case unions put forward relies heavily on customary and strongly held views of pay differences. One expectation of employers, managers and some workers is that the 1991 single-employer bargainers (the SGTs) will develop a flexible response to these and other considerations not adequately reflected in the Whitley and PRB structures.

Many of the NHS customary pay differences are part of the important gap between the earnings of female and male health workers. This is one of the industries in the UK in which women workers outnumber men, and yet at almost every level and for every occupation there are both men and women working side by side. This has major implications for workforce representation, management strategies of control and flexibility, and on the workers' own perceptions of fair wage comparisons.

The average gross weekly earnings of a full-time female nurse/midwife in April 1990 was £228.9 and this compared with £158.5 for nursing auxiliaries. How did this compare on average with other female workers in major NHS occupations? The equivalent figure was £169.5 for administrative and clerical staff and £139.1 for ancillary staff. Men, however, averaged quite different amounts: A&C £294.4, ancillary £166.6 and ambulancemen £232.3. These are averages and do not take account of part-time workers, hours worked, nor the distribution of earnings. Nevertheless, the picture that soon emerges is that men earn considerably more than women, that the job hierarchy is reflected in pay with doctors at the top and female ancillary workers at the bottom, and that these differences are strongly felt and well established in custom and tradition.

Another important element to be examined is the make-up of pay as between the occupations. These pay levels and other factors tell their own story of bargaining and representative patterns, as well as the power relations between and within the occupational groupings.

Some examples will illustrate the main themes in explaining and analysing occupational pay within the NHS. These include the customary nature of internal relativities; the distinctions in pay structures between the professions, the A&C grades and the manual workers; the ways in which the different groups argue for more pay; and the bargaining consequences of these factors.

Routh studied the long-term changes in pay of doctors and nurses as part of his wider research. In 1913/14 doctors' average pay was £422, but the spread of earnings varied from a lower quartile of £195 through a median of £370 to an upper quartile of £700. By 1955/6 the average was £2320 with a spread from £1794 through £2300 to the upper quartile of £2865. In general there has been some narrowing of differentials.[40] The figures for female doctors are harder to establish until the Pilkington Commission's findings in 1955/6. At that time female consultants averaged £2773 or 82% of the male average.

The average pay of a female nurse in 1913 was £55 and this had risen by 1960 to £424 (a 771% increase). 'In the nursing profession, differentials narrowed until 1955' as between staff nurses and ward sisters, but rose again from 1955 to 1960.[41]

Overall, between 1913 and 1978 real average pay rose by a factor of three in the UK, this means that 'the compounded rate of growth in real income per head has been a little over 1.7 per cent per year'.[42]

The central issues were the occupational shift from lower to higher occupations, the relative rise in female earnings, and the narrowing differentials within occupational groupings. As Routh notes, 'over the whole span, women have done better than men in every class except that of semi-skilled manual workers'.[43] Routh concludes with summary explanations for pay changes in the 1960s and 1970s. As he says, for the decade 1960–1970:

> average pay doubled over the ten years. Amongst the men, the lower professions and semi-skilled did exceptionally well, with the unskilled running them close. Skilled manual workers and managers fell a long way behind, foremen did even worse and higher professionals worst of all. In the case of the women, forewomen, skilled manual and higher professionals did badly ... The unskilled did best ... and the lower professions came next.[44]

In particular doctors and dentists did much worse than the average while nurses moved ahead strongly. In the next ten years pay and prices rose at hectic speeds. Despite this there was little change in the male hierarchy with the exception of managers' substantial relative fall. Meanwhile women's pay increased faster than men's partly due to the early years of the 1975 Equal Pay Act. For example, a female laboratory technician earned, on average, 61% of male pay for the same job in 1970; this had risen to 78% by 1978 and 81% by 1988.

What this section shows is that in general NHS pay reflects wider pay developments, and that in particular there was a closing of the male–female differential, a narrowing of the spread of earnings within the professions and some narrowing as between the lowest paid manual workers and the higher paid professionals. These shifts in differentials were not uniform but the overall job hierarchy remained more or less intact. Thus customary differences, reinforced by bargaining practices and structures, remained part of the NHS work and wages equation from the late 1940s to the late 1980s. As Routh expresses this process:

> The *status quo* is constantly being disturbed, however, by trade unions or professional associations getting better terms for the occupations they represent or by employers unilaterally or by individual bargaining raising the pay of all or some of the occupations or individuals they employ. This is a never-ending process, though the speed at which it operates may show great variation from time to time, and, since there are always some occupations whose members feel aggrieved or that they deserve upgrading in the pay structure, it is unlikely that equilibrium can ever be attained. So the process draws its energy from an endless stock of hope and envy, of which trade unionism is in part an expression.[45]

Of course, there are special and important features about employment in the NHS. Most relevant is that for the professional workers – doctors, nurses and PAMs – there are few, if any, alternative employers. This has two notable consequences: first, because of multi-employer bargaining there is minimal competition as between health authorities in terms of pay and conditions. Secondly, the internal labour market in terms of promotion and specialism plays a highly significant role in pay determination. In order to allow for these factors, pay for these groups was determined partly on a historical basis and partly through the use of outside comparators developed through special pay inquiries, as with Halsbury 1974, Clegg 1980 and the wider findings of Megaw for the Civil Service in 1982.[46] This approach still dominates the cases put forward to the PRBs by the staff side. Of equal importance at present is the case for higher pay based on recruitment and retention difficulties. These refer to young people entering training, and the leakage of staff to other countries, other jobs, the private sector and, mainly, out of the profession for good.

For the professions recruitment is mainly from either the newly qualified or from returners (mainly married women on a part-time basis) at the bottom range, and from other hospitals at senior levels. There is some recruitment from overseas and this may well rise into the 1990s. Retention is a quite separate problem relating to the internal labour market of the business, as opposed to the external labour market for recruitment, and will create quite distinct employment policies often related to promotion and conditions of service rewards for long service.

In contrast with most of the professionals, other staff have transferable skills and work within a labour market dominated by external factors. Porters and cleaners, maintenance workers and secretaries, managers and drivers, can all, if required and given the right circumstances, work in some other industry. Thus their pay, still decided through Whitley, relies more heavily on comparative pay of directly comparable groups, but is also more vulnerable to local labour market conditions, the bargaining strategies of the larger unions, and bonus schemes. For example, in 1990, male ancillary workers worked on average 5.8 hours of overtime. Their average gross weekly earnings were made up as follows: total of £167.1, of which £28.1 was overtime, £13.3 pbr and £13.9 shift premium. That meant that 33.2% of their earnings were from additions to the basic rate. This contrasts with 2.7% for A&C staff. For female ancillary workers the proportion of total earnings from additions to basic was 18.8%. The breakdown for them was: total £139.1, of which £8.3 was overtime, £7.9 pbr and £10.0 from shifts.

This make-up of pay explains some of the bargaining arrangements and pressures and union structures and policies. For example, the bulk of nurses depend on basic pay for their earnings and this reflects national wage bargaining and therefore strong national union pressure. In contrast, the ancillary workers depend on overtime and payment-by-results, which generates an endless stream of grievances at the workplace encouraging local steward activity.[47]

It is not necessary to discuss job content and some of the elements that decide the relative levels of pay in the jobs hierarchy. Market forces do play a role, but these are mutated by institutional factors. Job mobility and skill substitutability are also significant. Managers know that they are paying too little when their secretarial staff leave to work down the road at a large insurance company, or when electricians leave to become self-employed, or when nurses just leave. You do not have to be an economist to know that, all you need to do is read the advertisements in the local press. The ability of managers to pay more to keep staff is controlled by their overall budgets, by the ease of substitution of the staff by lower grades, by the political impact on patient care of staff shortages, and by the agreed rate for the job. In the 1990s managers will be given, on paper at least, the authority to implement payment schemes aimed at resolving these difficulties with fewer institutional barriers to market forces than before. Whether this is a dream come true or a nightmare of uncontrollable monsters is not yet clear.

THE INDUSTRIAL RELATIONS TRADITION

This preliminary discussion is intended to place pay relativities and trade union/professional association activity as major themes in the industrial relations of the NHS. Since its inception the NHS has been characterized by five main organizational developments in the conduct of its industrial relations. These constitute a tradition which in part has its roots in earlier health services, but owes a great deal to the wider traditions of public sector industrial relations in the postwar period. The five factors are:

1. The more or less continuous growth in absolute numbers and density of the trade unions from 222 000 trade union members and 42.6% density in 1948 to 950 000 members with a density of 76% by 1978 and a concomitant growth in influence.[48]
2. The growth in numbers of all professional groups and an expansion of their trade union-like activities.

These first two related factors reflect what Carpenter called 'the phenomenal growth of most unions recruiting among health service staff'.[49] The rise in density of union membership relates to the factors of union growth widely identified elsewhere by Bain.[50] These include the continued willingness of employers to recognize the unions/associations for bargaining purposes; the impact of inflation and incomes policies in the 1970s on professional and white-collar workers; the recruitment strategies of some of the unions in terms of policies on women, part-time workers, workers from ethnic groups and young workers; and the use of more aggressive and militant trade union tactics.

3. The overriding dominance of centralized forms of collective bargaining for the vast majority of employees through Whitley.

4. The limited role of individual employers, the emphasis on the administrative functions of management rather than the discretionary decision-making functions, and the growth in importance of the personnel/human resource management function over time.
5. The changing nature of the government's view of its role in the management of the NHS from less to more direct intervention. This last issue relates to the abandonment of the state as model employer in favour of the state as just another employer but with tightly controlled central strategies.[51]

The ways in which these developments and collective bargaining institutions have been perceived by the staff and their organizations has played its own major role in the ability of employers and managers to enforce control mechanisms and therefore increase productivity while holding real pay relatively low.

Those staff with deeply rooted trade union traditions in health care, such as ancillary workers in NUPE or psychiatric nurses in COHSE or administrators in NALGO, generally welcomed both the setting up of the NHS and the adoption of Whitley, although they had some reservations about the final system of pay determination. For the first years of the NHS these unions and their members came to the view that the employers and senior managers sought to delay decisions and necessary changes whenever possible, and in this they were both backed and dominated by the largely incompetent and unimaginative Ministers of Health and their senior civil servants. One example of this with relevance to today is the refusal of the employers to grant a form of regional appeal open only to the trade unions.[52] Thus from the early 1950s the main trade unions shared a commitment to the NHS with a wary suspicion of management, employers and government interference.

In contrast most of the 'professions' had neither a trade union nor a bargaining tradition. Some, most notably the doctors with the British Medical Association, did have organizations which had the same objectives as trade unions – to defend the interests of members and promote future pay and employment prospects. The doctors, however, had adopted the classic small craft tradition based on narrow vested interests and favoured profession-specific protection from the state in the form of laws (what the Webbs described as 'legal enactment'[53] and Turner as closed union practices[54]). The success of protecting entry to the profession and thus controlling the labour supply enabled doctors and some other groups to eschew collective bargaining and therefore to ignore the trade union aspects of their defence organization.

To understand how professional associations and trade unions obtained recognition in the NHS, it is necessary to examine the historical development of negotiating systems for hospital staff prior to the introduction of the NHS in 1948. The mainspring for the Whitley system was a combination of existing and union-supported systems of wage negotiations in the health services, and the postwar enthusiasm for centralized and orderly national negotiating systems in the public sector based on the success of Whitley in local government and the Civil Service.

The main tradition of organized workers and bargaining was in the larger hospitals. For example, not long after the formation of the Standing Joint Conciliation Committee, the Association of Clerks and Stewards of Mental Hospitals obtained recognition from the Mental Hospitals Association to negotiate on behalf of administrative and clerical workers in mental hospitals. Thus, mental hospital staff achieved recognition to negotiate through joint bargaining machinery at around the same time as other public service staff.

In addition to the mental institutions, the other pre-NHS hospitals were local authority hospitals, which had previously been Poor Law Infirmaries which the local authorities had taken over in 1929 and the voluntary hospitals, which were generally independent, charitable organizations, notably the teaching hospitals. Before 1939 collective agreements were almost unknown in these hospitals and in the voluntary hospitals there were very few staff who were trade union members.

The war years saw major changes in the trade union activities and bargaining systems in hospitals. During the war labour was necessarily in short supply and civilians were 'directed' under wartime regulations into essential work. Hospital work was so designated, and with collective bargaining weak in hospitals, the government had to intervene to create the necessary negotiating machinery.

Thus, throughout the Second World War, collective bargaining procedures were created for the majority of hospital workers. Nurses, ancillary staff, doctors, administrative and clerical staff had all developed national negotiating forums. The notable exception to this trend was the members of the professional, scientific and technical staff, where no bargaining or negotiating arrangements existed in hospitals prior to 1945.

In considering how best collective bargaining could be undertaken in the newly created uniform health service after 1945, the government agreed that the Whitley system, which was already established in the Civil Service and in local authorities, would be the most suitable forum in which salaries and conditions of employment could be discussed.

The management side of the Whitley Councils was composed of representatives of NHS management (both 'lay' members and NHS officers) and Departmental civil servants. The Department of Health also provided the secretary to the management side and the secretariat. The staff sides were composed of those organizations which had members in the appropriate professions and occupations (Figure 1.1).

Originally, 41 trade unions and professional associations were able to represent their members in the NHS, but since 1948 several amalgamations have occurred. Table 1.2 lists the 36 organizations that in 1990 were the recognized staff side organizations.

In 1948 the density of trade union membership in the health service was 42.6%, in 1968 it had dropped to 37.9%, but by 1979 it had risen to 73.7%[55] Thus, initially trade union membership was low in the NHS when compared with other areas of the public sector. A sizeable proportion of staff were members of professional associations, notably the Royal College of Nursing (RCN), the British Medical Association (BMA) and those professional associations representing the Professions Allied to Medicine. The following two chapters examine the development of trade union membership in the NHS, looking at the experiences of some of the professional associations and multi-occupational TUC-affiliated trade unions and reveal the way in which government legislation and policies led to growth both in the number of certificated trade unions and the perceived benefits that such membership appeared to offer to most NHS employees.

Only ten of the staff side organizations recognized by the NHS are not certificated as trade unions. Twelve of the recognized staff side organizations are affiliated to the TUC. The issue of TUC affiliation while important, and extremely awkward in the mid-1970s, must not cloud the issue of the trade union behaviour and/or type of the organizations examined. For

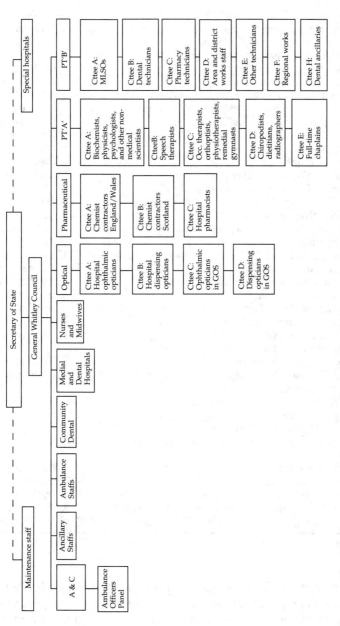

Figure 1.1 The Whitley structure. Since 1990 Committees B, C, E and H of PT'B' have merged to form committee T, and D and F are now committee W.

Table 1.2 Recognized staff side organizations

Organization	Status
Amalgamated Union of Engineering Workers	TUC trade union
Association of Clinical Biochemists	Trade union
Association of Dispensing Opticians	
Association of NHS Officers	Trade union
Association of Optometrists	Trade union
Association of Supervisors of Midwives	
British Association of Occupational Therapists	Trade union
British Dental Association	Trade union
British Dietetic Association	Trade union
British Medical Association	Trade union
British Orthoptic Society	Trade union
Chartered Society of Physiotherapists	Trade union
Company Chemists Association Ltd.	
Confederation of Health Service Employees	TUC trade union
Co-operative Union Ltd	
Electrical, Electronic, Telecommunication and Plumbing	Trade union
General, Municipal, Boilermakers and Allied Trades	TUC trade union
Health Visitors' Association	TUC trade union
Hospital Physicists' Association	Trade union
Manufacturing, Science, Finance	TUC trade union
National and Local Government Officers Association	TUC trade union
National Pharmaceutical Union	
National Union of Public Employees	TUC trade union
Pharmaceutical Standing Committee (Scotland)	
Royal College of Midwives	Trade union
Royal College of Nursing of the United Kingdom	Trade union
Scottish Association of Nurse Administrators	
Scottish Health Visitors' Association	Trade union
Scottish Committee of Ophthalmic Opticians	
Socialist Health Association	
Society of Administrators of Family Practitioner Services	
Society of Chiropodists	Trade union
Society of Radiographers	TUC trade union
Transport and General Workers Unions	TUC trade union
Union of Construction, Allied Trades and Technicians	TUC trade union
Union of Shop, Distributive and Allied Workers	TUC trade union

example, the HVA is a single-profession association yet has been TUC-affiliated since its early years, while NALGO, a large multi-occupational and multi-industry white-collar union, has been in the TUC only since 1964. More recently the EETPU, a traditional craft-cum-general union, was expelled from the TUC, while the Society of Radiographers affiliated after a membership ballot in 1990.

The trade union and professional association membership figures relate, in part, to the numbers of NHS staff and are relatively influenced by the differential growth and decline in certain staff categories. For example, ancillary workers have fallen in number due to subcontracting of services thus weakening the membership of unions such as NUPE, while the number of scientific and professional staffs has generally risen providing their representative organizations with more members and possibly more bargaining power.

CHANGES IN THE COMPOSITION OF NHS STAFF

As has been seen, the numbers employed in the NHS have grown over the years. The growth has been uneven both in speed and in direction. There has been a steady increase in doctors and nurses, but a recent decline in ancillary staff. The scientific and technical staff have grown the fastest. The essential mix of main categories has remained largely unchanged. The bulk of staff work in large district hospitals. The four main groups remain: ancillary, administrative and clerical, scientific and technical, and professional.

The NHS has now become one of the largest organizations in Europe, employing, in 1987, 1.2 million people. The latest wte figure for Britain in 1987 of about 975 000 indicates the amount of part-time employment there is in the NHS, since although, as will be seen below, there has been a reduction in overall numbers in certain groups of staff, the general trend in staffing levels has continued to climb. The size of the labour force means that industrial relations in terms of the costs of employment and control over work performance is one of the central management issues. These changes in workforce composition, alongside changes in the management functions, reveal the importance of the tensions between and within staff categories. One consequence of both the divisions among staff and within management has been the emphasis in some recent analyses on intra-organizational bargaining[56] – it emphasizes the importance of divisions within each side of the bargaining process such as trade union members and stewards, and personnel and line managers.

As would be expected with such a large number of employees, there is a great diversity of skills, expertise and abilities among the manual, white-collar, technical and professional staff who are employed in the NHS and an equally broad range of grades and salary levels. The nursing professions (including midwives and health visitors) have always been the largest single group of staff employed in the health service and they account for virtually half of those employed and command the largest salary bill. In terms of absolute numbers (which includes part-time and full-time) there were 514 000 in this category employed in 1987, the vast majority of whom were women.

As Table 1.3 shows, there has been an overall increase in the numbers employed by the NHS since its inception, but there have been important shifts in and between the relative representation of the different categories of staff. This has had important consequences for trade union strength and activities, and for the outcome of collective bargaining.

The constant rise in staff shown by Table 1.3, with its concomitant increase in expenditure, was of concern to governments that were determined to control public spending. In 1983, manpower 'targets' were set for all NHS staff. Regional Health Authorities were asked to monitor staffing levels closely and achieve a reduction in overall staff numbers of between 0.75% and 1.0% from the total employed at 31 March 1983.[57] Administrative, clerical, maintenance and ancillary staff numbers were expected to fall more sharply, between 1.35% and 1.8%[58] and health authorities were specifically asked not to fill vacancies automatically.

An important element in the distribution of staff for any analysis of the NHS and of industrial relations is the size of the various workplaces. While many staff work in relative isolation in the community, the majority work in hospitals.

In 1960 there were about 2400 hospitals with some 440 000 available beds in England. By 1988 there were 1737 hospitals with 297 342 beds. For most of this period the largest hospitals (those with more than 250 beds) contained about 70% of beds, and therefore, the majority of hospital staff work in hospitals with more than 250 beds. This feature of NHS employment allows parallels to be drawn from studies of industrial relations

Table 1.3a Number of staff employed in NHS hospitals by category, United Kingdom

Year (at 31 Dec.)	Medical and dental staff (whole-time)	Nurses and midwifery staff[1]	Professional and technical staff[2]	A&C staff[2]	Domestic and ancil-lary staff[3]	Total
1951	11 375	188 580	14 110	29 021	163 666	406 752
1952	11 894	194 861	14 844	29 101	171 077	421 777
1953	12 036	201 564	17 061	31 429	151 700	413 790
1954	12 510	204 485	18 331	32 795	155 774	423 895
1955	12 866	206 567	19 404	33 421	157 917	430 175
1956	13 240	212 917	19 941	34 593	160 463	441 154
1957	13 523	218 331	20 383	35 904	163 548	451 689
1958	13 575	226 770	20 879	36 643	171 077	468 944
1959	19 198	236 717	22 970	37 212	201 624	517 721
1960	19 853	242 164	24 002	38 450	202 968	527 437
1961	20 345	249 571	27 460	40 877	210 308	548 561
1962	21 095	264 657	28 555	42 675	215 528	572 510
1963	21 684	267 725	29 850	44 075	215 245	578 579
1964	22 147	275 537	31 060	45 667	217 410	591 821
1965	22 939	290 338	32 720	47 872	218 191	612 060
1966	23 605	303 338	34 353	50 110	224 005	635 411
1967	24 652	315 896	36 112	51 902	229 596	658 158
1968	25 680	320 142	36 929	51 434	227 039	661 224
1969	26 604	330 684	38 763	54 097	227 461	677 609
1970	27 398	343 664	41 696	56 877	229 313	698 948
1971	28 852	361 980	43 089	60 050	235 642	729 613
1972	30 379	382 652	45 343	64 551	236 940	759 865
1973	31 670	392 387	47 785	69 184	231 050	772 076
1974	33 026	408 146	47 015	89 999	230 944	809 130
1975	34 817	445 720	57 011	106 454	235 209	879 211
1976	35 759	452 882	65 204	113 637	242 212	909 694
1977	36 796	452 258	65 357	114 206	241 823	910 440
1978	37 981	450 042	69 024	116 080	241 047	914 174
1979	39 525	460 683	72 390	118 691	239 419	930 708
1980	40 618	476 182	74 558	121 528	240 791	953 677
1981	41 465	502 581	78 269	125 275	241 718	989 308
1982	42 159	509 454	80 543	125 483	239 865	997 504
1983	43 006	509 656	82 505	126 914	239 565	1 001 646
1984	43 315	509 708	86 893	127 522	239 319	1 006 757
1985	43 799	514 962	88 872	128 567	221 429	997 629

[1] Whole-time and part-time.
[2] Excluding part-time staff in Scotland.
[3] Including works, maintenance, ancillary, ambulance and transport staff.
Source: Annual Abstract of Statistics.

Table 1.3b Health service staff numbers 1978–1989 (wte)

	1978	1979	1980	1981	1982	1983	1984	1985	1986	1987	1988[7]	1989
Health service staff and practitioners: total	968 733	986 500	1 010 402	1 047 803	1 058 297	1 059 474	1 048 863	1 043 894	1 029 794	..		
Regional and area health authorities/ boards and boards of governors staff: total	915 678	932 034	954 617	990 572	999 975	999 833	987 919	981 930	969 849	..		
Medical staff: total	41 261	42 648	43 784	44 706	45 351	46 114	46 375	47 040	47 355	47 119	48 873	50 290
Hospital medical staff total[1]	37 819	39 179	40 290	41 152	41 808	42 558	42 848	43 456	43 784	43 741	45 438	46 906
Consultant and senior hospital medical officer with allowance	12 726	13 004	13 482	13 777	14 017	14 349	14 699	14 978	15 281	15 512	15 974	16 517
Staff grade[7]	..	..	..			..	..	..	..	..	..	33
Associate specialist	1013	1020	1039	1014	1035	1019	995	935	884	865	859	877
Senior registrar	2688	2808	2933	3046	3079	3187	3142	3254	3326	3322	3351	3488
Registrar	6479	6613	6764	6787	6995	7099	7054	7014	7108	7097	7385	7297
Senior house officer including post registration house officer	9668	10 285	10 590	10 904	11 023	11 137	11 142	11 351	11 228	10 994	11 623	12 407
Pre-registration house officer	3149	3291	3355	3419	3411	3553	3483	3518	3493	3478	3566	3637

[1] Whole-time equivalent. Figures exclude locums and general medical practitioners participating in Hospital Staff fund.
[7] New grade introduced in 1989.
Sources: Department of Health; Scottish Health Service Common Services Agency; Welsh Office.

Table 1.3b (continued) Health service staff numbers 1978–1989 (wte)

	1978	1979	1980	1981	1982	1983	1984	1985	1986	1987	1988[7]	1989
Other staff[2]	91	81	71	66	58	37	89	36	40	54	23	17
Hospital practitioner	134	165	210	242	251	252	262	257	262	249	231	233
Part-time medical officer (clinical assistant)	1871	1912	1846	1898	1940	1924	1982	2113	2162	2170	2426	2402
Community health medical staff[3]	3442	3469	3494	3554	3543	3557	3527	3586	3571	3377	3435	3384
Dental staff: total	3235	3286	3288	3360	3397	3372	3350	3370	3322	3168	3128	3092
Hospital dental staff: total[1]	1288	1350	1366	1408	1440	1433	1487	1498	1492	1470	1465	1475
Consultant and senior hospital dental officer with allowance	433	452	471	477	485	489	506	508	503	517	511	512
Associate specialist	74	76	91	91	101	103	105	99	103	93	84	81
Senior registrar	112	111	100	108	106	112	98	97	118	121	118	129
Registrar	190	206	204	199	211	210	229	230	223	201	216	204
Senior house officer	174	182	186	196	197	202	218	232	215	236	223	246
Dental house officer	154	170	159	170	180	166	170	171	168	152	138	129
Other staff[2]	16	12	10	10	8	5	5	3	4	5	4	3
Hospital practitioner	7	12	16	15	17	17	15	14	12	13	12	14

[1] Whole-time equivalent. Figures exclude locums and general medical practitioners participating in Hospital Staff Fund.
[2] Figures include Senior Hospital Medical/Dental Officers (SHMO) without an allowance and other ungraded staff.
[3] Whole-time equivalent. Figures exclude locums and occasional seasonal staff.
[7] New grade introduced in 1989.

Sources: Department of Health; Scottish Health Service Common Services Agency; Welsh Office.

Table 1.3b (continued) Health service staff numbers 1978–1989 (wte)

	1978	1979	1980	1981	1982	1983	1984	1985	1986	1987	1988[7]	1989
Part-time medical officer (clinical assistant)	128	128	130	142	136	128	142	145	146	134	160	158
Community health dental staff[3]	1948	1936	1921	1952	1957	1939	1863	1872	1831	1697	1663	1617
Nursing and midwifery staff: (excluding agency): total[8]	424 304	433 490	448 824	474 497	481 873	483 061	482 215	486 607	487 273	397 902.5	397 641.0	397 641.0
Qualified nurses and midwives[8]	226 904	233 249	240 462	256 921	265 109	270 736	276 602	284 116	287 715	239 354.0	241 782.0	
Student and pupil nurses and midwives[8]	92 433	91 043	91 983	96 255	97 044	94 167	91 369	86 485	83 148	64 563.8	62 933.0	
Other nursing and midwifery staff[8]	104 967	109 198	116 379	121 321	119 720	118 158	114 244	116 006	116 410	93 984.5	92 927.0	
Professions allied to medicine staff[8]							36 193	37 992	39 215	34 941.2	35 638.3	
Scientific and professional staff[8]	68 650	72 097	74 153	77 887	80 299	82 084	11 433	11 845	12 297	10 863.2	11 604.3	
Professional and technical (excluding works) staff[6,8]							51 562	52 184	52 419	33 170.1	32 532.4	

[3] Whole-time equivalent. Figures exclude locums and occasional seasonal staff.
[6] From 1 April 1984, Operating Department Assistants (ODAs) were transferred from Ancillary to Professional and Technical 'B' Staffs Council. Therefore figures for these staff groups prior to September 1984 are not comparable with those for September 1984 onwards (accounting for approximately 3000 wte in September 1984).
[7] New grade introduced in 1989.
[8] 1987 and 1988 are figures for England only.

Sources: Department of Health; Scottish Health Service Common Services Agency; Welsh Office.

Table 1.3b (*continued*) Health service staff numbers 1978–1989 (wte)

	1978	1979	1980	1981	1982	1983	1984	1985	1986	1987	1988[7]	1989
Works and maintenance staff[8]	30 867	31 243	32 166	32 977	32 971	32 650	32 087	31 566	30 973	24 046.4	22 524.2	
Administrative and clerical staff[4,5,8]	115 107	118 078	120 492	124 426	124 863	126 220	126 652	127 594	128 439	110 699.7	112 311.5	
Ambulance officers, ambulancemen/women and other ambulance staff[8]	20 707	20 223	20 934	21 435	21 590	21 697	21 441	21 595	22 465	19 010.2	18 760.7	
Ancillary staff[6,8]	211 547	210 969	210 976	211 284	209 631	204 635	189 023	175 319	159 109	114 497.6	107 051.3	

[4] Figures exclude ambulance officers.
[5] Includes Family Practitioner Service administrative and clerical staff and General Managers
[6] From 1 April 1984, Operating Department Assistants (ODAs) were transferred from Ancillary to Professional and Technical 'B' Staffs Council. Therefore figures for these staff groups prior to September 1984 are not comparable with those for September 1984 onwards (accounting for approximately 3000 wte in September 1984).
[7] New grade introduced in 1989.
[8] 1987 and 1988 are figures for England only.

Sources: Department of Health; Scottish Health Service Common Services Agency; Welsh Office.

in other industries in which the size of the workplace is relevant. Size of establishment was considered to be one of the three main factors in union recognition, the other two being ownership and size of enterprise. These three factors were also important determinants for the existence of joint consultative committees at work, and pay levels tended to be higher in larger establishments.[59] The significance of this for trade union membership, shop steward activity, and managerial practices is considerable and will be explored further in Chapter 7.

The recent loss of staff among ancillary workers may presage a change in the NHS's employment policies with fewer directly employed staff. Some SGTs may use their new freedom to reduce staffing levels in some areas of operation. Such changes will have serious implications for the size of the workforce, the salary bill, the composition of the workforce in terms of part-time and female labour, and for trade union/professional association bargaining power. However, as the fall in figures has revealed, the greatest drive in 'efficiency savings' came through the policy of the 'contracting-out' of some hospital services. The competitive tendering process for ancillary services has resulted in an instant fall in staffing levels when contracts have been awarded externally, and even where contracts have been awarded 'in-house', there have generally been reductions in staff. Between 1983 and 1985 there was a reduction of approximately 20 000 wte ancillary staff employed in England. This reduction obviously had serious implications both for those staff involved and for the trade unions to which they belonged.

The changes of the 1990s represent the second major readjustment in use of labour and the attitude of staff in labour organizations since 1948. In the 1950s there were staff shortages within the NHS, and partly as a result of this and due to other factors there was a slow and painful transition among hospital doctors and nurses towards a system of wage labour. Nurses remained largely untouched by trade unionism with the important exception of psychiatric nurses in COHSE. The profession was dominated by conservative and authoritarian matrons, and their main professional body, the RCN, reflected this. The PAMs were in a similar position: they had very limited trade union and collective bargaining traditions and were very much in the hands of the civil servants who dominated Whitley behind the scenes and senior members of the professions who ran their Colleges and Societies as clubs for the protection of their own interests.

In the 1960s much of this began to change with a new generation of health workers brought up in the shadow of the NHS, and with wider social and labour market forces creating a larger and better educated workforce. By the 1970s, in line with other professional and white-collar employees, these professions grew rapidly in membership, became trade unions, and became increasingly concerned with industrial relations at both national and local level. The most spectacular change came with nurses, who flooded into the three main competing organizations – NUPE, RCN and COHSE. The 1980s saw the continued growth in membership and activity of all of these groups, which is significant given the national trend of decline amongst other trade unions. All these groups have further extended their trade union and industrial relations operations, and in 1991 they stand as one of the most unionized and best served group of public employees.

Overall the four decades since the founding of the NHS have seen a very large, if uneven, increase in the main staff groups; a huge rise in the membership of trade unions and professional associations; and an increase in trade union activity and in local and national collective bargaining. The position in 1991 is one in which all staff groups are represented by a trade union or professional association with strong industrial relations support, with changing internal structures of these organizations to incorporate the shifts in the relative importance of industrial relations issues, and with recent involvement in industrial action and/or political demonstration. In short, the 1990s, whatever else they witness, will experience a continuation of the strong movement towards a commonality of interest and approach amongst health workers, and this will be encouraged by government reforms, decentralized bargaining, staff shortages, and the continued expectations of patients and the wider population with regard to the survival of the NHS and the staff who work within it.

MANAGERS, EMPLOYERS AND THE GOVERNMENT

Before a more detailed look at the 'labour partnerships' for health workers it is useful to summarize the position regarding the management and employer structures and their relationship to politicians and senior civil servants. It is the Secretary of State for Health who has the power in law to fix the wages and conditions of all staff employed in the NHS. The Secretary of State invokes statutory powers after seeking the advice of a range of bodies for different NHS occupations and these generally consist of representatives of NHS staff and management. The agreement that is referred to the Secretary of State is the result of collective bargaining and the forum at which such agreements are reached for the vast majority of NHS employees are the Whitley Councils and Pay Review Bodies.

One of the fundamental contradictions upon which the operation of the NHS is based is that between the employers and the government. Here is the classic formulation of a system in which inexperienced and Treasury-dominated civil servants control the negotiations and their outcomes behind the scenes, while their appointees amongst the employers are the men and women who actually sit across the table from the trade union representatives during negotiations at Whitley. At local level it is the managers who tend to negotiate on behalf of employers. This pattern gives rise to several analytical methods: the intra-organizational bargaining model that accounts for delay and confusion among employers and managers, especially during industrial disputes; the separation of operational management needs and objectives from strategic decision-making; and the accusation that the delivery of health care is a secondary consideration to the saving of public expenditure.

The NHS is funded by central government from monies drawn from general taxation and NHS National Insurance contributions, although throughout the 1980s the NHS was increasingly expected to raise additional revenue from charges for certain NHS goods and services. The central allocation of financial resources is voted annually by Parliament and it is a major function of the successive Secretaries of State for Health to negotiate within the Cabinet for an appropriate proportion of the public expenditure budget and they are then accountable to Parliament for the proper use of those funds. The Secretary of State is accountable not only for the determination of a national policy for the NHS, but also for the actions that are carried out by, or on behalf of, individual health authorities. They are expected to have detailed knowledge of, and influence over, the NHS. It is also the case that the actions of the Ministerial and Health Departmental staff are subject to examination by the Social Services Committee of the House of Commons, as well as the Public Audit Office.

While in each of the four parts of Britain the health service is the direct statutory responsibility of the appropriate Secretary of State, and each has a health department staffed by civil servants to help in this task, it is not the government which is the employer. It is the Regional and District Health Authorities, who employ the staff, provide the buildings and equipment and have to ensure that patients receive care. In England there are 14 Regional Health Authorities (RHAs) and 190 District Health Authorities (DHAs). In Scotland and Northern Ireland there are 15 and four Health Boards (rather than Regions) respectively, while in Wales, some of the functions of the RHAs in England are the responsibility of District Health Authorities and others are carried out by the Welsh Health Common Services Authority or the NHS Directorate of the Welsh Office. This was the situation before April 1991.

The Regional and District Health Authorities currently comprise a chair and between 16 and 19 members. It is the Secretary of State who appoints the chairs and members of RHAs/Boards as well as the chairs of the DHAs. The relevant RHA/Board members then appoint the DHA members and in so doing are required to consult various local interests and appoint a representative of the appropriate university. Between four and six of the DHA members are directly appointed by relevant local authorities and many of these are selected on the advice of professional bodies and trade unions. In September 1990 there was another shift away from local accountability when the government announced the direct appointment of authority members without the need for community representation.

There have been two major structural reorganizations of the NHS. In 1974 hospital and community services were unified under regional and 'area' health authorities and at this time the ambulance and local authority dental services were transferred from local authority control into the NHS.[60] Then, in 1982, the government removed the 'area' tier of management, reducing this to simply RHA (Board in Scotland and Northern Ireland) and DHA (Area in Scotland) levels of management.[61]

Since 1977 government has allocated money to RHAs on the basis of a formula which sought to identify the health care needs of each region's population. The formula was known as RAWP (Resource Allocation Working Party).[62] Each year, when allocating finances to regions, the government decided how far actual allocations should move towards the target shares that were indicated by the formula. It is planned to remove this system of resource allocation and introduce, over a two-year period from April 1990, a system to fund RHAs on a weighted capitation basis.[63]

In 1989–90 the total gross expenditure on the NHS had increased to £26 billion from £8 billion in 1978–9, an increase of 40% after allowing for general inflation. With pay accounting for over 70% of all NHS expenditure it is obvious why pay bargaining in the NHS has such a high political profile.

CONCLUDING COMMENTS

This opening chapter has sought to argue the case that industrial relations is a central part of the current financially driven reforms. The labour-intensive nature of most of the industry and the managerial imperative to raise labour productivity place wage determination and wider reward packages ('market' relations) and performance controls ('managerial' relations) at the heart of the operational needs of the new NHS businesses, i.e. the self-governing trusts and the directly managed units behaving *as if* they were self-governing trusts. The ability to control and influence these factors within health provision will be fought out between the varied and divided representatives of the staff and the managers seeking to apply new managerial systems and cultures in place of strong traditions and customs. One major battlefield, and the one that will largely determine the extent and nature of the battle, will be the collective bargaining procedures and agreements.

NOTES

1   Routh, G. (1980) *Occupation and Pay in Great Britain 1906–1979*, Macmillan Press, London, p. 1.
2   Ibid., p. 1.
3   Thorold Rogers, J. (1923 edn), *Six Centuries of Work and Wages*, Fisher Unwin, London, p. 523.
4   Phelps Brown, H. (1979) *The Inequality of Pay*, Oxford University Press, Oxford, p. 7.
5   Ibid., p. 142.
6   Flanders, A. (1970) 'Industrial Relations: What is Wrong with the System?', in *Management and Unions: The Theory and Reform of Industrial Relations*, Faber, London.
7   For criticisms of the pluralist approach adopted by Flanders and the Donovan Commission see amongst others, Goldthorpe, J. (1974)

'Industrial Relations in Great Britain: A Critique of Reformism', *Politics and Society*, IV.

8 Donovan (1968) *Royal Commission on Trade Unions and Employers' Associations*, Cmnd 3623, HMSO, London.

9 Whitley, J. (1917) *Interim Report on Joint Standing Industrial Councils*, Cd 8606, HMSO, London.

10 Fox, A. (1966) *Industrial Sociology and Industrial Relations*, Research Paper 3, Donovan Commission, HMSO, London.

11 Miliband, R. (1973) *The State in Capitalist Society*, Quartet Books, London, p. 73.

12 Pollard, S. (1968) *The Genesis of Modern Management*, Penguin.

13 Goodrich, C. (1920) *The Frontier of Control*, G. Bell and Sons, London.

14 Smith, A. (1776) *The Wealth of Nations*, 1910 edn, Everyman, London, p. 59.

15 ACAS (1983) *Collective Bargaining in Britain: Its Extent and Level*, Discussion Paper 2, ACAS, London.

16 ACAS (1987) *Labour Flexibility in Britain*, Occasional Paper 41, ACAS, London. Atkinson, J. (1984) 'Manpower Strategies for the Flexible Firm', *Personnel Management*, August, pp. 28–31.

17 Abel-Smith, B. (1960) *A History of the Nursing Profession*, Heinemann, London.

18 Minute from the 1982 Annual Report of the then NUG&MWU (now the GMB), p. 130.

19 Wootton, B. (1962 edn), *The Social Foundations of Wage Policy*, Unwin University Books, London.

20 Priestly (1955) *Royal Commission on the Civil Service 1953–55*, Cmnd 9613, HMSO, London.

21 Clegg, H. (1980) *Nurses and Midwives Standing Commission on Pay Comparability, Report No. 3*, Cmnd 7995, HMSO, London.

22 Trade Union Congress Health Services Committee (1981) *Improving Industrial Relations in the National Health Service*, TUC, London, p. 60.

23 Cleminson, J. (1989) *Review Body ...: Sixth Report on Nursing Staff. Midwives and Health Visitors*, Cm 577, HMSO, London.

24 Bett, M. (1991) *Review Body ...: Eighth Report on Nursing Staff, Midwives and Health Visitors*, Cm 1410, HMSO, London pp. 25–6.

25 Cleminson, J. (1987) *Review Body ...: Fourth Report on Nursing Staff, Midwives Health Visitors*, Cm 129, HMSO, London.

26 Holdsworth, T. (1991) *Review Body on Doctors' and Dentists' Remuneration: Twenty-First Report*, Cm 1412, HMSO, London, p. 60.

27 Wilkins, G. (1989) *Review Body on Doctors' and Dentists' Remuneration: Nineteenth Report*, Cm 580, HMSO, London.

28 Bett, M. (1991) *Review Body ...: Eight Report on Professions Allied to Medicine*, Cm 1411, HMSO, London p. 19.

29 PT'A' staff side evidence 1990, paper 2, p. 19.

30 Bett, Cm 1411, op. cit., p. 14–20.

31 PT'A' staff side evidence paper 1, p. 17.

32 Wootton, op. cit., p. 125.

33 Ibid., p. 125.

34 Ibid., p. 126.

35   Ibid., p. 131.
36   Ibid., p. 133.
37   NALGO 1990 pay claim for NHS members, p. 1.
38   Ibid.
39   NUPE 1990 pay claim for NHS members.
40   Routh, op. cit. p. 60–1.
41   Ibid., p. 70–1.
42   Ibid., p. 119.
43   Ibid., p. 123.
44   Ibid., p. 164.
45   Ibid., p. 200.
46   Halsbury (1974) *Report of the Committee of Inquiry into the Pay and Related Conditions of Nurses and Midwives*, DHSS, London. Clegg (1980) op. cit. Megaw (1982) *Report of an Inquiry into Civil Service Pay*, Cmnd 8590, HMSO, London.
47   McCarthy, W. (1966) *The Role of Shop Stewards in British Industrial Relations*, Research Paper 1, Donovan Commission, HMSO, London.
48   Mailly, R., Dimmock, S. and Sethi, A. (1989) 'Industrial Relations in the NHS since 1979', in Mailly, R., Dimmock, S. and Sethi, A. (eds), *Industrial Relations in the Public Services*, Routledge, London, p. 116.
49   Carpenter, M. (1982) 'The Labour Movement in the NHS: UK', in Sethi, A. and Dimmock, S. (eds), *Industrial Relations and Health Services*, Croom Helm, London, p. 76.
50   Bain, G. (1970) *The Growth of White-Collar Unionism*, Clarendon Press, Oxford. This is one of several works by Bain on the causes of union membership growth.
51   Fredman, S. and Morris, G. (1989) 'The State as Employer: Setting a New Example', *Personnel Management*, August.
52   General and Municipal Workers Union (1949) *Journal*, December, 12(12), p. 370.
53   Webb, S. and Webb, B. (1897) *Industrial Democracy*, 1920 edn Longmans, Green & Co., London. The Webb's views on the functions and doctrines of trade unionism are taken up in Chapters 2 and 3.
54   Turner, H. (1962) *Trade Union Growth, Structure and Policy*, George Allen and Unwin, London. Turner's concept of a 'closed' union is discussed in more detail in Chapter 2.
55   Bain, G. and Price, R. (1983) 'Union Growth: Dimensions, Determinants and Destiny', in Bain, G. (ed.), *Industrial Relations in Britain*, Basil Blackwell, Oxford, p. 15.
56   Walton, R. and McKersie, R. (1965) *A Behavioral Theory of Labor Negotiations*, McGraw Hill, New York.
57   Mailly *et al.*, op. cit., p. 133.
58   Health Circular 83[6], DHSS, 1983.
59   Daniel, W. and Millward, N. (1983) *Workplace Industrial Relations in Britain*, Heinemann Educational Books, London, pp. 20, 130 and 270. Millward, N. and Stevens, M. (1986) *British Workplace Industrial Relations 1980–1984*, Gower, Aldershot, pp. 62, 138, 246.

60 See White Paper, *National Health Reorganisation: England* (1972), Cmnd 5055, HMSO, London.

61 For summary comments on the 1982 reorganization see Chaplin, N. (1982) *Getting it Right: the 1982 Reorganisation of the National Health Service*, IHSA, London; and Levitt, R. and Wall, A. (1984) *The Reorganized National Health Service*, Croom Helm, London.

62 See *Report of the Resource Allocation Working Party* (1976), HMSO, London.

63 *Working for Patients* (1989), HMSO, London, pp. 31–2.

Chapter 2

The professions and their associations

INTRODUCTION

The professions are the most numerous and influential category of staff within the NHS. They fall largely into three groups: doctors and dentists; nurses, midwives and health visitors; and the professions allied to medicine (PAMs). All these groups have traditionally sought to defend their pay, status and job territory through legal enactment based on narrowly conceived vested interests. The doctors have long demanded state support for their activities while maintaining their control over the supply of labour. One consequence of this is that doctors and their representative organization have until recently eschewed collective bargaining and the concomitant trade union functions.

In industrial relations terms these groups have behaved like 'closed' craft unions[1] in which the main features include:

1. control over the supply of labour (through control over qualifications and professional discipline);
2. organizational independence and integrity found in their reluctance to affiliate to the TUC (notable exceptions are the HVA and more recently the SoR) and to merge into larger groupings;
3. fierce protection of their job through a combination of legislative support, sociocultural perceptions of the importance of the undiluted nature of their profession, and the policing of their own standards.

The extent to which these professions have also exhibited some other characteristics of trade unions depends on definitions[2], but the methods used to protect jobs and pay have tended to be more concerned with political influence and public support than with industrial action and collective bargaining. This varies with each profession and grouping them together must not allow the error of assuming that there are no sharp differences between and within the professions. The majority of doctors and dentists are self-employed and/or have important elements of work outside their NHS employment. This puts them in a special category in bargaining and trade union terms. In contrast, the vast majority of nurses are employees of the NHS, but differ in place and type of work, qualifications and attitudes to trade unionism. These divides are reflected in the fact that nurses belong to several organizations including the three largest NHS unions: two, COHSE and NUPE with TUC affiliation and with non-nurse members, and the third, the RCN, outside the TUC and recruiting only nurses. Other unions also recruit nurses but in relatively small numbers, such as the GMB and NALGO. The divisions between and among the PAMs are even more deeply felt: radiographers work almost exclusively in departments in large hospitals headed by consultant radiologists, many physiotherapists work outside large centres and have their own heads of department, and orthoptists tend to work alone.

The professions mainly belong to organizations with high levels of membership density and with relatively strong financial positions. This enables even quite small ones to survive without undue stress and to continue their professional and industrial relations functions. This may now change. The volume and importance of non-national bargaining, at either collective or individual level, will put greater strains on the internal relationships within the organizations as between industrial relations and professional concerns, and will force most of these bodies to adopt more trade union-like activities and stances. This has already happened to some extent and will be given a further impetus by the advent of the single-employer bargainer.

Historically the staff who are employed in the NHS have been commonly defined by the type of work that they perform and this division applied for pay, negotiating and representation purposes. It is also the case that by statute an appropriate recognized professional qualification is required in order for the medical, nursing, professional and scientific staffs to gain employment in the NHS. For example, the Professions Supplementary to Medicine Act 1960 established for each of the professions concerned – chiropodists, dietitians, medical laboratory scientific officers, occupational therapists, orthoptists, physiotherapists and radiographers – a Registration Board with the general function of promoting high standards of professional education and conduct. The Boards cover the UK and are responsible for maintaining registers and for approving courses of training, qualifications and the institutions in which the training will be carried out. The Boards operate under the general supervision of the Council for Professions Supplementary to Medicine (CPSM) whose membership is composed of representatives of the eight professions, plus eight medical and seven lay members.[3]

While the Act itself does not prevent unregistered members of the professions practising, in 1964, when the Act became fully operative, regulations were made which prevented the employment of unregistered members of the professions in the NHS (though not outside it). Comparable regulations apply to speech therapists.

The title of 'Professions Supplementary to Medicine' was amended by the government in 1984 to become 'Professions Allied to Medicine', although the regulatory body is still known as the CPSM.

The Nurses, Midwives and Health Visitors Act (1979) provides for a single United Kingdom Central Council (UKCC), supported by powerful national boards in each of the four parts of the UK. The UKCC has a duty to prepare and maintain a central register of qualified nurses, midwives and health visitors and, as with the CPSM, to determine the education, training and other requirements for admission to the register.[4]

The General Medical Council is the regulatory body for the medical profession with a similar brief.[5] These are examples of how the professions have sought to protect their members' conditions of service through special legal status, self-regulation and public esteem.

The main theme of this book, however, with regard to the professions and their associations, is that while they started within the NHS as reluctant participants they soon adapted and developed their major strategy for survival and improvement. This is taken in general to be profession-specific protection, through the law, of their job territory and so of their status, pay and conditions of service. It is still an important part of their political strategy. As the current reforms unravel so they create ever sharper tensions within these bodies as to how best to defend their interests: through collective bargaining and/or through political pressure groups and special protective laws. In the words of the Webbs, these groups sought to defend their vested interests through 'legal enactment'[6], and this might no longer be adequate.

The Webbs wrote about the functions, methods and doctrines (or principles) of trade unionism about one hundred years ago. What they had to say remains the best account of 'labour partnerships' and in part applies with great accuracy to the single-profession associations found in the NHS in the 1990s. In the early years of the nineteenth century, trade unionists, along with other pressure group representatives, put great store by acts of Parliament remedying wrongs and/or protecting their interests. *Laissez-faire* dominance for most of the nineteenth century made such activities worthless until the last decade of the century when the extension of the franchise again made workers push for legislative protection, notably for the limitation of hours of work. While there were considerable disadvantages in gaining the help of the law such as delay, expense and frustration, yet there was a glittering prize if successful:

> once the Common Rule is embodied in an Act of Parliament, it satisfies more perfectly the trade union aspirations of permanence and universality.[7]

Their thesis is that the best unit of organization is the trade, and that common conditions for its regulation are best achieved through legal enactment rather than by collective bargaining. There can be little doubt that this is what the 'trades' or professions in the NHS have sought to maintain.

The Webbs considered that trade unions had two major economic consequences which they refer to as 'devices'. These were the Common Rule and Restriction of Numbers. Many unions might adopt such objectives, and doctors and nurses clearly do, but their actual policies will depend on the selection as between the three main doctrines: vested interests, supply and demand, and the living wage. The doctrine of vested interests is the one most commonly utilized by the NHS professions: it encourages demarcation disputes, long training periods, limiting the numbers qualifying, the defence of customary pay and conditions, and fierce resistance to any threats to its privileges.[8]

Most of the professional associations representing NHS professionals have based their protection of interests on the method of legal enactment and its associated parliamentary influences in order to defend their control over the labour supply and customary common terms of employment through the principle of vested interests.

The argument continues that this one-dimensional approach has been undermined and to some extent replaced by its major alternative – the protection of interests through collective bargaining if, and when, the professions became increasingly subject to supply and demand rather than to state protection. This process has been rough and ready, but it is there. The tension between traditional methods of influence and new more trade union-like methods has shown itself in several forms. In practical terms there has been an increase in the numbers of full-time officials involved in industrial relations and there is now an impressive record of training stewards. It is apparent in the development of internal decision-making processes which have opened up to activists avenues for policy control previously closed. In other ways the pronouncements of leaders of the associations and their role in the reforms, cutbacks and industrial action within the NHS in the 1980s have shown a hesitant and often unhappy expression of the realities of market forces as exchanged for the comforts of Whitehall influence.

Whatever the current changes and tensions the stated objectives of the various professional associations that operate in the NHS remain:

> to promote the development of the profession, to maintain professional standards, to uphold the status of the profession and to provide representation upon, and protection for, the interests of the profession as a whole and the welfare of its members. They also set out to provide the human and financial resources necessary for fulfilling these objectives.[9]

In order to meet such aims, the professional associations provide educational facilities, research grants and scholarships (within the limits of their funds) and almost half of them have examining-body status and provide post-registration courses of various types.

Their constitutions and charters establish their role as the watchdogs of the profession on all legislative and administrative proposals and this, together with their stated concern for the welfare of their members, has caused them to maintain and develop trade union activities. Indeed, it was in recognition of the growing importance of such activities that the Royal College

of Nursing extended its objectives to include more specifically
the promotion of 'the professional standing and interests of
members of the nursing profession'.[10] It is through this interpretation and development of their objectives that most of the
professional associations became actively involved in industrial
relations.

Table 2.1 lists these professional associations, the year in
which each was established, their membership numbers for the
years 1979 and 1987 and gives the percentage change that
occurred. The issues that are currently of importance to these
associations and their members include how far down the road
of traditional trade unionism will they go? The radiographers
recently affiliated to the TUC, the health visitors merged with a
large general union (MSF), most associations have appointed
new industrial relations staff, often from large TUC-affiliated
unions, and the training of stewards continues at a high rate and
increasingly involves bargaining as part of the courses. These
developments depend on recent reforms which strengthen
managerial powers and weaken the traditional security and
prospects of individual health professionals. Other factors
involved include size of employment unit with the concentration

Table 2.1 Professional associations: some examples of their membership figures in 1979 and 1987

Professional association	Year est.	No. of members 1979	1987	% increase
Association of Clinical Biochemists (ACB)	1953	1998	2407	20
British Association of Occupational Therapists (BAOT)	1936	6139	9047	47
British Dental Association (BDA)	1880	12 027	15 808	31
British Dietetic Association (BDA)	1935	1650	2119	28
British Medical Association (BMA)	1832	52 859	82 359	56
British Orthoptist Society (BOS)	1937	665	1229	85
Chartered Society of Physiotherapists (CSP)	1895	14 619	24 376	67
Health Visitors' Association (HVA)	1896	11 300	16 435	45
Hospital Physicists Association (HPA)	1943	873	1480	70
Royal College of Midwives (RCM)	1881	17 465	33 487	92
Royal College of Nursing (RCN)	1916	122 420	281 918	220
Society of Chiropodists (SoC)	1945	4408	4750	8
Society of Radiographers (SoR)	1920	8050	11 500	43

of staff in large district general hospitals, the type of work with increased technology and changed patterns of patient care, and the changing composition of the members of the profession in terms of background and training.

Most of these professional associations registered as independent trade unions in the mid-1970s in response to the then Labour government's legislation on issues such as Health and Safety and trade union rights.[11] They also grew in numbers with the growth of their professions and developed trade union status with appointments of specialist staff. There were major efforts, only some successful, to forge new ties with TUC unions despite some local difficulties. In the late 1970s the 'competition between TUC and non-TUC professional associations intensified',[12] but by the mid-1980s this had been replaced by uneasy cooperation and later by positive initiatives for a joint response to joint problems. A few district level TUC unions maintained their hostility and separateness from the non-affiliates, but this reminder of the inability of some unions and union activists to change with the times has increasingly diminished.

With NHS cutbacks and pay cash limits in the 1980s many of the professions felt left out in the cold in terms of influence on the government and frustrated by their inability to secure better deals. This exploded with industrial action in the early 1980s which directly led to the setting up of a Pay Review Body for nurses, midwives, health visitors and for the PAMs. But the health reforms and cuts continued to the disadvantage of the associations and their members. By 1991, therefore, they were in a situation of rapid change and internal turmoil. Despite some better than NHS average pay settlements the overall security and conditions of employment were not in line with expectations and the professions decided to continue with a range of strategic developments. This included, for some of the PAMs and some nurses, a move to higher level qualifications as a defensive labour market response, but also to closer links with TUC unions. In general all these changes have not had a substantial impact on the way the associations are run, but this may well be round the corner.

The structure of most of these professional associations is similar with their executive body – often known as the association's Council – being elected from amongst the membership, lay officials similarly elected at workplace levels and a varying number of full time industrial relations staff employed at the association's headquarters as well as, for the larger organizations, at Regional levels. The following examples provide a more detailed insight into the structure of some of these professional associations. It is worth noting that these bodies are excluded from recent legislation requiring that their senior officers be elected. This exclusion is justified in legal terms by defining them as special register bodies under the 1971 Industrial Relations Act, but the political purpose behind such exceptions is strongly related to a government strategy of rewarding (or appearing to reward) those representative bodies which eschew industrial action and which lend support to some of the government's reforms.

In addition, the influence of powerful lay members and an enduring concern for professional standards (an amalgam of status, job protection and care) mean that the balance of power as between their trade union activities and their professional activities is a constant source of tensions in terms of funds, staffing and, at crucial times, policy. Most of these bodies have a Council and a Secretary which are primarily concerned with professional matters, and the industrial relations is controlled by an industrial relations committee serviced by a secretary and a team of industrial relations officers in their own department. In recent years there have been some bitter clashes between the IR departments and the Councils reflecting both the uneasy move to more collective bargaining, the more political nature of the IR department and the influence it gains through steward training and case work. This latter activity may well tread on the toes of those senior members of the organization in management positions with a strong voice on the Council.

Most of these bodies are a single-profession organization with a classic 'closed' union structure. This implies that the membership integrity of the organization is more important as a device for survival and success than size. Indeed some of these bodies are quite small (the BOS has about 1200 members), but they are financially viable and professionally independent. The recent changes in the NHS employer structures and the ever changing nature of the technology has meant a tendency for deskilling among some of the professions. This deskilling for some staff has been matched by the trend towards the multi-skilling and concentration of skills of others. This has led to a series of tough-minded debates about their futures which have included further labour market control strategies such as the move to an all graduate profession, as for radiographers and physiotherapists and Project 2000 for nurses, and at the same time some enhancement of one loose federation of PAM unions known as the Federation of Professional Organizations (FPO).

These bodies have until now known limited local bargaining which has been largely confined to personal cases in discipline and grievance, and some disputes involving work organization issues. The recent regrading of the nurses, midwives and health visitors generated a substantial number of grievances and the rare outbreak of local industrial action. In addition, the fact that nurses work shifts, and that junior hospital doctors work overtime, and that radiographers work oncall has meant some involvement for these groups in employer-level bargaining. The new situation, however, will further embroil them in collective bargaining at single-employer level and this means both new forms of bargaining structures and alliances, and new relationships between industrial relations officials and their members and their Councils. These points are further developed in Chapter 8. The rest of this chapter examines the professions and their organizations in more detail.

DOCTORS AND DENTISTS

Workforce composition

The Royal Commission on the NHS pointed out that 'the vast majority of people will, when they are ill, expect the doctor to diagnose what is wrong and prescribe treatment'.[13] Although hospital doctors account for only 6% of the NHS workforce, they are responsible for initiating most of its expenditure and have increasingly become involved in assuming a role in the management of the financial resources and of the service itself.

The number of hospital doctors more than doubled between 1948 and 1978,[14] at an average growth rate of over 3% per annum. In fact, there were 13 635 hospital doctors and about 20 000 GPs in 1949 and this had risen to 34 784 hospital doctors and just over 26 000 GPs by 1977. By 1988 the NHS employed over 54 000 hospital doctors, of whom over 17 000 were consultants[15] (Table 2.2). It is important to recognize differences within the doctors: there are hospital-based doctors and GPs; within hospitals there are differences between specialisms which sometimes also reflect the proportion of part-timers, women and

Table 2.2a Doctors and dentists in the National Health Service in Great Britain: 1988 and 1989

	1988 med.	1988 dent.	1989 med.	1989 dent.	Change (%) med.	Change (%) dent.
Hospital medical and dental staff[1]						
Consultants	17 386	637	17 854	644	2.7	1.1
Associate specialists	1018	111	1034	104	1.6	−6.3
Staff grade	—	—	33	—	—	—
Senior registrars	3726	145	3848	157	3.3	8.3
Registrars	7727	267	7614	248	−1.5	−7.1
Senior house officers	11 705	228	12 476	255	6.6	11.8
House officers	3567	138	3642	129	2.1	−6.5
Hospital practitioners	947	59	948	63	0.1	6.8
Clinical assistants	8635	849	8881	879	2.8	3.5
Other	77	8	23	7	−70.1	−12.5
Total	54 788	2442	56 353	2486	2.9	1.8
Community medical staff[1]						
Regional and district medical officers			170		169	−0.6
Specialists in community medicine			469		462	−1.5
Special salary scale staff			12		7	−41.7
Trainees in community medicine			330		345	4.5
Senior clinical medical officers			1401		1375	−1.9
Clinical medical officers			2077		2036	−2.0
Other medical staff			2630		2577	−2.0
Total			7089		6971	−1.7
Community dental staff[1]						
Regional and district dental officers			130		137	5.4
Assistant district dental officers			31		32	3.2
Senior dental officers			396		425	7.3
Dental officers			1455		1377	−5.4
Other dental staff			106		113	6.6
Total			2118		2084	−1.6

[1] At 30 September.
Source: DDRB, 1991, p. 60.

Table 2.2a *(continued)* Doctors and dentists in the National Health Service in Great Britain: 1988 and 1989

	1988 med.	1988 dent.	1989 med.	1989 dent.	Change (%) med.	Change (%) dent.
General practitioners						
General medical practitioners[1]						
unrestricted principals	30 277		30 631		1.2	
restricted principals	170		179		5.3	
assistants	276		261		−5.4	
trainees	2165		2239		3.4	
General dental practitioners						
principals[2]	17 144		17 436		1.7	
assistants[2]	296		394		33.1	
salaried health centre dentists[3]	85		68		−20.0	
Ophthalmic medical practitioner[4]	930		882		−5.2	
Total	51 343		52 090		1.5	
Total: NHS doctors and dentists	117 780		119 984		1.9	

[1] At 30 September.
[2] At 1 October. Provisional figures for 1990 are available; those for 1989 are used for consistency.
[3] At 30 June. Figure at 30 June 1990 was 53.
[4] At 31 December.
Source: DDRB, 1991, p. 60.

those from other countries. The spread of doctors by region varies, with Scotland having had nearly twice as many per 10 000 population as Trent in 1977 and the West Midlands having the most hospital medical staff of all the regions in 1987.[16] About one in three hospital doctors are consultants, and a disproportionate number of these are men born in Britain.

The vast majority of dentists are in partnerships, with remarkably few in hospitals. As a result they are similar to GPs. This category enjoy a peculiar status. Most of them are self-employed employers who contract to provide services for the NHS. Their trade union and industrial relations needs are therefore much reduced, although their general need for protection and influence in those corridors where pay is decided remains high. The Review Body for doctors and dentists

Table 2.2b Hospital medical staff (England): analysis by grade and sex

		1978		1983		1984		1985		1986		1987		1988	
		No.	wte	No.	wte	No.	wte	No.	wte	No.	wte	No.	wte	No.	wte
All staff:		38 527	31 013	42 709	35 112	42 728	35 322	43 495	35 920	43 992	36 305	43 957	36 250	45 445	37 559
	M	31 044	25 202	33 077	27 349	32 764	27 258	33 077	27 453	33 101	27 437	32 875	27 200	33 667	27 872
	F	7483	5812	9632	7762	9964	8064	10 418	8467	10 891	8868	11 082	9050	11 778	9687
Consultant and Shmo[1] with allowance		11 640	10 382	12 892	11 824	13 185	12 131	13 458	12 374	13 785	12 651	13 992	12 831	14 300	13 177
	M	10 450	9349	11 333	10 449	11 526	10 657	11 711	10 825	11 913	11 001	12 048	11 113	12 227	11 331
	F	1190	1033	1559	1375	1659	1473	1747	1549	1872	1650	1944	1718	2073	1845
Associate specialist (formerly medical assistant)		913	760	939	785	906	760	849	710	809	675	792	667	779	655
	M	516	461	524	474	516	469	474	429	451	406	459	419	453	421
	F	397	299	415	310	390	291	375	281	358	268	333	248	326	234
Senior registrar		2614	2228	3084	2678	2988	2638	3132	2755	3253	2857	3215	2865	3182	2861
	M	2139	1844	2367	2087	2252	2038	2351	2114	2443	2178	2365	2147	2316	2118
	F	475	384	717	591	736	600	781	642	810	678	850	717	866	743
Registrar		5369	5087	5821	5560	5755	5504	5749	5483	5849	5614	5873	5661	6146	5886
	M	4390	4226	4531	4392	4455	4317	4465	4307	4497	4372	4492	4370	4684	4525
	F	979	861	1290	1168	1300	1187	1284	1176	1352	1242	1381	1291	1462	1362

Note: Numbers are as at 30 September each year.
[1] From 1987 Senior hospital medical officers with allowance are included with other staff.
Source: Health and Personal Social Services Statistics.

Table 2.2b (*continued*) Hospital medical staff (England): analysis by grade and sex

		1978 No.	1978 wte	1983 No.	1983 wte	1984 No.	1984 wte	1985 No.	1985 wte	1986 No.	1986 wte	1987 No.	1987 wte	1988 No.	1988 wte
Senior house officer[2]		8346	8260	9627	9558	9589	9537	9792	9722	9690	9622	9457	9372	9960	9884
	M	6336	6307	6896	6863	6687	6675	6632	6612	6437	6424	6128	6098	6352	6324
	F	2010	1954	2731	2694	2902	2862	3160	3110	3253	3198	3329	3274	3608	3560
House officer		2525	2516	2826	2825	2773	2772	2838	2837	2813	2811	2790	2782	2862	2861
	M	1734	1726	1753	1753	1727	1726	1737	1736	1614	1613	1593	1589	1595	1595
	F	791	789	1073	1073	1046	1046	1101	1101	1119	1198	1197	1193	1267	1267
Other staff and Shmo without allowance		108	61	49	30	142	74	41	22	79	28	93	40	62	14
	M	92	53	44	28	101	54	34	20	63	23	71	31	47	11
	F	16	8	5	3	41	20	7	2	16	5	22	9	15	3
Hospital practitioner		466	117	882	221	903	228	845	205	850	210	894	212	853	200
	M	433	110	821	207	834	211	785	191	789	194	809	194	787	185
	F	33	7	61	13	69	17	60	14	61	16	85	18	66	16
Para. 94 appointment		6546	1604	6589	1631	6487	1679	6791	1813	6864	1840	6851	1821	7301	2021
	M	4954	1126	4808	1096	4666	1111	4888	1221	4894	1226	4910	1238	5206	1363
	F	1592	478	1781	536	1821	568	1903	591	1970	614	1941	582	2095	659

Note: Numbers are as at 30 September each year.
[2] Prior to 1984 figures include post-registration House Officer.
Source: Health and Personal Social Services Statistics.

recommends an intended average net remuneration for GPs and GDPs.

These divisions within the profession are of real importance for industrial relations. They provide a constant source of contradictory demands on the BMA and BDA policy-makers. They reflect status differentials which in turn may reflect attitudes to colleagues, patients and change. In the future they may well experience quite different pay and conditions with the coming of decentralized and performance related pay bargaining, and the newcomers to the profession may feel, as they showed in the 1975 junior hospital doctors dispute,[17] that they are as capable of taking industrial action as any other health worker.

Pay determination

The pay of doctors and dentists in all their NHS forms has been decided for many years (since 1971 as the Review Body on Doctors' and Dentists' Remuneration, the DDRB) through the system of the unions (BMA and BDA) providing evidence and the employers and DHSS providing other evidence to the members of the Review Body. It in turn submits recommendations to the Secretary of State (see Chapter 6). In April 1988 the government accepted the recommendation of 7.3% for GPs and 8.1% for hospital and community doctors. In April 1989 the government implemented the 8% pay recommendation. Throughout the 1980s doctors and dentists have achieved better pay rises than most other NHS staff and have compared favourably with the average earnings index.

The most recent case put forward by doctors and dentists is very similar to that produced by all other NHS staff organizations. High on the list of Pay Body considerations are the labour market issues of recruitment and retention linked to motivation and morale. This is the line of the government and the health departments that pay should reflect the labour market situation within wider guidelines of affordability. Where the DDRB's concerns vary from the other Review Body is that there is more interest shown in internal labour market issues of promotion and discrimination against women hospital doctors than with comparability associated with the external labour market.

However, the line on comparability is much more interesting, as the Review Body noted: 'the Departments repeated their view that doctors and dentists could not occupy an unchanged position in a historic earnings league'.[18] The argument continued that doctors and dentists had done very well, among the best, within the public sector, with real pay increases of 36% in the 1980s. The question of comparators is the crux of this particular debate: doctors and dentists wish to remain broadly in line with NES figures for other higher professionals such as lawyers and accountants, while the government, through the Departments, suggests that this is unrealistic and unacceptable in social and economic terms.

While most of the arguments simply reflect the concerns of the day, the important point remains about long-term customary pay differences between professions and within them in terms of the original labour pool (highly qualified and motivated graduates) in which they all fish. This shift in position by government reflects the need to convince the doctors and dentists that to earn more they have to enter the more risk-based and market-centred earnings merry-go-round of those they wish to use as comparators. This might well happen in the self-governing trusts where a series of possible futures for doctors can be imagined, including their exclusion from direct employment and the development of partnerships of consultants hired back on medium-term contracts and/or by the session.

The relative success of the 1980s for these professions has meant a limited role in bargaining for their organizations, and less urgency in the pay determination contests. This has recently changed. The NHS reforms both in management/employer structures and in financing have generated a new round of debates on bargaining strategies, political pressure group activities and the role of the industrial relations officers. The BMA has appointed more and more Industrial Relations Officers (IROs) and have linked them with influential Place of Work Accredited Representatives (POWARs).

In addition, the anticipated policy of some single-employer bargainers suggests that some doctors will have their pay decided away from Pay Review and that most will have elements of their pay decided at the employer's discretion. As part of this process, performance related pay and the concomitant individual pay contract loom large in the fears of many doctors and present some nice issues for the BMA and BDA. A central point here is the measurement of performance. None the less, conventional managerial wisdom is in line with the arguments from workload and productivity which are associated with some of the half-digested economic theories and practices that the Review Bodies and Ministers seem to accept. These are examined in Chapter 8.

The 1990 pay round brought basic pay for hospital doctors ranging from £11 255 as the minimum for a house officer to £43 075 for the maximum for a consultant. Community doctors and dentists range from £16 790 to £34 375, and the intended average for GPs is £34 680 compared with £29 740 for dentists. In addition, there are the agreed fees and allowances: these are made up of merit and distinction awards that vary from A+ up to £43 075 to a low C of £6935. There are then a plethora of other allowances, supplements, oncall payments, fees that add up to significant amounts of money and influence earnings. All of this is outside any private income doctors and dentists may have. Earnings, therefore, will be considerably in excess of pay rates.

The 1991 Pay Review Body report was the first since the enactment of the NHS and Community Care Act 1990. The BMA and BDA put greater stress than usual on comparisons with like employment outside the NHS, and the Review Body commented that:

> The data considered as a whole suggest that earnings for doctors and dentists increased more slowly between 1989 and 1990 than those for comparable groups in the private sector. This is one of a number of important factors we have taken into account.[19]

Overall the 1991 report repeated the labour market arguments and comparability studies of previous years, although it felt constrained to tinker with internal relativities by giving consultants and GDPs slightly more than the others.[20]

The solutions which the BMA in particular will develop in the face of the problems facing its members and all doctors in the 1990s will combine the well-tested dual approaches of political influence and employer-based bargaining. This latter will develop in line with traditional structures, and despite the claims of today's health service managers and employers, the system they advocate will more closely mirror a previous form of industrial relations than any new formulations. With this in mind, it is worth examining the main collective bargaining customs of doctors, and in particular the BMA's stormy entrance into the NHS.

The BMA and the NHS

What kind of trade union and bargaining traditions did the doctors have? Prior to 1939, the Askwith Committee[21] recommended rates for doctors in local authority and mental hospitals which were principally followed. In 1946, following the Spens Reports,[22] which set the pay of GPs, dentists and consultants and specialists, respectively, the BMA met the British Hospitals Association (BHA) and the Mental Hospitals Association (MHA) on a formal basis to fix revised rates pending the result of the Danckwerts Award.[23] This subsequently adjusted the Spens settlements upwards.

As Table 2.1 indicated, the BMA and the BDA are the oldest professional associations, having been established in 1832 and 1880 respectively. Only the BMA was recognized as being involved in negotiations before 1948 and that recognition continued with the creation of the NHS. An interesting element of this was that the BMA was granted the right to represent all doctors whether they were members or not, and a continuing consequence of that is that non-BMA members can sit on (and even chair) local negotiating committees of the BMA with the employer. The BDA's negotiating status was formally recognized in 1950. Since that time, these two organizations have been the only professional associations to be fully recognized by the Department of Health as being eligible to negotiate on behalf of doctors and dentists. The BMA won sole negotiating rights under the Whitley system when the NHS was set up.

The Labour government granted this despite the formidable and often ill-tempered fight the BMA leadership put up against many aspects of the NHS. Eckstein is not alone in characterizing the BMA's campaign against the NHS as ill-founded, and as the ill-considered reaction of the conservative-dominated leadership. As he says: 'as soon as the Government became serious about reforming the medical system, a sort of nameless fear of what might ensue gripped the profession's representatives'.[24] This is an intriguing view since it indicates the extent to which the BMA feared for its special protections under a Labour government, and thereby exposed its ignorance of both Labour politics and its awareness of the privileges granted to the profession in the past. Eckstein goes on to show that the vast majority of doctors, and nearly 80% of hospital doctors, favoured a 'free and complete hospital service'.[25] Hence the official BMA policy reflected not the views of its members but of its political allies in the Conservative Party.

This initial opposition to the NHS did not prevent the BMA from following an essentially practical series of policies with regard to their members' pay, conditions of service and job control. This pragmatism behind a mask of professional aloofness and disciplined self-control, is nearer the heart of the BMA's decisions within the NHS rather than the odd hysterical outbreak of reactionary élitism. It's reaction to the NHS can be traced back to its origins. In 1832 the Provincial Medical and Surgical Association was founded in Worcester in an endeavour to counter the dominance of London in matters of medical practice. The meeting that set it up was held 'in the boardroom of the Worcester Infirmary... more than fifty practitioners were present'.[26] It was not until 1853 that the association first allowed London practitioners to join the association and three years later that the title became the British Medical Association.[27] At the same time, the association's publication became known as the *British Medical Journal*. From its earliest days, the BMA's powerful political lobby was in evidence and one of its first major successes was the Medical Act of 1858 which established the General Medical Council – the regulatory body for the medical profession.[28] Little concludes his centenary history of the BMA with reference to a major debate about the nature of the funding of health care and the remuneration of doctors. As he says:

> the position of the voluntary, and indeed of the municipal, hospitals has changed very considerably during recent years, partly through the drying up of many of the large subscriptions from charitable donors, partly to the development of contributory schemes which encourage working-class people to subscribe regularly to their local hospitals, and partly to the passing of the Local Government Act of 1929 which clearly envisages the improvement and greater use of the old poor law hospitals (now municipal or council hospitals). Fortunately the Association had forseen these developments, and began in 1920 to prepare the mind of the profession for the inevitable changes. When hospitals were institutions for the 'relief of the sick poor' medical men were glad to give their services gratuitously. But when they became (as they are rapidly becoming) places supported largely by the collective contributions of workmen and employers, and by funds derived from contributory schemes which are of the nature of insurance against the risk of the need of hospital treatment –

> when hospitals found themselves obliged to demand payment
> from patients according to their means, and above all as hospitals
> become more and more the resort of people who could not be said
> to be 'poor persons' – then it became obvious that the members of
> the medical staffs could no longer afford to give their services
> gratuitously.[29]

This hesitant and half-understood move from self-employment
to a form of employment as an independent professional was
taken a step further with the founding of the NHS and the development of doctor as employee.

The authors of the second volume of the BMA's official
history (1932–1982) noted with some annoyance that 'the most
important event for the BMA in the 50 years covered by this
volume was not the war or the therapeutic revolution, but the
nationalization of medicine 1946–8'.[30] This term 'nationalization'
conveys the BMA's distaste for the NHS, and certainly many of
its leaders have never settled for the public ownership of health
provision. From the start the BMA's official position was very
hostile to Bevan, and the *BMJ* summarized the fears of the profession: it did not like doctors being full-time salaried employees
of the state, it wanted full representation of doctors on all
administrative bodies, it supported the rights of doctors and
patients to be 'free to choose', it opposed 'the proposal to disin-
herit the voluntary hospitals', and feared a 'whole-time salaried
state medical service'.[31] The BMA, while opposing reform,
simultaneously prepared for it, and mounted a campaign
amongst its members to secure support for the BMA's negotiating position with government.

Through a series of plebiscites the BMA publicized the doctors' worries and views. The results were not always as clear cut
as the official history maintains, and many doctors had grave
reservations about the BMA's leadership. By May 1948 the BMA
agreed to cooperate with the NHS after Bevan made concessions.
The authors' explanation for the BMA's opposition was that, 'so
long as the Minister of Health exhibited a high-handed, truculent
attitude towards the medical profession the doctors were united
against him'.[32]

Almost immediately Bevan and the government paid the
price for their concessions to the doctors and the virtual exclusion of other health workers and their organizations from most
major committees. The doctors were unhappy with their pay and
in 1948/9 the Spens reports moved towards certain principles for

government to follow. In January 1950 Medical Whitley met for the first time, but as with other employees the doctors felt it 'too cumbersome, too slow, and too much inhibited by Government policy'.[33] In 1952 doctors' pay went to arbitration and Danckwerts developed a pay formula which in 1954 was extended to hospital doctors. In 1957 there was a Royal Commission into doctors' pay under Pilkington[34] which established a Pay Review Body as the BMA had wanted and which first reported in 1962. For the rest of the 1960s pay awards for doctors, like everyone else, became bogged down in incomes policies and National Board for Prices and Incomes (NBPI) referrals. In 1970 the government agreed to a new independent pay review system under Halsbury,[35] but even that was not safe from types of incomes policies such as phasing, as in 1978 and again in 1990/1.

It is of lasting importance that when the Labour government established the NHS it faced a protracted dispute with the BMA over doctors' remuneration and the terms on which they would practise in the NHS. Since the government was anxious to persuade the BMA to encourage doctors to join the NHS, the association was able to win major concessions for its members, some of which set the parameters within which the NHS would be organized. The BMA's role in the foundation of the NHS remains an issue of controversy and moment – it illustrated the hostility of the major profession to the nationalization of medicine, and it showed the ability of the doctors through the BMA to secure a powerful place in any system of health service provision. The extent to which leading figures in the profession opposed the NHS in 1948 is remarkable. As the official NHS historian noted:

> the serious newspapers were inundated by letters from doctors concerned that their fundamental liberties were under threat. These fears were exacerbated by increasingly impassioned letters and speeches from the BMA leadership.[36]

He suggests that 'ideally the BMA leadership wanted abandonment of the entire scheme'.[37] Bevan was the *bête noire* to be fought tooth and nail. As Webster coolly announces, 'the credibility of the BMA Council rested on its policy of vigilance, which retrospectively looks like overreaction'.[38]

Later he writes about the 'reckless and emotional BMA leadership'.[39] The fierce opposition to Bevan, the man and his scheme on health, came not only from the doctors but also from nearer home, from his own senior civil servants, some Ministers, and the voluntary hospital lobby. Some nurses, through the RCN, initially opposed a nationalized service, but by the start of the NHS most had been persuaded to accept the inevitable. As Jenny Lee remembers about Nye Bevan,

> at a time when he was locked in endless stormy negotiations with the British Medical Association, the violence of the attacks on him frightened some of his colleagues. They urged that more concessions be given to his critics. While cold feet under the Cabinet table were making life difficult for Nye in private, hot-heads, led by the Socialist Medical Association, were lambasting him in public.[40]

The Socialist Medical Association (SMA) was an important pressure group of doctors in support of the NHS, and their anger with Bevan stemmed in part from his refusal to acknowledge their contribution to the debate.[41] Jenny Lee also quotes Bevan as saying he was aware of, but unworried by, the imperfections in the NHS such as private beds and the failure to secure a full-time salaried medical staff. As he said, 'no future government will dare undo it'.[42]

Another biographer of Bevan remarked about the BMA's position on the NHS Bill that

> even so it was astonishing to him that the leaders of the medical profession had identified themselves in such a spirit of partisanship with the Conservatives. The spokesmen of some elements of the profession had become the most reactionary politicians in Great Britain.[43]

His taking over of the voluntary hospitals was seen as 'a very carefully prepared measure of highway robbery'.[44] As Brome records, 'a dramatic statement from Dr. Dain, Chairman of the BMA Council, said that Aneurin Bevan would become "complete Medical Services dictator".[45] The eventual compromise with the doctors which Bevan saw as a necessary act of *realpolitik* was bitterly criticized by many in the Labour Party, seeing it as not a compromise with the doctors as much as one with the policies of the wartime coalition.[46]

Bevan played a unique role in the original formation of the NHS. His battle with the doctors, or more precisely with the militant wing of the BMA's Representative Body and most of the national leadership, is legendary. The doctors' position was made up of several elements, as Foot explains:

On the doctors' side, opposition to the form of national health service proposed by Bevan was compounded of many elements. At best, it derived from a deeply entrenched belief that almost any system of State control over medicine would destroy the doctors' clinical freedom ... Much the strongest bent in the medical mind was a non-political conservatism ... finally, with these other emotions went a powerful streak of professional arrogance.[47]

It was therefore Bevan's task to, 'persuade the most conservative and respected profession in the country to accept and operate the Labour Government's most intrinsically socialist proposition'.[48] The BMA had strong support from the Conservative press, but in Foot's judgement the excessive attacks on Bevan and the NHS from the BMA generated a strong hostility to the doctors and their attitude to the popular reform of health.

The BMA's bitter opposition to Labour governments and Labour Party policy in general cannot be doubted. The BMA opposed the attempts by Labour in 1965–8 to phase private beds out of the NHS. The BMA's view was that this meant 'a substantial loss of income' for part-time consultants.[49] In 1975 the BMA considered the Labour government's efforts to separate private practice from the NHS as 'the greatest threat to the independence of the medical profession' since the NHS was started.[50] This battle continued with the BMA threatening sanctions over the terms of the 1979 Royal Commission until Lord Goodman achieved a compromise between the BMA and the government.[51]

In contrast, the BMA accepted without opposition the Conservative government's 1974 reforms of the NHS.[52] In more recent years, however, the BMA has attacked Conservative reform proposals. In 1989/90 a great deal of time and money was spent in personal and policy indictments, and this campaign succeeded in gaining some limited changes in the reform proposals and some improved bargaining position for the doctors. The decision to take such a committed stand against the government was bitterly fought through all levels of the BMA and surprised as well as angered Ministers. As in all cases, there are many doctors who dislike the BMA's conservative policies and approach and are prepared to counter the present efforts to individualize doctors' pay and privatize the NHS. But even their fondest friends could not claim that such groups had substantial support.

This sketch of the BMA's original opposition to the NHS is intended to illustrate the complex nature of the relationships between a highly esteemed profession working *as if* they were self-employed (as many are) within a state-funded industry which is often controlled by conservative Civil Servants and which involves the expenditure of enormous amounts from the public purse. It shows how the Labour Party has been caught too often in the trap of underestimating the power of the BMA and overestimating the bargaining strength of the doctors themselves. In industrial relations terms the early fights within the NHS persuaded political leaders of both main parties that the best way to deal with doctors' pay was to leave it to a Review Body and in the main implement its recommendations even when they outraged government policy on public sector pay. Political advisers have long memories when it comes to damaging disputes with powerful groups, and doctors have benefited from their willingness to fight hard and to secure the help of other powerful vested interests and from the weaknesses of politicians, especially those in the Labour Party caught in the timeless trap between their principles and their political futures.

Trade Union aspects of the BMA

The BMA was the first of the professional associations in the NHS to obtain certification as an independent trade union. Its general policy is decided by an Annual Representative meeting of 600 members, who are elected on a 'craft' or geographic basis, that reflects all branches of the profession. The BMA's Council, or central executive, usually meets on five occasions a year. In order to comply with the 1984 Trade Union Act, 46 of its members are now voted for by the membership as a whole in a single, annual ballot. Only these elected members have voting rights.

After what the BMA refers to as the 'nationalization' of medicine, many members felt that the BMA required a more trade union element. In order to get around some political and legal aspects relating to the status of the organization under the Companies Acts the BMA set up the British Medical Guild as its trade union wing.[53] It was used in the 1957 pay dispute, and again in 1965 and 1970.[54] The BMA, along with the BDA, RCN and RCM, wanted exemption from the 1971 Industrial Relations Act and won it under sections 84–86 which set up a Special Register of bodies not subject to the Act. This was preserved in the 1974 Trade Union and Labour Relations Act. In general the view was that, doctors are individualists, not collectivists, and there are many features of trade unionism that are anathema to them: the political levy, the closed shop, the strike ... and picketing.[55]

There is a network of 18 Regional Services centres that covers the whole of the UK and the activities of the full-time regional staff who are employed in these centres are coordinated by the Membership and Regional Services for England, in close collaboration with the regional offices in Scotland, Wales and Northern Ireland (Figure 2.1). This regional system started after 1977, and was a victory for the reformers after several years of battle within the BMA relating to its essentially London-dominated and undemocratic system of government. This constitutional aspect of internal political differences shows itself from time to time in the tensions between the Council and the Representative Body.[56] The political differences are more important than revealed by the BMA's official historians.

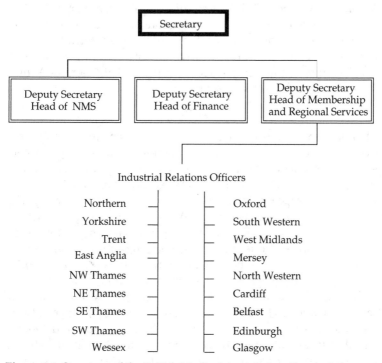

Figure 2.1 Structure of the British Medical Association. For clarity, some divisions which report directly to the Secretary have been omitted. (*Source:* BMA head office.)

There are some 500 Place of Work Accredited Representatives who work in hospitals, universities, community medicine and community health sectors and provide the 'grassroots' level of representation and advice. The BMA's Professional Relations Unit provides the liaison between the BMA nationally and its regional representatives and divisions and sends out regular information bulletins.

There are four main committees with sole negotiating rights which represent the interests of doctors who are employed in the NHS. These are: General Medical Services (for General Practitioners); Central Consultants and Specialists; Community Medicine and Health; and Hospital Junior Staff. In addition, members receive advice and help from the legal department and through their Regional Service.

Finally, the BMA has full-time press, parliamentary and information officers to provide the necessary publicity and public relations support, and its weekly publication, the *British Medical Journal*, which in 1989 had a circulation of more than 100 000.[57] The wealth and influence of this professional association was perhaps never more evident than in its often vitriolic media campaign against the Conservative government in general, and the Secretary of State in particular, during 1989 when the White Paper *Working for Patients* was published.

This account of the pay determination system for doctors and dentists and then of the BMA's reaction to the setting up and subsequent reforms of the NHS reveals a strong profession in a dominant position within the NHS and at hospital level. The profession's representative association, the BMA, is a hybrid organization, part pressure group and part trade union, with a healthy financial position, strong professional wing and increasing industrial relations function used to fighting in many ways on many fronts for the perceived interests of its members. It has recently increased its overall membership and now claims to have about three-quarters of the medical profession within its ranks. As befits a closed craft union based on a single profession, its current concerns revolve around job regulation and labour supply issues, although there is increasing interest in single-employer pay bargaining and in particular worries over individual performance related pay contracts and increased managerial controls over individual doctors.

A leading BMA official stated in a letter to the author that the BMA and its members faced two major issues in the 1990s: the decentralization of bargaining (Chapter 8), and problems from recent management changes.

> An important objective of these changes was to reduce substantially the extent of the medical profession's participation in local health authority management, bringing finally to an end a tradition of consensus management which had prevailed in the NHS since its inception in 1948. It is the BMA's view that a health service cannot be run both effectively and in the interests of the patients without the full participation of clinicians in all aspects of management.

NURSES, MIDWIVES AND HEALTH VISITORS

Workforce composition

Table 1.3 shows this staff group to be the largest in the NHS, commanding the largest salary bill. In 1966 there were 252 111 nursing staff working in the NHS. By 1977, that figure had risen to 379 699,[58] and as Table 2.3 indicates, in 1989 the total had reached 490 000 (wte). Thus, in two decades the numbers of nursing staff had almost doubled. Of these 64% were qualified professionals, 13% were in training and the remaining 23% were auxiliaries and assistants. This low proportion of qualified staff caused the RCN a great deal of concern.[59] The high cost of employing nurses is emphasized by Clay, who points out that their pay bill accounts for £3 out of every £100 that the government has to spend.[60]

Midwifery and health visitors' statistics are always included within the 'nursing' totals. They have long been recognized as separate professions, even though the majority are trained nurses.

Unlike the doctors and dentists, this group of health workers have had their pay and conditions determined through the Whitley Council system until the setting up of a Pay Review Body for them in 1984. In addition, nurses have been members of several trade unions and in particular they belong to the three largest of the NHS unions: the RCN, NUPE and COHSE. There are nurses in other unions such as NALGO and the GMB. The RCN is dealt with in this chapter while NUPE, COHSE, the GMB and NALGO are discussed in Chapter 3. This section, however, looks at the pay and pay determination for nurses and the infor-

Table 2.3a Nursing and midwifery staff (England): analysis by area of work and grade

		1983	1984	1985	1986	1987[1]	1988[1]
All nursing and midwifery staff[2]	Total	394 683	393 739	397 031	397 240	397 909	397 647
Administrative nursing staff		2339	2627	2543	2340	2512	2601
Nursing staff in centrally based services		1702	1669	1724	1775	1898	1854
Blood transfusion service staff		1144	1140	1131	1151	1115	1145
Administrative midwifery staff		220	179	171	179	187	198
Hospital nursing staff	Total	329 965	328 268	329 959	330 830	331 172	330 669
Qualified	Total	171 295	174 693	179 273	182 319	184 373	186 689
Senior nurses 1–5		221	268	264	440	654	749
Senior nurses 6–8		5411	5611	5744	5458	5428	5608
Tutorial nursing staff		4307	4701	4570	4935	5030	5003
Other registered nurses		95 955	97 648	101 235	104 613	107 187	110 986
Enrolled nurses		65 401	66 466	67 460	66 875	66 074	64 343
Learners							
Post-registration student nurses		1959	1959	1983	2169	1950	1769
Post-enrolment student nurses		1674	1475	1572	1648	1521	1568
Pre-registration student nurses		50 535	50 963	49 422	48 350	47 370	48 008
Pupil nurses		18 336	15 094	12 333	10 358	8310	6179
Unqualified	Total	86 165	84 083	85 375	85 987	87 649	86 453

Note: wte as at 30 September each year.

[1] Figures include 'Other Statutory Authorities' staff. Prior to 1987 figures for these authorities were not collected in the Annual Manpower Census.

[2] Excludes agency staff.

Source: Health and Personal Social Services Statistics for England, 1990 edn, pp. 54–5.

Table 2.3a (continued) Nursing and midwifery staff (England): analysis by area of work and grade

		1983	1984	1985	1986	1987[1]	1988[1]
Other nursing staff[3]		86 097	84 053	85 357	85 981	87 644	86 453
Nursing cadets		69	30	18	6	5	—
Hospital midwifery staff	Total	18 156	18 535	18 597	18 722	19 008	18 993
Qualified	Total	13 403	13 795	14 219	14 543	15 029	14 978
Senior nurses 1–5		17	24	25	28	47	50
Senior nurses 6–8		628	603	614	579	526	499
Tutorial midwifery staff		545	540	550	534	563	621
Other state certified midwives		12 214	12 627	13 030	13 403	13 893	13 807
Learners: student midwives		4753	4740	4378	4179	3979	4015
Primary health care nursing staff	Total	37 467	37 464	38 866	38 116	37 916	38 081
Senior nurses 1–5 and above		72	82	82	91	125	144
Senior nurses 6–8		1226	1409	1334	1254	1211	1191
Health visiting							
Health visitors[4]		9640	9251	10 240	10 393	10 333	10 313
Other registered		948	1053	871	460	641	689
Other enrolled		112	104	100	93	91	102
Student health visitors		1023	971	866	832	785	786
Other nursing staff		162	188	204	224	260	235

Note: wte as at 30 September each year.

[1] Figures include 'Other Statutory Authorities' staff. Prior to 1987 figures for these authorities were not collected in the Annual Manpower Census.

[3] Include nursing auxiliaries and nursery nurses.

[4] Includes Health Visitor Fieldwork Teachers, HV School Nurses, TB visitors with HV certificates and Bank HVs.

Source: Health and Personal Social Services Statistics for England, 1990 edn, pp. 54–5.

Table 2.3a *(continued)* Nursing and midwifery staff (England): analysis by area of work and grade

	1983	1984	1985	1986	1987[1]	1988[1]
District nursing						
District nurses[5]	8999	8767	8998	9119	8691	8648
District nursing tutorial	60	46	50	43	43	42
Other registered	1543	1782	1876	1315	1732	1763
Other enrolled[6]	3898	4047	4216	4296	4232	4221
Student district nurses	577	648	704	680	650	608
Other nursing staff	2594	2717	2998	3203	3300	3264
School nursing service						
Registered nurses[7]	2445	2442	2493	2485	2473	2415
Enrolled nurses	218	219	189	182	162	142
Dual/triple duty posts						
Health visitor/district nurse/midwife (and health visitor/midwife)	68	49	45	37	30	25
District nurse/midwife (and SRN/midwife)	684	584	503	457	391	339
Enrolled nurse/midwife	5	6	4	—	—	3
Other registered nurses	1161	1167	1179	1207	1095	1214

Note: wte as at 30 September each year.

[1] Figures include 'Other Statutory Authorities' staff. Prior to 1987 figures for these authorities were not collected in the Annual Manpower Census.

[5] Includes District Nurse Practical Work Teachers and Bank District Nurses.

[6] Includes enrolled nurses with District Nursing Training.

[7] Includes school nurses and other registered nurses working in the school health services.

Source: Health and Personal Social Services Statistics for England, 1990 edn, pp. 54–5.

Table 2.3a (*continued*) Nursing and midwifery staff (England): analysis by area of work and grade

		1983	1984	1985	1986	1987[1]	1988[1]
Other enrolled nurses		296	280	321	368	364	459
Other unqualified staff		1738	1654	1594	1378	1308	1481
Community health midwifery staff	Total	3713	3858	4041	4128	4101	4106
Senior nurses 1–5 and above		—	2	1	—	1	3
Senior nurse 6–8		119	133	134	117	111	107
Other midwifery staff		3594	3723	3906	4011	3989	3996
Agency nurses (Hospital)[8]		2191	3426	3716	4866	5665	5632
Agency midwives (Hospital)[8]		200	220	261	268	252	319
Agency nurses (PHC)[8]		43	101	143	282	215	280
Agency midwives (PHC)[8]		7	—	—	35	1	2

Note: wte as at 30 September each year.

[1] Figures include 'Other Statutory Authorities' staff. Prior to 1987 figures for these authorities were not collected in the Annual Manpower Census.

[8] Not included in the totals.

Source: Health and Personal Social Services Statistics for England, 1990 edn, pp. 54–5.

Table 2.3b Whole-time equivalent numbers of nursing staff in Great Britain at 30 September 1989[1]

Pay grade	Whole-time equivalents	
	No. (000)	%[2]
Senior nurse grade 8 and above[3,4]	3.6	0.7
Grade I	6.5	1.3
Grade H	10.4	2.1
Grade G	64.0	13.0
Grade F	30.8	6.3
Grade E	81.9	16.7
Grade D	72.1	14.7
Grade C	26.1	5.3
Grade B	19.2	3.9
Grade A	95.6	19.5
Student nurse	57.9	11.8
Pupil nurse	4.7	1.0
Teaching staff[5]	6.5	1.3
Post-registration student	9.8	2.0
Other nursing staff	1.4	0.3
Total[2]	490.5	100.0

[1] Excludes agency staff.
[2] Totals may not equal the sum of components because of rounding, and percentages have been calculated from unrounded figures.
[3] Although senior nurses and midwives are not dealt with in this report, they are included in this table for completeness.
[4] Includes senior nurse grades 8 to 1 + (Staff Support — education).
[5] Includes all education staff except those mentioned in footnote 4.
Source: PRB for nurses 1991, p. 25.

mation provided applies for the nurse members of the other unions representing nurses. This split reflects, to some extent, the training, status and specialisms of nurses as well as the origins of the organizations. It also reflects the unions' structure in terms of open recruitment or a closed single-profession base, which in turn impinges on the policy priorities as between the unions.

RCN and the nurses

In 1941 the Ministry of Health fixed minimum salaries for student nurses. Subsequently, a Nurses Salaries Committee was created – the one for England and Wales being chaired by Lord Rushcliffe and the one for Scotland initially by Professor Taylor and later by Lord Guthrie.

The professional associations represented on the Rushcliffe Committee were established before the NHS came into being. The Royal College of Midwives (RCM) was founded in 1881, the Health Visitors Association (HVA) in 1896 and the Royal College of Nursing (RCN) in 1916. In recent years all have expanded their full-time officer support to their members, particularly with regard to industrial relations work, and the RCN, RCM and HVA were amongst the first of the NHS organizations to appoint union stewards. Dyson and Spary claimed that, in 1979, 'the RCN's training programme for stewards [was] unquestionably the best developed of any NHS professional association and [might] be considered to compare favourably with that of the long established multi-occupational unions'.[61]

The RCN membership, according to head office figures, has risen as follows since the formation of the NHS:

1950	44 239
1960	43 465
1971	49 551
1981	181 111
1989	280 000 approx.

This makes it the largest NHS trade union along with NUPE (counting only NUPE's members in the NHS) and COHSE. It has increased its membership in the past two decades while that of NUPE and COHSE has fallen during the 1980s. This reflects both the different composition of the health service membership of the different unions as well as the increased unionization of nurses when faced with uncertainty and a more explicit managerial and industrial relations work environment. By the late 1980s the RCN had about 280 000 nurse members compared with about 120 000 in COHSE (of whom about a quarter are psychiatric nurses), 80 000 in NUPE and about 7000 in the GMB.

There are many books on the history of the nursing profession, but there is only one history of the RCN and that concentrates on professional matters.[62] The RCN started life in 1916 as the College of Nursing Ltd to promote the education and training of nurses, to keep a register of qualified nurses, and to promote Bills in Parliament to achieve these aims. During the Second World War the RCN achieved a major breakthrough in the determination of nurse pay and conditions of service. In 1940 a Local Authorities Nursing Services Joint Committee was established, and in 1941 the government set up a nurses salaries committee, the Rushcliffe

Committee. The RCN wanted Whitley-type bodies, but the ones established fell short of that model of joint determination. The main issue was that the Committee's recommendations were not binding on the employees. COHSE had been fighting for these reforms before the RCN took up the bargaining rights of nurses, and these early successes must be mainly attributed to COHSE's organization allied with the RCN's Whitehall Influence.

In 1943 the Nurses Act provided professional protection on the registration of nurses, but the RCN felt that the role of nurses was underplayed in the totality of health care provided for in the White Paper on the NHS. In 1945 the non-trade union status of the RCN was being attacked by some Labour-controlled local authorities, and the College issued this statement:

> The Royal College of Nursing supports – and has always sup-
> ported – the view that under modern conditions nurses should be
> organized on a national basis, but feels equally that each nurse
> should be free to choose for herself the particular organization to
> which she would like to belong, and which she feels is best able to
> meet her professional needs.[63]

The RCN, along with the RCM, HVA, ANA and ASM, was involved with the Rushcliffe Committee which negotiated pay and conditions for nurses and midwives before 1948.

In 1948 the RCN's annual conference was held at about the time of the setting up of the NHS itself. As the 1948 Annual Report records:

> The year 1948 has seen the implementation of the National health
> service Act which may well prove to be an epoch in the history of
> nursing ... Strenuous efforts have been made, and will continue to
> be made, to secure a still greater degree of nurse representation
> on all appropriate bodies set up to implement the National health
> service.[64]

The same report noted that 'many regional Hospital Boards have asked the College to nominate nurses to serve on Hospital Management and other Committees'. And that 'of the 41 members representing the staff side, the Royal College of Nursing has 12 representatives',[65] and nine on the standing committee on nurses, three for midwives, three for public health and four for mental health nurses.

The RCN generally supported this system, which it dominated. As the 1948 Annual Report says:

The establishment of Whitley Council machinery for the nursing profession marks the realization of the policy of the College that negotiating machinery should be set up in order to agree uniform salary scales and conditions of service. This policy has been pressed by the College for many years, and its memorandum submitted to the Ministry of Health Inter-Departmental (Athlone) Committee on the Nursing Services in January, 1938, contained a strong recommendation for the establishment of negotiating machinery for the nursing profession.[66]

The RCN runs as a professional body with extensive nurse education and award activities. The industrial relations has been traditionally dealt with by the Labour Relations Committee set up in 1938 and reconvened after the war in 1947. Its task is to advise the Council on matters relating to the settlement of salaries and conditions of service; negotiating machinery and all other matters within the field of industrial relations.[67] While the RCN supported the setting up of Whitley for nurses it shared the views of the other nurse representative bodies in the early years that it delayed settlements, and it failed to deal with startling pay anomalies. The RCN, however, benefited as an organization from this government-led central system. As Abel-Smith argues,

> The central government by its intervention, by its basic choice of representatives on official committees, by its ratification and financial support of the decisions of those committees, strengthened the position of the professional associations.[68]

In addition, the RCN gained strength from its association with the trade unions representing nurses. It gained from the tougher negotiating traditions of the unions, and it may well be as true today as in the early 1950s that 'to some extent the skill of the trade unions in collective bargaining promoted the status and membership of the Royal College of Nursing'.[69]

As Dyson and Spary note, 'for the first 25 years of the NHS, the industrial relations activities of the professional associations were concentrated centrally within the Whitley Councils'.[70] This bald statement hides some significant variations in detail, and perhaps ignores the real meaning of that central involvement. For example, in 1962 the RCN, through the relevant Whitley Committees, failed to agree with the management on a range of issues: pay, and board and lodging charges (later agreed after a reference to the Industrial Court); hours of duty reduction to 39; payment of training allowances; and the attempt by management to introduce special payments for certain duties such as working on Sunday.[71] In addition, the RCN campaigned against government cuts in the funding of the NHS, and these elements of conflict with government in the economic crisis of the early 1960s began the painful process of re-education that led the RCN to reformulate its structures and policies in the 1970s.

Indeed, the fast-moving events of the mid-1960s led to the RCN coming under attack from within its own ranks and from outside on a series of issues, and the first tentative response in 1967 was to amend its constitution to give more power to the Representative Body and to reform the branches. The RCN leadership was fearful of being outflanked by other nurse organizations and sought to extend its membership. This meant letting in members of the Student Nurses Association, and approaching members of the National Association of State Enrolled Nurses.[72] The tensions within the RCN over its professional and trade union activities were often made worse by tensions between senior nurse managers and the large number of staff nurses. This vertical recruitment is common to associations and unions that organize professional staffs. The debates of the 1970s and the developments in policy in the 1980s to some extent reflect the changing nature of the managerial structures in the NHS and the increasing influence of rank-and-file nurse members of the RCN.

By 1970 the RCN along with many other public sector unions was recruiting rapidly and moving to a phase of pay confrontation with government based in part on the sufferings under incomes policies, in part from the increased bureaucratization of the public services, and in part from the changing nature of the expectations of members. Other reasons for the growth in union density among nurses included the inflationary pressures on living standards, and the copycat element from other professional groups such as teachers outside the NHS and ancillary workers inside.

In 1970 the RCN embarked on its 'raise the roof' campaign. Its origin lay in the 1968 Report of the Prices and Incomes Board on nurses' and midwives' pay. The RCN felt that on two major issues the recommendations were unacceptable: nursing education and salary ceiling. The campaign was based on a major public statement of the nurses' case, and as the RCN claimed, 'suffice to say, the membership, the profession, the public, press and parliament alike gave magnificent and touching support by raising the roof in one way or another'.[73] This campaign was part of a wider NHS series of disputes such as the 1968/9 laboratory technicians and the 1970 electricians disputes; these fed into three years (1972–6) of major national disputes, which in turn were followed from 1976 to 1977 by a series of local disputes.[74]

The watershed year was 1974. The incoming Labour government brought with it not only a series of labour laws designed to encourage collective bargaining and trade union membership, but also a deep commitment to incomes policies. These combined with high expectations of Labour supporters to trigger off major demands from all groups within the NHS. The RCN, along with most other professional associations, applied and succeeded in becoming trade unions. But, 'despite these developments, the general Whitley Council failed to establish new procedures for collective bargaining at national level'.[75] The RCN announced a further reorganization of its structure in 1974 with the setting up of 'centres' and the development of more strongly based regional industrial relations activities.[76] It threatened the new Secretary of State, Barbara Castle, with 'drastic action' unless something happened on pay. Two things did: first the government accepted the recommendations of the Briggs Report, and it then agreed to set up an independent pay inquiry under Lord Halsbury.[77]

The RCN felt that 'the standing of the RCN, in the sphere of labour relations has been enhanced by it becoming a certificated independent trade union'.[78] This was further accompanied by the establishment of a RCN official in every region of the NHS, and the successful build-up of trained RCN stewards with the development of the RCN Stewards National Committee in 1978. That year it highlighted its concern about the use of job evaluation for the grading of nurses, and was involved in early moves to coordinate the trade union side's responses to new management initiatives. By the late 1970s the RCN, and nurses in general, were caught up with the wave of unrest based on the government's use of incomes policies and public expenditure cuts. The RCN's campaign based around the slogan 'pay not peanuts' pushed the government to make nurses a special case, and the RCN argued for a reduction in the working week to 37.5 hours. Along with this increased activity went the further development of the industrial relations and collective bargaining side of the RCN's organization.[79]

By the early 1980s the RCN membership gains were spectacular. Its trade union activities complemented its professional image to provide an overall service for members. This reflected a general disillusion with the NHS as a 'model employer'[80] and with the state as a protector of its employees' rights. With the Conservative's aversion to arbitration in the public sector and its imposition of cash limits came a period of harsh cutbacks and low pay settlements that threatened the RCN's credibility. In 1982 the RCN feared the consequences of the Megaw report which signalled the government's determination to stop comparability as a method of public sector pay.[81] The RCN adopted the slogan 'nurses' pay – bridge that gap' which referred to comparable salaries in the private sector.[82]

In 1982 another landmark was reached. This time pressure from RCN members forced votes on both TUC affiliation and the deletion of Rule 12 against strikes, and although both were lost, they were indicative of the desperate mood of significant numbers of active members. The RCN leadership was walking an ever thinner tightrope. On the one hand it welcomed the government's efforts for greater efficiency in the NHS, but on the other it worried about the effects on patient care. At the same time the RCN with other NHS unions were pushing for a higher pay rise than allowed for under cash limits, and after many threats and some action the government agreed to both a pay rise and the setting up of a Pay Review Body for nurses, midwives and health visitors, and for the PAMs.[83] Trevor Clay, RCN General Secretary at the time, claimed that the RCN's no strike policy helped to recruit nurses during the 1979 and 1982 strikes.[84] Although Clay misreads the pay settlement solutions for nurses, he at least was aware of two important points for the RCN leadership to note:

> two myths about industrial relations and nurses need to be shattered. The first is that nurses are not powerful as a group in society and the second is that the public always loves the nurses.[85]

Pay determination

The arguments and methods used to advance the pay claims of nurses have varied over time, and important differences have been made more acute by the competition between NUPE, COHSE and the RCN for nurse members and between the RCN and RCM for midwives, and between the RCN and the HVA for health visitors. In practice, most health visitors remain within the

HVA (newly merged with MSF – about 16 000) and most mid-wives stay with the RCM (about 33 000). The division of nurse members as between the large unions reflects status, regional, political and bargaining differences within the profession. In the mid-1970s wage militancy by nurses helped COHSE to recruit members[86] and the feeling was that the RCN's traditional image was unattractive to many new nurses at that time.

The nurses themselves, such famously selfless workers in the public's imagination, fall within several conflicting categories and their pay levels and make-up of earnings reflect this. First the importance of the issue: in 1989 the pay bill for NHS nursing staff was over £5.5 billion. This was paid to nearly half a million wte nurses. The vast majority (80%) are within grades A to G with fewer than 20 000 (4%) in senior management positions. The bulk of nurses are on clinical grades, and nearly 100 000 on grade A, the bottom grade. For an adult nurse this grade in 1990 ranged from £5950 to £7355 for the standard full-time week. The top of grade G is £16 195. In terms of earnings the pay bill is divided between 85% on basic, 10% on special duty payments and the rest a small amalgam of allowances, leads and overtime. The NES provides some guide to the range of earnings as between nurse managers, nurses and nurse auxiliaries.

Table 2.4 illustrates the ways in which nurse/midwife managers can be divided from most clinical nurses/midwives and again from nursing auxiliaries. The pay spread reflects qualifications and responsibilities, but since it is associated with different trade union membership patterns and current changes in the ways in which nurse pay is determined it becomes more significant. There are two points worth noting: (1) that the ratio of lowest to highest decile for nurses is 2.5 compared with 1.8 for both managers and auxiliaries. This indicates the potential for

Table 2.4 The distribution of gross weekly earnings amongst traditional nursing grades in 1990

	Lowest decile	Lower quartile	Median	Higher quartile	Highest decile
Nursing administrators	£214	£281	£316	£346	£379
Nurses	£129	£180	£226	£276	£327
Nursing auxiliaries	£114	£133	£155	£176	£209

Source: New Earnings Survey for full-time adult females. All figures are rounded up to the nearest £.

the introduction of performance related pay for the managers and for narrower pay bands for auxiliaries. (2) When these figures are indexed using £114 (the cut-off of the lowest decile of auxiliaries) as the 100 base then the highest paid auxiliaries receive less than the median for nurses and the lowest decile for managers. The highest decile for managers is 332 and for nurses 287 compared with 183 for auxiliaries, a factor of more than three between the best and worst off nurse. This figure will grow considerably with the new pay systems and will have profound consequences for the unity of the profession and the perception of nurse managers by the increasingly relatively lower paid auxiliaries.

A summary of this was given in the previous chapter with the conclusion that nurse managers and nurses had pulled away from the low paid auxiliaries and that RCN members therefore had fared relatively better than those nurses in NUPE and COHSE. This view needs to be tempered by the importance of regional spread of the unions' power bases. The RCN has a disproportionate number of better qualified, higher grade staffs in London and many larger teaching hospitals. COHSE and NUPE tend to recruit from the lower grades of staff, from specialists like psychiatric nurses, from those in the Midlands and the north of the country, and from many outside main centres of population. This competition for nurse members has meant traditional hostilities between the RCN and the other nurse unions, and this will hinder developments in the SGTs towards single-table bargaining, prime union recognition and union efforts to prevent staff reductions.

In 1987 the Pay Review Body considered that there had been a sharp deterioration in the recruitment and retention situation for nurses and that this would become a major argument in pay determination for the next few years.[87] The DHSS and the Regional Health Authority chairs carried out a survey of staff shortages to augment the rather anecdotal accounts usually quoted. The overall view was that there was a shortfall of about 9% among qualified staff but none among the unqualified, which suggested that authorities were substituting unqualified for qualified nurses as part of their cost savings through skill mix changes. The staff side in its evidence was much sharper about both the issue itself and the employers' and government's complacency over the looming staff crisis. The PRB summarized its views as:

we are satisfied from the evidence we have received that the areas of difficulty are too widespread and the outlook too potentially serious for us to fail to take account of them in our recommendations this year.[88]

The other main pay argument fostered by the government is that of affordability, and in the 1987 report the PRB essentially rejected the Department line and embraced the more traditional method of the independent arbitrator, namely comparability. It commented:

in order to recommend what we believe are appropriate levels of pay, we take into account not only cash limits but also a number of other important factors ... but any recommendations that we might frame within the constraints of the cash limits would, in our judgement, fail to meet the needs of the emerging manpower situation.[89]

The RCN and the rest of the staff side unions put the greatest emphasis on pay comparability. While the government through the Departments contested this principle, the PRB took the line that to resolve the staffing crisis nurses' pay must at least be competitive with outside equivalent occupations. This debate between the most appropriate means of determining nurses' pay will become sharper and more relevant once that pay is determined by health authorities and trusts acting as single employers. Figure 2.2 shows the movement of nurses' earnings compared with the average earnings index between 1983 and 1991.

Within the staff side variations in demands are more acute than in analysis and/or argument. NUPE wanted a flat rate increase to underpin the low levels of pay for nursing auxiliaries and assistants. The RCM again asked for higher awards for its members than for nurses on corresponding scales, and the HVA asked for the restoration of the Health Visitor grade to parity with the Sister I grade.

In 1988 the new clinical grading system came in with a range of formidable industrial relations issues. The RCM put together an angry and determined additional evidence presentation for the 1988 Review Body in which it sharply questioned the Review Body's acceptance of the Department's figures on midwife shortages.[90] It restated the special responsibilities and duties of the midwife. To this end the RCM supported proposals on new grades which would allow for a Midwife grade equivalent to seven increments above the minimum for Sister II. In addition, a

April 1983 = 100

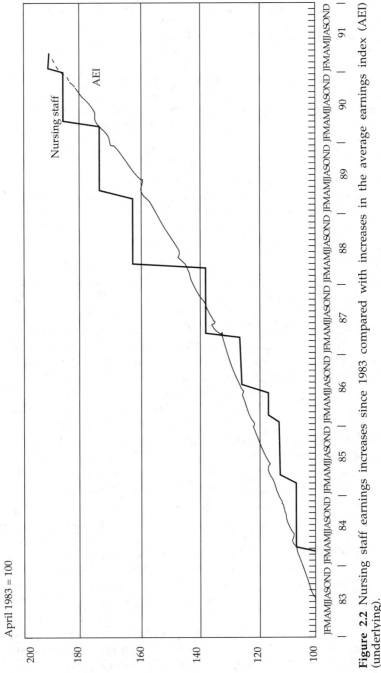

Figure 2.2 Nursing staff earnings increases since 1983 compared with increases in the average earnings index (AEI) (underlying).
(*Source*: PRB for nursing staff 1991, p. 42.)

large salary increase is merited due to staff shortages and development in skills.

One major aspect of the RCM's evidence was the poor quality of evidence about midwives presented by the Departments to the Pay Review Body and the apparent acceptance of that inadequate data. This raises serious questions both about the real ability of the government to control labour planning and therefore the NHS, and about the managerial ability to do so at health authority and SGT level.

The RCM showed particular concern over certain aspects of the new grading schemes. Five points were considered: (1) the grading of student midwives; (2) the appropriateness of grade D for midwives; (3) the grades of community midwifery sisters relative to their hospital counterparts; (4) whether midwifery training should be regarded as a second specialist qualification; (5) whether the same criteria for grading can be used for nurses and midwives.[91] The vast bulk of the staff midwives had been transferred to grade E although this varied across the regions. In East Anglia 92% of staff midwives were put on E compared with 57% in Mersey. This suggests that the regions may have used the regrading exercise as a local labour market experiment in recruitment and retention. This was not its avowed purpose, but may well have been its practical use.[92]

This point is further illustrated when it is noted that 8.4% of midwifery sister posts in Wales went to scale F compared with 24.6% in England.[93] The Social Services Committee concluded that:

> we have identified three main problems with the recent regrading of midwives. First, the Government's insistence on grading newly qualified midwives on grade D will act as a disincentive to nurses to train as midwives. Second, it may actually cost more to fill grade D vacancies with agency midwives if midwives do not apply for these posts. Third, no financial recognition is given for the extra training midwives receive … These concerns lead us to the conclusion that the present arrangements for linking the pay and grading of midwives to those for nurses may not be satisfactory.[94]

There are a variety of points that need to be made about this type of analysis. First, it indicates the extent to which many pay reforms within the NHS are not thoroughly worked out, and have unintended consequences of an expensive and muddled nature. This can be seen as one example of a wider malaise.

Second the regradings of this group of staff as well as those
carried out for most of PTB and currently being negotiated for
PTA, suggest a clear management policy. The truth is that the
staff side have argued for these changes for several years, but the
employers and the Departments have agreed them now due to
labour market factors in the short term and not due to any
longer-term view of the nature of the industry and/or the
relevant occupations.

Third are the specific industrial relations issues that emerge
from regradings. These include assimilation questions and the
numbers involved in 'red circling' (pay protection). They include
the favoured method of assigning new grades such as job evaluation. In addition, the role of the unions before, during and
after the new gradings are developed is crucial. Failure to
consult and agree before and during may mean prolonged
grievances after the event. This has happened with a vengeance
for nurses and midwives.

Fourth, what are the implications for the future single-
employer bargainers? What type of grading scheme will they
adopt? What role will be ascribed to the unions? How will
grievances be dealt with and how will these be resolved if no
agreement is reached at the level of the employer?

Between 1989 and 1991 the Pay Review Body gave awards
once again based on the norms of government policy and the
arguments for pay. In 1989 the Review Body was apprehensive
over the assimilation disputes and felt that some of the benefits
of the new structure might be lost in delay and conflict. Once
again the main cases were based on the labour markets, pay
comparability, cash limits or affordability, and to a less extent
workload and productivity. The staff side were very anxious
about the low pay of the nursing auxiliaries but the Review Body
felt that the internal pay differences should remain unchanged.[95]
The recommendation of 6.8% on the salary bill took the top of
grade G to £14 860.

In 1990 the surveys on vacancies by all the staff side unions
again indicated the impending crisis of staffing levels. These
carried great weight with the Review Body. Again the real
debate was over comparability, with a COHSE survey showing
that over half the respondents were dissatisfied with their pay.[96]
The Review Body accepted the general case on comparability but
with one eye to the future began a discussion of flexible pay[97] in
which the Departments argued strongly for local management

discretion. This was opposed by the staff side. The Review Body went some way to accepting the argument for flexible pay, but only wanted a relatively small amount set aside for its implementation this year. The total cost of the recommendations was 9.6% of the nurse pay bill.

In 1991 the story was familiar. A full survey of nurse vacancies was carried out by the Office of Manpower Economics (OME) and the recruitment and retention problem highlighted. The Departments considered pay to be less important in this area than non-pay measures, and this view was supported by the regional chairs. The unions took a more serious view of staff shortages, especially amongst the lower A and B grades.[98] The recommended settlement, which the government immediately decided to phase, took clinical grade pay from £6050 from the bottom of A to £21 470 at the top of I.[99]

Structure of the professional associations

a)   The Royal College of Nursing

The RCN was founded in 1916, incorporated by Royal Charter in 1928 and certificated as an independent trade union in 1977. The College is governed by a Council which consists of 18 members who are elected by postal ballot, 14 of whom are from England, with one each from Scotland, Wales and Northern Ireland and one student member. There are also ten members who serve *ex officio*, including the President and Deputy President. The General Secretary of the RCN (in common with the chief executives of the PAM professional associations) is secretary to its council and is the chief executive officer with ultimate responsibility for the total work of the College as a corporate entity. The RCN employs an impressive range of senior level full-time officers and chief officers six of whom are directors of HQ departments. There are three Board Secretaries and four Regional Secretaries, and there is at least one office/officer in each English RHA, three in Scotland, two in Wales and one in Northern Ireland.

Industrial relations has its own department which is headed by a director and it is this department that holds the prime responsibility for trade union activities of the RCN, both nationally and locally. In addition to its representative and legal functions, the RCN's labour relations and legal department is responsible for the administration of their Indemnity Insurance scheme which, again in keeping with the PAM professional associations, covers all fully paid-up members against claims of professional negligence. This department is also responsible for the organization of the safety representatives' scheme (see below).

The membership structure of the RCN is based locally on RCN branches which are established throughout the UK, not specifically as trade union branches, but as 'the sole focal point for all RCN activities in a particular locality'[100]. It is the regional officers who are expected to ensure that the RCN is represented on consultative committees, as well as providing advice and assistance to the elected RCN stewards. A steward structure has been developed with committees at district, regional and national level and at local level the RCN stewards are expected to work closely with the RCN branches (see Figure 2.3).

Both RCN branches and the members at their place of work are able to nominate safety representatives, who are expected to have been employed for at least two years. Once they have been accredited, the RCN provides training courses for the safety representatives who are, in turn, expected to work closely with the RCN stewards to keep the local membership informed about their activities.

The RCN's industrial relations has long been dominated by powerful regional secretaries, and there has been a dearth of national policy for the conduct of industrial relations in hospitals and the community. The head office function of the IR department has been restricted to developing the case for the Review Body and attending many outside meetings of relevant bodies. Membership participation is low, although this is partly compensated by an active stewards' network linking members to the union.

An issue that always receives publicity whenever any form of industrial dispute affects the NHS is the 'no strike' clause contained within the RCN's rule book (Rule 12) which forbids members from taking strike action. Although there have been several ballots over this issue, it is still the case that the RCN's membership do not wish to see this rule amended.

b)   The Royal College of Midwives

Midwifery is a distinct profession with its own history and institutional development. The Midwives Institute was founded

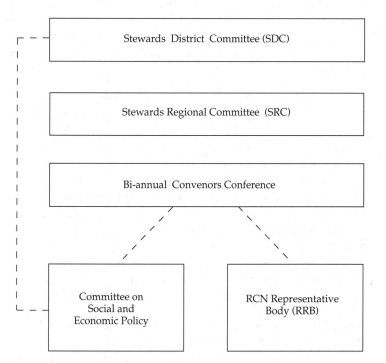

Figure 2.3 Royal College of Nursing stewards structure. (*Source*: RCN.)

in 1881 and was the main organization for midwives until it became the College of Midwives in 1941 and received its Royal Charter in 1947. In 1976 it became a certificated trade union. A major element in the RCM's pay and conditions proposals has been the fight on three fronts:

for the maintenance of professional recognition ...; the conferment of the status that the midwife deserved; and the demonstration of that status in salary scales.[101]

By 1985 the College had over 28 000 members with another 2500 student members. Each member belongs to one of the 214 local branches which have their own branch leadership and activities. In general the RCM accords with the model of professional associations run by a Council and with leading officers such as a President. In recent years it has developed an influential and highly professional industrial relations department with several permanent officials. These have in turn encouraged and developed a successful local stewards network based on extensive training and expert support (Figure 2.4).[102]

c)   The Health Visitors' Association

Health visitors are also a distinct profession, but by their nature are based in the community and not in hospitals. This gives the occupation a unique place in public health provision and a distinctive trade union tradition. The Health Visitors Association was founded in 1896 as the Women Sanitary Inspectors' Association. It became a trade union in 1918 and affiliated to the TUC in 1924. This early decision places the HVA in a special category with regard to trade union and collective bargaining traditions, and means that its organization more closely resembles a trade union than a professional association. It became the HVA in 1962, and by 1985 it had 15 000 members with over 500 local representatives. Its government is based on an Executive Committee with a General Secretary and other full-time staff concerned with both professional and industrial relations matters (Figure 2.5). In 1990 it merged with MSF as part of its strategy to protect its members' interest through bargaining strength, and in recognition of the difficulties its members will face in the 1990s. The vote was 7797 in favour with 341 against on a 47% turnout.[103]

PROFESSIONS ALLIED TO MEDICINE (PAMS)

Workforce composition

The PAMs covered by the Professions Supplementory to Medicine (PSM) Act of 1960 have numbered seven since the merger, in 1985, of the Society of Remedial Gymnasts with the Chartered Society of Physiotherapists. Within the NHS, one of these groups – the Medical Laboratory Scientific Officers (MLSO) – is not part of the same employment group. Included within the PAM category are those professions who have 'direct' patient contact, such as physiotherapists, radiographers, dietitians,

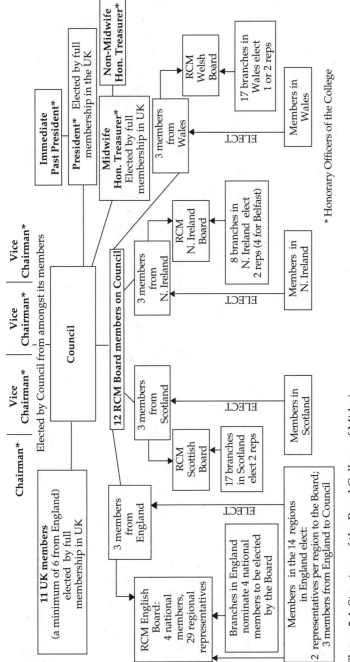

Figure 2.4 Structure of the Royal College of Midwives.
(*Source*: RCM Steward's handbook.)

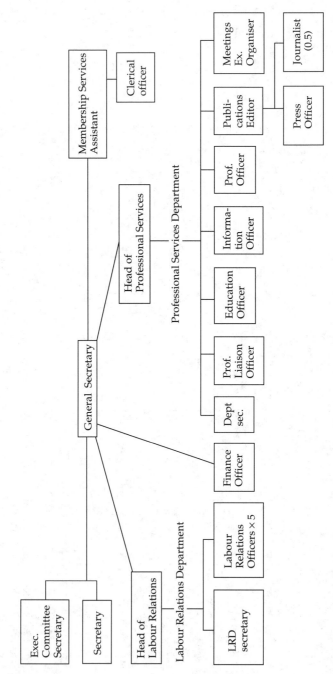

Figure 2.5 Proposed organizational structure of the Health Visitors' Association. (*Source*: HVA)

orthoptists, chiropodists and occupational therapists. While not included within the PSM Act, technical instructors, and helpers and footcare assistants fall within the scope of the PAM group. The MLSOs are included among other scientific and technical staff in Chapter 3.

Table 2.5 reveals that in the 12 years from 1977 to 1989 there was a 61% overall rise in PAMs employed in the NHS. Occupational therapists (+120%) and dietitians (+107%) accounted for the largest increases.

Table 2.5 Total PAMs, related grades and helpers (wte) in the NHS

Occupation	1977	1989
Art and music therapists	—	340
Chiropodists	2484	3500
Dietitians	755	1560
Occupational therapists	2774	6090
Orthoptists	457	620
Physiotherapists	7073	11 620
Radiographers	7754	10 210
Remedial gymnasts	351	n/a[a]
Helpers and footcare assistants	4798	5810
Technical instructors	—	2930

[a] Merged with physiotherapists in November 1985.

Bargaining arrangements

No bargaining or negotiating arrangements existed before 1945 for professional and technical staffs in hospitals. In 1945 the professional organizations formed the Professional Staffs Association (PSA) and a formal Joint National Council (Hospital Staffs) (JNC(HS)) was created. The management side consisted of the BHA, MHA and local authorities and the staff were represented by the PSA. The JNC(HS) covered all PSM grades.[104] (As previously noted, this group of staff's title has, since 1984, been amended to the Professions Allied to Medicine.)

With the exception of the Association of Clinical Biochemists (ACB), Table 2.1 shows that these associations were all formed before 1948. The associations which represent staff within the PAM group have very strong membership, particularly the five smallest associations, and the variations in size between organizations largely reflects the variation in the size of the profession.

All of these Professional associations are certificated as trade unions and perhaps the most important factor in strengthening the industrial relations role of these associations has been the rapid development of a local steward/representative network. Dyson and Spary pointed out in 1979 that 'as stewards' of these associations become trained, the local service to the members is likely to be impressive by ordinary trade union standards'.[105]

All the organizations that make up this group act independently with their own distinctive traditions, professionalism and policies. The common ground between them, however, is sufficient to enable them to form a single body for negotiations at national level through Whitley Council PT'A' and the Pay Review Body, and for them to come together in close relations at local level. In addition, they are formally linked through a loose federation under the umbrella title of the Federation of Professional Organizations (FPO). The industrial relations functions overlap, and the officials meet on a regular basis. The two dominant groups are the physiotherapists and the radiographers. They have the largest and most strategically placed memberships, and as with the other groups, they enjoy a very high density of membership.

The organizations behave, in their trade union activities, as single-profession and mainly closed unions. They control the qualifications of their professions, and act to enhance and protect the labour supply side of their activities. In terms of pay and conditions of service their activities have been concentrated on national level joint bargaining and they share common pay systems through the Whitley PT'A' Council. In its Eighth Report in 1991, the Pay Review Body noted that there were nearly 34 000 qualified staff in this group on a wte basis. On this calculation there were some 11 500 physiotherapists, 10 000 radiographers and 6000 occupational therapists. These figures do not correspond with the actual numbers working in the NHS and therefore with the union membership figures. For example, about 40% of the physiotherapists are part-time workers and so actual numbers are much higher. In general, for all the groups about a quarter of staff are on the Basic grade, and over half on either Senior I or II. These proportions vary by profession: there are proportionately more radiographers on the Basic grade than physiotherapists, with virtually no chiropodists at that level[106] (see Table 2.6).

Overall, 90% of this group's earnings come from basic pay, and 3.6% from oncall and standby payments.[107] Again this varies

Table 2.6a Professional and technical staff (England): analysis by occupation

	1978	1983	1984	1985	1986	1987[1]	1988
Total NHS professional and technical staff[2]	57 237	68 691	72 656	74 298	76 083	78 975	79 775
Professions allied to medicine: total	24 213	30 141	30 741	32 466	33 548	34 631	35 237
Chiropodists	1913	2392	2293	2366	2445	2644	2617
Dietitians	616	819	938	1016	1086	1137	1192
Occupational therapists	2385	3377	3611	3995	4334	4605	4873
Orthoptists	376	444	432	455	474	487	516
Physiotherapists	6458	8091	8535	8901	9153	9329	9587
Radiographers							
Diagnostic (includes MMR and others)	5618	6700	6797	6943	7049	7143	7249
Therapeutic	693	739	806	853	893	905	936
Teaching	104	137	147	195	201	206	217
Helpers in							
occupational and industrial therapy	3059	3950	3530	3648	3662	3413	3202
physiotherapy departments	1664	1833	1734	1815	1839	1902	1948
other departments	126	321	307	346	361	390	409
Other professions allied to medicine[3]	1200	1338	1611	1936	2051	2471	2491

Note: wte as at 30 September each year. Students are not included, except for junior medical laboratory scientific officers, student and junior technicians, pharmaceutical students and post-graduate pre-registration pharmaceutical students.
[1] Prior to 1987 figures for 'Other statutory authorities' (e.g. Public Health Laboratory Service and Health Education Authority) were not collected in the Annual Manpower Census. Figures for 1987 onwards are therefore not directly comparable with those for earlier years.
[2] On 1 April 1984, operating department assistants transferred from the Ancillary to the PT'B' Staffs Council, thus totals for 1984 are not comparable with those for earlier years.
[3] Includes art and music therapists and instructors, technical instructors, handicraft teachers, unspecified PAM grades and other statutory authorities.
Figures for individual years are not strictly comparable.
Source: Health and Personal Social Services Statistics, 1990 edn, pp. 58–9.

Table 2.6a *(continued)* Professional and technical staff (England): analysis by occupation

	1978	1983	1984	1985	1986	1987[1]	1988
Scientific and professional staff: total	7119	9168	9518	9870	10 249	10 863	11 604
Chaplains (whole-time staff only)	125	180	165	177	170	174	197
Speech therapists							
Audiology	65	108	82	63	48	39	32
Other	1322	1865	2064	2275	2460	2592	2697
Biochemists							
Health authorities	954	1289	1251	1198	1175	1106	1142
Other statutory authorities	—	..	..	..	..	278	275
Physicists	498	662	697	723	768	788	827
Psychologists (clinical)	863	1307	1365	1516	1623	1697	1960
Child psychotherapists	59	65	55	79	84	92	135
Other scientists[4]	257	363	383	396	453	547	592
Pharmacists and opticians: total	2976	3329	3343	3304	3256	3240	3360
Opticians							
Ophthalmic	104	102	108	99	94	73	106
Dispensing	18	15	14	18	14	12	14
Pharmacists	2405	2786	2726	2829	2749	2851	2883
Post-graduate pre-registration pharmaceutical students	444	360	251	346	355	297	350

Note: wte as at 30 September each year. Students are not included, except for junior medical laboratory scientific officers, student and junior technicians, pharmaceutical students and post-graduate pre-registration pharmaceutical students.
[1] Prior to 1987 figures for 'Other statutory authorities' (e.g. Public Health Laboratory Service and Health Education Authority) were not collected in the Annual Manpower Census. Figures for 1987 onwards are therefore not directly comparable with those for earlier years.
[4] Includes regional scientific officers and audiology scientists.
Figures for individual years are not strictly comparable.
Source: Health and Personal Social Services Statistics, 1990 edn, pp. 58–9.

Table 2.6a (*continued*) Professional and technical staff (England): analysis by occupation

	1978	1983	1984	1985	1986	1987[1]	1988
Other pharmacists and opticians	6	67	244	12	44	6	7
Other scientific and professional staff[5]	—	..	114	139	213	311	388
Professional and technical 'B' staff: total (excluding works)	25 906	29 382	32 397	31 962	32 286	33 480	32 934
Medical Laboratory Scientific Officers							
Health authorities	13 089	14 718	14 554	14 542	14 624	14 519	14 221
Other statutory authorities	—	..	..	..	..	955	956
Technicians: total[2]	12 328	14 467	17 208	17 269	17 509	17 713	17 463
Animal technicians							
Health authorities	29	57	32	14	16	15	17
Other Statutory Authorities	—	..	..	..	..	20	20
Artificial kidney assistants	111	131	126	124	123	127	136
Cardiographers	291	466	416	430	443	445	446
Dark room technicians	1147	1168	1131	1077	1020	957	839
Dental therapists	288	256	237	216	206	187	161
Dental hygienists	89	146	116	117	120	123	106
Dental surgery assistants	2935	3111	3071	3029	2985	2879	2790

Note: wte as at 30 September each year. Students are not included, except for junior medical laboratory scientific officers, student and junior technicians, pharmaceutical students and post-graduate pre-registration pharmaceutical students.
[1] Prior to 1987 figures for 'Other statutory authorities' (e.g. Public Health Laboratory Service and Health Education Authority) were not collected in the Annual Manpower Census. Figures for 1987 onwards are therefore not directly comparable with those for earlier years.
[2] On 1 April 1984, operating department assistants transferred from the Ancillary to the PT'B' Staffs Council, thus totals for 1984 are not comparable with those for earlier years.
[5] Includes psychological technicians, speech therapy helpers, part-time and assistant chaplains, other S&P staff and other statutory authorities.
Figures for individual years are not strictly comparable.
Source: Health and Personal Social Services Statistics, 1990 edn, pp. 58–9.

Table 2.6a (*continued*) Professional and technical staff (England): analysis by occupation

	1978	1983	1984	1985	1986	1987[1]	1988
Dental technicians	642	646	658	632	609	594	580
Electronic technicians	165	74	86	162	253	264	244
Medical artists	22	25	27	36	30	25	26
Medical photographers	332	352	346	352	336	324	323
Medical physics technicians							
Health authorities	1505	2241	2211	2190	2144	2126	2249
Other Statutory Authorities	—	..	..	..	..	79	79
Operating department assistants[2]	—	..	2705	2693	2665	2633	2360
Pharmacy technicians	2036	2499	2569	2674	2762	2793	2778
Physiological measurement technicians							
Audiology	623	785	787	781	798	775	779
Cardiology	766	928	933	931	943	876	916
Neurophysiology	276	274	285	290	296	277	285
Post-mortem room technicians (anatomical pathology)	364	460	460	465	481	481	482
Radiography helpers	126	155	162	192	0	273	360
Other technicians	580	693	852	864	1049	1441	1487
Other professional and technical (excluding works)[6]	489	197	635	152	153	293	294

Note: wte as at 30 September each year. Students are not included, except for junior medical laboratory scientific officers, student and junior technicians, pharmaceutical students and post-graduate pre-registration pharmaceutical students.

[1] Prior to 1987 figures for 'Other statutory authorities' (e.g. Public Health Laboratory Service and Health Education Authority) were not collected in the Annual Manpower Census. Figures for 1987 onwards are therefore not directly comparable with those for earlier years.

[2] On 1 April 1984, operating department assistants transferred from the Ancillary to the PT'B' Staffs Council, thus totals for 1984 are not comparable with those for earlier years.

[6] Includes driver/technicians, hearing therapists, teachers of the deaf, supervisors and assistant supervisors (PS Scales) (in 1984). Also includes staff in Other Statutory Authorities (OSAs) not elsewhere specified or shown separately.

Figures for individual years are not strictly comparable.

Source: Health and Personal Social Services Statistics, 1990 edn, pp. 58–9.

Table 2.6b Distribution of whole-time equivalent numbers of NHS staff in Great Britain at 30 September 1989

Profession	Basic	Senior		Chief				District[2]	Teaching staff[3]	Others	Total[4,6]
		II	I	IV	III	II	I				
Art and music therapy	20	160	120	10	10	0	0	0	0	6	340
Chiropody	[5,6]	1790[5]	910[5]	190	210	20	0	180	30	160[5]	3500
Dietetics	320	340	540	60	90	0	0	180	0	20	1560
Occupational therapy	1270	1350	2000	330	630	170	110	170	40	30	6090
Orthoptics	30	220	230	20	40	[6]	0	40[7]	40	10	620
Physiotherapy[7]	2510	3180	3850	470	890	160	150	180	150	60	11 620
Radiography	3900	2500	1870	460	780	160	120	150	240	40	10 210
Total qualified staff[4]	8060	9550	9530	1540	2660	510	380	900	500	310	33 940
Technical instructor											2930
Helper and footcare assistant											5810

[1] Or Superintendent or Head.
[2] A small number of district posts (District III in occupational therapy, and District III and Designated District in physiotherapy) are not separately identifiable and are therefore excluded here.
[3] Includes only those student teachers remunerated on the student teacher scale.
[4] Totals may not equal the sum of components because of rounding (to the nearest 10).
[5] Includes sessional chiropodists.
[6] Less than 5.
[7] Graded as Head I or Head II.
[8] Including remedial gymnastics, which merged with physiotherapy in November 1985.
[9] Additionally, at the same date, there were some 160 (wte) staff who could not be allocated by profession or grade.
Source: PRB for PAMs 1991, p. 19.

across the professions, with radiographers earning more from oncall than the others. As with other groups, the Pay Review Body gave much weight to the labour market issues of recruitment and retention. The data for the PRB's analysis were provided by the Joint National Professional Manpower Initiative. They found serious problems in filling vacancies, especially among occupational therapists. The staff side again stressed, as it had in previous years, the need for flexible working patterns as well as better pay to improve retention and encourage returners. The government's view, which remained unchanged for several years, was that the overriding consideration was one of affordability within government guidelines, and that the rate of inflation and comparability should not count towards pay determination. (See Figure 2.6 which shows the movement of PAMs' pay with the average earnings index 1983–91).

As usual, the staff side argued strongly the case for pay in line with both inflation and average earnings. The PRB took account of both the labour market considerations on filling vacancies and the comparability arguments of the pay of outside professions. As they concluded:

> Our recommendations are intended to reduce the differences between starting salaries in the professions within the NHS and the general level of starting salaries for graduates in the economy as a whole.[108]

Their recommendations meant that as from April 1991 a Basic grade would start on £10 800 and the top of Senior I would become £17 000. The highest paid PAM would now receive £25 750 for a District I and £26 725 for a teaching Principal. The top pay to go to a technical instructor would be £13 675 and for an adult helper, £8230. This represented no change in internal relative pay, but some marginal catching up with some grades of nurse. The government decided in February 1991 to phase the settlement again, to the annoyance of both the staff side and the PRB. This meant the quoted salaries would only be achieved in December 1991 and that the percentage annual increase is 8.4% and not the 10.8% recommended.

The debate within the Pay Review Body as to the validity of the opposing arguments remains unresolved. The PRB are now able to claim, as they were in 1986, for example, that 'the contribution of pay levels to the ease or difficulty of recruitment is open to dispute'.[109] In 1986 the Review Body still saw external comparisons as very important, and productivity and workload

April 1983 = 100

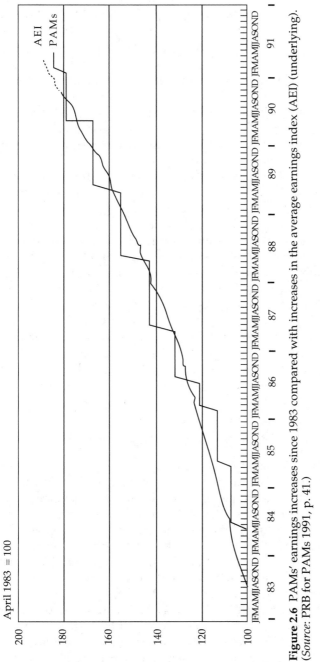

Figure 2.6 PAMs' earnings increases since 1983 compared with increases in the average earnings index (AEI) (underlying). (*Source*: PRB for PAMs 1991, p. 41.)

measures as of doubtful use for these professions despite the counter-arguments from the Departments.[110] Their recommendations meant that a Basic grade started in April 1986 on £6695 while the top of Senior I was £11 020. The reports for 1987–90 provide a similar digest of argument and data, but seem to result in awards roughly in line with those for other health service professions. Within this, two elements have become more important: flexibility of both pay and non-pay conditions, and regrading. Despite several months of intense negotiations the two sides failed by March 1991 to resolve their differences and no new grading structure has been agreed.

The PAMs form an ever growing part of the professions within the NHS, and their individual representative bodies act as well-organized and well financed closed unions. Their experience of bargaining at health authority level has been limited to personal cases, usually taken by full-time officials, and some disputes. The current reforms, the growing importance of PAMs' contribution and the increase in active stewards will change this. They are increasingly like traditional trade unions, and as with the doctors and the nurses inside the RCN, the tensions between the industrial relations and professional activities and policies are creating greater strains within the organizations. This in part may be reflected in the ways in which they move closer together within the FPO. For now, it is worth a brief consideration of the way the two largest organizations operate.

Structure of the professional associations

a)   The Chartered Society of Physiotherapists

The CSP was founded in 1895. In 1920 it was granted a Charter and in 1976 was certificated as an independent trade union. Since 1948 it has been the principal negotiating organization for physiotherapists in the NHS. With some 24 000 members, it has 75 local branches and 17 regional boards. The Council of the CSP is elected by members and works through committees which are assisted by a number of specific interest groups. The CSP journal, *Physiotherapy*, with a circulation of 27 000, is read in almost a hundred countries.

The CSP is responsible for professional as well as trade union matters and at its central London headquarters a staff of almost 60 is employed to service the membership. The Industrial Relations Committee (IRC) is a standing committee of the CSP's

Council and the Industrial Relations department is the executive arm of the IRC, with its trade union work significantly expanded in recent years.[111]

The IR department is headed by a Director of Industrial Relations and staffed by seven full-time officers, who, in addition to their representative and advisory responsibilities, organize and train a network of 600 stewards and 650 safety representatives throughout the UK. The stewards and safety representatives are elected by members at their workplace and are organized on a District and Regional structure under a Regional steward. Figures 2.7 and 2.8 show the CSP steward network and the CSP industrial relations structure.

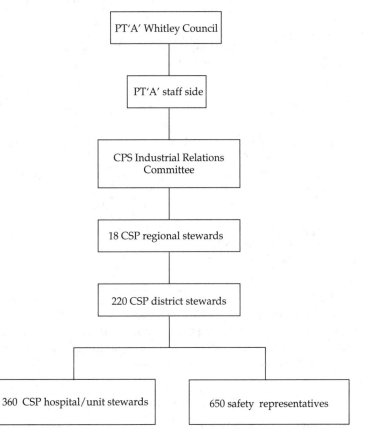

Figure 2.7 Industrial relations structure of the Chartered Society of Physiotherapists.
(*Source*: CSP head office.)

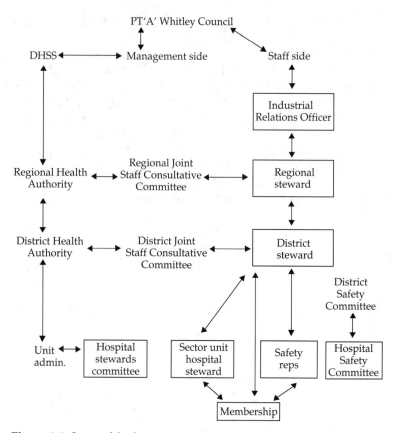

Figure 2.8 Steward/safety representative network of the CSP and its relationship with the NHS.
(*Source*: CSP head office.)

The training for the elected stewards includes week-long courses on negotiating skills and procedures, health and safety at work courses, a range of shorter courses for regional representatives, and specialist courses on pay bargaining, SGTs and links with other unions .

b)   The Society of Radiographers

The Society of Radiographers was founded in 1920 with the initial aim of enhancing the status and improving the training of radiographic technicians.[112] In 1976 the Society became a registered independent trade union and at the same time formed the

College of Radiographers as a charity to look after the training and professional development of radiographers.

The governing body of the Society and College of Radiographers is again its Council, which is made up of 22 members, elected by a postal ballot from the membership every three years. The majority of these members of Council (12) are elected on a regional basis and are the senior lay trade union representatives. The remaining ten members of Council are elected by a national ballot. The Council members annually elect from their ranks a President and Vice President as well as chairs of the three major subcommittees of Council.

It is the Industrial Relations Committee that is responsible to Council for the organization of trade union matters, and all the regional representatives plus two additional Council members and two members who are annually elected at the Delegates' Conference, form this committee. While the General Secretary has executive responsibility to Council for the management of both the Society and College business, there is an Assistant Secretary (IR) and three full-time industrial relations officers who organize and run the day-to-day business of the trade union and represent, advise and support a membership that has increased over the past few years.

The representative structure of the Society consists of more than 400 local and district representatives and 400 health and safety representatives, who are all elected on a three-year basis at their place of work. There are 15 branches throughout the UK and the Republic of Ireland and 12 sub-branches. At least two of the district or local representatives, as well as the regional representatives, are members of the branch committees which are Society – not College – branches and meet on at least ten occasions each year, electing their branch committees from amongst their local membership. The Society has, since 1979 held regular Delegates Conferences which have played a crucial role in deciding policies. Affiliation to the TUC was one such policy that came from the Delegates Conference. In 1990 the Society did affiliate after a postal ballot in which 4483 voted in favour with 2127 against in a turnout of 55%.[113]

CONCLUDING COMMENTS

It was only from the early 1970s that the professional associations established their status as trade unions and developed local involvement in industrial relations. They became certificated as independent trade unions under the Trade Union Labour Relations Act (1974) and the 1975 Employment Protection Act. As such they can be regarded as single-profession trade unions, in contrast with the multi-occupational trade unions such as COHSE, MSF, NALGO and NUPE, which are discussed in the following chapter.

The main features of note are the extent to which they organize the majority of members of their professions within the NHS, their financial strength, their multi-faceted defence strategies based on control of the labour supply, legislative enactment and collective bargaining. The growth in membership throughout the 1970s, and their continued growth in the 1980s, was in contrast to the decline in members among other trade unions in the NHS in the past few years. The growth in trade union activities, especially through the well-trained and well-supported steward systems, goes against the efforts of the government and managers to find alternatives to traditional trade union representation and functions.

Most members of these professions subscribe to a strong 'felt-fair' pay tradition in which comparability and protection against inflation are seen as far more important than suspicious looking productivity deals and the probably short-lived use of individual performance related pay systems.

NOTES

1   Turner, H. (1962) *Trade Union Growth, Structure and Policy*, George Allen and Unwin, London.
2   Blackburn, R. (1967) *Union Character and Social Class*, B. T. Batsford, London. This book develops the notion of 'unionateness' to place representative bodies of workers along a continuum from TUC affiliated traditional unions to staff associations.
3   Merrison, A. (1979) *Royal Commission on the National Health Service*, HMSO, London, p. 172 on CPSM, Cmnd 7615.
4   Ibid., pp. 200–1 on the UKCC.
5   Ibid., p. 278 on the GMC.
6   Webb, B. and Webb, S. (1897) *Industrial Democracy*, 1920 edn, Longmans, Green & Co., London.
7   Ibid., p. 255.
8   Ibid., p. 562–3.
9   Dyson, R. and Spary, K. (1979) 'Professional Association', in Bosanquet, N. (ed.), *Industrial Relations in the NHS*, King Edward's Hospital Fund for London, London, p. 145.

10 Royal College of Nursing (1981) *Members' Handbook*, RCN, London, p. 6.
11 The legislation included the Health and Safety at Work Act of 1974, the Trade Union and Labour Relations Act of 1974, and the Employment Protection Act of 1975.
12 Carpenter, M. (1982) 'The Labour Movement in the NHS: UK', in Sethi, A. and Dimmock, S. (eds), *Industrial Relations and Health Services*, Croom Helm, London, p. 85.
13 Merrison, op. cit., p. 207.
14 Ibid., p. 209.
15 Wilkins, G. (1990) *Review Body on Doctors' and Dentists' Remuneration: Twentieth Report 1990*, Cm 937, HMSO, London, p. 54.
16 Merrison, op. cit., p. 16.
17 Gordon, H. and Iliffe, S. (1977) *Pickets in White – the Junior Doctors' Dispute of 1975*, MPU Publications, London. Treloar, S. (1981) 'The Junior Hospital Doctors' Pay Dispute 1975–1976: 'An Analysis of Events, Issues and Conflicts', *Journal of Social Policy*, 10, pp. 1–30.
18 Wilkins, G. (1989) *Review Body on Doctors' and Dentists' Remuneration: Nineteenth Report 1989*, Cm 580, HMSO, London, p. 6.
19 Holdsworth, T. (1991) *Review Body on Doctors' and Dentists' Remuneration, Twenty-First Report 1991*, Cm 1412, HMSO, London, p. 7.
20 Ibid., p. 8.
21 Clegg, H. and Chester, T. (1957) *Wage Policy and the Health Service*, Basil Blackwell, Oxford, p. 8.
22 Spens, W. (1948) *Report of the Interdepartmental Committee on the Remuneration of Consultants and Specialists*, Cmd 7420, HMSO, London.
23 Webster, C. (1988) *The Health Services Since the War*, HMSO, London, pp. 198–201.
24 Eckstein, H. (1959) *The English Health Service*, Harvard University Press, Cambridge, Mass p. 142.
25 Ibid., p. 148.
26 Little, E. (1932) *History of the British Medical Association*, vol. 1, *1832–1932*, BMA, London, p. 24.
27 Ibid., pp. 74–7.
28 Ibid., pp. 64–5.
29 Ibid., p. 334.
30 Grey-Turner, E. and Sutherland, F. (1982) *History of the British Medical Association, vol. 2, 1932–1981*, BMA, London.
31 Ibid., pp. 52–4.
32 Ibid., p. 75.
33 Ibid., p. 106.
34 Ibid., pp. 147–64, and Pilkington, H. (1960) *Report of the Royal Commission on Doctors' and Dentists' Remuneration 1957–1960*, Cmnd 939, HMSO, London.
35 Grey-Turner and Sutherland, op. cit., p. 162.
36 Webster, C. (1988) *The Health Services since the War, vol. 1, Problems of Health Care: the National Health Service before 1957*, HMSO, London, p. 45.

37 Ibid., p. 61.
38 Ibid., p. 107.
39 Ibid., p. 110.
40 Lee, J. (1980) *My Life With Nye*, Jonathan Cape, London, pp. 176–7.
41 Webster, op. cit., p. 79–82.
42 Lee, op. cit., p. 177–8.
43 Brome, V. (1953) *Aneurin Bevan*, Longmans, Green & Co., London, p. 168.
44 Ibid., p. 168.
45 Ibid., p. 168, quote from the *British Medical Journal*, 16 November 1946.
46 Ibid., p. 172.
47 Foot, M. (1975) *Aneurin Bevan*, vol. 2, 1945–1960, Paladin Books, London, p. 101.
48 Ibid., p. 104.
49 Grey-Turner and Sutherland, op. cit., p. 142.
50 Ibid., p. 143.
51 Ibid., p. 144.
52 Ibid., pp. 126–7.
53 Ibid., p. 296.
54 Ibid., pp. 297–301.
55 Ibid., p. 295.
56 Ibid., p. 284–6.
57 British Medical Assocciation (1989) *The BMA: 'Friendly and Scientific'*, BMA, London, p. 1.
58 Clay, T. (1987) *Nurses: Power and Politics*, Heinemann, London, p. 21.
59 Ibid., p. 22.
60 Ibid., p. 136.
61 Dyson and Spary, op. cit., p. 15.
62 Bowman, G. (1967) *The Lamp and the Book: the Story of the RCN 1916–1966*, The Queen Anne Press, London. This book concentrates on the professional matters and personalities within the first fifty years of the RCN, but it does provide some comment on the trade union and industrial relations issues.
63 Ibid., p. 133.
64 Royal College of Nursing (1948) *Annual Report*, p. 4.
65 Ibid., p. 5.
66 Ibid., p. 5.
67 Ibid., p. 7.
68 Abel-Smith, B. (1960) *A History of the Nursing Profession*, Heinemann, London, p. 208.
69 Ibid.
70 Dyson and Spary, op. cit., p. 163.
71 Royal College of Nursing (1963) *Annual Report*, p. 12, and Bowman, op. cit., pp. 174–7.
72 Royal College of Nursing (1967) *Annual Report*, p. 7–9.
73 Royal College of Nursing (1970) *Annual Report*, p. 9.
74 Bosanquet, op. cit., p. 6; and Morris, G. (1986) *Strikes in Essential Services*, Mansell Publishing, London, chapter 6.

75 Dyson and Spary, op. cit., p. 165.
76 Royal College of Nursing (1974) *Annual Report*, p. 2.
77 Royal College of Nursing (1975) *Annual Report*, p. 10. Briggs, A. (1972) *Report of the Committee on Nursing*, Cmnd 5115, HMSO, London.
78 Royal College of Nursing (1977) *Annual Report*, p. 12.
79 Royal College of Nursing (1978/9) *Annual Report*, p. 12.
80 Fredman, S. and Morris, G. (1989) 'The State as Employer: Setting a New Example', *Personnel Management*, August.
81 Megaw, J. (1982) *Report of an Inquiry into Civil Service Pay*, Cmnd 8590, HMSO, London. Brown, W. and Rowthorn, B. (1990) A Public Services Pay Policy, Fabian Tract 542, Fabian Society, London.
82 Royal College of Nursing (1981/2) *Annual Report*, p. 6.
83 Royal College of Nursing (1982/3) *Annual Report*, p. 7 and 17.
84 Clay, op. cit., p. 126.
85 Ibid., p. 129.
86 Taylor, R. (1978) *The Fifth Estate*, Routledge and Kegan Paul, London. p. 253.
87 Cleminson, J. (1987) *Review Body...: Fourth Report on Nursing Staff, Midwives and Health Visitors 1987*, Cm 129, HMSO, London, p. 2.
88 Ibid., p. 11.
89 Ibid., p. 13.
90 Royal College of Midwives (1987) *Evidence to the Review Body for Nursing Staff, Midwives, Health Visitors and Professions Allied to Medicine for 1988*, RCM, London.
91 Social Services Committee of the House of Commons (1989) *Resourcing the NHS: Midwives' Regrading 1988–89*, Fourth Report, HMSO, London.
92 Ibid., p. vii.
93 Ibid., p. viii.
94 Ibid., p. xi.
95 Cleminson, J. (1989) *Review Body ...: Sixth Report on Nursing Staff, Midwives and Health Visitors 1989*, Cm 577, HMSO, London, p. 11.
96 Cleminson, J. (1990) *Review Body ...: Seventh Report on Nursing Staff, Midwives and Health Visitors 1990*, Cm 934, HMSO, London, p. 7.
97 Ibid., p. 17–19.
98 Bett, M. (1991) *Review Body ...: Eighth Report on Nursing Staff, Midwives and Health Visitors 1991*, Cm 1410, HMSO, London, pp. 4–5.
99 Ibid., pp. 20–1.
100 Royal College of Nursing (1986) *Constitution for RCN Branches*, RCN, London. p. 1; Royal College of Nursing (1986) *What the RCN Stands For*, RCN, London.
101 Cowell, B. and Wainwright, D. (1981) *Behind the Blue Door: the History of the RCM 1881–1981*, Ballière Tindall, London, p. 91.
102 Royal College of Midwives (1986/7) *Members' Handbook*, RCM, London.
103 Health Visitors Association (1985) *Local Representatives' Handbook*, HVA, London. For details of the merger ballot see *The Health Visitor*, 63(7), July 1990, p. 219.

104   For the history of bargaining for the PAMs and technical staffs see the brief comment in Trades Union Congress (1981) *Improving Industrial Relations in the National Health Service*, TUC, London, p. 21.

105   Dyson and Spary, op. cit., p. 155.

106   Bett, M. (1991) *Review Body ...: Eighth Report on Professions Allied to Medicine 1991*, Cm 1411, HMSO, London, p. 19.

107   Ibid., p. 20.

108   Ibid., p. 10.

109   Greenborough, J. (1986) *Review Body ...: Third Report on Professions Allied to Medicine 1986*, Cmnd 9783, HMSO, London, p. 13.

110   Ibid., p. 11.

111   Chartered Society of Physiotherapists (1987) *Source Book*, CSP, London.

112   Moodie, I. (1970) *The Society of Radiographers. Fifty Years of History*, Society of Radiographers, London.

113   For details of the affiliation ballot see *Radiography Today*, August 1990, p. 1.

Chapter 3

The trade unions and their members

INTRODUCTION

Most of the trade unions that organize health workers are general unions with members in a range of occupations in a range of industries. Most of them existed when the NHS was founded and gave full support to its initial collective bargaining system. These unions, their members and leaders, have been at the heart of most of the campaigns to improve the service and to protect it from cutbacks, undemocratic reorganizations and the contracting out of services. Their basic methods of operation have been similar: recruit members where possible, develop local steward networks, campaign through the media and local politicians when appropriate, and take industrial action when necessary. This broadly common approach does not disguise severe differences between and within the unions, nor does it hide the damage done by competition for members between the unions, but it does provide the ground upon which cooperation has been based often through the TUC health services committee.

These unions aim to achieve a standard rate for the job and bargaining over the nature of that job. The crucial development, as described by the Webbs, was the move away from individual contracts to collective agreements:

> But if a group of workmen concert together, and send representatives to conduct the bargaining on behalf of the whole body, the position is at once changed. Instead of the employer making a series of separate contracts with isolated individuals, he meets with a collective will, and settles, in a single agreement, the principles upon which, for the time being, all workmen of a particular group, or class, or grade, will be engaged.[1]

Such schemes give rise to a series of related issues: the determination of this Common Rule, the mechanisms of joint determination, the enforcement of the rate through arbitration and/or industrial action, the organization of the union, and the enforcement of the union's rules on individual members. The economic purposes of such collective bargaining were noted in the previous chapter as not only the setting of the standard rate but also the restriction of the labour supply. For most members of these general unions the latter is much harder to achieve than for the professional associations.

While the professions sought to achieve their aims through legal enactment and vested interests, the general unions in the NHS have adopted collective bargaining and the principles of supply and demand, and the living wage. The former doctrine involves attempts to control the labour supply through mechanisms such as the closed shop and/or by recruiting into membership all workers in the relevant trade and/or employer. Supply and demand removes trade union demands beyond that of custom to that of what the market will bear. So in good times efforts are made to force wages up. Such activities may result in union leaders, activists and policies which emphasize the tough discipline of fighting for more in the market and they will combine with anyone who can share in that struggle.[2] This might apply to sections of MSF, the GMB and the EETPU. It might well apply to some of the arguments used by the unions (NUPE, COHSE and the GMB) in the 1989 ambulance staff dispute.

The living wage doctrine was developed to counter the fall in earnings during the trade slumps. It was powerfully expressed by Sam Woods MP (Vice-President of the Miners Federation of Great Britain) and quoted with approval by the Webbs:

> They held it as a matter of life and death that any condition of trade ought to warrant the working man a living. They held that it was a vital principle that a man by his labour should live, and notwithstanding all the teachings of the political economists, all the doctrines taught by the way of supply and demand, they said there was a greater doctrine overriding all these, and that was the doctrine of humanity.[3]

This argument, in its national minimum wage form, is increasingly used by NUPE and COHSE to combat the lower terms of employment offered in contracted-out services, and to support their members in the lowest paid jobs – often part-time women workers.

Most of these unions are characteristically 'open' in their structure, unlike the professional associations. This means that they tend to recruit all similar categories of staff within any given employer, and that they concern themselves more with pay and conditions than with labour supply issues. It may also mean that they are more likely to merge and that they embrace collective bargaining as the mechanism they most favour.[4]

The unions of most interest are NUPE and COHSE: they both recruit nurses and ancillary workers, they both were involved in pre-NHS union organization of health workers, they both welcomed and have continued to support the NHS as a service for the people of Britain, and they account for nearly half a million trade union members in the NHS. The only other organization to have anywhere near that size of membership in the NHS is the RCN. The major difference between the two unions is that COHSE is essentially a single industry union, while NUPE has large membership in local government, the old public utilities and universities.

The other two important NHS unions are NALGO and the MSF (formerly ASTMS and TASS). These are large white-collar unions with less than 10% of their membership in the NHS. In the case of NALGO these are mainly A&C staff, although they also recruit from managerial grades among nurses and ambulance staff. From the start of the NHS, NALGO too gave strong support, but for many years was bedevilled by membership rivalries. MSF's main presence in the NHS comes from ASTMS members based in the scientific and technical grades. This union expanded rapidly in the 1970s, and now with ex-TASS members forms a powerful and growing NHS group including health visitors merged through the HVA in 1990. All four of these unions are in the TUC and correspond to the general image of trade union behaviour and organization.

The other group of traditional unions includes the TGWU, GMB, UCATT and EETPU. These all have important NHS sections, but compared with their general concerns they tend to be marginalized by the other unions and the collective bargaining system. They have lost members in the NHS in recent years, and often have very few of a given type of member in any one location/occupational group.

Six of these multi-occupational trade unions, as Table 3.1 reveals, principally represent craft, works, maintenance and ancillary staff although the GMB and the TGWU have some ambulance personnel and A&C staff in membership. The GMB recruits nurses through its white-collar section, APEX.

Table 3.1 NHS membership of six of the multi-occupation trade unions

Trade union	Membership	No. members
AUEW	Members in crafts grades as engineers and engineering craftsmen	n.a.
EETPU	Members in craft grades as plumbers and electricians. Also a few works officers	10 000
GMB ⎤ APEX ⎦	Members in ancillary and ambulance grades ⎤ Section of the GMB, has members in nursing, ⎬ administration and clerical ⎦	40 000
TGWU	Members in A&C, ambulance and ancillary grades	30 000
UCATT	Members are works officers, building and maintenance operatives	7000
USDAW	A few members who work as dental technicians	n.a.

As Chapter 5 will reveal, neither the AUEW nor the EETPU have national representation on the Whitley Councils, UCATT and USDAW represent members on one of the Professional and Technical Councils and the GMB and TGWU's national representation in the NHS is principally with the ambulance and ancillary staff. It is the remaining four multi-occupational trade unions who have the largest NHS membership and the widest range of influence at the Whitley Councils. Table 3.2 lists the overall and NHS 1988 membership of these four unions –

Table 3.2 Multi-occupational trade unions: four examples of overall and NHS membership figures for 1988

Trade union	Membership totals	
	Overall	In NHS
COHSE	218 321	218 321
MSF	653 000	approx. 50 000
NALGO	750 000	approx. 70 000
NUPE	620 000	approx. 250 000

Source: Annual Report of the Certification Officer, 1989.

COHSE, MSF, NALGO and NUPE – and this is followed by a brief examination of the structure and history of each of these four unions' health service sections along with some analysis of the pay and pay determination of their members.

CONFEDERATION OF HEALTH SERVICE EMPLOYEES (COHSE)

COHSE organizes nurses, administrative and clerical staffs, ambulance staff and officers, ancillary staff, technicians and helper grades. Only NUPE and the RCN have more members in the NHS. COHSE's historical and current strength is among nurses: from its early years before the First World War until the mid-1970s this was overwhelmingly among psychiatric nurses (in 1980s this was 70% of nurse members) and as a result COHSE's membership and policy remained somewhat limited to this group. From the 1974 action over nurses' pay to the early 1980s COHSE's membership grew very rapidly and more and more general nurses joined. In 1988 this trend was given a further boost by the nurses' regrading dispute. COHSE sources give the following membership figures:

1947:	40 000
1967:	66 240
1977:	200 455
1980:	216 482
1989:	209 344

COHSE perhaps more than any other union has been responsible for the development of trade unionism in the NHS, especially amongst nurses. Its strong traditions and clear stance for better terms and conditions of service have enabled it to recruit and represent more and more health workers. The membership belong to geographically based branches, although some of these are also workplace branches. The members elect their branch committee, and increasingly stewards are elected to represent specific groups of members. The union has 13 regions which correspond to the NHS management regions, and each has full-time officials based in a regional office. At the centre is the NEC serviced by full-time officials, including the powerful General Secretary. The Annual Delegate Conference remains the supreme governing body, and conference delegates drawn from the branches decide policy based on motions presented to local branches[5] (Figure 3.1).

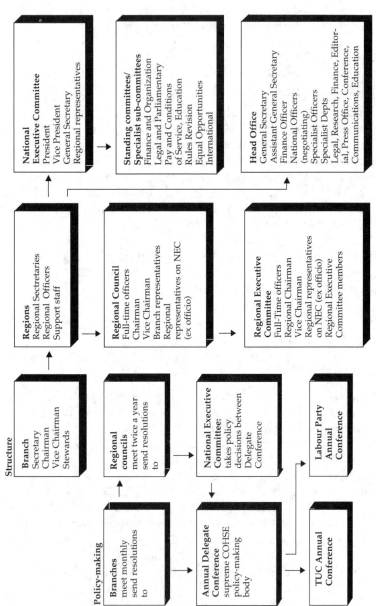

Figure 3.1 Organizational structure and policy-making process within COHSE. (*Source*: COHSE Steward's handbook.)

In the case of COHSE, the detailed analysis about their members' pay and pay structures is dealt with elsewhere – for nurses under the RCN in Chapter 2 and for ancillary workers and ambulance staff under NUPE later in this chapter. In the case of ancillary and ambulance staff there is no distinctive COHSE line at the moment since it has devised a shared policy and approach with NUPE and the other Whitley unions, GMB and TGWU. In the case of nurses this applies to NUPE but not to the RCN. COHSE is currently in talks with NUPE and NALGO over a merger, and that means that in public, at least, any policy and strategy differences are minimized. COHSE has been active in sounding out the views of its members on a range of issues. The 1990 Review Body for nurses noted the COHSE membership survey carried out in the summer of 1988 in which half the respondents to the questionnaire stated that they had considered leaving nursing due to low morale, low pay and high levels of stress.[6] This parallels another survey of their members in ancillary jobs which asked similar questions with similar results.[7] Table 3.3 gives the results of that survey.

The history of COHSE outlined below suggests that it has been less willing to change tack and to innovate in organizational terms than some other unions, and its position on the right of centre of the Labour Party has meant that it has not enjoyed the support of some of the other main TUC-based NHS unions. But it has a record of struggle and organization within the NHS second to none, and has played a major role in pushing the case of low pay for women and the organization of nurses and ancillary workers to the fore of industrial relations.

The origins of COHSE go back a long way into an obscure part of working-class history. As Carpenter's history of COHSE covers this adequately there is only the need for a summary here.[8] The first formal landmark was the founding in September 1910 of the National Asylum Workers Union (NAWU) based mainly in Lancashire.[9] This was itself the result of several earlier attempts to organize nurses and attendants in asylums. By July 1911 there were 4000 members in 44 institutions from all over England and Wales.[10] By 1914 the NAWU had had its first strike and had affiliated to the Labour Party. By 1920 membership reached its interwar peak of 18 000. In 1918 the Poor Law Workers Trade Union (PLWTU) was formed for grades below that of clerk working for local Boards of Guardians. This was mainly London-based and started with about 5600 members, but

Table 3.3 Results of COHSE membership survey, summer 1988

Because of the lack of key statistical data, COHSE conducted a survey of
  a sample of its members on overtime working, recruitment and
  retention problems, staff turnover and morale.
A total of 383 questionnaires were returned.
They demonstrate that health authorities are using overtime and agency
  staff to deal with high vacancy rates.
Almost three-quarters of the respondents had seriously considered
  leaving their job in the NHS over the previous 12 months.

Main reasons for seriously considering leaving the NHS

Reason	No. of staff giving it as the first reason	% of first reasons	% of respondents to question who listed it as a reason
Level of pay	193	39.1%	85.6%
Low morale	62	12.6%	69.2%
NHS cuts	56	11.4%	67.3%
Level of stress	51	10.0%	60.3%
Management	46	9.3%	57.1%
Workload	44	8.9%	50.0%
Working hours/patterns	16	3.2%	42.6%
Other	15	3.0%	21.6%
Long hours of work	10	2.0%	37.2%

NB: Some respondents gave more than one first or main reason for
seriously considering leaving the NHS.

By far the most important reason was pay.

by 1920 it peaked at 14 000 members. By 1922 it had become the
Poor Law Officers Union (PLOU). These early unions reflected
both the divisions of health care between local government and
hospital associations, and the possibility of organizing health
workers in trade unions when and where they were not dominated by professional bodies and found themselves working in
an essential service for awful pay and in exceptionally bad
conditions.

The 1920s and 1930s saw the setting up of a permanent Joint
Consultative Committee (JCC) between the Mental Hospitals
Association and the NAWU, but it also saw most individual
employers ignore any agreements reached. This has strong
parallels with the schools system, and one lesson for the trade
unions was that in future national agreements must be forced
upon all employers. In 1923 the NAWU affiliated to the TUC,
and in 1931, with changes in the status of attendants to nurses,

the NAWU became the Mental Hospitals and Institutional Workers Union (MHIWU). Meanwhile the PLOU became the National Union of County Officers (NUCO) in 1930 and affiliated to the TUC in 1933. In 1937 the Guild of Nurses was formed within NUCO, and in 1943 it became the Hospitals and Welfare Services Union (HWSU) based in municipal hospitals. These changes in name and form were mainly the consequence of changes in local government responsibilities and in the operations of mental institutions. Other features of these years such as falling membership and TUC affiliation both reflected more general trends amongst the unions as they sought to counter the depression in the economy, and their efforts to come to terms with more centralized and state-related economic decision-making.

In 1946 the MHIWU and the HWSU merged to form COHSE. Part of the impetus for this merger was the coming together in the war years of health service and local government activities, the shortages of labour, and the development of national pay rates for nurses. In 1943 the Rushcliffe Committee gave more pay and better conditions to nurses,[11] and more important, the notion of national pay determination came in despite opposition from both employers and the nurse managers.[12] Other staff shortages forced the government to act and the Hetherington Report on female domestic workers provided an impetus for national bargaining on their behalf. As Carpenter says: 'the best hopes for improvement lay in the achievement of national bargaining for all support staff'.[13] Both the HSWU and NUPE backed this. The HWSU also tried to organize and win national pay for ambulance workers through the Ambulance Services Guild.

COHSE gave enthusiastic support to both the NHS and the Whitley system. This principled support for the NHS was restated by COHSE in its submission to the Royal Commission thus: 'COHSE is wholly committed to the maintenance of a service which is free to the patient at the time of need'.[14] As Carpenter notes: 'The NHS started life with an enormous fund of goodwill of its staff, its most precious resource.'[15] However, poor pay and conditions, and exclusion from decision-making, slowly dissipated this initial asset. The staff shortages of the 1950s combined with the Conservative government's determination to control public expenditure and pay put pressure from the start on the Whitley system, which was complex enough due to the

differentiated nature of the workforce, existing wide local variations in pay, and the divisions between groups of staff and their
organizations. As Carpenter points out, the general problem of
functional councils and the Labour government's refusal to
make joint consultation compulsory was intensified in the case
of COHSE which was represented on most councils but dominated none of them.[16] The 1950s witnessed in Carpenter's words
'abysmal pay and deteriorating working conditions which
exacerbated existing staff shortages'.[17] The watershed year was
1959: the change was made within the union from mainly male
psychiatric nurses to more general nurses and more women, and
by 1963 membership had risen to 67 000. Throughout this time
COHSE was in conflict with the RCN, which sought to continue
the dominance of the matron, refused to accept reforms, and
opposed most methods of securing better pay and conditions.

From the mid-1960s to the mid-1970s two themes emerged:
health service work was becoming more remote from patient
contact and the new style of management made control more
functional and impersonal. In other words hospital work began
to resemble work in other large organizations, and the industrial
relations that emerged often mimicked those found elsewhere.
The centralization of the service 'gave immense potential power
to strike at the jugular veins of the district general hospitals'.[18]
Dyson in his study of the ancillary workers' dispute in Leeds in
1972/3 took this point to heart and has argued ever since that
decentralization would remove much union power.[19] The
centralization of the service based on the twin needs of greater
Treasury control over expenditure and the economies of scale to
be found in management operations and large district general
hospitals, further alienated health workers excluded even more
from any say in the decisions that affected their working lives.
Even COHSE, never a radical union, felt that 'there is room for
worker-participation in the sense that there must be full
involvement of staff *before* decisions are taken'.[20]

In the 1970s, however, the move created a situation which did
give more power to local stewards, and this sparked off the
enormous growth in stewards throughout the NHS, which had
started in a small way with ancillary workers after the introduction in 1967 of the NBPI-inspired bonus schemes. This occurred
with incomes policies which normally affected public sector
service workers worse than any other group. The combination of
these factors led to the 1974 nurses' pay dispute which ended

with the Halsbury Inquiry which granted pay rises. COHSE's leading role in this dispute enabled it to recruit nurses and other workers, and for the next six years it expanded rapidly.

By the late 1970s the professional associations had begun to regroup. The legislation of the Labour government forced them to become trade unions, which they did. And by 1978 the RCN had rebuilt itself and presented a real challenge to the other nurses' trade unions. This was compounded by Lord McCarthy's report on Whitley which 'sanctioned the position of professional associations within the system'.[21] The 1980s saw cutbacks, reorganization, management reforms, regradings, Pay Review Bodies and industrial unrest. COHSE managed to hold its membership and its policies during this period, but the RCN fared much better. The situation is one in which private medicine and the privatization of many services has reduced the NHS and the power of the some of the general unions within it considerably. In this process the rights of patients and of staff have been reduced as the new employers and the general managers dominate the operational side, and ministers and powerful private companies dominate policy. What remains true, as Carpenter suggests, is that, 'what was clear, even before its inception, was that the NHS and its industrial relations, would never be far from the centre of the British political stage'.[22]

Today COHSE remains a large and powerful NHS trade union. It is involved in detailed merger talks with NUPE and NALGO, and this indicates both some internal difficulties and the external force of a changed bargaining situation within the NHS. In particular COHSE has kept a firm hold on its nurse members and their more militant tradition, and has managed to unite important groups of workers in hospitals across traditional occupational lines and status divides. It has done so with a moderate political image, an unreformed constitution and the considerable support of lay members.

COHSE has opposed most of the current round of reforms, but has accepted the new pay arrangements for nurses, and was one of the unions involved in the 1989 ambulance dispute which fought to create a new pay determination system outside of Whitley. Its current membership is composed of about 120 000 nurses, 60 000 ancillary staffs, 5000 ambulance staff, and the remainder are scattered among A&C and PT'A' and PT'B' staff groups. Throughout the 1980s about 80% of COHSE's members were women. The key to COHSE rests in its moderate and gradual approach to bargaining issues with employers and within the TUC, and its growth steeped in militant tradition. As Carpenter noted:

> a dramatic change in its fortunes occurred following the nurses' pay campaign in 1974 when, alone among staff side organizations, it initiated a programme of industrial action. By 1979 it was the twelfth largest union in the TUC – a remarkable achievement for a union recruiting in such a limited membership field crowded with competing organizations.[23]

At local level it is active in hospital-based Joint Consultative Committees and has a strong steward base supported by regional full-time officers. It is well placed to confront the employers in the new trusts, but recognizes that recognition and fragmented bargaining may require the creation of some kind of confederal NHS union approach.

As Hector MacKenzie of COHSE said in a personal communication to the author,

> COHSE believes that the imposition of the so called internal market and opted out hospitals is simply a stepping stone to full privatisation and the selling off of large sections of the service, [and that the best way to defeat this is to work closely with NALGO and NUPE and to present] 'a united front to employers and co-ordinate our activities at local level in a successful effort to enhance our bargaining strength.

MANUFACTURING SCIENCE AND FINANCE (MSF)

MSF was formed in 1988 by the merger of ASTMS and TASS. This created a TUC-affiliated union with over 650 000 members – the fifth largest union in Britain. Most of its members are white-collar and technical and professional staff in the private sector, and only about 50 000 are in the NHS.

Its NHS membership is mainly based on the old ASTMS membership, although the recent merger with the 16 000-strong Health Visitors Association has altered this balance. ASTMS's largest membership in the NHS is drawn from the Medical Laboratory Scientific Officers, pharmaceutical staff and speech therapy profession, although it has members amongst the PAM professions and related grades. The TASS membership in the NHS was negligible and confined to a handful of dental technicians through their membership of NUGSAT (National Union of Gold, Silver and Allied Trades).

The groups of staff now represented by MSF grew very rapidly in number throughout the 1970s. In 1987 there were nearly 80 000 wte professional and technical staff in the NHS in England. About 35 000 of these were PAMs. Of the rest about 11 000 were scientific and professional staff with pharmacists (2851) and speech therapists (2631) the largest groups both represented by ASTMS. The remainder are the PT'B' staff of nearly 34 000. Over 14 000 of these are the MLSOs and the rest a variety of technicians such as dental surgery assistants (2879), pharmacy technicians (2793) and operating department assistants (2633) (Table 2. 6, pp. 97–100).

This rapidly increasing and influential group suffered from dispersion of numbers and uncertainty of professional status. By 1980 ASTMS, with its 25 000 NHS members had members in scientific, technical, laboratory, PSM, pharmaceutical, optical and medical grades. ASTMS was represented on four Whitley functional councils and ten subcommittees. It had two seats out of 22 on the Optical Council, eight out of 24 on the Pharmaceutical Council, two out of 22 on PT'A' but dominated committee A for biochemists, physicists and psychologists; and committee B for speech therapists. On PT'B' it had three of the 21 seats but dominated committee A for MLSOs. TASS had no representation worth mentioning although it was a recognized union.[24]

ASTMS was itself the product of a merger between ASSET and the AScW in 1968. The new union was dominated by its extraordinary General Secretary, Clive Jenkins. It grew at a phenomenal rate and soon merged with the National Union of Insurance Staffs, the Medical Practitioners Union and the Guild of Pharmacists.[25] Between 1964 and 1974 ASTMS had grown by 347% to a total of 325 000 with some 72 full-time officials and assets of nearly £2 million. In the 1970s about two-fifths of its members were in engineering, about another fifth in banking and insurance, with smaller numbers in the NHS (20 000), chemical workers (7 000) and 10 000 in petrochemicals. Throughout the 1980s ASTMS lost members along with most other private sector general unions, and by the late 1980s was experiencing some financial problems and internal realignments based on the changing composition of its membership.[26]

In contrast, TASS was based on a traditional craft union recruiting draughtsmen. The General Secretary of the

Draughtsmen and Allied Technicians Association (DATA), Jim Mortimer, was a very influential figure in the labour movement, becoming head of ACAS and General Secretary of the Labour Party.[27] It experienced rapid growth of 91% from 1964 to 1975 when it had 126 000 members. After an uneasy loose federation with the AUEW, TASS split away and formed the other part of MSF under its influential and tough-minded left-wing General Secretary, Ken Gill. At the time of the merger TASS had about 240 000 members and ASTMS 390 000. By 1989 MSF had 653 000 members.

There are more than 20 separate staff groups in the professional, scientific and technical services of the NHS. They range in size from the few medical artists (of which, in 1977, there were 11 wte) to the many thousands of MLSOs. Medical laboratory technicians were represented only in informal discussions with the BHA and local authorities and their pay scale rates were fixed directly in 1946 and 1947 until, in 1948 a JNC (Medical Laboratory Technicians) was formed. Other groups include amongst their members university trained biochemists, physicists and psychologists and grades for which there are no specific educational requirements above 'O' level or the equivalent. JNCs to cover other groups of hospital technicians followed shortly afterwards.

The scientific and technical staff have a mixed, complex and at times obscure history with regard to the start of the NHS. Their numbers were limited and they were scattered throughout the service. In the 1960s their numbers expanded very rapidly with the development of technology in medicine and with the intensification of scientific methods within the service. The main union which tried to recruit these staff was ASTMS. It had some partial success, and in keeping with its spectacular rise elsewhere it played a role out of proportion to its size or tradition with the NHS trade unions. It recruited more qualified staff, and a majority of men. The main expansion elsewhere was amongst lower grades of staff, often part-time women in NALGO and NUPE.

MSF have one national health sector officer although one or two of their regional full-time officers who have health service responsibilities within their overall remit also fulfil a 'national' role in the representative and bargaining processes. There is a research department upon which the national officer is able to call. As a 'general' trade union, while in some parts of Britain (London for example) there are specific health service branches, in many others the health service members are part of a general branch and as such are part of a wider employment group. All of the NHS professions in which MSF have members, such as speech therapists, MLSOs, and some radiographers, have as their main representative forum a specific national advisory committee, and it is here that issues that relate to each individual group in the NHS are considered. At local level, MSF stewards are, in general, elected to represent all of the membership in the hospital or health authority, and not to represent a specific group.

As with other Whitley Council unions, MSF has fought to improve the relatively poor pay of its NHS members. In 1988 MSF in its claim on behalf of MLSOs argued that 'they are rewarded for these considerable efforts with inadequate incomes, an outmoded grade structure, and inferior conditions of service'.[28] They provided evidence of low morale and high turnover. The main case was a comparability one with Scientific Civil Service grades. The case suggests that for junior grades the gap is 14% but closes to 8% for senior staff. Before 1980 the MLSO pay was tied to that of the Civil Service, but that link was broken when the government abandoned comparability as a pay argument. The claim for higher pay was associated with a reduction in working hours, the removal of holiday anomalies, and progress towards a six-week holiday entitlement.

In the 1989 claim MSF repeated its comparability case and insisted on protection from the increasing inflation rate. In addition, a new grading scheme was requested with the removal of the lowest point in each grade, more flexibility for qualified staff on rotation, and an effective training grade for pathology technicians.[29]

The 1990 claim asked for a 12% pay rise on all points of the pathology pay spine, a 35 hour week, six weeks holiday and independent arbitration if negotiations failed to secure a satisfactory agreement. In 1991 all the arguments recently employed were again used, but this time they were supplemented with arguments based on workload and demand.[30] In 1990 the bottom of the MLSO pay scale was £8862 and the top for an MLSO4 was £24 570. From 1981 to 1987 pay rises had varied from 4% to 6% per annum for all staff, and only once in 1986 had the settlement been significantly higher than the rate of inflation. In 1988 the settlements varied from 11% at the bottom to 24% at the top, with inflation at 4%.

There was a change in the bargaining arrangements for some staff in 1990. A new PT'B' subcommittee, Committee T (incorporating Committees B, C, E and H), was formed to negotiate conditions of service for Medical Technical Officer and Dental Auxiliary grades. This committee had representation from five unions: NALGO (6), MSF (5), COHSE (4), NUPE (4) and USDAW (1) (26 March 90 PT'B' Council memo from joint secretaries). At the same time another new subcommittee, W, was formed from committees D and F. By September 1990 the Department of Health's Advance Letter (PT'B') 3/90 contained the details of the new agreement. Paragraph 11 stated that:

> Agreement has been reached on the introduction of:
> – a facility to enable local management to supplement pay points where this would assist in addressing proven recruitment and retention problems;
> – new rules relating to use of the scale advancement facility;
> – discretion on the starting pay of new appointments.

In another Advance Letter, (PT'B') 6/90, the use of local pay flexibility was further articulated.

> The aim of local pay supplementation, as with the A&C agreement, is to help recruit and retain suitably skilled staff. It is expected that pay flexibility will be used selectively as part of a package of conditions which incorporate the improved nationally agreed grading structures providing enhanced career opportunities and within which employing authorities now have considerably increased discretion.[31]

The MSF is an open union which recruits a relatively small proportion of its members in the NHS. None the less, it has grown within the NHS through mergers with a range of professional and technical staffs' organizations and offers, therefore, an important challenge to less traditional and aggressive unions in their policies on representation. In addition, most MSF members in the NHS remain in PT'B' with important influence in PT'A' and through the health visitors on the Nurses and Midwives Council. This concentration of membership makes it more influential and powerful than other general unions with comparable NHS membership, such as the GMB.

John Chowcat, the MSF national officer for health services, indicated in a personal communication to the author his union's view that,

Given current Department of Health pressures to introduce greater numbers of support staffs in professional departments and to move towards deploying proportionately fewer skilled professional staffs, MSF believes that a period of widespread local productivity bargaining is emerging, in which our function is to protect professional standards of service to patients and the job security and income of our membership in relevant grades. We must be fully prepared for this development.

NATIONAL AND LOCAL GOVERNMENT OFFICERS ASSOCIATION (NALGO)

The numbers of administrative and clerical staff grew rapidly in the 1960s and 1970s, but have remained steady in the 1980s. Most belong to NALGO, although some specialist and more senior staff belong to a variety of management associations. Following the Griffiths Report (1983) into the management of the NHS, the government introduced the general management concept into the service. General managers were initially appointed at regional, district and unit level and by 1987 there were over 800 such high level managers in post. The concept of 'general' management was subsequently applied to specific, as well as overall, areas of management responsibility with the creation of such posts as 'In-patient Services Managers' and 'Directors of Nursing and Personnel'. Many of these managers have resisted trade union membership as they seek individual contracts and solutions to their own problems. Some functional managers either stay in their professional associations or seek protection in a range of professional bodies.

NALGO is the union, however, which recruits mainly among the A&C grades. It, like NUPE, gave full support to the NHS at the start and welcomed the bargaining system of Whitley. It soon found that, as with the manual workers, too much power rested with Whitehall and too little initiative with local employers and mangers. They in turn tended to exclude staff from any participation in the service, and by the end of the 1950s the A&C grades were in disarray.[32] By the end of the 1960s NALGO had joined the TUC and presented itself as one of the new style white-collar unions with spectacular growth, a decentralized stewards system, and increasing democratic union government.[33] In the 1980s, however, NALGO lost members in line with general trends, and within the NHS its members experienced acute changes with job redesign, new technology and a series of management and employer reorganizations.

NALGO is the fourth largest trade union in Britain and has about two-thirds of its members in mainly white-collar staff in local government (nearly 500 000 out of a total in 1988 of about 760 000). The second largest category of NALGO members, although a long way behind those in local government, are members in the NHS – nearly 67 000 or about 9% in 1988. This represents a fall of NALGO's NHS membership from a peak in 1981 of about 90 000, and a fall in density from about 65% in 1980 to about 50% by 1989. The bulk of these fall within the general staff category of Administration and Clerical, and NALGO dominates the A&C Whitley Council. It is also represented on the Nurses and Midwives Council, and on PT'A' and 'B'. The spread of the membership between occupations and within them reflects both NALGO's origins and the movement of responsibilities between local government and health services over the years.

NALGO head office gives the following figures for membership in the NHS 1981–8:

1981:	89 500
1982:	86 400
1983:	80 500
1984:	75 900
1985:	71 300
1986:	69 200
1987:	68 900
1988:	66 500

The breakdown of the A&C category in the 1980s would be approximately of the order of half the group as clerical, about 20% as administration, 12% as secretarial and 10% as typists, with a further 10% miscellaneous for England only (Table 3.4). The large increase in this category of staff came with the 1974 reorganization, and was maintained by the introduction of information technology and the various schemes to privatize the NHS in the late 1980s.

From the mid-1980s on, NALGO, in common with many other public sector unions, began to change its overall structures and approaches to bargaining. In 1985 NALGO's pay claim on behalf of A&C staff in the NHS had low pay as its first listed objective, and it nominated a minimum rate based on two-thirds of the national average male manual earnings, at that time £5408. In

Table 3.4 Breakdown of administrative and clerical staff in the NHS in England

	Unit	1978	1983	1984	1985	1986	1987	1988
Total NHS administrative and clerical staff	No.	117 940	129 616	130 057	131 316	131 907	136 404	139 010
	wte	100 302	109 965	110 304	111 048	111 351	114 595	115 951
Senior administrative[1]	wte	5968	7386	7799	7998	9168	10 802	12 006
Junior administrative[2]	wte	14 448	14 954	15 081	15 883	16 037	16 652	17 731
Clerical[3]	wte	47 747	50 727	50 729	50 578	50 040	50 158	49 926
Medical secretaries[4]	wte	—	4467	5627	7677	8801	8912	8812
Secretaries[5]	wte	15 981	13 186	12 459	10 857	9600	9798	10 154
Typists and machine operators (including supervisors)	wte	7176	8069	7689	7486	7502	7625	7512
Ex-local health authority staff	wte	—	464	379	311	264	218	185
Other staff (excluding support services)	wte	339	278	259	257	396	617	477

[1]Principal Administrative Assistant (Grade 9 and above), includes general managers.
[2]Below Principal Administrative Assistant (Grade 9) and above Higher Clerical Officer – including regional/national trainees.
[3]Includes Higher Clerical Officer, excludes storekeeper clerks.
[4]Medical secretaries cannot be separately identified prior to 1981.
[5]Prior to 1981 included some supervisory staff. From 1981 onwards these staff are included in typists and machine operators.
Source: Health and Personal Social Services Statistics for England, 1990, p. 61.

Table 3.4 (*continued*) Breakdown of administrative and clerical staff in the NHS in England

	Unit	1878	1983	1984	1985	1986	1987	1988
Support services: total	wte	5284	6958	6795	6582	6138	5916	5507
Laundry and linen[6]	wte	357	652	599	578	523	468	458
Farming[6]	wte	17	18	18	11	10	9	10
Catering[6]	wte	1360	1970	1985	1959	1910	1919	1930
Domestic services including wardens	wte	2268	2352	2248	2124	1771	1603	1534
Central sterile supply department[6]	wte	341	511	527	532	544	531	543
Storekeeper clerks[6]	wte	917	1455	1418	1378	1380	1388	1032
Dental Practice Board	wte	1392	1481	1501	1482	1497	1425	1272
Prescription Pricing Authority staff	wte	1967	1996	1987	1938	1910	1784	1669
Other Statutory Authorities staff[7]	wte	—	—	—	—	—	686	698

[6] Prior to 1981 showed managers only. From 1981 onwards includes all staff.
[7] Prior to 1987, figures for Other Statutory Authorities (e.g. Public Health Laboratory Service and the Health Education Authority) were not collected in the Annual Manpower Census.
Source: Health and Personal Social Services Statistics for England, 1990, p. 61.

addition, NALGO asked for an £8 plus 8% increase to 'compensate for the erosion of real wages by comparison with other staff and movements in the rate of inflation and average earnings'. It also wanted a review of the entire pay structure and 'restoring the pay links with the Civil Service which were broken in 1980'.[34] On service conditions the emphasis was on a shorter working work (35 hours), a minimum of 30 days' annual leave, and improvements in long service leave.

The detailed case that followed took non-manual women's earnings as the base, since more than 80% of the A&C workforce are women. The base year used for the argument was 1972 when the NHS earnings for clerical and secretarial staff matched the average pay for all non-manual women, but by 1984 this had become a 17% gap against the NHS staff. In addition to this fall relative to all other non-manual women, there was also a fall compared with equivalent Civil Service staff and with NHS staff covered by Pay Review Bodies. In 1984 the A&C grades won a 4.5% rise against 7.5% for the index of average earnings. The case continued with arguments from inflation added to the comparability ones.

The key element of the claim was the offer of a restructuring which it was hoped would improve pay and meet some of the needs of the employers in the post-Griffiths management. In 1985 there were 14 general grades, 41 numbered scales and 17 lettered scales. The attack on the structure included criticism of the number of increments within scales, and the illogical degree of overlap between scales. Most people did not understand the structure, promotion within it was a lottery, and it had lost any claim to be a 'felt-fair' system. NALGO urged the introduction of a salary spine 'capable of application across the entire A&C structure'.[35]

In October 1985 an agreement was reached which reduced the working week from 40 hours to 39, kept the existing structure, and provided a 4.7% pay rise. In 1986 NALGO submitted its claim asking for a £20 per week increase, and again seeking a review of structure and special treatment for the low paid. They argued that 'pay should be fair when compared with similar employment'.[36] In particular they showed that from 1980 to 1985 A&C average pay had risen 28.1% compared with inflation of 43.4% and an average earnings index of 58.2%.[37]

In 1987 NALGO again asked for a £20 per week award across the board, and again the case was based on comparison with average earnings, NHS Pay Review staff and the Civil Service. This time NALGO pointed out that they wished to reserve the right to go to arbitration if there was a dispute over pay which could not be resolved in Whitley. By April 1987 the range of the numbered scales was from a minimum of £6884 for scale 1 to a maximum of £30 980 for scale 41 extended to point A. General grades varied from £3301 for a copy typist to £10 958 for a senior administrator.[38] In 1988 the same debate with the same data was repeated with NALGO now asking for £24 per week rise coupled with a 35 hour week and 30 day's annual leave.[39]

The breakthrough eventually came in 1989 with an agreement on a new salary structure. The pressures on NALGO to make concessions in exchange for long cherished objectives on better pay, especially for the low paid, combined with the pressures on the management to win greater flexibility through a more business-like pay structure to produce a new agreement. Once again NALGO asked for a £15 per week or 10% rise and this time linked it more explicitly to labour market considerations of recruitment and retention. In other words the NALGO claim looked more like a submission to a Pay Review Body and took into account managerial requirements as part of the overall argument on comparability.[40]

The 1989 agreement issued by the DHSS in July included the new structures, assimilation agreement, a 6.25% pay rise and, of crucial significance for the management, 'the introduction of the facility for local management to supplement pay points where this would assist in addressing proven recruitment and retention problems', new starting salaries, and a reduction in hours.[41]

In 1990 NALGO returned to its familiar themes with the emphasis on too many women clustered around the low pay grades, and therefore asked for 12% or a £18 per week rise as the main element of the claim. In addition to its usual arguments NALGO added the one about extra workload based on its members' responsibilities under the new systems. The 1990 settlement was for 7.7% or £8 per week.[42]

NALGO's origins like that of many modern trade unions explain much about their internal government and policy dispositions. With NALGO there were three separate developments within local government of relevance: the growth of professional associations among groups such as civil engineers in the late nineteenth century; the coming together on the pensions issue of senior and chief officials in 1894 in the Municipal Officers

Association; and the efforts to organize all local government officers started by Blain in Liverpool in 1896 with the Liverpool Municipal Officers Guild.[43] In 1905 the last two groups merged to form NALGO with about 5000 members.[44] By 1920 NALGO members had voted three to one to become a recognized trade union; at the same time it became embroiled with the early versions of Whitley.[45] By 1941 NALGO was fully committed to Whitley 'as the only means of securing the national salary scales, conditions, and status which were now its main objectives'.[46]

The war years, as with COHSE, transformed the union's NHS staff with the NJC (National Joint Council) administrative, professional, technical and clerical rates applicable to all local authority hospital staff. In addition, administrative and clerical staff in voluntary hospitals and mental hospitals merged their organizations in 1942 to form the Institute of Health Service Administrators which fixed rates with the employers, the BHA and local authorities.

At the time of the NHS's formation NALGO had a long history of negotiation and organization, and was fully committed to both the NHS and its Whitley system. Very soon, however, certain facts of life emerged which have dominated the NHS ever since. Spoor describes them as well as anyone:

> the negotiating machinery was complex and divided, the issues confused by political pressures, the chief antagonist all-powerful but inaccessible, and the Whitley Councils often powerless to negotiate, to compromise, or to reach firm agreements.[47]

These problems arose from the NHS's necessary rationalization of the previous system of health care based on municipal and voluntary hospitals and services. The old service had been managed by 'a complex of appointed agencies'[48] essentially dependent on central government for funds.

As Spoor notes in horror about the operation of the Whitley Council:

> worse, none of the employers' sides had any effective power to negotiate. Since all were financed from the national Exchequer, none was allowed even to discuss, let alone agree, any improvements in pay unless the Treasury approved. And the Treasury was not represented on the Whitley Councils at all.[49]

The composition of the staff sides was equally messy. The staff of the former voluntary hospitals were organized in 'a bewildering variety of professional societies'[50] – most were small, with no experience of wage negotiations and opposed to trade unionism. As Spoor explains:

> if this complex and irrational negotiating structure was inevitable in the circumstances in which the health service was established, its results were equally inevitable – endless delay, frustration, and denial of justice to the staffs for whose well-being it had been created.[51]

In the early 1950s all this became apparent when inflationary pressures forced staff to demand more pay from a government not prepared to listen or act. The consequences of staff pressure were familiar in the words of Spoor commenting on staff pay claims:

> all shared the common experience of staff side claims left unanswered for months; of Whitley councils meeting to be told that the Minister's representatives were not ready with counter-proposals; of these representatives waiting on Treasury approval; of Treasury refusing to sanction any increase, however meritorious, lest it prompt other pay-claims elsewhere; of a complete absence of negotiation; and of staff sides being forced to take their problems to the Industrial Court.[52]

It is not surprising that this led to growing unrest amongst the staff and laid the basis for trade union expansion and a growing determination to take action in the next two decades.

This government indifference and management powerlessness created a familiar story: staff shortages as the NHS failed to recruit new young staff and lost the middle ranks to other industries. The Treasury's short-sighted meanness created the crisis. In 1956 another often repeated farce was acted out: the management side of A&C promised a review of salaries after rejecting the 12.5% pay demand under instructions from the Minister. When MPs urged the Minister to improve salaries,

> he rebuked them. Pay in the health service, said his Parliamentary Secretary, was settled by Whitley Councils. Intervention by the Minister ... would be quite improper.

As Spoor rightly attests, 'to those who knew the truth, this answer was barefaced sophistry'.[53] This failure to solve the pay problem was exacerbated by the use of incomes policies in 1957 and led to NALGO's first industrial action in the NHS. This took the form of an overtime ban of its 23 000 NHS members. The ban and the political campaign that accompanied it had three benefits for NALGO: it stimulated recruitment; it helped the media realize the news potential of trade union actions; and it helped remove the image of NALGO as a local government union only.[54]

Spoor's excellent account of the deficiencies of Whitley and the appalling level of mismanagement by government and civil servants alike ends in the early 1960s with NALGO campaigns for better pay for nurses, for A&C and for a host of smaller groups. His part of the history of NALGO ends with the story of affiliation to the TUC in 1964.[55] His mantle is taken up by Newman.

When NALGO affiliated to the TUC it did so with nearly one-third of a million members.[56] This was substantially more than either NUPE or COHSE. NALGO's development in the 1970s was based on opposition to the Conservative legislation on industrial relations and cautious acceptance and then opposition to the Labour government's attempts at incomes policies. It experienced rapid growth in membership and density along with many other white-collar and public service unions. In the early 1970s NALGO undertook serious internal reforms in part as a reaction to the reorganizations in the NHS and local government. It also experienced poaching of its members by more aggressive and militant unions such as ASTMS and NUPE.[57] As Newman notes,

> the story of the reorganization of the NHS is one of frustration, indecision, delay and absolute dismay for those in the service ... and to the unions trying to guide and protect their members.[58]

Under Sir Keith Joseph's watchful stare the NHS was regrouped into 14 Regional Health Authorities and 70 Area Health Authorities with the DHSS as the central planning and management organ. Opposition was strong and the general lack of consultation and employee involvement angered the unions. But anger stopped short of industrial action.

By the end of the 1970s NALGO's opposition to government policy was in line with that of the TUC although NALGO refused to join NUPE over its 1978/9 pay campaign for low paid workers in the NHS and local government.[59] Throughout the 1980s NALGO campaigned against NHS cuts, against privatization of the service, for more employee involvement, against pay beds and for closer links with other health workers. For example, merger talks with NUPE and COHSE were supported by the NEC and conference in 1986;[60] and more democracy within the NHS was agreed.[61] On pay, NALGO has been involved in a succession of campaigns for all its NHS members and opposed individual performance related pay for managers and other grades.[62]

In its Health Section, NALGO employs a national officer, a deputy national officer and three assistant officers with full-time support provided by legal and research departments in their London headquarters. In each health authority NALGO employs full-time officers, one of whom often has the responsibility for a specific group of staff in a district. All members belong to a branch which elects the branch officials at the annual general meeting and stewards are elected annually at their place of work. The make-up of these branches and the subsequent remit of the local stewards is dependent upon the perceived needs of the local membership with some representing a wide spectrum of members within the branch and others being specifically related to an employee group.

At district level there are service conditions committees which feed into a national committee for health, and this committee appoints NALGO representatives to the National Joint Council for the service. It also reports back to, and takes instructions from, a group meeting of Conference delegates for that service[63] (Figure 3.2).

NALGO's emergence as a key public sector union of the 1990s dates from the crucial years of the mid-1970s. As Taylor notes, quoting an article from NALGO's journal, *Public Service*, in May 1975: 'comfortable, uncomplaining and isolated from the trials and tribulations of the world outside'[64] summed up NALGO the union. In 1970 the union sanctioned its first ever strike in Leeds, and 'the radicalism of a growing section of NALGO activists brought a new stridency into the union ... the militancy paid off'.[65] In general the union swung to the left in the 1970s, consolidated its enormous membership growth, adopted a more pragmatic attitude to industrial action, and yet, as Taylor concluded, at the end of the 1970s 'for the present the union remains strangely muted and slightly on the defensive'[66]. In the 1980s NALGO's hold over its membership growth faded, and the need to fight incessant attacks on the amounts spent in local government, education and health coupled with the problems of the privatization of some of its members' employers made it

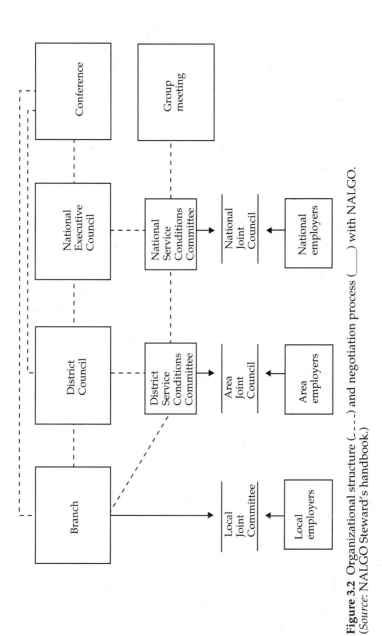

Figure 3.2 Organizational structure (_ _ _) and negotiation process (___) with NALGO.
(*Source*: NALGO Steward's handbook.)

even more cautious as a trade union although it made it more political as a pressure group.

While it retained this position until the late 1980s, its membership figures then began to decline steeply, primarily as a result of the 'competitive tendering' initiatives in local government. Thatcherism's ideological imperatives to compel both the health service and local authorities to put many of their service provisions out to tender pushed NUPE to amend its constitution so that, by the end of the 1980s it is now able to recruit non-public sector employees, which is in line with NALGO's constitution.

NALGO as the main union for the A&C grades still maintains its dominant position amongst this type of white-collar worker in the NHS. Some senior managers have quit the union over the past few years and have either not joined any union or have sought refuge in non-TUC groupings such as FUMPO. NALGO has remained one of the largest and best run unions and has maintained its centre left political position with the election of Alan Jinkinson as General Secretary in succession to John Daley. The union has kept a traditional bargaining position within the NHS and has fully utilized the customary arguments on pay differences. Its recent achievement in winning a new pay structure was seen as of vital importance in the run-up to the single-employer bargaining of the 1990s, and one task of the union is to motivate, and maintain unity amongst, large numbers of low paid and often young female workers.

NATIONAL UNION OF PUBLIC EMPLOYEES (NUPE)

Workforce composition

In this section we shall look at manual workers within the NHS, both skilled and unskilled, the majority of whom are ancillary workers. They are made up of part-time women workers and full-time men involved in hospital activities such as catering, domestic services, portering and laundry. The manual workers in the NHS include works and maintenance staff who are mainly craftsmen employed on building and engineering maintenance, mainly at unit level. Ambulance staff are also dealt with here.

Tables 3.5, 3.6 and 3.7 provide figures for numbers employed in these categories in England from 1978 to 1988. It can be seen that ambulance staff numbers have risen slowly from 17 402 wte to 19 010 wte. The total NHS ancillary staff wte fell dramatically in these years from 172 791 to 115 063 (about 33%). In contrast, the number of works and maintenance staff wte fell slightly from 25 342 to 24 179, although the decline since 1982 has been more marked. In total these groups accounted for about 160 000 wte staff in England in 1987.

Table 3.5 Ambulance officers and ambulancemen/women (England)

	Unit	1978	1983	1984	1985	1986	1987	1988
Total	No.	17 588	18 518	18 265	18 392	19 392	19 678	19 389
	wte	17 522	18 397	18 103	18 188	18 966	19 010	18 761
Ambulance officers and control assistants	wte	3221	3249	3174	3139	3124	3037	2980
Ambulancemen/ women	wte	14 301	15 148	14 930	15 049	15 841	15 973	15 781

In 1971 the NBPI report on the pay and conditions of NHS ancillary workers[67] noted that throughout the 1960s the number of full-timers had risen very slightly from 152 730 in 1961 to 153 194 in 1969, while the numbers of part-timers rose from 58 061 in 1961 to 79 869 by 1969. The vast majority of these were women. In many ways that summarizes the health service recruitment pattern in these years of expansion: mainly low paid part-time jobs for women. Of the 220 000 total ancillary workers in 1969 nearly three-quarters were women. In fact of the 81 000 part-timers 77 000 were women, while of the 139 000 full-timers just over half were women. In particular the largest three categories were domestic (114 000), catering (44 000) and porters (23 000). In domestic work there were only 9000 men in total, and of the 105 000 women 60 000 were part-time. In catering there were 12 000 men to the 32 000 women, and again nearly all the men were full-time while one-third of the women were part-time. In the portering group there were no women and over 90% were full-time. This pattern of employment matters in several ways since it influences the recruitment and activist profile of the relevant unions, their policies towards the different type of employment, managers ability to control and contain labour costs, and the ability of the unions and workforce to mount campaigns in their defence.

Table 3.6 Ancillary staff: analysis by occupation (England)

	Unit	1978	1983	1984	1985	1986	1987	1988
Total NHS ancillary staff	No.	219 128	215 329	198 968	184 153	167 577	157 325	148 439
	wte	172 177	166 184	152 202	139 379	124 267	115 063	107 619
Laundry	wte	8748	7988	7563	7013	6357	6008	5521
Farms, gardens and ground maintenance	wte	3481	3081	2810	2566	2286	2122	1829
Catering	wte	30 033	27 839	26 056	24 373	21 959	20 546	19 212
Ward orderlies	wte	11 382	10 269	9293	7644	6430	4454	3550
Domestic services (including ward housekeepers)	wte	68 843	66 393	61 384	54 220	44 772	40 503	38 251
Central sterile supply departmental staff	wte	3601	3902	3880	3888	3726	3528	3469
Drivers[1]	wte	3078	3307	3229	3118	2985	2823	2717
Operating department staff[2]	wte	3579	4054	1234	1257	1215	1163	1101
Porters[3]	wte	24 022	23 608	22 710	21 905	20 861	19 940	18 763
Stokers	wte	1640	776	633	472	325	270	178
Stores staff	wte	2754	2648	2538	2469	2374	2201	1978
Telephonists (including supervisors)	wte	4144	4137	3994	3841	3642	3393	3147
Other ancillary staff	wte	6776	8107	6803	6538	7258	7548	7335
Dental Practice Board	wte	43	34	32	32	32	34	43
Prescription Pricing Authority	wte	52	41	43	44	46	48	44
Other Statutory Authorities[4]	wte	—	—	—	—	—	484	481

[1] Includes Blood Transfusion Service Drivers.
[2] Includes operating department orderlies and operating theatre attendants only from 1984. (Operating department assistants transferred to Professional and Technical Staff Council 'B' on 1 April 1984.)
[3] Includes incinerator attendants.
[4] Prior to 1987, figures for Other Statutory Authorities (e.g. Public Health Laboratory Service and the Health Education Authority) were not collected in the Annual Manpower Census.

Table 3.7 Works and maintenance staff: analysis by occupation (England)

	Unit	1978	1983	1984	1985	1986	1987	1988
Total NHS workers and maintenance staff	No.	25 486	26 825	26 244	25 851	25 000	24 196	22 671
	wte	25 443	26 083	26 227	25 838	24 983	24 179	22 653
Works staff: total	wte	5579	5971	6001	6081	5843	5708	5323
Regional works architectural, engineering and surveying staff		2116	2191	2055	2000	1813	1680	1508
Works staff (other than at RHA): total[1]		3463	3780	3956	4080	4030	4028	3815
District works officers[1]		249	386	760	849	921	1184	1151
Engineers		2102	2002	1883	1800	1754	1499	1396
Building officers		885	1069	999	1018	962	840	811
Other engineers/builders[2]		—	—	128	336	321	425	359
Works assistants		184	33	29	25	22	17	12
Other works staff		43	288	156	52	48	40	64
Dental Practice Board		—	1	1	1	1	1	1
Prescription Pricing Authority		—	—	—	—	1	1	1
Other Statutory Authorities[3]		—	—	—	—	—	22	20

[1] Includes unit works officers and district and unit works support. The increase from 1983 is largely due to the effects of the 1983 reorganization of works staff.

[2] Due to the introduction of new codes from 1984 it is now possible to identify some staff, previously shown as 'other works staff', as either engineers or builders.

[3] Prior to 1987 figures for Other Statutory Authorities (e.g. Public Health Laboratory Service and the Health Education Authority) were not collected in the Annual Manpower Census.

Source: Hospital and Personal Social Services Statistics for England 1990, pp. 60 and 62.

Table 3.7 (continued) Works and maintenance staff: analysis by occupation (England)

	Unit	1978	1983	1984	1985	1986	1987	1988
Maintenance staff (including craftsmen and labourers): total	wte	19 864	20 832	20 216	19 758	19 140	18 471	17 331
Engineers		6563	6859	6634	6548	6479	6401	4776
Electricians		4028	4267	4161	4064	3995	3947	5104
Plumbers		1248	1524	1370	1322	1209	1166	949
Building operatives and other maintenance staff		8025	8155	8025	7798	7414	6848	6395
Dental Practice Board		—	13	12	11	10	11	10
Prescription Pricing Authority		—	14	14	16	15	14	14
Other Statutory Authorities[3]		—	—	—	—	—	84	83

[3] Prior to 1987 figures for Other Statutory Authorities (e.g. Public Health Laboratory Service and the Health Education Authority) were not collected in the Annual Manpower Census.
Source: Hospital and Personal Social Services Statistics for England 1990, pp. 60 and 62.

NUPE's membership

The main representative trade union for these workers is NUPE, although other large unions do recruit some of the more specialist workers, such as the TGWU, UCATT and the EETPU. These are all trade unions in the traditional sense, and NUPE accords well with the image of a general union. It is TUC-affiliated, based on branches with an extensive local stewards network and full-time officials answerable to an NEC and regional bodies – the whole being accountable to an annual delegate conference (Figure 3.3). When the NHS started, NUPE already recruited some health workers, and it gave full support to both the principles and the practice of the new health service. Its then General Secretary, Bryn Roberts, was a friend of Bevan and the success of the NHS was seen as a major step forward for the bulk of working people in Britain. NUPE secured recognition from the start and recruited strongly among ancillary workers, but very slowly among nurses until the mid-1960s.[68]

The rapid growth of NUPE in the late 1960s through to the late 1970s depended on several general factors,[69] but in particular the development of local stewards and bargaining after the 1967 NBPI productivity bonus deal,[70] the concentration of health workers into large employment units, and the consequences of incomes policies. As NUPE grew in size so it became more and more influential within the TUC and Labour Party, but the famous strikes in the winter of 1978/9 against the Labour government's incomes policy proved to be a crisis point for NUPE; since then it has lost members. In the NHS it has fought hard to resist privatization of many of the services which employ NUPE members. Overall its recent policies and campaigns to improve employment rights for part-time workers, young workers, female workers and for workers from ethnic minorities have met with some success. In addition, its role in anti-government propaganda and demonstrations has helped maintain some morale amongst the members. Finally its involvement in a controlled way in industrial disputes, especially during the ambulance dispute of 1989/90, has enabled it to play a leading role in the proposed merger with NALGO and COHSE.

NUPE, like COHSE, has a long history of organizing health workers and, like NALGO, of organizing local government workers. Although within the NHS it mainly represents ancillary workers, ambulance staff, and nurses, it does also represent

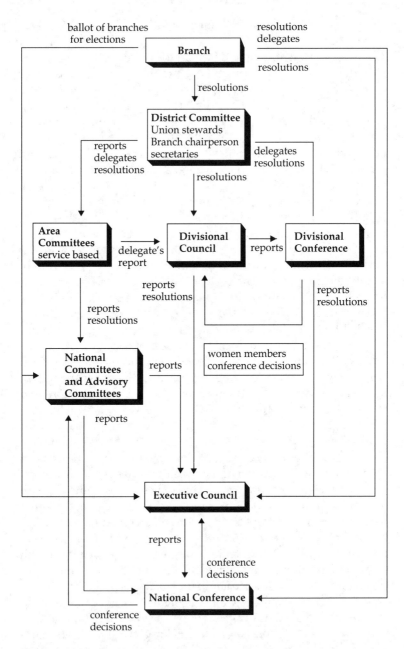

Figure 3.3 Organizational structure and policy-making process within NUPE.
(*Source*: NUPE Steward's handbook.)

groups within A&C, PT'A' and PT'B' and others. Like many other public sector unions, but unlike several large manual worker unions, NUPE grew rapidly in the 1970s but has declined in the 1980s partly due to tendering out of services within which its members work. NUPE membership figures show that in 1989 the union had about 605 000 members in all, with about 250 000 in the NHS (or 40%).

1970	305 000
1979	712 000
1989	604 912

NUPE's membership is composed of about 70% women, many part-time workers and many low paid workers. A large number of these workers are foreign or from ethnic minorities. Its largest membership is in the ancillary grades. The kind of difficulty NUPE faces in recruiting members and representing them can be seen from the 1979 Clegg Commission report on NHS ancillary staff, where of the 270 000 total staff numbers about half were full-time and half part-time. Of the full-time staff about half were men and half women, but the part-time staff were nearly all women. These workers were grouped into 18 pay groups and were represented by NUPE, COHSE, GMWU and the TGWU.[71]

In contrast to this very mixed group, the ambulance staff represent a more cohesive category of workers, with the vast majority being full-time men. The division between those with some paramedical training and those without has become increasingly significant following the 1989 dispute and the advent of SGTs.

In 1974 the NHS became responsible for the provision of the ambulance service throughout Britain. In England and Wales the service was transferred from the control of local authorities, which effectively reduced control from 142 separate services to 53. At the same time, in Scotland, the service was transferred from the St Andrew's Ambulance Association and in Northern Ireland the service became the responsibility of the four Health and Social Services Boards, rather than the Northern Ireland Hospitals Authority.

The breakdown of ancillary staff in 1983 shows that of the 166 000 wte in English hospitals the largest category – about 40% – were domestic workers, followed by about 17% in catering, 13% porters, 10% orderlies and 5% in laundry, with 15% in miscellaneous groups such as telephonists, vehicle drivers, stokers, storekeepers and workers in central sterile supply departments and gardens. This represents marginal changes since 1974 with a slightly higher proportion of porters and domestic workers and slightly lower for laundry and catering.

In 1989 in a memorandum to the Social Services Committee[72] the Department of Health reported that the reduction in ancillary staff in the UK between 1978 and 1987 was from 211 700 to 140 000. The Department pointed out that:

> it is not possible to ascribe what proportion of that reduction has occurred as a result of management action on manpower levels, competitive tendering and the introduction of new technology. The Department does not have data showing either the overall manpower consequences of competitive tendering or the number of staff working for private contractors in hospitals.[73]

The large number of ancillary workers in the NHS and their importance for the operations of the hospitals has meant that, on the surface, the workforce and their main unions should be in a strong bargaining position. In practice this has not tended to be the case due in part to the composition of the workforce, internal divisions and the unions' own attitudes. The large numbers of part-time female ancillary staff as well as a disproportionate number of young workers, non-UK workers and shift workers, allied with some high staff turnover ratios, have meant a nightmare for union organization and participation. In addition, this was the first group of NHS workers to receive significant local pay systems from the late 1960s. These tended to fragment bargaining and cement the already strong differences among ancillary staffs. The 1971 NBPI report mentioned above concentrated on the issue of low pay and pay principles.

Pay bargaining

In 1970 ancillary pay varied from £16.25 to £21.6 for basic grade men and from £12.76 to £18.12 for basic grade women.[74] The ancillary workers were under the day-to-day operational controls of managers working for the health authorities although their pay and conditions were determined by Whitley. The key comment of the report, which echoes down to us twenty years later with a chilling ring is that, 'there has been a failure to adopt a coherent strategy, backed up by sufficient resources, either at the centre or in the regions for the introduction of schemes for raising pay and efficiency'.[75]

In 1979 the Clegg commission looked at ancillary staff in the NHS as well as ambulancemen.[76] Its brief was to establish 'acceptable bases for comparisons'[77] of the groups under examination with others. Of the 18 pay groups three-quarters were in the lowest three groups of pay.[78] The issue of low pay dominated the union evidence for ancillary workers, and the unions complained at the lack of local pay bargaining for the majority of their members.[79] The Clegg findings were based on benchmark jobs used as key external comparators. For the NHS ancillary workers these included domestic assistants, porters, drivers and cooks.[80] This report sought to develop a scientific formula for pay determination based on job evaluation schemes and trend lines. It was soon overtaken, however, by the events of the 1980s which greatly reduced the numbers of ancillary workers through contracting out, and the very pay principles secured through Clegg were abandoned by the employers.

Eight years later the unions were back to square one. In April 1987 NUPE put forward its claim for ancillary workers on behalf of all the Whitley unions (COHSE, GMBATU, NUPE and TGWU). The unions wanted a flat rate increase with a target minimum rate of £125 per week for all staff; more shift pay and a review of shift working; the consolidation of bonus payments; a move to harmonization of service conditions through a 35 hour basic week, more annual leave and better holiday provision. They also wanted the right to go to arbitration.

The case was based on several arguments, but the main one, as usual, was comparability:

> the gap in average earnings between male, full-time manual workers in the health service and the earnings of manual workers throughout the economy now stands at £45.70 a week.[81]

The pay link with average manual earnings was 74% in 1986 for male staff and 58% for female. Using virtually any comparator the results were the same – NHS ancillary staff came near the bottom of all pay leagues. The claim therefore was particularly concerned about low pay and the cluster of women on low paid jobs. There are strong parallels with the NALGO claim and those of other groups within the Whitley system.

In April 1988 NUPE again presented the staff side claim. This time they asked for a £14.62 pay rise and a reduction in hours to 39. The case opened with the equal value argument:

> in their 1986 claim, the trade unions argued that the grading structure was not only increasingly antiquated in terms of

technological change, but failed to reflect changing social values, particularly in relation to the value of jobs traditionally done by women. Our claim was that the structure was discriminatory in terms of the equal value amendment.[82]

The case also referred to increased workload and productivity, and the new labour market faced by many employers.

The case opens the door for the single-employer bargain, and NUPE's position rests on a combination of a nationally agreed minimum with employer additions bargained over at the level of the employer and/or plant. The unions put the argument that the need is for a better trained and more skilled ancillary workforce which is genuinely incorporated into health care teams.[83] This again is a significant argument based on the realities of falling numbers of ancillary workers, and the realization of the trend to marginalize their members' work and therefore the union.

In October 1986 there were agreed changes in the flexibility of staff deployment, but this was not rewarded by more pay.[84] In April 1989 NUPE again set out the claim. This time a major objective was to secure the wider use of the job evaluation schemes to secure equal pay for work of equal value. This claim was made on the twenty-second anniversary of the NBPI report which had highlighted low pay.

> The situation twenty years on is that ancillary staff feel that they are the neglected backbone of the health service, their skills and dedication unrecognised and their morale at rock bottom. They are bitter about not being paid a decent wage.[85]

This statement was true for the majority, but it was used to put pressure on employers about to embark on their own experiments in staffing and industrial relations in which future uncertainties loomed larger than traditional resistance to union demands. The unions emphasized changing labour markets and workload, and the loss of over 100 000 ancillary jobs since 1984.

All evidence allowed the case to be prosecuted with vigour: 45% staff turnover rates, massive use of overtime and subcontracted labour to cope with staff vacancies, and the NAHA evidence to the House of Commons Select committee admitting the low pay and high levels of staffing problems, and this was echoed by the NAHSPO evidence.[86]

The April 1990 ancillary claim repeated the same sentiments with the same evidence. The case was tied to the new reforms and their introduction. In October 1990 in a joint campaign with COHSE, the GMB and the TGWU the unions launched their 1991 claim under the banner of 'there's got to be a better way'. The campaign was based on parity with local government manual workers, much more training for staff, and the right to go to arbitration if the 1991 offer were rejected.[87]

In April 1990 ancillary workers' rates ranged from £101 to £118 per week for lettered pay scales A to D, and from £115 to £131 for numbered pay scales (supervisory grades I to IV). It is worth comparing the pay of some of NUPE's diverse membership through a main category male ancillary (a hospital porter) and an ambulanceman and a female ward orderly. In April 1990 the average gross weekly earnings for an ancillary in the NHS was £167 for men and £139 for women. This compared with rates for nurses of £256 for men and £234 for women, and of £232 for male ambulance staff.

Table 3.8 shows the differences between groups on the basis of occupation and gender, and illustrates the high dependence of the lowest paid on overtime and shift working. For the porter, basic is about 66% of earnings, for the ward orderly it is 88% and for the ambulanceman it is 95%. This influences bargaining arrangements, levels of membership activity and interest in the pay mechanisms and therefore the union. It will be taken into account in the single-employer pay variations and staff reductions into the 1990s.

Table 3.8 Pay comparisons of some ancillary grades and ambulancemen

	Average gross weekly earnings	Over- time	pbr	Shift	Hours Total	O't	Median
Ambulanceman	£234	£10.6	—	—	40.8	1.9	£227
Male porter	£167	£28.1	£13.3	£13.9	45.3	6.5	£161
Female ward orderly	£141	£4.7	—	£12.2	38.8	1.3	£135

Source: New Earnings Survey, 1990.

NUPE's history and structure

Overall NUPE still dominates the coalition of ancillary staff unions, and with its merger talks with COHSE, they outweigh the other two general unions. NUPE, like NALGO, has fought hard on the equal pay front and the low pay issue. Its task is made more difficult by the large number of young and part-time workers, by the large number of establishments in which it has members, by the considerations of competitor unions, especially in the area of nursing, and by the poor quality of line management in charge of its members. None the less, NUPE has remained one of the largest of the UK trade unions, and has maintained its bargaining position in the public sector in hard times. It, like NALGO, has a left-of-centre leadership and policies under General Secretary Rodney Bickerstaff. In a letter to the author he argued that NUPE,

> will continue to work for the elimination of low pay in the health service and will pursue equal value challenges and other initiatives to end workplace discrimination, particularly against women part-time staff. Across the board NUPE will seek to safeguard national bargaining agreements against the threat of opted-out hospital trusts.

Dick and Williams point out that 'when the National Union of Public Employees was established in 1928 it stood firmly on the foundation stones of a history stretching back for almost forty years'.[88] As the concentration of people in large cities continued so the need for local government services became more acute. Many such services were provided by private companies sub-contracted to the local authority, and groups such as London dustmen were paid by the load. The fragmentation of workers by activity, employment situation and locality was reflected in the fragmented origins of municipal workers' trade unionism. For example, one early union was called the Carmen and Roadmen's Union of the Parish of Camberwell.[89] By 1890 the membership had spread and it changed its name to the South London Vestry Employees' Labour Union.[90] Most members were employed by the vestries in London, but in the early 1890s its base spread to London County Council workers as well. It collapsed in 1900 partly owing to the breakaway in 1894 of the London County Council Employees' Protection Association.[91] The majority of its members came from the drainage service with a few asylum workers as well. In 1899 it became the National Association of County Authority Employees to reflect its growth outside London.[92] That same year it affiliated to the TUC and changed its name to the Municipal Employees' Association.[93]

The MEA started to grow rapidly through the ability to merge with the numerous small local unions such as the Battersea

Vestry Workers and to pick up members from the collapse of rival unions such as the National Municipal Labour Union.[94] There were also problems with rival unions such as the Gas Workers and the National Amalgamated Labour Union.[95] In addition, the MEA suffered fierce internal divisions which proved an enormous handicap in fighting off the larger general unions. As a result a split developed and in 1907 the National Union of Corporation Workers was formed,[96] based mainly in London. Much of its rapid early growth came from poaching MEA members and branches. Soon afterwards the MEA merged with other unions to form what eventually became the GMB.

The 1920s gave the municipal trade unions their first taste of Whitley. As with the school teachers,[97] they strongly supported a system of national wage bargaining, but found that there were two major disadvantages: first the slowness of the negotiating process, and secondly that too many local authorities refused to be bound by the national agreements. Through the difficult years of the mid-1920s and the General Strike the NUCW became an increasingly influential force within the TUC and labour movement, and it was able to survive these years of setback better than most unions.[98]. In 1928 the NUCW called a special delegate conference and adopted the name the National Union of Public Employees. Dick and Williams explain the motivation for this:

> from time to time branches and members had suggested that the title of the union should be changed to one which would embrace all workers employed in local government service. These sug- gestions had been given a new sense of immediacy when the Minister of Health had announced that he intended to introduce a Bill to the autumn session of parliament with the objective of reforming the machinery of local government.[99]

These few notes on the early history of NUPE indicate the considerable difficulties in recruiting and retaining members among low paid and often unskilled workers employed by local authorities. It also shows that as with other public sector unions, there are important links between the structure and government of the unions and government legislation and policy. In addition, the constant conflict with other unions has hindered the devel- opment of a strong union response to employers' initiatives. Finally this review has shown that NUPE has witnessed a changing employment situation for its members from local government to health services to private contractors and back again. This has always been forced on the union rather than the union being able to forestall it.

By 1933 NUPE's membership stood at 13 000 and its finances were precarious. But under the leadership of Bryn Roberts its fortunes picked up and by 1939 it had over 50 000 members and a strong financial base.[100] In 1943 the Hetherington Committee proposed that JCC rates should apply compulsorily to ancillary staff who were employed in all mental hospitals, that the rates set by the four provincial NJCs should apply to all local authority hospitals and that certain prescribed rates should apply to voluntary hospitals. These recommendations were generally, but not universally, applied. In 1945 a NJC for Staff of Hospitals and Allied Institutions in England and Wales, chaired by Lord Mowbray, was set up to fix national minimum rates for ancillary and domestic staff. Since this did not cover mental hospitals, a Mental Hospitals Committee replaced the JCC domestic committee and fixed a single national rate which was above the provincial average.

In the 1930s when Bryn Roberts became General Secretary the pay and conditions for ancillary health workers were deplorable, and this was in part due to the divisions among both employers and employees and the virtual absence of trade union organization among this group.[101] In 1941 for nurses and in 1945 for hospital and institutional domestic staff NJCs were set up in the wake of wartime needs, and both were replaced by Whitley in 1948.[102] Bevan was an old friend of Roberts and NUPE welcomed both the NHS and Whitley with great enthusiasm.[103] At the start NUPE was on five of the nine functional councils, and Craik claims that by then 'NUPE had already become the chief hospital trade union'.[104] The 1950s were a period of staff shortages and high labour turnover due to low wages and long hours. By 1955 there were 130 000 full-time and 40 000 part-time ancillary staff, but they were hard to organize in trade unions, although nurses were harder still.

The slow growth of trade union membership was due to several factors: the small size of employment units; the isolation of many workers both geographically and socially; the strong anti-union sentiments amongst nurses; and backward-looking managers.[105] The first properly negotiated settlement brought pay rises and shorter hours for thousands of ancillary workers and helped NUPE recruit.[106] The difficulties in negotiating have been well expressed by both Carpenter and Spoor, and Craik quotes from Bryn Roberts in a similar vein:

> Every effort has been made through the appropriate negotiating machinery to obtain these reforms of better wages and shorter working hours. They have not succeeded owing to the attitude of the Ministry of Health – and the responsibility for the growing chaos in the NHS rests squarely upon this unimaginative Department.[107]

This helped NUPE to recruit amongst ancillary staff, but nurses were much more difficult. The growing shortages of nurses allied with a change in attitude to nursing as a means of earning a living very slowly encouraged a few nurses to join the union. As Roberts pointed out, nursing was a 'hard, thankless and underpaid job'.[108] By the mid-1950s, however, there was no progress. Meanwhile Roberts and NUPE were concerned with the lack of consultation and employee involvement in the management decision-making process. Roberts pushed hard for the development of joint consultation, but was over-optimistic when he claimed that 'the Labour Government's National Health Act brought the hospitals out of their hole-and-corner privacy into conformity with democratic public requirements'.[109]

For many years in the 1960s and into the 1970s NUPE fought off challenges from rival unions for representation of certain groups of members: for ancillary and some other staff this came from the TGWU and GMWU, both with traditions in local government as well as the NHS, and both with strong ties into transport and among male manual workers. The competition to recruit nurses came mainly from COHSE in the years of expansion after 1974 and from the RCN in the 1980s, although in the 1970s NUPE had recruited nurses who before would have joined the RCN. NUPE long favoured a closer relationship with COHSE, and in the early 1960s this was proposed from both the TUC and NUPE.[110] In 1965 NUPE merged with NASA (National Ambulance Services Association), thus becoming the dominant union for ambulance staff.[111] There were problems with NALGO over the recruitment of a range of clerical and ancillary staffs. NUPE tended to be a more aggressive union, with dominant and powerful general secretaries, while NALGO and COHSE tended to underplay their membership size and in the case of NALGO much impetus and activity was stifled by its dominant committee system.

From 1967 to 1977 NUPE grew from 250 000 members to more than 600 000. Under the control of Alan Fisher its reputation for militant defence of public services created its powerful image. The crucial impetus to NUPE's modern development came from Report 29 from the NBPI. As Taylor rightly points out, 'the report emphasised the extensive under-utilisation of labour, the lack of shift allowances, incentive payments and service increments'.[112] Taylor goes on to argue that 'NUPE has been the main militant union defending the social wage and public expenditure from attack since the mid-1970s'.[113] NUPE was behind the mass demonstration in November 1976 which formed the march on Parliament – in this public statement against cuts in the public services NUPE worked closely with NALGO.

Membership was rising fast and changing in nature. The reasons for both included incomes policies, more radical young and women workers, centralization and reorganization in the NHS and local government, the greater impact of local bonus schemes, the burden of economic crisis pushed on to public services, and the end of anti-leftist domination of trade unionism. NUPE was forced to recognize that its style of work, limited policies, crouched position on industrial action, and undemocratic structures were inadequate. The union called on academics from Warwick University to analyse the state of the union and propose change. The result was published in 1974 by Fryer, Fairclough and Manson. They recorded that in 1973 NUPE had 470 000 members in 1709 branches, of whom 300 000 were women.[114] The traditions of NUPE were in favour of national bargaining, industrial unionism and industrial democracy.[115]

In the late 1960s membership participation rose with the coming of shop stewards on the back of local productivity bargaining. In 1971 came NHS recognition of the steward. In 1970 39% of branches had no steward and this fell to 11% by 1974.[116] In the NHS a range of disputes, the question of pick-eting, and the power over emergency cover pushed the process rapidly along. As the state's role blossomed so large general unions such as NUPE depended more and more on full-time officials, including some full-time branch secretaries.[117] Rapid growth with national bargaining created the dangers of member-ship isolation given that over half of NUPE's women members in the NHS were part-timers.[118] The Warwick University study carefully analysed the role of the steward, branches, areas/divisions, the NEC, the full-time officials and the annual conference. The main findings were that the stewards should be brought more fully into the union's machinery, that there should be more regular consultation with the membership, and that there was a need to develop structures and forms of work which promoted participation of women and widened the democracy of the union.

In the critical issue of member and officers relationship the Warwick report was at its best:

> one of the most striking characteristics of NUPE is the key role played in the organization by its full time officials ... reliance upon the officers also owed much to the widely dispersed and fragmentary nature of NUPE membership ... while this dependence upon Officers was understandable and even necessary, it was also open to the possibility of becoming self-confirming ... a dependence upon full time officials is conducive neither to democracy nor necessarily to effectiveness ... recent developments in membership involvement and awareness ... may be seen as helping to counteract membership dependence.[119]

In 1982 NUPE members were involved in an eight-month dispute, and in 1983 it led the successful strike of water workers. Bickerstaffe replaced Fisher as General Secretary in 1982, and with that came a strengthening of the full-time union officials and union organization. As the 1990 Diary says:

> despite the attacks of the Conservative Government on the Public Service, NUPE's membership remains high, standing at over 650 000. The Political Fund Ballot at the end of 1985 which resulted in a 84% vote to retain our Political Fund, strengthened the Union's organization and reinforced our ability to defend the public services.[120]

In 1988 and 1989 NUPE members in nursing and other health workers fought to prevent changes in the NHS, and of course NUPE members played a major role in the ambulance dispute of 1989/90.

NUPE's health section has two national full-time officers whose sole responsibilities are with health service members. They then have full-time 'divisional' officers, each of whom has two assistants, one of whom has responsibility for health matters within that division and the other, local authority issues. Beneath this tier of organization there are full-time area officers who again have a 'general' remit for NUPE members within their area. At local level, NUPE health authority branches elect their officers from within their membership and finally, shop stewards are elected to represent a range of occupations.

Throughout the late 1980s, NUPE and NALGO began formal discussions regarding a merger and they were subsequently joined by COHSE in this venture. In 1989 each of the three organizations' annual conferences agreed that the merger discussions should continue with the issue likely to go out to their membership for a decision early in the 1990s. The latest statement of intent from the three general secretaries of the relevant unions claimed that the new merged union would be the largest TUC-affiliated union, with 1.5 million members. It would provide 'greatly enhanced bargaining strength' and be able 'to build on the high quality of services'. The statement indicates the financial resources of the new union, its ability to match government and employer expertise, and that the 1992 annual conferences will approve merger for membership ballot in November 1992, for vesting day in March 1993.[121]

CONCLUDING COMMENTS

It has been shown that the minority of the staff organizations in the NHS are multi-occupational trade unions which are nearly all affiliated to the TUC. These unions have members in virtually every employment group within the NHS – with the four described above being particularly influential. The proposed amalgamation of three of these four large unions would not only create the largest trade union in Britain, but would undoubtedly have serious implications for industrial relations in the NHS. This is one of many consequences that the government and NHS employers did not consider when they drew up their reform proposals. If the merger does occur, it could lead to 'single-union' deals and the end of the recognition arrangements that have always existed within the NHS.

The main NHS trade unions have been on the receiving end of policy changes in the health service which resulted in loss of membership, weaker finances and some scrabbling around for policy direction. Their traditions and commitment to a public health service will allow them to adapt and survive, and they should benefit in terms of influence and recruitment from the possible mix of national and local bargaining arrangements based on a restructured Whitley system and single-employer schemes.

NOTES

1   Webb, S. and Webb, B. (1897) *Industrial Democracy*, 1920 edn, Longmans, Green & Co., London, p. 173.
2   Ibid., p. 581.
3   Ibid., p. 589.
4   Turner, H. (1962) *Trade Union Growth, Structure and Policy*, George Allen and Unwin, London.
5   COHSE (1976) *Union Steward's Handbook*, COHSE, London, pp. 10–19.
6   Cleminson, J. (1990) *Review Body ...: Seventh Report on Nursing Staff, Midwives and Health Visitors 1990*, Cm 934, HMSO, London, pp. 3 and 7.
7   NHS ancillary staff case 1989, p. 7.
8   Carpenter, M. (1988) *Working for Health: the History of COHSE*, Lawrence and Wishart, London.
9   Ibid., pp. 45–7.
10 Ibid., p. 48.
11 Ibid., p. 226.
12 Ibid., p. 225.
13 Ibid., p. 230.
14 COHSE (1977) *Memorandum of Evidence to the Royal Commission on the National Health Service*, COHSE, London p. 37.
15 Carpenter, op. cit., p. 247.
16 Ibid., p. 266.
17 Ibid., p. 341.
18 Ibid.
19 Dyson, R. (1974) *The Ancillary Staff Industrial Action*, A survey and report prepared for the Leeds Regional Hospital Board.
20 COHSE (1977) op. cit., p. 39.
21 Carpenter, op. cit., p. 369.
22 Ibid., p. 247.
23 Carpenter, M. (1982) 'The Labour Movement in the NHS: UK' in Sethi, A. and Dimmock, S. (eds), *Industrial Relations and Health Services*, Croom Helm, London, p. 77.
24 Trainor, R. (1987) *A Directory of the NHS Whitley Council System 1986–7*, Health Services Manpower Review, University of Keele, pp. 47 and 52.
25 Taylor, R. (1978) *The Fifth Estate: Britain's Unions in the Seventies*, Routledge and Kegan Paul, London, p. 271. In 1974, for example, the Guild of Hospital Pharmacists voted 894 in favour and 147 against merger with ASTMS: see Fish, J. (1983) *The Guild of Hospital Pharmacists 1923–1983*, ICI.
26 Smith, C. (1987) *Technical Workers*, MacMillan, London.
27 Ibid.
28 MSF claim for MLSO 1988, p. 1.
29 MSF claim for MLSO 1989, pp. 2–3.
30 MSF claim for MLSO 1990, p. 1.
31 Advance Letter (PT'B') 6/90, paragraph 8.
32 Spoor, A. (1967) *White-Collar Union: Sixty Years of NALGO*, Heinemann, London.

33   Newman, G. (1982) *Path to Maturity: NALGO 1965–1980*, NALGO, London.
34   Claim by NALGO for A&C staffs 1985
35   Ibid., p. 5.
36   Claim by NALGO for A&C staffs 1986, p. 1.
37   Ibid., p. 3.
38   Claim by NALGO for A&C staffs 1987.
39   Claim by NALGO for A&C staffs 1988.
40   Claim by NALGO for A&C staffs 1989.
41   Advance Letter (AC) 9/89.
42   Claim by NALGO for A&C staffs 1990.
43   Spoor, op. cit., p. 11–13.
44   Ibid., p. 18.
45   Ibid., p. 76.
46   Ibid., p. 222.
47   Ibid., p. 347–8.
48   Ibid., p. 348.
49   Ibid., p. 348.
50   Ibid., p. 349.
51   Ibid., p. 349.
52   Ibid., pp. 350–1.
53   Ibid., p. 352.
54   Ibid., p. 359.
55   Ibid., pp. 533–61.
56   Newman, op. cit., p. 81.
57   Ibid., p. 241.
58   Ibid., p. 377.
59   Ibid., p. 482.
60   NALGO, *Annual Report* 1986, pp. 87–8.
61   Ibid., p. 142.
62   Ibid., p. 141.
63   NALGO, *Members' Handbook* 1989, p. 7.
64   Taylor, op. cit., p. 240.
65   Ibid., p. 244.
66   Ibid., p. 247.
67   NBPI (National Board for Prices and Incomes) (1971) *The Pay and Conditions of Service of Ancillary Workers in the National Health Service*, Report No. 166, Cmnd 4644, HMSO, London.
68   Craik, W. (1955) *Bryn Roberts and the National Union of Public Employees*, George Allen and Unwin, London.
69   Taylor, op. cit., p. 247.
70   NBPI (National Board for Prices and Incomes) (1967) *Pay and Conditions of Service of Manual Workers in Local Authorities, the National Health Service, Gas and water Supply*, Cmnd 3230, HMSO, London.
71   Clegg, H. (1979) *Local Authority and University Manual Workers; NHS Ancillary Staffs; and Ambulancemen: Standing Commission on Pay Comparability*, Report No. 1, Cmnd 7641, HMSO, London, p. 3.
72   Social Services Committee of the House of Commons (1989) Third Report, paragraph 1 of Appendix II.
73   Ibid.

74 NBPI (1971), op. cit., p. 13.
75 Ibid., p. 22.
76 Clegg (1979), op. cit.
77 Ibid., p. 1.
78 Ibid., p. 3.
79 Ibid., p. 9.
80 Ibid., p. 27.
81 Claim by NUPE for ancillary staffs 1987, p. 2.
82 Claim by NUPE for ancillary staffs 1988, p. 3.
83 Ibid., p. 6.
84 Claim by NUPE for ancillary staffs 1986, p. 7.
85 Claim by NUPE for ancillary staffs 1989, p. 3.
86 Ibid., pp. 7–9.
87 Claim by NUPE for ancillary staffs 1990.
88 Dix, B. and Williams, S. (1987) *Serving the Public: Building the Union. The History of NUPE, Volume I 1889–1928*, Lawrence and Wishart, London, p. 9.
89 Ibid., p. 36.
90 Ibid., p. 39.
91 Ibid., p. 71.
92 Ibid., p. 74.
93 Ibid., p. 75.
94 Ibid., p. 96.
95 Ibid., p. 101.
96 Ibid., p. 134.
97 Seifert, R. (1987) *Teacher Militancy: A History of Teacher Strikes 1896–1987*, Falmer Press, Sussex.
98 Ibid., p. 223.
99 Ibid., p. 227.
100 Claim by NUPE for ancillary staffs 1990, p. 14.
101 Craik, op. cit., p. 147.
102 Ibid., p. 148.
103 Ibid., p. 149.
104 Ibid., p. 151.
105 Ibid., p. 154.
106 Ibid., p. 155.
107 Ibid., pp. 158–9, from an article by Roberts in the September 1954 issue of the NUPE *Journal*.
108 Ibid., p. 167.
109 Ibid., p. 169.
110 Craik, W. (1968) *Sydney Hill and the National Union of Public Employees*, George Allen and Unwin, London, p. 88.
111 Ibid., p. 90.
112 Taylor, op. cit., p. 248.
113 Ibid., p. 252.
114 Fryer, R., Fairclough, A. and Manson, T. (1974) *Organisation and Change in the National Union of Public Employees*, Department of Sociology, University of Warwick, p. 10.
115 Ibid., p. 11.
116 Ibid, pp. 12–15.

117   Ibid., pp. 16–18.
118   Ibid., p. 21.
119   Ibid., pp. 16–18.
120   NUPE Diary, 1990, p. 17.
121   Statement on NUPE–NALGO–COHSE merger from the three
        general secretaries, March 1991.

Chapter 4

Employers, managers and the conduct of industrial relations

INTRODUCTION

Until the late 1960s administrators and hospital secretaries carried out the duties of today's managers. In industrial relations there was little to do. Pay and conditions of service were largely determined at central level of the national system, and hospital and health authority managers implemented Whitley. In the field of 'managerial relations' such as discipline and grievance the employers and managers held sway with few rights for individual staff unless they were doctors or dentists. The system fed off the low level of trade union activity at the level of the employer, and the highly centralized and undemocratic nature of most of the representative organizations at national level. The democratic 'deficit' that characterized much NHS decision-making was nowhere more apparent than in the attitudes and activities of these pre-managerial managers.

This chapter explores the recent changes in management activities, the growing 'professionalization' of the personnel function, and the employers' organization and powers. These developments were caused by a range of factors including increased concern over the expenditure of public money, the escalating demand for more and more sophisticated health care, and the implementation of management information systems. In industrial relations terms the changes were a response to shifts in the labour market which created uneven supply of different types of health worker, and the rapid growth in the level of membership and activity of the trade unions and professional associations.

Strategic developments in the business operations of hospital and community services, through government reforms of the financial system, have generated a new managerialism based on elements of private sector management methods in dealing with a range of issues. Changes in the labour market for the less skilled workers in favour of employers in many regions led to the demand for either subcontracted services or for local flexibility to reduce staffing levels and reduce the terms of employment. At the same time the tighter labour market for some technical and professional grades meant staff shortages in areas of crucial operational need and, therefore, the demand for labour flexibility took the form of a more intensive use of current staff (skill concentration) and higher rewards to attract more staff. Allied to these solutions were the possibility of altering the skill mix by simultaneously deskilling some jobs and demanding multiple skills from other staff.

The major internal jolt to the personnel management system came from the inability of employers and managers to cope with the workplace consequences of local bargaining, the growth of powerful shop stewards and the local impact of national disputes. For the first 20 years of the NHS the membership of trade unions and professional associations was modest (except for the medical and dental professions) and there were virtually no union stewards or representatives to encourage such development.

This situation began to change in the late 1960s and early 1970s with the introduction of bonus schemes for ancillary staff, craftsmen and ambulance staff following the reports of the NBPI in 1967 and 1971.[1] At that time as Mailly, Dimmock and Sethi explain:

> There seems no doubt that in those health authorities in which the schemes were introduced, the explicit emphasis on the 'cash nexus' and the use of work study assisted the development of a trade union consciousness amongst ancillary workers.[2]

Equally, the impact of incomes policies on NHS employees caused the ancillary staffs' first national dispute in 1972, when their pay link with local government workers was broken. Their action spread from a local dispute in Bristol and has been seen as a watershed in NHS industrial relations. In the following years recruitment by trade unions, particularly NUPE and COHSE, increased significantly.

Soon after this the Code of Practice, associated with the 1971 Industrial Relations Act, gave positive support to the role of the steward and recommended agreed procedures for discipline, dismissal and grievance matters and the establishment of joint committees to establish procedures where necessary.[3]

This legislation was ultimately replaced by the Trade Union and Labour Relations Act (TULRA) of 1974, and under the provision of the Employment Protection Act (EPA) in 1975 three new codes of practice were introduced which replaced the 1971 Code. These extended local collective bargaining to cover procedures relating to discipline, time off for trade union stewards and the disclosure of information.[4] Subsequently the provisions of the Health and Safety at Work etc. Act (1974) further extended the role of trade union representatives in workplace bargaining.[5]

The legislation encouraged most of the professional associations to seek legal certification as trade unions and at this time, for example, the BMA, RCN, RCM, CSP and SoR became certificated trade unions. There were two notable exceptions to this. The IHSA decided that NALGO should take over its industrial relations role and the Guild of Hospital Pharmacists chose outright merger with a multi-occupational trade union – ASTMS (later MSF).

The development of trade unionism amongst the professions was formalized through their certification. In addition, they developed trade union structures, stewards' networks and some links into the health authority consultation systems. This process was slow and uneven and presented little threat to the control mechanisms of the managers. The combined trade union and professional association membership and bargaining power was impressive, but it failed to materialize in a coherent and challenging manner due to divisions within and between the staff groups. When this challenge became more direct, through industrial action in the late 1970s and early 1980s, then managers pressed their employers and the government to alter the balance of managerial control and authority away from the staff and their organizations.

One cause of the weaknesses within the staff side was the attack on the role of the professional associations. This was first publicly identified in the 1976 McCarthy report[6] but was again, 13 years' later, restated by MSF to the members of the House of Commons Social Services Select Committee,[7] the argument being that these associations 'rode on the backs' of the multi-occupational trade unions because the professional associations were too small in industrial relations' activities and lacked the resources and expertise to provide adequate representation for their members.

This claim is one that Dyson and Spary disparaged in 1979 when they pointed out that those professional associations with memberships that exceeded 10 000, such as the BMA, BDA, RCN, RCM and CSP,

> have a significantly high ratio of full time officers to members and have been rapidly and successfully developing the role of their lay officers. These figures compare favourably with many established trade unions affiliated to the TUC and in several cases the financial resources of these established single-profession trade unions are considerable.[8]

It has been shown that since 1979 even the smallest of the professional associations that are certificated trade unions have employed specialist industrial relations staff and have developed a network of lay industrial relations and health and safety representatives. Indeed, one of the characteristics of many of these small organizations is the low ratio of members to stewards, with the stewards being trained on day release and residential courses, which according to Dyson and Spary, 'match those of the multi-occupational trade unions'. Equally, 'the high ratio of participation in the role of steward helps to ensure a very effective form of representation at local level and makes for a highly motivated membership with many activists'.[9]

Then there is the question of those employees who are members of both a professional association and a trade union. In other words they hold 'dual membership'. This concept was originally fostered by the TUC affiliated trade unions, particularly COHSE, because it stressed the separateness of the professional and trade union functions of the organizations. The complementary nature of this relationship was, particularly in the early days of the NHS, accepted as totally legitimate for those professional staff who had a strong sense of commitment to trade unionism at a time when the multi-occupational trade unions offered the only way of fulfilling this commitment. However, since the mid-1970s, as the professional associations developed their own trade union roles, so they have increasingly challenged this concept. In parallel the traditional trade unions, such as COHSE, have started to increase their professional side.

It has been amongst the nurses, midwives, radiographers, physiotherapists and scientists that this membership battle has been at its most intense.

Another debilitating issue among the staff organizations was that of the TUC. This division between the TUC affiliated and non-affiliated trade unions within the NHS is often less clear cut than it may appear. Several of the professional associations have balloted their members during the late 1970s and 1980s on affiliating to the TUC. Between 1979 and 1989 the RCN twice balloted their members on this issue, as did the CSP in 1979. Each of the postal ballots received a negative response, although in the latter case, the margin for rejecting the proposal was extremely small. The SoR held a ballot in 1989 which failed to get the 55% majority stipulated by the Council, but another ballot on the matter in 1990 led to its affiliation later that year. Then, prior to its seeking certification as an independent trade union, the British Dietetic Association had agreed in principal to NALGO formally taking over its industrial relations' role, but when it was time for the BDA membership to subscribe to NALGO, they simply withheld payment and the arrangement was cancelled. The TUC/non-TUC divide took another twist when the EETPU was expelled from the TUC over its behaviour during the print workers' dispute at Wapping.

The issue of industrial action is another matter that is perceived to divide the TUC-affiliated trade unions from the professional associations, but, while the RCN and RCM have specific rules precluding the withdrawal of services by their members, there have been occasions – particularly in 1974, 1979 and 1982 – when members of many of the professional associations have taken industrial action in pursuit of both claims over pay and conditions of service.

An example of this occurred in 1979 when the short-lived Clegg Commission's report on pay comparability for PAMs[10] proposed an increase in pay that was conditional upon an equalization of working hours to 36.5 a week. The fact that physiotherapists worked 36 hours, radiographers 35 and speech therapists 33, led to several 'days of action' being held by these groups and the equalisation proposals being dropped.[11]

Following the range of disputes that occurred in the NHS during 1979, the Conservative government, which had been elected in May that year, issued in the following December a circular entitled 'If Industrial Relations Break Down' (HC{79}20).

It was partly in response to requests from regional personnel officers for some national guidance on the handling of disputes. The circular advised on the options that were available to management including suspension, withholding pay, using volunteers and contingency planning. It acknowledged that its suggestions, if applied by hospital management, could provoke an escalation of the dispute and lead to a deterioration of local industrial relations (this point is developed in Chapters 6 and 7).

The government had not consulted the trade unions over this matter and the circular was received with a great deal of hostility. In an attempt both to get the circular withdrawn, and to provide guidelines for the conduct of industrial disputes, the TUC issued, in 1981, its own Code of Practice for NHS industrial disputes. For those unions in the NHS whose constitution does not preclude taking industrial action, it is this code of practice that is generally followed. Its purposes included attempts to safeguard the good name of the trade unions and the TUC, to win over public support for the action, and to control media attacks on the Labour Party through its association with the largest of the NHS unions.

(i)   Any Action which restricts services to patients due to an industrial dispute should be consistent with respect for human life, safety and dignity.

(ii)   In the event of an industrial dispute it will be a matter for each union or unions to consider the action that is necessary in the light of the circumstances of the dispute.

(iii) For the duration of an industrial dispute, the union(s) involved should make arrangements in advance and with due notice, in consultation and, preferably, by agreement, with the employer, or appropriate senior member of staff, for the maintenance by their members of supplies and services essential to maintain emergency services and services to high dependency patients.

(iv)   Emergency services are those which directly involve the life, limb or ultimate safety of a patient, for example, 999, renal dialysis, terminal discharges, maternity, radiotherapy or serious accident patients.

(v)   High dependency patients are those whose life, limb or ultimate safety might be at serious risk without the maintenance of services, for example, children, severely mentally handicapped people or elderly patients.

(vi)   No services should be reduced to a level where satisfactory cover cannot be maintained in respect of emergency and

high dependency patients. In particular, delivery and distribution of drugs, food, oxygen and fuel should not be
impeded.

(vii) Unions may wish to give additional and more detailed
advice on instructions to their members appropriate to the
particular circumstances of the dispute.[12]

The 1982 nationwide dispute in the NHS following an 'across
the board' claim of 12% by the staff side and a counter offer by
the government of 4% to ancillary and clerical staffs and 6.4% to
nurses, was often bitter and tense. Clay reports that 61 954
nurses in RCN membership voted on this offer, with almost two-
to-one against acceptance (41 297 against and 20 657 for).[13] Some
of the tensions between the affiliated unions and the professional
associations were partially resolved by the decision to coordinate
action through the TUC Health Services' Committee. Following
an increased offer to the nurses of 7.5%, the RCN again put this
to their members and with an increased vote of almost 30% to
86 600, a massive 58 143 again rejected the offer.[14] It was at this
point that the government began to discuss the establishment of
a Pay Review Body for nurses and PAMs, and eventually a two-
year pay package included this proposal. Both the nurses and
the PAMs accepted the offer and the other health workers
accepted a 6.4% increase. However, they were not offered any
form of independent arbitration over pay. This action was seen
by some managers as a defeat for the TUC unions representing
ancillary staff and a vindication of the need for greater management discretion at employer level tied into clearer strategic
guidance from the centre. It was, however, a victory for the
nursing staff and PAMs because they were able to force from the
government a pay review system which would prevent, at least
for some years, the introduction of discretionary pay for their
members at employer level.

Because of the nature of their work, as the TUC Code of
Practice makes clear, industrial action in the NHS has to be
carefully organized and sympathetically presented. It is true of
all staff side organizations that there is recognition that whether
in pursuit of claims for more resources for the service generally,
or for improved pay or conditions for a specific group of staff,
withdrawal of labour is a difficult weapon to use and in many
cases political, rather than industrial pressure is applied. An
example of this was the fact that during 1986 the RCN spent
£250 000 on full-page advertisements in national newspapers

over several days, in order to publicize their concern about the loss of nursing influence at senior management level that the Griffiths 'General Management' scheme would cause.

The media attention that is immediately focused – particularly in London – by any form of industrial action in the NHS, is only positive as long as no patient can be found to have suffered as a direct result of this action. As the ambulance staff discovered in their dispute at the end of 1989, fulfilling a commitment to emergency calls, in accordance with the TUC guidelines, may win public acclaim, but in the face of government intransigence and employer objectives to divide and privatize the service it is an empty gun that points at the employers' head.

The common method of the pursuit of improved pay and conditions of service by single and multi-occupation trade unions has, during the late 1970s and 1980s, narrowed considerably the differences that some of the larger trade unions saw as being immovable. At both national and local level the 'affiliated' and 'non-affiliated' trade unions more willingly worked together. As the local shop steward/representative networks grew, as the single profession unions provided training courses for their lay officials that were at least as good as many of the larger affiliated unions, so throughout most of the country the Joint Shop Steward Committees face their management sides containing representatives from both the multi-occupational and single profession trade unions. There are, however, important local exceptions to this which are jeopardizing the current negotiations on new bargaining arrangements for the self-governing trusts.

These halting and uneven developments that have brought some health unions and workers closer together are partly responsible for the changes in management and employer structures and operations. This is linked with the labour market situation in which the demand for the services of health workers is moving in an uneven and unpredicted manner. The ever-growing demands for health care have increased the numbers of medical, nursing and scientific staffs in the NHS, and this has meant an increase in the membership of the trade unions/professional associations to which they belong. In contrast government initiatives to 'privatize' most of the ancillary services and sell off 'unwanted' NHS land and properties, have caused a large reduction in the membership of some of the multi-occupational unions – particularly NUPE. Subcontracting hit several government targets at the same time. As Mailly, argued:

> In the case of the NHS, there was a determination to see areas of its 'hotel services' being provided by private enterprise. This was in part an ideological commitment based on the belief that these types of service could be delivered more efficiently and cheaply by private companies. However, it also offered the prospect of reducing labour costs, and therefore NHS expenditure, in one single process.[15]

Thus, as the NHS approaches the twenty-first century, the providers of health care and the staff organizations that represent them face an uncertain future. For many of them the fact that they are more knowledgeable and practised in industrial relations issues than many of their management counterparts, brings some consolation.

In line with other industries, although not at the identical moment, the NHS experienced an explosion of trade union activity. It was in response to this seizure of the bargaining initiative by the unions that managers, employers and government devised a counter-strategy to regain control at the point of production and the place of work. Purcell and Sisson have argued in their comments on developments in the private sector in the 1970s and early 1980s that management sought to regain control that had been lost to the unions in the previous decade. The form of this re-appropriation of managerial rights was linked to Donovan-type analysis: the institutionalization of conflict and the removal of collective bargaining from the point of production through the introduction of payment schemes. As they argue:

> This involved, firstly, introducing a variety of procedures to institutionalize industrial conflict; and, secondly, restricting the scope of collective bargaining and avoiding it altogether, if possible, at the point of production.[16]

The argument for British industry in general applies, more or less, with equal force to the NHS from the late 1970s onwards. The government, the employers and the line managers together sought a coalition to raise labour productivity through greater management rights and labour flexibility. These objectives would achieve, if successful, lower public expenditure for government, more powers for employers, and greater opera-

tional controls for managers. The form and direction of the
changes in employer and manager powers have been mainly
determined by the influence, size and policies of the various
trade unions and professional associations. So the outright opposition of NUPE and COHSE to management reforms of ancillary
related services generated the policy of contracting-out. In
contrast, the continued market and political power of consultants has led to the introduction of individual performance
related pay bargaining.

MANAGEMENT IN THE ASCENDANT

The advent of large-scale trade union growth, workplace-and
authority-based trade union organization through stewards and
other lay activists, and industrial disputes by nearly all groups of
staff, triggered the management reforms and rethinking
discussed below. This account of the growth and development of
trade union activity within the NHS and its consequence in
increased levels of individual and collective disputes has
dominated management and government's view of the conduct
of industrial relations. Throughout the 1950s and 1960s and even
into the early years of the 1970s NHS managers had limited
contact with industrial relations proper, and their activities were
narrowly limited to traditional personnel issues such as pensions
and training. In the mid-1970s this changed with the developments in British industrial relations in general arising from rapid
increases in union membership, new laws and government
policies, and worries about the control of labour markets and
labour productivity. The NHS was part of this change, and by
the late 1970s union membership and activity along with
incipient shifts in financial policy and management roles meant
that industrial relations became a more important element of
managerial activity. By the 1980s this had been reinforced
through successive management changes, and the continual
financial squeeze creating national and local problems of pay,
performance and recruitment and retention of staff. In other
words, the conduct of industrial relations and the organization
of employers and managers in the 1980s owes a great deal to a
government response, partly encouraged by some sections of
employers and managers, to changes in trade unionism and
worker activity. The rest of this chapter outlines current
managerial and employer organization with regard to the main

concerns against this backdrop of powerful multi-union structures, complex labour market considerations, and the generation of commercial type priorities in the provision of the service.

This chapter, then, is concerned with employers and managers as they impinge upon industrial relations and not with their functions and duties in general. Much of the reform process of the 1980s has concentrated on the management of the NHS and has done so in technical and ideological ways. The task, therefore, is to unpick from the various threads of change those that impinge on industrial relations issues. The two major ideological changes that have gone hand in hand with more practical reforms were centred around the 1983 Griffiths Report[17] which heralded the change from administration to general management, and the 1989/1990 reforms with their emphasis on the purchaser of health achieving value-for-money through competition.

Specifically this chapter lays out the current and future nature of NHS employers, the changes in managerial industrial relations strategies, the management of managers, and the managerial arguments for more decentralized pay determination with or without the concomitant bargaining arrangements. The task is to show the damage done to the NHS owing to a lack of coherent strategies by managers in industrial relations, and to show how this illustrates both the tendency of the present government to deal in the short term and its desire to maintain tight central financial and employment controls over the public sector.

THE EMPLOYERS

At present the NHS itself does not employ anyone. There are 240 legally independent NHS employing organizations such as the District Health Authorities, Health Boards, Regional Health Authorities and Special Health Authorities. Another four organizations can be added to this list, which include the civil servants (NHS Management Executive Members amongst others) who deal directly with the NHS. The number of NHS employing authorities before April 1991 was:

England	190
Wales	9
Scotland	15
N. Ireland	4

Special HA	8
Regional HA (Eng)	14
Total	240

In addition, private contractors, especially in the hotel and catering services since 1982, have provided a growing source of varied employment for many staff working within NHS premises.

Regional Health Authorities

Regional Health Authorities, of which there are 14, exist only in England. Their main role has been as part of the management control mechanism over the 190 English District Health Authorities. In general their industrial relations role is limited, but since 1984 it has been enhanced by the practice of the Secretary of State to consult with regional chairs to determine pay strategy. The Regions have no direct employment responsibilities for DHA staff, with the exception of medical consultants.

The regions have traditionally employed administrative staff for the task of review of the DHAs, but also they have employed staff who run a series of operational and management services deemed best provided by region. These include distribution centres, ambulance services, blood transfusion services, legal, information and management services. After 1984 some of these services were cut back, and either delegated to the DHAs or given to the private sector. In 1989 the West Midlands RHA, for example, agreed to a management buy-out of its 320-strong management services division which provided computing and consultancy services.

Scotland, Wales and Northern Ireland do not have a regional structure. For these countries the coordination between the Health Boards or Authorities is undertaken through their respective Health Departments. In Scotland the Common Services Agency plays a major role in the coordination of central services, and is as yet untroubled by government pressures to reduce its functions.

Health authorities

The vast majority of NHS staff are employed by the various health authorities. They have wide discretion over whom they employ, but until recently there has been little discretion over the terms of that employment. Those were determined by Whitley agreements: indeed the front page of the General Whitley Council handbook states that these agreements are 'mandatory' for both employers and employees. Central control of the employment relationship with major government involvement represented a fundamental break with the systems that preceded the NHS. The emphasis since 1984 has been on a national service directly managed as a nationwide system. The principle for employment was, therefore, national practices based on national standards.

The main employment function of the health authorities has been to decide the numbers, types and proportions of staff to be employed within given financial resources. The allocation of resources is of course one of the great questions of economic and social policy. Within the NHS the total budget tended to be allocated on an incremental basis with exceptions for political and/or technical considerations. This fairly haphazard and random method of allocation was, and was seen to be, both unfair and inefficient, and by the early 1970s calls were made to improve the allocation mechanism. The first response was to replace historical accident with bureaucratic formula. This was the setting up of the Resource Allocation Working Party (RAWP).[18] The main element of the system was to try to allocate resources as between regions and districts on some notional estimate of demand based on proxy measures such as the catchment population stratified by special categories (such as women over 60, children under 5).

The current reforms, despite some denials from Ministers, seek to replace formula funding based on population profiles with what the government considers to be the only mechanism available for the efficient (and in the long term, *ipso facto*, fair) allocation of resources: the market.

The most important issue here is the discretion over expenditure that health authorities had in relation to staff. They had considerable scope to vary the numbers and skill mix of staff across specialisms. The evidence for this comes from an analysis of the types of staff employed in different health authorities. This freedom to decide the composition and size of the workforce contrasts with the lack of freedom to determine their employment conditions. This limitation is very real: in 1956 the Guillebaud Committee on the costs of the NHS strongly opposed local pay,[19] and the 1977 NHS Act (schedule 5) as amended by the 1983 Act empowers health authorities to employ staff on such pay and conditions of service as they may determine subject to 'any regulations or directions the Secretary of State may make'. Regulation 3(1) of the legally binding regulations made under that Act states that, in the case of remuneration approved by the Secretary of State, health authorities may pay 'neither more nor less, either from extra or other sources'.

In the case of conditions of service other than pay, health authorities must include in the conditions of their employees the conditions approved by the Secretary of State, but may grant other additional conditions (Regulation 3(2)). Such additional conditions were very rare.

Since health authorities can only vary the pay and conditions of their staff with ministerial approval, and since such a process is tortuous and arduous, the health authorities have bent the rules and have been engaged in grade drift and other workplace practices widespread outside the NHS. The extent to which the 1991 reforms will change all this is explored in Chapter 8.

Some employer discretion

While central control through national agreements has been the norm, there have always been exceptions. Some national agreements have had elements of local discretion, such as the GWC agreement on removal expenses and another allowing service away from the UK to count as NHS service when deciding incremental starting points. Similarly there are national grading systems, but since the implementation of these partly depends on the organization of work at hospital level, and since this is locally determined, so health authorities have been able to vary grades on this basis. This was a source of conflict with staff organizations where they felt that the grades did not correspond to national guidelines.

Since 1987 grading systems have been subject to change and more local discretion. As the NAHA reported to the Social Services Committee:

> the over-rigid grading system again gives rise to fabricated job descriptions which enable authorities to bend or break national Whitley rules, but which give rise to coercive comparisons by staff between authorities.[20]

A familiar management refrain, supported by government statements, is that national Whitley agreements are too detailed and too prescriptive. The management view is that national agreements should set out broad principles while the details are determined at workplace and/or employer level. In practice several procedural agreements have been of this type: grievance, disciplinary and trade union facilities.

The development of employer based disciplinary procedures steeped in the legislation of the 1970s enabled both management and staff organizations to negotiate at workplace level. This in turn helped to develop both shop steward organization and the personnel function. Even though it gave the opportunity for local decision-making in general it was used in a very limited and narrow manner, and once again managers have recently declared their frustration with the operation of these procedures.[21]

The most recent batch of national agreements reflect the inching process towards some employer flexibility. For example, extra discretionary payments for scarce skills, as for speech therapists, computer staff, MLSOs and pharmacy staff. Another example from 1989 was the agreement for A&C staff which gave the right for discretionary increments and increased rights to employers to pay salary additions of up to 20% outside London and up to 30% in London for 'difficult to recruit' staff. A more limited experiment in 'local pay' is going on through the Pay Review Body for nurses. In contrast, the 1990 PRB report for PAMs rejected Department of Health proposals for regional and/or flexible pay on the grounds that there was a national labour market for PAMs.

In 1990 the NHS general managers received even greater elements of employer flexibility in the application of the national agreements. In practice the variations in basic pay for this group remain limited. The performance related pay element is, as it must be, based on employer decision. This performance related pay system now covers about 7000 managers in addition to the 900 general managers in the first agreement of this kind.

The national pay and conditions system that existed from the early years of the NHS has come under increasing pressure to allow for employer-based variation. In the 1970s some of this pressure came from trade unions representing staff who felt they had a bargaining power not reflected in Whitley mechanisms and in pay outcomes, and in the 1980s these pressures have come from managers seeking greater controls over staff and associated costs and some professional staff frustrated by staff shortages and lack of reward.

Other types of employer

a)   Contractors

Between 1978 and 1987 the number of ancillary staff employed within the NHS fell from 211 780 to 148 000. A major part of the reduction was caused by the introduction of competitive tendering of services after 1982. The Department of Health, which provided these figures, could not provide data for the numbers of staff working for contractors in NHS hospitals nor any detailed analysis of the staffing impact of the changes. Most tenders (82%) were won by in-house groups, but only at the expense of numbers employed and their pay and conditions. The absence of hard analytical data in the wake of these changes and of clear thinking about the role of health authorities as both employers and as users of contracted out services is a worry at a time when similar changes are being introduced for clinical and allied areas of the service.

The industrial relations consequences of tendering out are of real significance since they broke important elements of the mould of NHS employment relations. For example, redundancies and reduced staff conditions of employment not only undermine the image of the service as a 'good' employer as part of the state's image as a 'model employer', but also generate uncertainties amongst all staff which are not conducive to the nature of NHS employment. An interesting possible future development for subcontractors is the introduction of 'contract compliance' initiatives common in the USA to enforce better employment practices from companies wishing to win government/state sector contracts. The National Audit Office has stated that:

> savings [from privatization] have arisen mainly from the need to draw up specifications including the rationalization of existing operations [in domestic services], less favourable conditions of employment, greater use of part-time staff, changes in working practice and increased productivity.[22]

The employment elements of this were emphasized in a 1986 Treasury report which said that:

Contractors in the ancillary services usually offer similar basic rates of pay ranging from 10% less to a few percent more in some cases, but they eliminate costly bonus schemes and overtime working, providing little if any sick pay and avoid national insurance payments by means of more part time working. The differences in total labour cost may typically be in the order of 25%. Pensions are the main single element in it.[23]

NUPE's evidence to the Social Services Committee bitterly complained that,

> as a result of competitive tendering in the NHS, a stable, committed and established work force has been replaced by a casualised, almost entirely part time staff, paid even less than regular NHS employees, and expected to work even harder for their small wage packets.[24]

NUPE pointed out that staff turnover rates rose and that in general all staff become thoroughly demoralized. NUPE condemned those employers that resorted to such policies:

> a system which sacrifices people to the demands and dictates of a 'market' which is nothing to do with quality or caring and everything to do with short-changing the work force and patients is not only inhuman but inefficient. The limited experience of introducing 'competition' into the health service has made the 'market' reality for thousands of health workers. A market where their jobs are sold to the lowest bidder![25]

The government supports and encourages those NHS employers that have adopted such an approach. It argues that since competitive tendering started in full, in 1983, there have been savings of about £120m per year (about 17% of previous costs). The government additionally claims that the new system generates 'clearer performance criteria, improved productivity, innovatory ideas and techniques, and better management'.[26]

The White Paper *Working for Patients* states that competitive tendering has broadened out to a whole range of support services, and in 1990 was worth about £1 billion. Other services include hotel provision, estate services, linen removal, computer services, security, distribution, design and package contracts. The government now believes that 'there is scope for much wider use of competitive tendering, beyond the non-clinical support services ... This can extend as far as the wholesale "buying in" of treatments for patients from private sector hospitals and clinics'.[27] The new list will include radiography and laboratory services. Throughout the new health service, both within self-governing trusts and in directly managed units, the implications of tendering out remain the same: redundancies and reductions in terms and conditions of service. The leaked document for senior managers on industrial relations in self-governing trusts (the so-called 'Trent Document') makes it quite clear how redundancies and lower conditions of service will be necessary and implemented for some staff groups.[28]

It is obvious that in addition to a belief in the efficacy of market forces, the government wants to rid the health service of trade unions, or at least to weaken their position radically. Tendering out achieves this objective quite simply, and therefore, in the view of the government and many senior managers, will remove the threat of union growth and industrial action experienced in the 1970s and in the 1982 strikes and 1989 ambulance dispute. Such theorizing indicates a remarkable inability to see beyond the immediate problems, and fails to take account of the reasons why governments and employers and managers have favoured trade union recognition and collective bargaining as the primary means of regulating industrial relations. The power of customary pay differences and job regulation, and the advantages of running a complex business with a varied staff with staff representative organizations has, for the moment at least, been overshadowed by more pressing financial considerations.

b)   General practitioners

General practitioners (GPs) in the NHS are the original subcontractors to the NHS. They are not employees, but work for the NHS under contracts. Their pay is composed of a mixture of factors: capitation fees based on the numbers of patients on their lists, targeted incentive payments and a set of additional allowances and/or items of service payments. Despite their unusual role within the NHS their 'average remuneration' is recommended by the Doctors' Pay Review Body and fixed by the government. They are contractors who are on a fixed-price contract and whose price is recommended by an outside body.

In recent years GP practices have increased in size, and current government changes provide incentives for larger practices. In addition GPs employ other staff including receptionists, secretaries, cleaning staff, nurses and nursing auxiliaries. More recently some practices now employ physiotherapists. Most of the costs of employing these staff can be recouped by the GPs subject to the agreement of the Family Practitioner Committee.

The government's plans allow practices with more than 9000 patients to become budget holders. This enables them to purchase services from health authorities, and provides an incentive to offer their own treatment and diagnostic services. Examples might include cold surgery, laboratory services, health visitors, physiotherapy, chiropody and dietetic services.

GPs, therefore, will remain contractors while becoming employers of health staff. The pay and conditions of such staff might well be determined on a practice-by-practice basis with GPs bidding up salaries of some staff and reducing conditions for others. Two elements emerge: first, when GPs become employers who determine the pay and conditions of their staff, can they maintain the relationships within the practice? Second, what will be the impact upon national pay and recruitment patterns?

c) Self-governing trusts

Under the government reforms some health authorities and/or units within health authorities will be able to become self-governing trusts (SGTs). In these circumstances they will become employers in their own right independent from the health authorities in which they are based. They will be able to determine the pay and conditions of their staff independently from national NHS agreements. This has been one of the major carrots dangled before managers in their search for managerial freedom from civil service dictat and trade union bargaining power. Since April 1991 57 SGTs have been established and there are over 200 more with applications for trust status in what are referred to as second and third wave trusts.

The government believes that this form of employer is the best suited to carry out health services, and hopes that all 2000 or so NHS hospitals will become trusts alongside other units of activity such as ambulance services. The notion of large numbers of independent employers providing health care to millions of citizens is a fundamental change to the thinking of all other postwar governments. The nature of industrial relations in these new single-employer bargaining companies will be discussed in Chapter 8.

The industrial relations implications of large numbers of competing employers are, whatever else happens, that there will be increased variation in the pay and conditions of employment of health staff as between and within employers and staff groups. One view is simply that scarce labour will force its price up when faced with competing buyers of labour. As the Social Services Committee noted, 'it is feared that, in the current climate of specific skill shortages, greater local flexibility will result in spiralling wages increases as the SGTs compete for scarce staff'.[29] For other staff the labour market will count against them, as NAHA warned: 'staff in low paid jobs could see relative if not absolute losses in either their pay or conditions of employment or both'.[30]

One group of staff in particular will face radical contractual changes under the Trust system: hospital consultants. Currently their contracts are held at regional level, but those that work for Trusts will be directly employed by the Trusts. As the White Paper notes:

> the Government sees it as particularly important that Trusts should employ their own consultants. Where consultants also work for other NHS hospitals or in the private sector, a Trust will need to employ them on a part-time basis consistent with a commitment to the trust's hospital.[31]

This fulfils a longstanding objective of many managers to get greater direct control over consultants' contracts.

A major feature of SGTs will be the way in which the supply of services responds to changes in the pattern of demand. This customer-driven system allied with new budgetary controls will result in a fall in perceived need for certain categories of staff, and redundancies will follow as at Guy's Hospital in London in April 1991. This crucial manipulation of demand for specific types of health care may be based on some doubtful, but popular, assessment methods. The most famous at the moment is that known as the 'Oregon Experiment'. At its craziest there are suggestions that health care priorities be decided by taking the democratic path of abiding by 'citizen network' decisions. Local people are asked to attend meetings where they vote on a series of mutually exclusive proposals – more money for heart bypass against more for infertility for example. The issue as to resource allocation is thus turned into a mechanical ranking exercise by the local people.[32] This corresponds well with the phoney democracy peddled by right-wing think-tanks in the UK about patient choice and the citizen as taxpayer being a sovereign decision-maker. Market health care is prone to madcap solutions to what are non-market issues.

MANAGEMENT AUTHORITY IN INDUSTRIAL RELATIONS

The unity of the NHS as a source of national employment conditions with associated national staff organizations and management policies stems from the Whitley system and the Treasury control over NHS budgets. The essential difficulties faced by employers and staff organizations when implementing these national controls at workplace and/or employer level have been highlighted by the changes in the nature of health treatment and by significant changes in the labour market conditions for most groups of health workers. The dominant feature of NHS managers, like their counterparts in the Civil Service, has been government policy and its relative neglect of NHS industrial relations. McCarthy summed up the majority view of managers and trade union officials in his paraphrase of Henry Clay's analysis of Whitley: 'employers who do not pay and paymasters who do not employ'.[33]

Overall NHS managers have been in the Civil Service tradition of implementing and enforcing national rule-based agreements and decisions, and have been often frustrated by any lack of coherent policy and strategy on industrial relations within the service. Most government decisions have been forced on them by other events: incomes policies for both Labour and Conservative governments to try to fend off, or at least to be seen to try to fend off, a fantastical wage–price spiral of inflationary forces; cash limits mainly to implement cutbacks whatever the veneer of argument about accountability; and inventions to deal with immediate and politically harmful unrest within the ranks of health workers as with pay inquiries in 1974 (Halsbury) and again in 1979 (Clegg), and Pay Review Bodies following the disputes in 1982.

In 1990 the government finally produced a version of strategic reform which on the surface appeared to be coherent: the end of national pay bargaining. The decentralization of decision-making allied with employer independence to allow for direct employer–employee agreements on pay and conditions cuts out staff organization and Civil Service intervention at a stroke. But with tighter financial controls, inadequate costing and performance measurement systems, and fierce resistance from staff and their organizations, such an objective looks unobtainable.

The industrial relations management of the NHS cannot in any simple way be either decentralized or removed from public accountability. As the Trent Document and other sources have indicated, industrial relations faces years of muddle, ineffectiveness and conflict. As I recently noted:

> In both health and education the job of personnel managers will be to secure consent and to bypass oppositions, but if it is achieved by the crude application of private sector practices, it will bring years of resentment, inefficiency and muddle.[34]

It was to avoid these demons that the original system was devised. Since 1948 the government has been charged with the provision of:

> a comprehensive health service designed to secure improvement in the physical and mental health of the people of England and Wales and the prevention, diagnosis and treatment of illness.[35]

It is the government, therefore, which is directly responsible for the state of the NHS at all levels. It is this direct accountability that makes the NHS such an important political weapon, and provides one element in the answer as to what lies behind the current changes, namely, the removal of the first and last great act of socialization in postwar British society in order to reduce public expenditure and increase private enterprise. An important corollary of this is the reduction in the role of the state as employer and, therefore, in the politically awkward nature of pay and disputes in the public sector. Specifically the White Paper makes the point:

> the running of the hospital service cannot, however, be administrated in detail from Whitehall by Ministers or by civil servants. The Government's main task must be to set a national framework of objectives and priorities. Local management must then be allowed to get on with the task of managing, while remaining accountable to the centre for its delivery of the Government objectives.[36]

Operational decisions are to be made by the managers within general policy restrictions, and this includes industrial relations decisions.

The new NHS structures and regulations reflect this division. It therefore makes it harder for MPs and/or members of the public and/or staff organizations to put the blame for NHS troubles on to the government of the day. Several recent cases have shown how the new employers and their managers are prepared to take severe disciplinary action against staff members who reveal to the public problems in the hospitals. For example, a consultant at the Christie Hospital publicized the withholding of a cancer drug on the ground of cost. The subsequent internal inquiry criticized the doctor and warned of measures to be taken against future 'whistle-blowers', even if the troubles, such as hospital closures, industrial action or staff shortages, are directly the result of government policy. This looks even stranger in terms of passing the buck when in recent years the same government has increased ministerial patronage and reduced public control, with the Secretary of State having powers to appoint the chairs of all health authorities, the members of the NHS policy board and of the Management Executive. In addition, the Secretary of State can prevent the appointment of general managers.

This discussion is aimed at determining the sources of managerial decision-making power with regard to industrial relations issues so as to be able to analyse better the role of staff organizations and the future for collective bargaining and joint consultation within the new employer structure.

The demand for clear line management responsibilities within industrial relations in the NHS has been a recurrent theme of reformers from all aspects of the political spectrum, and simply reflects the frustrations of local practitioners when faced with delay, inconsistency and indifference. ACAS in its submission to the Royal Commission in 1978 criticized the lack of strategic thinking in industrial relations within the NHS and recommended organizational change linked to 'the delegation of authority and responsibility for devising a comprehensive local personnel policy to staff at local level'.[37] The 1983 Griffiths Report echoed this main finding. It established a Supervisory Board for policy-making and a Management Board for the implementation of policy. This model failed.

The currently supported reforms have a Policy Board for strategic policy-making and a separate Management Executive chaired by a Chief Executive. The Policy Board is chaired by the Secretary of State and includes a variety of business moguls: Sir

Graham Day of Rover, Sir Robert Scholey from British Steel, and Sir Kenneth Durham of British Aerospace. These men were deemed to 'have extensive experience of giving direction to large and complex organizations'.[38]

The Management Executive becomes the body that operates the health service. It will set objectives for health authorities and it will monitor their performance. The role of Ministers in this set-up is unclear, and the Social Services Committee said:

> we believe that in the last analysis it is not practicable to separate policy from management in this way at the highest level. It is an illusion to suppose that in the last analysis the Policy Board can take full responsibility for NHS policy.[39]

The fears were based on financial controls. If such parliamentarians are worried by the inability of Ministers to keep away from management decisions and of the Treasury to let go purse strings, then everyone else should doubly doubt their intentions.

The implication of the design of the new structure, and perhaps more importantly of the nature of the people called in to advise, is that sections of the NHS will be moved into the private sector and that industrial relations will become increasingly confrontational as part of a management strategy to weaken the trade unions and therefore the bargaining power of health staff at a time of change and labour market uncertainty.

The intention is to develop a 'clear and effective chain of management command' which runs from RHAs down to DHAs, the self-governing trusts and family practitioner committees. The DHAs are expected to devolve decisions to directly managed units. These changes mean that the regional senior managers and especially the regional chairs will have more responsibility for strategic policy-making, especially in the area of industrial relations. The Secretary of State will appoint the regional chairs and they report directly to the Secretary of State. The clarity of management structure is clouded by the nature of some of the new relationships: the link of the Management Executive with regional general managers and from RHAs to the RGMs, and also from Ministers to the Policy Board and to the Management Executive. An NHS management bulletin in May 1989 emphasized that regional chairs will be subject to continuous policy and strategy control by the government. In other words, it appears at present that the new management structures and the apparent disengagement of the NHS control systems from

Ministers are just another attempt to resolve the longstanding issue of government intervention in the running of the NHS.

Within this, now as always, lies the role of senior civil servants at the Department of Health. The Civil Service has had an important role in industrial relations in the NHS. The management side secretaries of the Whitley Councils are civil servants. In the Whitley Councils for nurses and PAMs a voting majority of the management side are civil servants. In 1976 when Lord McCarthy took evidence on the working of Whitley, the Civil Service came in for justified criticism from most parties. This recurred in evidence given to the 1989 Social Services Committee in its examination of the role of Whitley Councils.

The thrust of the criticism by both managers and trade unionists is that the management side of Whitley cannot negotiate agreements because of Civil Service intervention. Roger Poole, a leading NUPE official, illustrated the frustrations of many when he said:

> the Management Sides of both Whitley Councils do not move a single inch without the Secretary of State's representative's say so. I know that when I am negotiating around the table I do not have to look at the Management Side's faces when I am trying to put an argument of one sort or another. I look at the Secretary of State's representative's face. If he is nodding when I am speaking I keep going, and if he is shaking his head, I find another track ... there is one person and one person alone that matters and that is the Secretary of State's representative.[40]

The NAHA argued along similar lines.

The members of the new NHS Management Executive will all become, if they are not already, civil servants. They rely heavily on the advice and support of the civil servants from the Department of Health. In industrial relations civil servants are renowned for their amateurish approach and lack of continuity in post. The management side secretaries, for example, may not have any NHS or industrial relations experience and/or knowledge. Some of this is changing with Duncan Nichol, the NHS chief executive, who has replaced many civil servants with ex-NHS professionals or outside business advisers.

This element within NHS industrial relations is important for two main reasons: firstly because within a state run NHS there must be some bureaucratic controls and institutions in which civil servants and ministers play dominant parts. This, despite the endless criticisms, is not a bad method of operation. It does lead to tensions and frustrations for managers, but it also provides safeguards for the public purse, and, more importantly, safeguards against short-term and localized policies pursued by managers seeking to maximize their own unit's activities at the expense of other parts of the NHS. In other words Civil Service involvement helps maintain the 'national' in the NHS.

Secondly, as long as civil servants are involved and Ministers with them, there remains public and political control over health. When, as now, these begin to fade, then a private service is round the corner. A privately funded and controlled health service would, by definition, remove the outstanding complaint of government interference and Civil Service dead hands. But it would also remove public accountability and a free service. Managers and trade union negotiators have a right to complain at inadequate negotiating machinery and government meddling in pay settlements, but their complaints should be seen as part of a dynamic of pressures and counter-pressures which will eventually create an NHS that, more or less, those involved in it want.

NATIONAL MANAGEMENT POLICY AND STRATEGY: ISSUES AND PROBLEMS

Policy refers mainly to the setting of objectives in line with wider ideology and policy elsewhere within the government's control. So the drive for greater 'efficiency' within the NHS is part of policy. The major ways to achieve this, such as tighter line management controls and the enforcement of market practices on the NHS, are also part of policy. There can be no doubt that there are policies of this corporate and general nature. *Strategy* is the laying down of the major practices and procedures required to achieve those policy objectives. These include the encouragement of self-governing trusts and the reduction in the importance of Whitley Council agreements. When these strategies are worked out in practice they come up against opposition from a variety of groups. Problems of implementation mount as difficulties with their original formulation become evident when the reality they seek to change appears to differ from the evidence with which they were originally presented. As these obstacles to implementation become greater so the divisions within management, as between for example tiers of authority and between and within professions and general managers, deepen. As the process unfolds the ability to achieve policy objectives appears to weaken, and the result is often a set of unforeseen, unprepared for and contingent events. Overall bitter in-fighting and muddle may rule the day, and short-term goal-setting and attainment dominate. Within this general picture of current NHS corporate planning lies a secondary set of issues and decisions which specifically relate to industrial relations and to the introduction of a fashionable management strategy: human resource management.

Much of this policy and strategy confusion stems from the contradictions within the NHS that confront the managers, and nowhere are these clearer than in the workings of the Whitley Council system (see Chapter 5). There have been two major reviews of Whitley in the past 14 years as all parties to the agreements have felt, for different reasons, dissatisfied. The first was Lord McCarthy's *Making Whitley Work* published in 1976. Five years later the TUC published its findings in *Improving Industrial Relations in the NHS*. Many of the criticisms that both reports noted reappeared in much of the evidence submitted to the Social Services Committee of the House of Commons in its Third Report in 1988/9 as part of the analysis of current reforms.

The two most compelling criticisms of the Whitley system in the NHS have been its high level of centralization, and that on the Management Side the relationship of government power to health authority power is unbalanced and unclear. The most recent evidence for management frustration over this issue has come from the Warlow Report which expressed the views of many general managers in the NHS. These managers feel that they lack the freedom to manage, and that their freedom is curtailed by both the trade unions and the civil servants. One difficulty in assessing the parties' comments on Whitley is to distinguish between principled and expedient lines of argument. The reason why it is important to do so is that the former may enable a reformed system to be created, while the latter may dismantle without substituting a system which meets the needs of industrial relations in the NHS. In addition, the tensions so frequently noted as between central government control and employer influence cannot be resolved within a socially owned and controlled public service operating in a private system of capital ownership. Such tensions are inevitable. The question has always been not how to remove them, but how to ensure that the

policies and structures that have been evolved to cope in practical ways with these contradictions remain capable of delivering
the service. The present government is seeking to remove the
tensions by simply removing major elements of the NHS from
public provision, and leaving the remainder under greater
central control.

McCarthy attempted to re-establish parts of Whitley to enable
the system to survive, and he recommended that more influence
be given to the employers. On pay the line was taken that while
the civil servants set the overall figure, the employers dealt with
pay structures and priorities. He also recommended the beefing
up of the personnel function at unit level and a more actively
strategic role for regional personnel and industrial relations
departments. Some of this has been undone in the past few
years.

A string of further reports amplified McCarthy's findings.
Many of them were directed at the management side's lack of
coherent strategy, lack of accountability and slow-moving
decision-making and implementation. In industrial relations the
criticisms also included poor quality of information on pay and
conditions, and the lack of local flexibility. Some of the
McCarthy recommendations that were implemented in 1976
were overturned in 1984.

THE MANAGEMENT OF THE MANAGERS

In the past few years the pay and performance of the general
managers within the NHS has been seen as an important part of
the government's NHS strategy. The argument from the government has been that the NHS has the resources to deliver a good
enough service, but is bad at managing those resources. In the
rhetoric of the White Paper managers need incentives to perform
better, and the managers demand ever increasing measures of
performance in order to achieve the performance related
elements of their pay packages. It was the 1983 Griffiths Report
that formally started the shift from administration of things to
the management of people. This was signalled with the appointment of unit and district general managers, although their
impact on industrial relations has until now been slight.

The 1983 report on the management of the NHS under
Griffiths addressed areas of concern that had been partially
tackled in the 1974 reorganization. Prior to 1974 the Hospital

Secretary controlled the powerful Hospital Management Committee of which there were nearly 400 in England. These were administrators in the civil service and local government traditions. A combination of factors developed to enforce change. These included financial stringencies, the view of the Conservative Party that the public sector should be more effectively managed, and the increasingly popular proposal that there should be 'maximum delegation downwards, matched by accountability upwards'. These became the recurrent themes in all NHS reform packages since the early 1970s.[41]

The main objectives of these reorganizations included a thorough-going integrated approach to the efficient utilization of resources. This was to be achieved through the unification of the two separate services: Area and District. The attempt was made to weld these changes on to the existing traditions of management by partnership through born again consensus, and thus limited the influence of the doctors. It failed, and one lesson from the failure was that the real need was for strong line management authority with ultimate control resting away from the doctors.

Reorganization involves heavy costs in terms of disturbance, delay and uncertainty. Reorganizations generate over-optimistic views, especially among the managers, of their benefits. These findings from a study of the 1974 reforms should be well noted by the supporters of the 1990 versions.

The pay of the NHS administrator class until the Griffiths Report was based on an incremental system negotiated through the A&C Whitley. The terms and conditions of employment based on Whitley applied to them, and they had a similar legal status to other employees. Most senior administrators belonged to a union, and many held senior office in their NALGO branches. This parallels the active union role of headteachers in the NUT, and local government senior management also in NALGO. The model was one of job security, across-the-board salary rises, good pension schemes and other familiar beneficial conditions of state employment for the senior ranks.

For many managers there existed a trade-off of comparatively lower salary in return for job security. These rewards provided incentives for entering and remaining in the system and they have undoubtedly been effective in the past in recruitment and retention.[42]

The 1974 reorganization certainly caused significant distraction of effort, and in the opinion of many observers made a contribution to the escalation of industrial disputes in the NHS from 1973 to 1975.[43] It heralded the departure from the NHS of large numbers of experienced senior managers, and their replacement by equally large numbers of inexperienced managers. The Labour government which had inherited the early years of the reorganization implemented it without enthusiasm, and set up a Royal Commission in 1976 to investigate the NHS. The Commission reported in 1979 and while supporting the NHS in general was critical of some aspects of management. In particular it took the view that there were too many tiers of management, too many administrators, too slow decision-making procedures, and that these led to a waste of money. It should be noted that these points reflect a general perception of management problems throughout British industry in the late 1970s, and that the Royal Commission was saying about the NHS what was accepted as good management practice. The evidence for this view of the NHS and the rest of British industry is very hard to find, although that is not to argue that there were not serious faults with the management of the NHS in 1979, as in 1991.

In December 1979 the government published *Patients First*[44] as its answer to aspects of the Royal Commission. In Health Circular (80)8 it abolished the Area Health Authorities in England, and established the District as the vital unit of administration in the new structure. It also gave more power to unit and district administrators. At the time, the Conservative government still sought to conserve the NHS traditions. As was said,

> the Government has rejected the proposition that each authority should appoint a chief executive responsible for all the Authority's staff. It believes that such an appointment would not be compatible with the professional independence required by the wide range of staff employed in the service.[45]

Two elements of this response remained intact later in the decade: reducing costs and devolved decision-making. But its central tenet, that of limited line management control, was quickly overturned by Griffiths.

Again the close interdependence of corporate strategy and industrial relations can be seen. The 1982 dispute in the NHS was partly set off by these changes, and in itself generated the political will and coalition within the Conservative Party to pursue even more radical change. The final rites were administered to consensus management. Griffiths attacked both the management systems and the terms and conditions of employment of senior managers. In particular the report saw no method of evaluating management performance, there were no clear objectives to be achieved, there was little if any serious attempt made to measure the output of the health service, and the clinical and economic evaluation of particular practices was rare. The report reached its height of righteous indignation when it said 'if Florence Nightingale were carrying her lamp through the corridors of the NHS today she would almost certainly be searching for the people in charge'.[46]

The health circular that followed [HC(84)13] charged health authorities with the task of establishing regional, district and unit general managers. These appointments could be made from any source. The aim was to bring to the NHS management concepts, and to offer substantial incentives to doctors to become part of the management process. Day-to-day decisions were further devolved downwards, and health authority Chairs were given more freedom to decide management structures 'in the way best suited to local requirements and management potential'. This initiative went hand in hand with the so-called cost-improvement measures. Most of these changes were accepted by the hospital staffs with the exception of the nurses.

While general managers appeared to enjoy new freedoms to manage through the easing up of controls at local levels, the government tightened its central control of policy and policy implementation. What had been achieved in reality was a strong transmission system from the centre down to the units by managers integrated into a pay and authority mechanism and therefore able and willing to carry out government policy. This was in contrast to the previous regime in which managers and the professional staff were able to dilute and deflect government policy on its way down to the level of implementation. This new power at the centre was further enhanced by the establishment under government control of a Management and Supervisory Board at national level.

The industrial relations impact on the managers themselves was rapid and far-reaching. In 1985 managers in post were again in the position, as they had been in 1982, of applying for their own jobs. Thus insecurity of tenure among managers had been turned into a major tool of senior management. Staff from the private sector and armed forces were encouraged to apply for these jobs. Their contracts were to be short-term, and their pay was based increasingly on performance related schemes. This is a familiar practice in the private sector where middle managers and those with functional responsibilities such as personnel managers are regularly 'terrorized' by their superiors as a crude mechanism of control.

Griffiths and the government defended their use of short-term contracts with reference to general practices in the private sector. In fact there is no evidence to support such a claim. In most large private companies the managers are on normal contracts as part of the need to retain the most able within the company. IBM, the company from which Len Peach (NHS head of personnel and later Chief Executive) came, offers a high degree of security to its managers in return for high performance.

The contracts for managers abolished the right to compensation for unfair dismissal when the contracts expired or for redundancy at the end of the contract. Managers had to sign fresh contracts when they started, and this tactic of allowing managers their jobs if they agree to new, less secure, contracts has now been used more extensively within the NHS. Indeed management by contract seems to have replaced management by agreement and consensus.

The most important element of the new employment structures for the managers was the removal of the 800 regional, district/board and unit general managers from the Whitley Council system. This was a unilateral act by the government without any consultation with the unions representing those staff. The Secretary of State simply implemented his decisions of the terms and conditions of this group. As the Department of Health's senior representative said to the Social Services Committee, the new pay systems were a radical shift away from agreed systems and incremental structures. This was replaced by,

flat-rate basic salaries without annual increments; general managers able to establish managers basic pay relatively according to their responsibilities (local flexibility); annual appraisal of individual managers against preset objectives; performance-related pay added to basic pay according to the final assessment performance agreed by an equity assessor above the general manager; and contracts of employment which tie continuation of the contract to satisfactory performance in achieving objectives.[47]

Similar arrangements have been made for senior Civil Service managers. The package is intended to create a cadre of managers bound by contract and eventually by ideology to government policy to the exclusion of service traditions, trade union negotiations and long-term planning.

CONCLUDING COMMENTS

The distinction between employers and managers, as the representatives of the employer, becomes more important the closer any organization moves towards a market model of performance. The managers themselves are forced to conform to employer requests with less and less discretion, and the control mechanisms include the carrot of performance related pay and the stick of short-term contracts. The overall effect is to encourage managers to adopt short-term solutions, to hit set targets on paper and to enforce new working practices amongst staff under their line control.

NHS reorganizations in the past 20 years have not produced any startling improvement in its performance. The current reforms, which embody both an employer reorganization and a management one, will drive some decisions downwards to junior and middle management levels, but will reduce the scope for managerial initiative and innovation as managers are required to reach targets set at higher operational levels within a commercially framed strategic policy. The tensions that will result will be considerable, and the managers will be forced to reassess their relationship with staff. The flurry of employee participation schemes and the implementation of human resource management strategies will be of small moment in this process. The main issues will remain the level of pay and its determination, the bargaining arrangements, the conditions of service, and the strength of the trade unions and professional associations to protect their members from the 'new industrial relations' as practised in the new health services.

NOTES

1   NBPI (National Board for Prices and Incomes) (1967) *Pay and Conditions of Service of Manual Workers in Local Authorities, the National Health Service, Gas and Water Supply*, Report No. 29, Cmnd 3230, HMSO, London. National Board for Prices and Incomes (NBPI) (1971) *The Pay and Conditions of Service of Ancillary Workers in the National Health Service*, Report No. 166, Cmnd 4644, HMSO, London.

2   Mailly, R., Dimmock, S. and Sethi, A. (1989) 'Industrial relations in the NHS since 1979', in Mailly, R., Dimmock, S. and Sethi, A. (eds), *Industrial Relations in the Public Services*, Routledge, London, p. 115.

3   *1972 Industrial Relations Code of Practice*, HMSO, London.

4   ACAS (1977) *Disciplinary Practice and Procedures in Employment*, Code of Practice 1; *Disclosure of Information to Trade Unions for Collective Bargaining Purposes*, Code of Practice 2; *Time Off for Trade Union Duties and Activities*, Code of Practice 3, HMSO, London.

5   Health and Safety at Work etc. Act 1974.

6   McCarthy, W. (1976) *Making Whitley Work: A Review of the Operation of the NHS Whitley Council System*, HMSO, London.

7   MSF evidence to the Social Services Committee of the House of Commons, Third Report, 1/2/1989, p. 100.

8   Dyson, R. and Spary, K. (1979) 'Professional Associations', in Bosanquet, N. (ed.), *Industrial Relations in the NHS: the Search for a System*, King Edward's Hospital Fund for London, p. 169.

9   Ibid., p. 170.

10 Clegg, H. (1980) *Professions Supplementary to Medicine: Standing Commission on Pay Comparability, Report No. 4*, Cmnd 7850, HMSO, London.

11 Industrial action and days of action by members of the PAM unions. See report in the *British Journal of Industrial Relations*, November 1980, p. 390.

12 Trades Union Congress Health Services Committee (1981) *Improving Industrial Relations in the National Health Service*, TUC, London, pp. 163–4.

13 Clay, T. (1987) *Nurses: Power and Politics*, Heinemann, London, p. 138.

14 Ibid., p. 139.

15 Mailly *et al.*, op. cit., p. 135.

16 Purcell, J. and Sisson, K. (1983) 'Strategies and Practice in the Management of Industrial Relations', in Bain, G. (ed.), *Industrial Relations in Britain*, Basil Blackwell, Oxford, p. 103.

17 Griffiths, R. (1983) *NHS Management Inquiry*, DHSS, London.

18 *Report of the Resource Allocation Working Party* (1976), HMSO, London.

19 Guillebaud,C. (1956) *Report of the Committee of Enquiry into the Cost of the National Health Service*, Cmd 9663, HMSO, London.

20 NAHA evidence to the Social Services Committee of the House of Commons, Third Report, 18/1/1989, p. 46.

21 Warlow, D. (1989) *Report of the conditions of employment of staff employed in the NHS*, Department of Health.
22 National Audit Office (1987) *Competitive Tendering for Support Services in the NHS*, HMSO, London, paragraph 6f.
23 Treasury HM report (1986) *Using Private Enterprise in Government*, HMSO, London.
24 NUPE evidence to the Social Services Committee of the House of Commons, Third Report, 1/2/89, p. 132.
25 NUPE, ibid.
26 *Working for Patients* (1989), Cm 555, HMSO, London, p. 69.
27 Ibid., p. 70.
28 This was a confidential document prepared by senior personnel officers in the Trent RHA in 1989 and called, 'Paper for General Managers of Self-Governing Hospital Trusts: Personnel Policy and Practice – the Challenges of the SGTs'.
29 Social Services Committee of the House of Commons (1989), *Resourcing the NHS: The Government's Plans for the Future of the NHS*, Eight Report, HMSO, London, p. 69.
30 NAHA evidence to ibid. – 8th Report, p. 70.
31 *Working for Patients*, op. cit., p. 22.
32 Crawshaw, R., Garland, M., Hines, B. and Anderson, B. (1990) 'Developing Principles for Prudent Health Care Allocation: the Continuing Oregon Experiment', *Western Journal of Medicine*, 152, pp. 441-6.
33 McCarthy, op. cit., p. 11.
34 Seifert, R. (1990) 'Prognosis for local bargaining in health and education', *Personnel Management*, June, p. 57.
35 *National Health Service Act*, 1946.
36 *Working for Patients*, op. cit., p. 12.
37 ACAS (1978) *Royal Commission on the NHS: ACAS Evidence*, Report No.12, ACAS, London, p. 11.
38 NHS management bulletin, May 1989.
39 Social Services Committee of the House of Commons, Third Report, 1989, paragraph 5.6.
40 NUPE evidence to Social Services Committee of the House of Commons, Third Report, 1/2/89, pp. 122-3.
41 Ham, C. (1982) *Health Policy in Britain*, Macmillan, London.
42 Social Services Committee of the House of Commons, Third Report, 1989, p. 253.
43 Bosanquet (ed.), op. cit.
44 *Patients First: Consultative Paper on the Structure and Management of the NHS in England and Wales* (1979), DHSS, London.
45 Ibid., p. 7.
46 Griffiths, op. cit., p. 12.
47 Social Services Committee of the House of Commons, Third Report, 11/1/89, p. 14.

Chapter 5

Whitley and the survival of collective bargaining

INTRODUCTION

The Royal Commission on the National Health Service in 1979 made three general observations:

1. That some form of centralized bargaining is essential for an organization as diverse and large as the NHS, although some matters may best be settled locally
2. That there can be no escape from government involvement in negotiations, even when no formal incomes policy exists
3. That the government effectively acts as both employer and arbitrator in the process.[1]

The system of centralized collective bargaining was established in 1948 and has remained virtually unchanged since that time. The General Whitley Council (GWC) and the functional councils are where conditions of service for all NHS staff (with the exception of general managers) are determined and where for 40% of staff, pay is negotiated. It is through the appropriate functional Whitley Council that the annual submissions are made on behalf of the remaining 60% of staff, whose salaries and allowances are recommended by Pay Review Bodies. It is the GWC that establishes the procedures for the resolution of differences at local and national level and lays down guidelines for local joint consultative machinery. This chapter provides a summary of the debate on the reform and abolition of the Whitley system since its inception in the NHS. It then lays out some of the main mechanisms, the main results of the system, and some additional continuing problems.

By the early 1980s local management and unions had jointly determined forms of industrial relation machinery at health authority level with a relatively wide range of procedural and substantive agreements. Then, throughout the late 1980s, there was a concerted campaign by management sides for more local 'flexibility' to be introduced into the pay and grading structures. Many of the grading structures that were reviewed at this time, in particular that of the A&C grades, have in some way met these demands. Similarly, in 1989 the Nurses, Midwives and Health Visitors Review Body agreed to a Departmental proposal for a pilot study to be carried out into the feasibility of introducing some form of local pay supplements for nurses and midwives. In their 1990 submission the Department recommended the proposal should be applied to PAMs.

As the NHS enters its fifth decade, centralized bargaining faces a very uncertain future even though many of the national bargaining councils have acceded to some form of local 'flexibility'. The main reason for this does not lie, as is so often asserted, in the weaknesses of the Whitley system as such, but in the desire to end national bargaining as part of the process to prepare large sections of the NHS for private company takeover. Evidence for this proposition comes from a series of documents from the Centre for Policy Studies (the right-wing think-tank of the Thatcherite Conservatives). In one study they argued:

> It is nonsense for the NHS to build new hospitals in areas with a high proportion of insured people without taking this into account, and without considering the potential of extant, fully equipped private hospitals.[2]

In February 1989, the Secretary of State, Kenneth Clarke, stated:

> I do not like centralized pay bargaining, I do not like national pay bargaining. I do not think it is good for management or staff.[3]

As he spearheaded the government legislation for hospitals and other service providers to 'opt out' of health authority control and fix their own employees' levels of pay and conditions, the Social Services Committee believed that this 'could signal the death knell for the Whitley Councils in the NHS at least as currently constituted'.[4]

The Minister of Health had spelled out the government's plans for the future settlement of NHS staff's terms and conditions of service and in doing so revealed a belief that the government's 'step-by-step' approach, through the introduction of chief executives and senior management structures in each hospital, would assist in the abolition of a centralized system which the government saw to be both 'archaic' and 'inflexible'.

> We regard as one of the key components of a locally managed enterprise ... the ability to determine your recruitment policies and what you pay the staff you recruit, and so there is no doubt that as a hospital becomes self-governing so it will take on that responsibility and so there will be that many fewer people covered by national pay bargaining.[5]

While many of the trade unions support the proposals for some local 'flexibility', they are committed to the retention of a national bargaining system as are several management side groups who would be greatly affected by such changes. Both the National Association of Health Service Personnel Officers (NAHSPO) and the National Association of Health Authorities (NAHA) supported the retention of some form of national system for determining pay, and one general manager, in questioning the practicality of moving away from a national system, claimed:

> As a general manager, I do not want to see national pay bargaining cease; it is very important, because at this point I do not think health authorities have the resources or the capability to undertake local pay bargaining.[6]

NAHA and the King's Fund have been involved in the pay determination debate along with many others. Their main concern has been the development of flexible local bargaining arrangements in order to give greater discretion to local managers while keeping some form of national framework.[7]

It appears that the future of centralized bargaining in the NHS is, therefore, dependent upon the success of the government's plans for hospitals to 'opt out' of health authority control, and so utilize single-employer bargaining arrangements.

The measures introduced by government to restructure the system of NHS pay determination have to some degree been influenced by ideology,[8] but are mainly the product of economic and financial considerations. Various policies point to such a view: the abolition of the concept of pay 'comparability' for NHS staff and its replacement with the measure of 'affordability'; the creation of Review Bodies for 'moderate' staff and the rigid maintenance of the application of 'cash limits' upon the non-

Review Body groups; the compulsion put upon health authorities to seek competitive tenders for domestic and catering contracts; and finally the appointment of Departmentally approved general managers which ended the era of 'consensus management' in the NHS. These features of recent reforms point to a government determined to sell off some parts of the NHS to the private profit-making sector, and to reduce the cost of running what remains.

It is not just a national system of collective bargaining that is at stake but bargaining itself. The essence of collective bargaining is the recognition that the best way to determine pay and conditions of service for groups of employees is through joint regulation, bilateral rule-making, as between managers representing the employer and unions representing employees. This was explained in Chapter 1 as the traditional liberal pluralist approach of Donovan and of subsequent Labour governments, the TUC, the trade unions, and some sections of management and the Civil Service.

Joint regulation becomes, on this model, the prime objective of industrial relations. Its mechanics, its implementation and its ability to resolve disputes of right and interest through both internal procedures and the use of third party intervention assume centre stage. If the institutions of collective bargaining are secure, and the practices accepted, then whatever the results of the bargains the system itself should remain intact. It was this set of propositions that Metcalf and others on the new right have challenged.[9] Their position is that the corporate objectives of, for example, profit maximization and/or market power, should dictate the industrial relations objectives. In this model the main purpose of industrial relations in a labour-intensive industry must be to raise productivity and increase management controls at the point of production. In order to achieve such ambitions the NHS managers are increasingly embracing the 'new industrial relations' rooted in business performance concepts which now include total quality management (TQM) and just-in-time internal service arrangements.

These latter objectives may be achieved through collective bargaining, but will tend to entail decentralized bargaining, extensive use of job evaluation and payment-by-results pay systems, highly institutionalized local procedures for dealing with grievances and disputes, fewer recognized unions, reduced scope of negotiable issues, and enhanced authority for employee participation and human resource management initiatives. One key to this is flexibility, as discussed in Chapter 1 and again in Chapter 7. It is now clear that there are strong moves within government and NHS management to remove all forms of bargaining from the management equation. If this cannot be achieved, then in the immediate future there will be a switch from multi-employer to single employer bargaining and a reduction in the numbers of recognized unions.

THE END OF PAY COMPARABILITY

One important staging post in this overall corporate objective for the provision of health care is the removal from health workers, their representative organizations and wage-earners in general of the felt-fair system of pay determination based on comparability. The removal of links with the Civil Service and local authority employees affected the non-pay review groups more than those within the Review Body system, since, as the Review Body has emphasized on several occasions, 'affordability' is only one of the criteria taken into consideration. The staff sides of both the nurses/midwives and PAM councils regularly present, as part of their annual submissions to the Review Body, both internal and external salary comparisons (Chapter 2).

The strength of this felt-fair pay system among NHS staff should not be underestimated. It has been the driving force behind most of the industrial action in the service since 1978. The 1982 strikes, for example, resulted in the creation of the Pay Review Body system for nurses, midwives and health visitors and PAMs in order to satisfy the demand for an independent assessment of pay which would include comparability. (See Chapter 6 for a fuller account of the 1982 dispute and its consequences.[10]) The Pay Review settlement of the 1982 strike was presented by government as a reward to non-strikers.[11]

The government agreed to talks with the TUC-affiliated unions on long-term pay determination for non-Review Body staff. Although these meetings occur intermittently, COHSE reported in 1989 that they had achieved very little.[12] The multi-occupation trade unions independently and through the TUC, have consistently argued for an effective system of pay comparability for their NHS members, which has consistently floundered upon the 'affordability' rationale.

The official position of the government was to distance itself from public service pay fixing and to expose the latter to the discipline of market forces.[13]

In their evidence to the PAM Pay Review Body in 1989[14] the Department pointed out that since 1980, nurses, PAMs and doctors had had average pay increases worth 93.4%, 84.8% and 75.5% respectively. Between 1983/4 and 1987/8 the average yearly pay award for both nurses and PAMs had been higher than those for NHS ancillary, A&C, ambulance, professional and technical scientific and maintenance staff.[15] This has significantly altered pay relativities in the NHS, and NAHA maintain that 'many authorities feel strongly that the creation of pay review for nurses and the PAMs has exacerbated the problems of internal differentials'.[16] This disruption of pay relativities in the NHS is significant and is illustrated by the pay situation of Physiological Measurement Technicians (PMT). In 1982 newly qualified State Registered Nurses (SRNs) and PAMs earned on average only slightly more than a newly qualified PMT. By 1988 the differential had increased to over 20%. Similarly a State Enrolled Nurse (SEN) in 1982/3 earned 10% less than a newly qualified PMT. By 1989 the SENs earned over 15% more than PMTs.

The greater rewards which have been achieved for staff under the PRB system have led some groups of health service workers to seek admission to one of the review bodies. For example, the only two professional associations on the PT'A' functional council to be excluded from the PAM Review Body – the Hospital Physicists Association (HPA) and the Association of Clinical Biochemists (ACB) – have applied on several occasions to be included within its remit. As the HPA reported:

> In spite of repeated requests since 1983, Medical Physicists have been unable to obtain either an independent review of pay or admission to a pay review body to consider their salaries, although they conform with the criteria laid down for admission to a pay review body. No reason for our exclusion has ever been given.[17]

In an endeavour to resolve their pay dispute in 1989, the ambulance staffs' council called for a PRB to arbitrate on the pay of ambulance staff (see Chapter 6), but together with the government, the Social Services Committee in 1989 were against an extension of review bodies for all groups of staff. They believed that such a movement would lead to a further erosion of managers' control over the pay determination process. However, in their conclusions and recommendations to the government, the Social Services Committee stressed their conviction that much of the dissatisfaction with pay and low morale within the NHS 'lies in pay comparability both within the health service and externally'.[18]

An alternative method of pay controls other than the pseudo-arbitration of Pay Review is through the relentless application of market forces – supply and demand – for the least skilled and hardest to organize groups. One version of this is through subcontracting, as applied to the so-called 'hotel' services. As Brown and Rowthorn comment in their summary of pay developments in the 1980s:

> The employees who have fared worst throughout the public services are the least educated. A high proportion of these are women … the relative position of private sector low-paid manual workers has also worsened in the 1980s.[19]

It is obvious that one way in which the pay of manual workers in the NHS could be lowered was if there had been, *pari passu*, a relative fall in private sector wage rates.

In 1983 the government launched a competitive tendering initiative for domestic cleaning, catering and laundry services. Other support services, including portering, estate services, computer services and security, have been added to the list. In the White Paper *Working for Patients*,[20] the government proposed to extend competitive tendering beyond the non-clinical support services and by 1991 some parts of the service were actively considering the privatization of radiology and medical laboratory services.

The National Audit Office (NAO) put the annual cumulative savings to health authorities from the competitive tendering initiative at £73 million. They pointed out, however, that this had been achieved at considerable cost to NHS employees.[21] A Treasury report emphasized the point that 'most of the savings from contracting out arise because contractors offer poorer conditions of employment'.[22]

Since labour costs account for 75–90% of domestic service costs and a high proportion of catering and laundry budgets, it is necessarily the first target for those who win tenders, whether these be private or in-house contractors. In the initial stages of competitive tendering, contractors raised a number of complaints about the system, not least of which was that the tender conditions, such as the obligation to observe Whitley Council pay rates and conditions, were too stringent. In response, the government advised health authorities of the fact that the Fair Wages Resolution had been rescinded so that Whitley terms and conditions need not be specified.

Thus, contractors cut costs by eliminating bonus payments, reducing holiday entitlements, offering no sick or maternity pay beyond the statutory minimum, by not providing pension schemes and by reducing compensation payments for unsocial hours, shift and weekend work. A further tactic to reduce the hours of work means that employers do not have to pay national insurance contributions and employees have only limited employment rights. NUPE claim that the turnover of staff had increased by up to 800% within months of a service being contracted out.[23]

Contracting out has led to a reduction of virtually 70 000 NHS ancillary staff which has, in turn, seriously affected the membership of the trade unions involved – particularly NUPE – and led to widespread criticism of the quality of service that is now provided. The Social Services Committee recommended that the experience to date should be carefully reviewed before such schemes were extended to clinical services.

The unions and the labour movement in general oppose this process for two major reasons. Firstly it places these services under the control of private companies, and secondly it influences the pay and conditions of staff employed both in the private companies and those remaining in the NHS. As early as 1984 the Labour Research Department reported that the new firms would only recognize unions after a fight, that about one in four jobs would be lost, the conditions of service of the workforce were much reduced under the new arrangements and the workers had been used to break strikes by unionized NHS labour.[24]

More recently the five largest multi-occupational TUC unions issued a negotiators' guide to privatization. The services involved include ambulance, audit, catering, cleaning, computing, estates, finance, hotel, laboratory, laundry, legal, nursing, pharmacy, portering, radiation protection, renal units, security, supplies, and waste disposal. The emphasis of the advice is on how to be involved at all stages of the process, health and safety issues and redundancy.[25] The same unions, COHSE, NUPE,

GMB, NALGO and the TGWU, have formed an NHS privatization research unit. It claims that 'competitive tendering has brought even lower pay into the NHS'.[26]

Thus contracting out and efforts to undermine Whitley agreements are part of an overall government pay strategy. None the less, despite repeated reports of its death, by 1991 the Whitley system was still alive.

This system has, during its four decades of existence, changed very little. Staff groups were automatically transferred from their pre-NHS bargaining arrangements into formalized Whitley councils and those staff side organizations that had previously taken part in such negotiations obtained recognition at the appropriate functional council. While, during the mid-1980s the government tightened central control over the selection and deployment of management side members and removed (with the appropriate staff sides' approval) virtually 50% of staff from collective bargaining on pay, those staff side organizations originally recognized have retained their 'seat' allocations virtually unchanged and continue their national role unchallenged.

However, as will be discussed in Chapter 8, whether the Whitley system will survive at all, let alone retain its present form, is dependent upon the success or failure of the Conservative government's reforms. Before considering such issues, it is necessary to look at the way in which collective bargaining has been, and is now, carried out in the NHS through Whitley.

The majority of industrial relations substantive agreements on pay and conditions of service have been secured through this formal and national mechanism. Its faults have been well demonstrated, but its achievements have been overshadowed in recent years by accusations aimed at Whitley but designed to reduce multi-employer and multi-union national bargaining in favour of fragmented workplace bargaining between a single employer and a much smaller pool of trade unions.

THE ONCE AND FUTURE SYSTEM?

Rather than present a detailed history of Whitley it seems more appropriate to consider the main basis for its existence as a negotiating/consultation device, and how that has fared over the years. The start is Henry Clay's famously barbed and practical analysis of the then Whitley schemes published in 1929.

He took the view that Whitley reports were far from innovative, but simply reflected the conventional wisdom of industrial relations practitioners based on long-term developments. These included the growth in trade union membership, the spread of collective bargaining, and the increased nature of state intervention. The Whitley Committee itself was a subcommittee of the Reconstruction Committee set up by Asquith in 1916. Its rather vague terms of reference led to five separate reports, but only the first report was of any interest. Clay argued that the first report on Joint Industrial Councils was based on traditional attitudes and that 'its importance consisted in three things: it asserted the principle of trade union recognition, it embodied the outlines ... of any effective conciliation scheme, and it made a case for widening the scope of conciliation organization'.[27] Thus Whitley used collective bargaining as the basis for industrial relations, and noted the importance of any such conciliation scheme being permanent (which allows, *inter alia*, for regular planned meetings thus avoiding the negotiating messages likely to come from one side or the other calling meetings at specific times). The schemes would be national in scope but decentralized in action, a point that is of crucial concern at the present time. The extent to which Whitley represented the triumph of collective bargaining is stated by Clay:

> Collective bargaining, for which organized labour had been fighting for over a century, was authoritatively pronounced normal and necessary, and was extended, potentially if not actually, over the whole field of wage-employment for the market.[28]

By the time the Whitley system was established for the health service some of Clay's conditions for the need and success of such a scheme of conciliation were met: variable levels of organization amongst some of the workforce, growing collective bargaining, and increased state intervention both as an employer and in social and economic institutions. His argument that such a scheme would reduce disputes and stoppages and create a smooth application of industrial relations was largely realized, and his stress on agreements with national scope but locally implemented and with workplace conflict avoidance procedures (grievance, disputes and discipline) well justified. The growth of union membership and organization in the 1970s meant that his third condition was eventually met as well.

With the establishment of the NHS in 1946, the Labour government produced plans for a 'Whitley' system for the NHS. It initially proposed a General Whitley Council and eight 'functional' councils, but the number of functional councils was subsequently amended to nine, with the division of the Professional and Technical (PT) Council into 'A' for those professional and technical staff who had direct patient contact, and PT'B' for those who dealt indirectly with patients.

In September 1947 the TUC convened a conference of unions which had members in health care services and the government's proposals were generally accepted. One area of serious contention concerned a proposal that the GWC should have control over the decisions of the functional councils, including pay, and the government subsequently agreed to reduce the GWC's role to 'conditions of service other than general remuneration ... of general application'.[29] Hospital pharmacists were included on the Pharmaceutical Council and the Optical, Dental and Medical Councils were also agreed in principal. A Scottish Advisory Committee to the General Council was created to deal with any specifically Scottish matters.

In 1947, in order to agree the functional council staff side constitutions, the Ministry of Health convened a series of meetings of those staff side organizations which claimed to represent the various staff groups. Apart from a dispute with the BMA over the pay and conditions on which doctors would practise in the NHS, which delayed the establishment of the Medical Council, these were, in general, soon agreed. The levels of representation on the staff sides of functional councils were fixed at their creation in 1948 and these can only be changed by an amendment to the constitution of the functional council. Procedurally, such a change requires the consent of the GWC following the functional council's agreement and 28 days' notice of the amendment. Such complicated rules have been seen as a serious barrier to reform of the staff side at crucial times.

The main constitution of the GWC establishes that its functions are:

(a) 'to secure the greatest possible measure of cooperation between the management and staff of the NHS with a view to increasing efficiency and ensuring the well-being of those employed in the services';

(b) 'to provide machinery for the negotiations of pay and conditions of service'.[30]

It is the GWC that establishes the conditions of service that are commonly applicable to all NHS staff and such agreements, after being ratified by the Secretary of State, are published in the GWC Handbook. This council's agreements cover such general issues as facilities that must be provided for staff organizations (section 38), the rates for subsistence, travelling, mileage allowances (sections 22–24) and removal expenses (section 26), as well as establishing procedures that cover redundancy arrangements, service reorganization and the 'protection' of pay and conditions of service (sections 45–47).

The first seven years of Whitleyism in the health service were analysed and pronounced upon by Clegg and Chester. As they succinctly noted:

> The growth of trade unionism and collective bargaining in the health services was slow and patchy. Nevertheless, when the National Health Service was established on July 5, 1948, there existed a considerable number of negotiating bodies whose form affected the structure of the new Whitley machinery which was set up within the service.[31]

The dominant element of this settlement was then, as now, the hospital staff. The constraints of the new system included using existing machinery were possible, of recognizing the need for separate machinery for major staff groups, and balancing this with the need for a central and national overall body. Hence the General Council with its range of functional councils in attendance was created.

> The Mowbray Committee could pass over to become the Ancillary Staffs Council with little change in coverage. The Rushcliffe and Guthrie Committees were as easily converted into a Nurses and Midwives Council. The creation of an Administrative and Clerical Staffs Council involved the amalgamation of separate bargaining bodies for the three old types of hospital ownership, but since each of these had dealt with all grades from the junior clerk to the senior administrator, there were no insuperable obstacles to amalgamation.[32]

The only serious problem was with the professional and technical staff. As Clegg and Chester noted:

> Problems of prestige, however, were involved in the proposal for a single council for professional and technical staff. This would entail the cooperation of professional associations and the trade

unions, and dealing in the same negotiations with the remuneration of both professional workers who had paid for their own training and technicians who had served an apprenticeship.[33]

The solution was to split the Council into 'A' and 'B'.

A crucial area of concern was what happened if the staff side and the management side failed to agree. The original intention, which was never realized, was that either management or staff could seek arbitration within terms of reference given by the General Council. This was to be strengthened through regional joint committees and workplace consultative committees. The exact form of these bodies was left vague, and there were no arrangements for the right of appeal against disciplinary decisions.

One of the more famous elements of any analysis on Whitley has rested heavily with Walton and McKersie's penetrating account of intra-organizational bargaining.[34] At its most straightforward this tells of the importance of bargains within the opposing parties, and that the outcome of such bargains plays a major part in the factors which determine the final outcome of negotiations between the parties. Whitley institutionalized this by its definition of the staff and management sides of the committees, and hence created a more rigid framework within which the internecine warfare of both sides intensified.

The composition of the staff sides at the start was largely carried over from previous arrangements: the four unions on Mowbray carried on to the Ancillary Staffs Council, while NALGO and the IHA were the backbone for the A&C Council. But, as Clegg and Chester note, 'almost every Council had its problems'.[35] Again, the historic compromises which created the original balance of forces as between unions held the system together but also emphasized the tensions which, by the late 1970s, began to become unbearable.

One problem was that small organizations took up their places alongside very large unions on nearly every Council. Another problem was to sort out groups previously dependent on either local and/or trade terms, such as the engineering and building maintenance craftsmen. Other problems included trade unions sitting down with professional associations, and that seats were roughly allocated by representative numbers. This was bad enough, but 'representation on the management sides presented a much bigger problem'.[36] For the first time the only employers would be the Regional Boards and the Boards of Governors. Yet local authorities still employed large numbers of public health staff, and there were also the Executive Councils. Most significant was the representation on the employers' side of the civil servants from the Ministry of Health and the Scottish Department. There was no place on the Councils for representatives of the Hospital Management Committees, and the local authorities were greatly over-represented. The whole set-up was one dominated neither by the managers nor even the major health service employers. This laid the foundation for two of the continuing problems of NHS Whitley: the unrepresentative nature of the named management side, and their quite different selection and approach as compared with the staff side.

There was then, and remains now, a formal division of labour as to decisions on a variety of conditions of service. For example, General Whitley dealt with leave of absence and travelling expenses. Functional councils dealt with most other issues: national standard rates of pay and standardized conditions. Grievances and other matters were to be settled by Regional Appeals Committees as subcommittees of the functional councils. In June 1950 the two sides agreed this system with three persons selected by the relevant staff organizations and employers. Grievances could only be taken through a recognized staff organization, something the unions insisted upon.

Finally, the GWC provides guidelines for locally agreed disputes procedures (section 33), and reaffirms its commitment to joint consultation about 'any significant decision that is likely to affect the well-being of employees' (section 39), and then establishes the procedures that must be followed before, and when, unresolved grievances or disciplinary matters are taken to regional or national appeal (sections 32, 40).

The unions saw these regional bodies as additional negotiating forums and sought to widen agreements through their decisions, while the management tried to maintain their limited and narrow role. When Clegg and Chester completed their study there was still no agreement on disciplinary appeals nor on a system of arbitration. The key issue was whether it should be unilateral or whether arbitration was available if, and only if, both parties agreed. This has remained a serious problem throughout the public services with governments switching from one to the other as perception of political damage and costs of industrial action were weighed. If either side can force arbitration then it is compulsory and becomes a major disputes avoidance technique, but if they can only go if both agree, then government can force employers to refuse arbitration with the risk of open dispute instead.

In the case of pay, decisions have been made either by the management side and accepted by the staff or through the awards of arbitrators. On the management side the represent-atives of the government departments dominate, and so pay is largely determined by government subject to management advice and staff pressure. Despite this overall control there are practical issues which mediate the outcomes. Two issues in particular are frequently raised by the staff side in negotiations: shortage of labour – here according to Clegg and Chester the government takes note only if there is a political cost of ignoring the argument – and the cost of living argument: the management side were equally dismissive of this latter argument and tended to reduce it to a marginal consideration in their decisions.

The key area of wage determination was that of relativities. Both government and health service employers preferred this argument at the time, but who were to be the comparators outside health for the doctors and the nurses, for example? From 1948 to 1955 arbitration, therefore, played a major role in pay determination. Arbitration would seem to benefit the staff side: on a rough guide the unions won two out of every three referrals.[37]

Clegg and Chester conclude their account of health service bargaining from 1948 to 1955 with a chapter entitled 'The reform of Whitleyism?'. Their starting point, however, is the main-tenance of a workable system of national collective bargaining, and not, as in the 1990s, its demise. They take the view that on the management side the problems of local authority and ministry representation seem intractable, but the lack of management representation might be remedied. The lack of personnel managers in the service was seen as an obstacle to many of their reform proposals in the short-term. They saw no way forward to alleviate the criticisms of the staff side, namely that there are too many organizations. More relevant and more likely reforms were to be found in the conduct of negotiations in order to prevent the tiresome delays and reduce the recourse to arbitration.

As has been noted, it cannot be the purpose of this book to provide a detailed historical analysis of health service industrial relations. The next dozen years saw little change and the mid-1960s mark the start of Whitley's, and the government's, failure to deal adequately with public sector pay.

The GWC remained responsible for 'policing the structure and providing modifications to the machinery'[38] of the system. In particular there had been the establishment of a grievance procedure and additions to local consultative machinery. Since the mid-1950s the management side had altered in line with some of the problems outlined by Clegg and Chester, for example, with the addition of representatives from hospital management committees. This went with the 1956 Guillebaud[39] report which reduced the number of seats for the Ministry. The real problem, however, remained unchallenged: the lack of permanent conciliation machinery to service and police agreements when implemented.

The whole pay system had been jeopardized with the various attempts at incomes policies since the mid-1950s, with awards being put aside and delayed. Throughout the 1950s the staff side remained reasonably pleased to take arbitration to the Industrial Court or to the National Arbitration Tribunal. In 1959 the right to unilateral arbitration was abolished. Given that other differences tended to be resolved by *ad hoc* inquiries, this meant that the management side held almost total control over pay.

The lack of conciliation machinery and the difficulties of obtaining arbitration meant that within the NHS there was no effective avenue for disputes and grievances to be resolved. Communications between the parties were narrow and limited, and the use of industrial action essentially prevented owing to the nature of the industry. Apart from doctors and a few others in a self-employed capacity able to withdraw contracts from the service there was no effective sanction open to staff, and this had been carefully exploited by the management side. Although collective action and disputes were, therefore, limited by a hostile management side, individual grievances could be pursued.

In some cases the most important decisions are not made by the relevant Whitley Council, but by subcommittees, as with Committee B for doctors which covers those employed by regional hospital boards. But as before, the ultimate authority for the imposition of Whitley agreements is the Minister under the 1946 Act, and this, since the late 1950s, includes awards made by functional councils. By the late 1960s the Whitley councils still tightly controlled pay rates and prevented local variations.[40]

The staff side remained unchanged in formal composition in these years. A notable feature of the staff side, which in the 1960s became more serious, was recruitment battles between several of the unions and associations,and this took on a greater importance with the increasing possibility that Whitley representation might become proportional to union membership. But by the late 1960s Loveridge could still comment that 'union representation at local level is patchy and the antiunion attitudes of local hospital management and the staff themselves are a fundamental block to recruitment'.[41] Loveridge also noted two barriers to the professional associations' being more involved in collective bargaining: firstly, and of minor technical importance, was the legal position of these organizations as registered companies. Secondly, and much more to the point, was that the members did not want to be considered as trade unionists. If this is a correct assessment, then attitudes changed very rapidly indeed during the 1970s. In particular the nurses began to change their image and outlook around issues such as the rights of student nurses, career and grading structures, and competition amongst nurse unions for better pay during periods of income policies (see Chapter 2).

The major bargaining change since the mid-1950s came with the creation in 1962 of a standing Review Body on doctors' and dentists' remuneration.

By the mid-1970s, the conditions necessary for Whitley to continue to exist and to deliver a collective bargaining system for the NHS were under increasing strain. The cynicism of Clegg and Chester, expressed 20 years earlier, pointed out that governments would only show interest in NHS industrial relations if, and when, votes might be lost. This came true in 1975/6 when Lord McCarthy was asked to report on the Whitley system. In his report, *Making Whitley Work*, published in 1976, he said:

> The Whitley Councils for the Health Services therefore represent one of the largest and most complex bargaining units in Great Britain, representing as it does so many people in a wide diversity of occupational groups.[42]

Four major areas of concern emerged. Firstly, the role of government in the negotiations; secondly, the structure of the Whitley councils; thirdly, the methods of working of the councils, including the use of arbitration; and fourthly the consultative agreements. Later a fifth concern developed: the relationships within the staff side.

The staff in general strongly opposed a system in which the management side was composed of 'employers who did not pay and paymasters who did not employ'.[43] The consequences of this were gradually apparent as living standards of NHS staff fell, as management–staff relations deteriorated, as confrontation increased, as decisions were made in increasingly remote places, and as collective bargaining proper collapsed. Many managers agreed with this analysis. There were five main proposals for change which concentrated on 'the malfunctioning of the bargaining relationship'.[44]

The staff side favoured:

1. direct negotiations with the Health Departments, as the doctors, dentists and optical practitioners had;
2. reduction of Civil Service influence on the management side;
3. local bargaining – favoured by those unions wanting direct negotiations with their own employers;
4. a management side composed of ultimate decision-makers;
5. some of the professional associations wanted independent persons put on to the Whitley councils for mediation, arbitration and independent review.

It is not necessary to rehearse all the arguments of the day (some sound horribly familiar and some seem quite eccentric), but they tend to indicate that current government reforms, which are not primarily about industrial relations, have none the less been developed to try to resolve the central dilemmas of the Whitley system by seeking to provide employers/managers with budget-based discretion in negotiation, and to develop single-employer bargaining within pay review national limits. In other words, McCarthy's proposals sought to make the contradictions within the industry workable, while current reforms seek to abolish the source of the contradictions within a state medical service.

A range of more specific criticisms were made of the management side. These included the lack of representativeness of the employers, the poor quality of management information, and the feeling that managers were not interested in 'good' industrial relations. In response there was an explosion in the provision of personnel management services, and the growth of an industry within an industry of management information systems. The brief commitment to better industrial relations in the late 1970s was replaced by a less than conducive commitment to good human resource management in the late 1980s.

On the question of pay determination, a major option canvassed was the establishment of independent Pay Review Bodies based on the recent success of Halsbury (1974). Many of the large unions favoured this, including NALGO, NUPE and COHSE. The issue of pay level was closely associated with those of grades, spines and comparability. One specific idea which was taken seriously was that of an all-embracing spine for all staff based on job evaluation and 'felt-fair' job hierarchies. This has been recently rediscovered in some regions.

The trade unions generally favoured the continuation of the ten functional councils, but management and the Department of Health thought there were too many councils issuing too many orders. Of the ten, two never met in practice – the Dental (Local Authority) and the Medical and (Hospital) Dental. Their pay is decided by the Doctors' and Dentists' Review Body. Many of the proposed reforms revolved around chopping and changing the composition and numbers of the functional councils. McCarthy preferred to concentrate on their working methods and committee structures.

The three remaining issues covered by McCarthy were staff side representation, third party intervention and local bargaining. Again the focus will be on those areas which have re-emerged at the present time.

Much of the argument about staff side representation centred around the lack of preparedness of the professional associations for collective bargaining. In particular, the lack of local representatives and industrial relations' officials was noted. The TUC took a strong line at the time in its evidence: 'the HSC strongly consider that representation should be restricted to independent trade unions affiliated to the TUC',[45] a position quickly abandoned. McCarthy did favour reducing the number of staff organizations through backing larger trade unions as against the smaller professional organizations. This prompted most of the professional associations to register as trade unions under the legislation of the new Labour government and thus greatly to strengthen their industrial relations function.

McCarthy, along with many others, noted that NHS Whitley was one of the most centralized national schemes in existence. He also noted that local discretion was very limited and confined to matters such as pay on appointment. The only exception to this were the agreed local variations on the Ancillary Staffs Council, the Ambulancemen's Council and on behalf of maintenance staff. These were mainly local bonus schemes.

The perceived problems with national collective bargaining included inflexibility – pay could not respond to local circumstances. Management saw this as creating absurd problems such as not rewarding merit/ability, no recognition for accepting additional duties, and no skill flexibility. There was no local industrial relations outside the occasional grievance and this meant that local managers tended to ignore it. The pressures of everyday hospital management were so great at times that ways were increasingly found to avoid national agreements: phoney gradings and spurious promotions for example, which in themselves created greater morale and management problems.

Managers were overwhelmingly in favour of greater local management discretion over local industrial relations issues. In particular managers then, as now, were exercised by questions of labour shortages, reward of performance and the retention of key workers. At this time managers wanted unilateral control over these matters to the exclusion of local trade unions and collective bargaining. Of the trade unions, ASTMS pushed hardest for local pay bargaining with single employers through a fully developed local negotiating system. A more popular view was the notion of flexible national agreements such as 'broad banding' which existed in local government. As McCarthy pointed out 'objections to decentralization were raised by management, civil servants and the Departments'.[46] Their fears resolved into three concerns – lack of local expertise, support for a 'national service', and growth of anomalies.

Finally, McCarthy looked at conciliation, one of the issues that Henry Clay saw as problematic to the practical workings of centralized public service collective bargaining. Despite original intentions, there was still no NHS arbitration agreement by 1975, and the parties preferred to use national machinery such as ACAS. Majority opinion supported the use of ACAS when required but really wanted a 'ready source of conciliation'.[47] Allied with this issue of national negotiations has been the staff consultative machinery. Section 24 of the GWC handbook provides for joint staff consultation at hospital level. A model agreement tells of management and staff side representation and functions and includes the aspiration that they will 'prevent misunderstanding'. McCarthy, however, noted the unpleasant reality: 'the agreement was concluded in 1950 and in the period between then and 1974, the experience of joint consultation was not happy'.[48]

The 1974 NHS reorganization suggested a remedy through circular HRC (73)11 in which health authorities were pressurized to consult staff through their staff organizations. There is no formal regular consultation. Specific matters are dealt with between the Department and the staff side secretariat of the Whitley councils. The overriding problem has been a lack of proper consultation at local level, a failure partly explained by their lack of scope, the non-participation by the doctors, a lack of management commitment, and the composition of the staff side. McCarthy wanted consultation to be 'meaningful' and its scope to cover 'any significant decisions that are likely to affect the well-being of employees'.[49] He asked for formal consultative machinery at national, regional and local level, and that the negotiation and consultative systems should be integrated.

McCarthy's report was important and influential, and like the original Whitley reports themselves, he tended to support the current traditions of collective bargaining rather than to produce radical changes to the dominant system. The response to the report from various sources was informative in as much as it enabled the contestants for future policy to flex their options in public without pinning them too openly to any party political flag.

The report generated a fierce series of debates which have echoed down to the present attempts to reform and reduce the Whitley Council system. At its most basic the debate grouped the antagonists as between those who attacked McCarthy's report and wanted Whitley abolished in favour of the local exercise of managerial prerogative through market forces, and those who gave some support to McCarthy and wished to retain a Whitley lookalike national bargaining arrangement with some local variation.

Even before McCarthy's report some commentators were repeating the familiar criticisms of Whitley. It produced 'a rigid complexity of discrete bargaining units', it created an unfair wage structure and poor levels of remuneration for many health workers, and it lacked an effective disputes procedure.[50] In addition, the Regional Appeals system only dealt with disputes of right, ones of the interpretation of current agreements, but failed to tackle disputes of interest. These weaknesses in procedures and results fuelled the drive for change based on the introduction of incentive payment systems for ancillary workers in the early 1970s and the creation of local procedural agreements. Both enhanced the role of unions and local stewards, and were behind the 1972/3 industrial action which most experts agree was the turning point in postwar NHS industrial relations.

In other words, academic commentators close to NHS management and government felt that Whitley could not contain the pressures from below. It remained unreformed and uncontentious as long as there were no undue problems in the management of the workforce. Once health workers flooded into unions and the unions acted with conviction and organized at local level, then managers and the government became afeared of Donovan's Greek monsters of chaos and anarchy, as revealed in their modern forms of wage drift, unofficial stoppages and restrictive practices. This was then the challenge to McCarthy and the Labour government, and their response under intensive union pressure was to maintain, again as Donovan wanted, the extensive use of collective bargaining. The reforms would make that bargaining system more responsive to the operational needs of hospitals in face of stronger unions and labour shortages. This triggered off the move for more and better personnel managers to help the over-pressed line managers to cope with daily issues. Subsequently it was the line managers and corporate planners who came to dominate the personnel function, retitled 'human resource management', and sought their own more drastic solutions to labour market variations and commercial pressures.

Management response to the McCarthy report was guarded. Many welcomed the changes in the construction of the management side of the councils, the enhanced role of information for bargaining, and the better status and understanding of the personnel function. In other words, they welcomed a system that might give more say to line managers and which opened the door for more local bargaining.[51]

The trade union response tended to follow their more obvious needs. So NUPE General Secretary Alan Fisher wanted a more proportional staff side team but also wanted to reduce the role of the Royal Colleges, and this point applied with equal force to health authority level joint consultative committees.[52] COHSE's David Williams, at the time Assistant General Secretary, shared Fisher's views on proportionality but was less keen on local bargaining and a regional Whitley tier.[53] In contrast, the RCN through its Labour relations officer Val Cowie, opposed proportional representation and attacked McCarthy for his 'totally erroneous assumption' about the role and functions of the professional associations with regard to dual membership and their ability to represent their members in trade unions terms.[54]

The main pressures for technical reforms of Whitley, those designed to make it work better, came from the larger unions and senior managers. The main pressures to disband Whitley or to create much greater local flexibility came from line managers, the government and from some smaller unions representing technical and maintenance staffs who thought their bargaining situation and experience would be better served at health authority level.

By the end of the Labour government's term in office in 1979 there was a Royal Commission into the NHS, a standing commission on pay comparability and massive strikes by public sector workers, including those in the NHS. Reforms from above, even with national union support, proved no shield from demands from below based on basic feelings of deprivation inspired by low salaries and status and channelled through increasingly democratic and powerful unions. As the Conservatives came to power, radical changes were mooted. The general mood was pessimistic. As one senior manager noted:

> Managers in the National Health Service during the 1970s have seen their organization almost torn apart by conflict and turmoil. The service has moved from relative stability with modest growth, paternalistic management, an obedient and well motivated staff and high public esteem, to organizational crisis. This crisis is characterized by the instability of NHS organizational and management structures, recurrent financial problems, poor morale among staff who are constantly at odds with both their employer and each other, and mounting public unease and concern.[55]

This comment specific to the NHS reflected wider problems in the early 1980s. As Winchester has suggested:

> In sharp contrast, by 1980 it had become commonplace to consider the major source of instability in British industrial relations as lying in the relationships between governments and public sector trade unions.[56]

The government moved to a common public sector industrial relations policy based on the belief that public sector pay caused inflation through the mechanism of borrowing, and that incomes policies generated major national conflicts with public sector unions. This moved them to the practice of refusing arbitration of wage claims, and of replacing comparability with affordability as a major pay argument. Throughout the 1980s the future of Whitley as a pay system hung in the balance.

In 1981 the TUC restated its view that a fair level of pay for health workers was more important than any reform of the collective bargaining system, but that

> In our view, the functional council or committee is the principal collective bargaining forum in the Whitley system, and it is by negotiation in this forum that the very great majority of decisions on pay and conditions should be made.[57]

Here at least was one voice in favour of keeping the Whitley councils alive.

The alternative Conservative view has been presented by Dyson. On the back of the 1982 NHS pay dispute he argued for the government line to remove pay bargaining from Whitley. The crucial change advocated was to replace Whitley with a pay system devised to protect health professionals from market forces, political whim and dominant Civil Service controls and tied in with a public acknowledgement that the NHS should, if possible, be free from industrial action. The outcome of this process was the creation of Pay Review Bodies for 60% of the staff – nearly all the professionals. This further split the NHS workforce, between scarce and complex labour of professional workers amenable to political pressures from a Conservative government, and large numbers of more traditional workers belonging to multi-occupational TUC unions in opposition to government policies and reforms.

In 1980 and 1981 the pay awards to NHS staff 'constituted the breaking of the mould' through the use of cash limits. Dyson provided a list of five options: the market forces option with local pay flexibility (the one now adopted for many staff outside Pay Review); incomes policy option (being rediscovered by the Labour Party); the trade union option of pay indexation which the TUC also backed (and has been restated by Brown and Rowthorn); no solution and continued industrial action. The final option given is the one favoured by Dyson: the analogue system. This implies a form of permanent arbitration body, such as Pay Review, for the professions using customary pay links in

a controlled way, but does not really deal with pay determination for other staff.[58]

Three years later Dyson predicted the immediate collapse of
Whitley, and explained the failure of the McCarthy reforms. This
is based, according to Dyson, on the failure by staff side to
reform themselves, and the lack of political realism by McCarthy
and later the TUC in coming to terms with the government's pay
determination policies.[59]

In 1984 Whitley was reformed again, and this meant it
survived in a form presented below in more detail. The major
development was a continuation of some points made by
McCarthy, especially on the management side. As Leopold
noted, there are now 50 management side members as compared
with over 200 previously. The Secretary of State now appoints all
of them, which has brought forth from the unions the accusation
of a lack of public accountability. The picture by 1986 was of a
reconstructed system full of old tensions.

Pay determination was still to be decided as between
government policy, personnel directors, regional and Whitley
chairs, Pay Review Bodies and the various staff organizations
and their members.[60] A fuller account of this line of argument
utilized the theoretical construct of intraorganizational bargaining to explain failures of policy and practice by
government, Civil Service and management. Such arguments
are extremely useful in tackling specific cases of muddle and
failure, but must not be used to hide deeper political motives
with regard to the selling off of health services. Leopold and
Beaumont suggest that cash limits imposed by government fell
into place with the efforts to devise a stand alone management
strategy for NHS pay. This would be achieved by strengthening
the authority of regional chairs as the lookalike board of
directors. They would be assisted by better pay research, an
enhanced briefing system, and influence over and cooperation
with Whitley chairs.

They concluded with a special reference to two interesting
developments: the briefing link between Whitley members and
the NHS, and the development of a pay strategy committee of
regional chairs. These efforts to bring pay within a private profit
type corporate strategy have been partly frustrated by the Pay
Review Body system, and partly by the failure to replace the pay
principle of felt-fair comparability with an acceptable alternative
for other staff.[61]

So the argument goes on. The alternatives remain to keep Whitley as the collective bargaining structure which best represents the health service rather than the Department of Health civil servants, or single-employer bargaining and the exercise of supply and demand as the major criteria for pay determination.

STRUCTURE, ORGANIZATION AND FUNCTIONS

Whatever the issues for the continuation of Whitley in any shape or form, the determination of pay, pay systems and conditions of service for nearly one million workers in a complex multi-occupational industry remains a major activity. Whether single employers can and would want to negotiate or even impose settlements on all these areas for all their staff is uncertain. In the meantime, most health service employers will fall back on the Whitley agreements outlined below.

The conditions of service which apply to specific groups of staff are negotiated at their appropriate 'functional' Whitley councils and, as with the GWC, so each functional council has a Whitley Council handbook which sets out in detail existing agreements on pay and conditions of service which are constantly updated as new agreements are reached. These functional Councils' agreements will include such matters as the grading structure that applies to the staff within that council's remit, their hours of work, the arrangements for emergency duty provision and for approximately 40% of NHS staff, the functional council will also collectively bargain over pay-related issues.

The determination of the pay for the remaining 60% of NHS staff is either by Pay Review Bodies, or by the Secretary of State. Approximately 1% of staff – mainly those employed in the varying levels of 'general management' – have their pay determined directly by the Secretary of State, with the majority of NHS staff, falling within the Pay Review Body system of annual pay reviews.

It is necessary to stop the flow of argument for a moment to comment on one group of workers so far neglected. There were considerable problems from the start over where the pay and terms and conditions of craftsmen and maintenance staff should be negotiated. Prior to 1948, this group had been covered by an agreement that they would not receive less than the appropriate trade rate. In 1951, a subcommittee of the Ancillary Council, the

Builders subcommittee, was created which consisted of management and the National Federation of Building Trades Operatives. In 1955, the government informed authorities by regulation that from then on the pay of engineering craftsmen would be as agreed in direct negotiations between the Ministry of Health and the Confederation of Shipbuilding and Engineering Unions (CSEU). In 1968, after arbitration, building craftsmen achieved parity with engineering craftsmen and the Builders subcommittee was abolished. Subsequently, individual direct negotiations between the Department of Health, advised by NHS management, and the relevant unions took place for electricians, plumbers and engineering craftsmen. Separate negotiations also take place for building operatives. This group of NHS employees do not have a functional Whitley council.

Doctors and dentists are another atypical group. The conditions of hospital doctors and dentists continued, in practice, to be negotiated directly between the BMA/BDA and the Ministry of Health after 1948. The Whitley Medical Council simply met to elect representatives to the GWC. In 1957–60 the Royal Commission on Doctors' and Dentists' Remuneration (the Pilkington Commission) recommended that a Review Body should be established to advise on the pay of doctors and dentists. Since 1963 the Doctors' and Dentists' Review Body has annually recommended to governments the levels of payment it considers to be appropriate. This Review Body had to be reconstituted in 1971 following its resignation in 1970 when the government of the day, because of incomes policies, refused to implement the DDRB's recommendations in full.

Following the 1974 reorganization of the NHS, a new functional council was created for ambulance staff, who had previously been employed by local authorities and, with the transfer of community health services to the NHS, the Dental Council became the Community Dental Council. Thus, in addition to the General Whitley council, since 1974 there have been ten functional councils:

Administrative and Clerical
Ambulance
Ancillary
Dental (Local Authorities)
Medical and (Hospital) Dental
Nurses and Midwives

Optical
Pharmaceutical
Professional and Technical 'A'
Professional and Technical 'B'

As described above, the Medical and (Hospital) Dental Council and the Dental (Local Authorities) Council never meet in practice. The pay of doctors and dentists is based upon the recommendations of their Review Body and agreed in negotiating committees which also agree certain conditions of service. Community dentists have a similar negotiating committee. In all of these cases the management side consists entirely of reprsentatives of the Health Departments.

Section 66 of the National Health Service Act 1946 gave the Minister of Health (now Secretary of State) the power to make regulations:

> with respect of the qualifications, remuneration and conditions of service of any officers employed by any body constituted under this Act ... and no officer to whom the regulations apply shall be employed otherwise than in accordance with the regulations.[62]

Any agreements reached jointly through Whitley then require, by statute, the formal approval of the Secretary of State before they can be notified to employing authorities for implementation. Following the Secretary of State's approval, the regulations are then circulated throughout the service (under Advance Letter (A/L) cover) and become enshrined in the appropriate Whitley council 'handbook' as part of the employees' terms and conditions of service. In this way, agreements reached nationally at the GWC relate to the terms and conditions of employment that are common to the vast majority of NHS staff as well as establishing the procedures for local consultative machinery and settling differences in regard to employees' conditions of service.

Similarly, agreements on the terms and conditions of service (and pay for approximately 40% of NHS employees) that relate to specific groups of staff, are negotiated in the various functional Whitley councils. Again, the Secretary of State notifies the employing authorities by means of an Advance Letter which sets out the rates and conditions of service. These can neither be exceeded nor underpaid. In this literal and legalistic respect, the

Secretary of State is the arbiter of the terms and conditions of employment of all NHS staff.

The constitutions of the functional Whitley councils provide for a specified number of management side members to come from the English, Scottish and Welsh health authorities and from the three Health Departments. McCarthy made a number of recommendations on the composition of Whitley Council management sides. The main points he made were as follows:

- Regional Selection Committees should nominate one member to each functional Whitley council to represent the region as a whole and this Committee would act as a briefing and reporting back facility for representatives.
- That there should be a modest increase in the number of officers serving as members of the management side.
- The personnel function in the NHS should be developed and it should be personnel officers' responsibility to service and assist the Whitley member in the region.

Although these changes were implemented, in 1983 this representative system of appointment was abolished. The main principles of the changes which were adopted in 1984 were:

- Chairs and members of Whitley Council management sides would be appointed by the Secretary of State, on the recommendation of the NHS. They would be accountable to him/her, though reporting through the joint apparatus, for considering pay matters.
- There would be fewer members than previously and they would be expected to give substantially of their time. The Department recognized that this would mean the end of the representative system for council membership. Where possible, individuals might sit on more than one council.
- There would be a core of 'generalist' members chosen on the basis of their negotiating ability or experience, and officers with special expertise needed by particular councils.[63]

As noted above, this new system of appointments reduced the number of management side members in order to aid the realization of the declared reason behind the changes, namely the need for a more professional and committed management side on the Whitley councils. The appointment of management side members is now made by the Secretary of State on 'the basis of personal qualities'.[64]

The majority of NHS appointments are regional or district chairs, with health service managers in the minority – the ratio being approximately two to one in favour of health authority members.

A new 'briefing' system has been introduced whereby each regional health authority with a Whitley Council member, identifies a briefing officer (usually a personnel officer) who is responsible for organizing briefing of the member. Those regions without a member are 'clustered' together with represented regions and a single contact point is identified to gather the views of that region to feed into the briefing officer. Mailly *et al.* state that preliminary impressions of the new system suggest that members are happier now that they are receiving the views of NHS managers on topics under discussion,[65] although there is uncertainty whether the views of the briefing officer are representative of NHS management as a whole within a region. Equally, it is reported that briefing officers and contact points tend to be 'reactive' rather than 'proactive' in the sense of responding to management secretariat papers and staff side proposals, rather than assisting in strategies. In its Third Report, the Social Services Committee recommended that:

> All Regions, if they have not already done so, review their procedures for identifying pay priorities in conjunction with their Districts and routinely communicate their views on pay priorities to the appropriate Whitley Councils and to the NHS management Board. If pay priorities were agreed on in advance of negotiations, managers would then have time to prepare their briefing material for Management side representatives.[66]

Since the establishment of the Whitley system, the management sides' secretariat has always been staffed by civil servants from the Department of Health. This arrangement has long been a target for criticism. A major part of the problem of the Department providing the secretariat is perceived to be the fact that since the civil servants change their posts frequently, this leads to a lack of continuity in negotiations.[67] There is a feeling within the health service that the Secretariat is staffed by people with little direct experience of the service and that it is not accountable to health service managers. A spokesman for NAHSPO commented that 'the way in which the present Management Secretariat appears to work is not in an obvious partnership with practitioners in the field'.[68] In 1980, the Department established a committee to examine the advantages and disadvantages of creating an Independent Management Side

Secretariat, but its report has never been published. The Social Services Committee recommended that further thought should be given to setting up an Independent Management Secretariat or that this role should be given to the Office of Manpower Economics.

Unlike the management side of the Whitley councils, the staff side secretaries of each of the functional councils and of the GWC are elected annually. However, it is rarely the case that the organizations so elected lose these positions. It is equally the case that the staff side, again unlike the management side, elect the chair annually.

What now follows is a brief summary of each functional council's composition.

Administrative and Clerical Staffs Whitley Council (A&C)

The A&C Council deals with the remuneration and conditions of service for administrative and clerical officers, including personnel, finance, computer and secretarial staff.

Number of staff covered: (1987) 138 200 (including 3500 ambulance officers and control assistants).

The management side has eight generalists and four from the Health Departments. The staff side is dominated by NALGO, with 19 of the 32 seats. Other unions represented include four seats each for NUPE and COHSE, two for the Association of NHS officers, and one each for the TGWU, GMB and Society of Administrators of FPS.

The council has two major subcommittees:
The Joint Negotiating Committee
The Ambulance Officers' Joint Negotiating Committee
The management side of the Ambulance Council, with one additional member from the A&C management side, acts as the management side of the Ambulance Officers' Joint Negotiating Committee.

Ambulance Whitley Council

The Ambulance Council deals with the remuneration and conditions of service of ambulancemen and women. The council does not include ambulance officers and control assistants.

Number of staff covered: (1987) 19 100.

The management side contains three generalists, four specialists and four from the Health Departments.

The staff side is dominated by NUPE, with eight of the 20 members. The GMB and TGWU both have five members and COHSE has two.

Ancillary Staffs Whitley Council

The main staff groups within the council's purview are domestic (43%), catering (18%), portering staff (13%), transport (2%) and grounds and garden staff (2%).

Number of staff covered: (1987) 148 000.

The management side is composed of three generalists, three specialists and four from the Health Departments.

The staff side is equally divided, with four seats each between the GMB, NUPE, COHSE and the TGWU. NUPE provides the staff side secretary.

Professional and Technical Staffs 'B' Whitley Council (PT'B')

The PT'B' Council deals with the remuneration and conditions of service for a range of professional and technical staff within laboratories, dental services, pharmacies, works and medical support departments. The full council considers those items which apply to all PT'B' staff (e.g. annual leave, sick pay), while six standing committees (detailed below) deal with specific occupational issues (e.g. pay, grading and qualifications).

Number of staff covered: (1987) 46 600.

The management side is composed of five generalists, three specialists and four members from the Departments.

The staff side has 21 members. MSF has the most members with five. UCATT, COHSE, NALGO and NUPE have three seats each, and USDAW and EEPTU (EESA) each have two.

Committees: the council has six standing committees as follows:

Committee A – Medical Laboratory Scientific Officers
Committee B – Dental technicians
Committee C – Pharmacy technicians
Committee E – Other technicians
Committee H – Dental ancillaries
Committee W – Works staff

N.B. Since 1990 Committee B, C, E and H have been merged to form committee T.

Optical Whitley Council: Pharmaceutical Whitley Council (Scientific and Professional Staffs Whitley Council)

A management side of the Scientific and Professional Staffs Council was established in 1984 to deal with the pay and conditions of service for scientific staff (e.g. biochemists, physicists, clinical psychologists, speech therapists, hospital chaplains, pharmacists and optometrists). NHS staff sides have not recognized the council, which covers the Optical and Pharmaceutical Councils as well as those groups of staff of PT'A' who were not included within the PAMs Review Body. Thus, negotiations are undertaken with staff representatives of scientists, speech therapists and hospital chaplains and the staff sides of the Optical and Pharmaceutical Councils.

Number of staff covered: (1987) 12 700.

The management side has five generalists, three specialists and four from the Health Departments.

The staff side of the original Optical Council had 22 members with seven belonging to the Joint Committee of Ophthalmic Opticians. The Association of Optical Practitioners has four, with two each for the Parliamentary committee of the Co-op Union, the ophthalmic group of the Socialist Medical Association, the Federation of Ophthalmic and Dispensing Opticians, the Scottish National Committee of Ophthalmic Opticians, and the MSF. There is one seat for the Association of Dispensing Opticians.

The staff side of the Pharmaceutical Council has 24 members, with MSF having eight. There are six each for the National Pharmaceutical Union and the Scottish Pharmaceutical Standing Committee, two for COHSE and one each for the Co-op Union and the Company Chemists' Association.

The next three categories are for those groups recognized for Pay Review Reports.

Nursing and Midwifery Staffs Negotiating Council

The Nursing and Midwifery Staffs Negotiating Council is responsible for negotiating changes in terms and conditions of service. Since 1984 pay has been determined separately in the light of recommendations made by the Pay Review Body for Nursing Staff, Health Visitors and the Professions Allied to Medicine.

Number of staff covered: (1987) 489 000.

The management side has five generalists, one specialist and six from the Health Departments.

The staff side is dominated by the RCN, which has eight of the 29 members, with support from a group of smaller associations. NUPE and COHSE have four seats each with the RCM having three seats. NALGO and the HVA have two seats each, and a variety of smaller organizations have one. These are the Association of Nurse Administrators, the Association of Hospital and Residential Care Officers, the Association of Supervisers of Midwives, the GMB, the Scottish Association of Nurse Administrators, and the Scottish Health Visitors Association.

Professions Allied to Medicine and related grades of staff: (PT'A' Whitley Council)

The PT'A' council is responsible for negotiating changes in terms and conditions of service of art and music therapists, chiropodists, dietitians, helpers and assistants, technical instructors, occupational therapists, orthoptists, physiotherapists and radiographers.

Number of staff covered: (1987) 40 400 (this figure does not include hospital physicists and clinical biochemists).

The management side has three generalists, two specialists and five from the Health Departments.

The new PAM(PT'A') Council came into being in February 1986, following a two-year inter-regnum when the staff side resisted the Departments' attempts (with the introduction of the Pay Review Body) to abolish the PT'A' Council and include these groups under the new Scientific and Professional Council. However, both sides agreed that only those groups whose pay was recommended by the Review Body should, in future, be represented by this council and the official title of the PT'A' Council was amended to become the Professions Allied to Medicine and Related Grades PAM(PT'A') Council. However, until the negotiating arrangements for the clinical biochemists and hospital physicists has been satisfactorily resolved, the staff side composition remains as it has been since 1948. It must be remembered, therefore, that the organization's proportional seat allocation includes provision for speech therapists and hospital chaplains as well as clinical biochemists, hospital physicists and other scientists. The organizations who claim representational rights for these groups are mainly ACB, HPA, NALGO and MSF.

The staff side has 22 members, with the largest number of five allocated to the CSP. MSF, BAOT, COHSE, NALGO, NUPE and the Society of Radiographers each have two seats. The remainder have one seat each: ACB, BDA, BOS, HPA and the Society of Chiropodists.

Hospital Medical and Dental Staffs Whitley Council

The Hospital Medical and Dental Council for practical reasons is in abeyance and never meets. It exists in order that the staff side can be represented on the GWC. Negotiations take place in two Joint Negotiating Committees (see below) which also exercise any residual Whitley functions. Since 1963 the pay for hospital doctors and dentists, community doctors and dentists and general medical practitioners has been recommended by the Review Body on Doctors' and Dentists' Remuneration.

Number of staff covered: (1987) 50 300 (excluding locums).

There are two main committees:
The Joint Negotiating Committee (JNC) for Hospital, Medical and Dental Staff which is divided into two subcommittees: JNC(S) for senior staff and JNC(J) for junior staff
The Joint Negotiating Body for Doctors in Community Medicine and the Community Health Service.

Maintenance staff

As previously mentioned, there is no Whitley Council for NHS maintenance staff, but a Maintenance Staff Management Advisory Panel (MAP) has been established to advise on matters referred to it by the Health Departments and the NHS management in general. The Advisory Panel comprises management only, but for pay negotiations it meets the trade union representatives.

Number of staff covered: (1987) 23 000

The management side has three generalists, four specialists and four from the Health Departments.

The staff side has eight members: two from the EEPTU and one each from CSEU, UCATT, NUPE, COHSE, GMB and the TGWU.

The scope and seat allocation of the General Whitley Council (GWC)

The GWC maintains the Whitley constitution and deals with conditions of service and similar matters which are of general application. Except where provision is made to the contrary, GWC agreements apply to all staff within the scope of the Whitley Councils.

The constitution of the GWC differs from those of the functional councils since its membership is principally composed of members of each of the functional councils. The GWC has 56 members of which a maximum of 27 are management side representatives who are:

1. The chairs of the management sides of the following functional councils: A&C, Ancillary, Ambulance, N&M, PT'A' and PT'B'.
2. The chair for the time being of the management side of Committee A of the Optical Council.
3. The chair for the time being of the management side of Committee A of the Pharmaceutical Council.
4. Plus a maximum additional number of members as follows: 14 from the English and three from the Welsh health authorities, and five from the Scottish health boards. In addition there are five from the Departments.

The staff side has 29 members: four each nominated from A&C, Ancillary, Hospital Medical and Dental, and Nursing and Midwifery Staffs. Three each from Pharmaceutical, PT'A' and PT'B' Staffs, two from Ambulance Staff, and one each from Optical and Community Dentists.

AGREEMENTS FROM WHITLEY

The GWC deals with NHS staff conditions of service that are of general application other than those allocated to functional councils. The failure of an employing authority to meet these conditions or to apply them in a manner with which an employee feels aggrieved, entitles that individual, through his or her recognized staff side organization, to seek a satisfactory resolution of the problem through appeals procedures that are established by the GWC.

The GWC meets on four occasions a year, and the agreements that it reaches are circulated to all employing authorities and

subsequently published in the GWC Handbook. The agreements broadly relate to:
1. Leave of absence for annual and public holidays, and for special purposes.
2. Expenses.
3. Miscellaneous issues.
4. NHS reorganization.
5. Redundancy and premature retirement entitlements.
6. Protection of pay and conditions of service.
7. Employee relations and procedures for settling differences.

The first 17 agreements of the GWC Handbook relate to the annual and public holiday entitlements which apply to NHS staff and can be divided into three sections:
1. Sections 14–17 relate to employees' entitlements for leave to attend meetings of Whitley Council, local authority or community councils (local health council in Scotland) and to appear as a witness at a Whitley appeal hearing.
2. Sections 8–13 establish an employee's rights of absence for civil or military duties (such as jury service, magisterial duties, parliamentary candidature or training with the Reserve and Cadet forces).
3. Sections 1–7 include statutory and public holiday entitlements, leave for compassionate reasons, to attend a job interview with another employing authority and for maternity reasons.

The latter agreement (Section 6) defines the conditions under which women are entitled to paid maternity leave, the procedures that must be followed in order to receive paid leave (e.g. written notification of the expected week of confinement and the date upon which she intends to return to work), the entitlement to alternative employment during pregnancy, her entitlement to sick leave and time off for ante-natal care. Paragraph 8 of Section 6 stipulates an employee's right to return to her job under her original contract and on no less favourable terms and conditions, while paragraph 13 lays down the financial costs to an employee who, after notifying her employing authority of her intention to return to work, fails to do so.

Sections 22–27 cover the expenses entitlements which apply to all NHS staff. These are subsistence allowances, travelling expenses, expenses of candidates for appointment, reimbursement of telephone expenses, removal expenses (which include expenses and paid leave while searching for accommodation, 'bridging' loans, payment of removal expenses and excess rent allowances). In August 1987 Section 24 was amended to allow employing authorities, where they deemed it economic to do so, to offer Crown cars to employees who are required to travel regularly on NHS business. This section also specifies the mileage allowances and associated provisions, to which all eligible NHS staff are entitled.

Section 51 affirms the GWC's commitment to equal opportunities in employment within the NHS. Section 52 points out that any employee who is elected to Parliament will not receive any special facilities. Section 53 advises employees who wish to contest local authority elections. Section 54 establishes when annual salaries are to be paid. Section 55 contains advice to employing authorities with regard to providing reasonable facilities for staff to prepare for their retirement, and Section 57 briefly lists the qualifying days for Statutory sick pay. Each of the functional councils' handbooks have a section dedicated to this topic.

The GWC establishes procedures that have to be followed when staffing arrangements are changed following a reorganization within the service. The way in which staff compete for posts or simply 'slot' into a new post are described in Sections 62 for England, 65 for Wales and 68 for Scotland, and the Appeals systems for staff aggrieved under these arrangements are Section 63 (England), 66 (Wales) and 69 (Scotland).

Section 45 of the GWC Handbook covers the arrangements that apply to any NHS staff who are made redundant. The minimum qualifying period is: (a) 104 weeks' continuous service whole time, or 16 or more hours a week part-time; (b) five years' continuous service of eight or more hours a week, after reaching the age of 18. The redundancy payment is a lump sum dependent upon the employee's age and reckonable service when he or she ceases to be employed.

This agreement also lists those who are excluded from eligibility (e.g. those dismissed for misconduct), definitions of suitable alternative employment in terms of place and type of employment that an employer can 'reasonably' offer an employee and the entitlement to early release from an employing authority of redundant employees who wish to take up employment outside the NHS. Finally, paragraph 12 of Section 45 asserts that if an employee is dissatisfied with an employing authority's calculation of redundancy payment, this matter is not subject to the normal channels of regional or national appeal, but is referred to the tribunal provided in Section 112 of the EP(Consolidation)Act 1978.

The immediate payment of superannuation on premature retirement is agreed under Section 46. It provides for such payment for eligible employees on redundancy 'in the interests of the efficiency of the service', and where 'in contemplation or furtherance of organizational change (statutory or managerial), the premature retirement would be in the interests of the service'.

In this agreement 'retirement age' means the age at which, under any written condition of employment, an employee may be required to retire, or if there is no such condition, age 65. In all cases the employee must be aged between 50 and retirement age and have at least five years' service within the NHS superannuation scheme, and the levels at which volunteers will be selected for premature retirement on organizational change are then established.

It can be seen that for those NHS employees who are made redundant the GWC redundancy agreement is little better than the statutory minimum, and for those ineligible to premature payment of superannuation as outlined in section 46, redundancy is certainly not a good option in the NHS.

The protection of pay and conditions of service for all NHS staff is enshrined in Section 47. This agreement applies to any employee who, as a consequence of organizational change, is required by management to move to a new post or suffers a reduction in basic hours worked within the standard working week. Long term protection of basic wage or salary is provided where downgrading is involved. An employee who is moved from one post to another and who is downgraded as a result of the move, is entitled to full protection of basic wage or salary, with benefit of any subsequent improvements or increments applying to the scale until the period of years specified expires.

The other occasions when 'protection' of salary would cease are when the normal basic wage or salary of the new post equals or exceeds the protected one, when the employee moves to a post with another authority on his/her own application, where the basic wage or salary is lower or equal to that of the existing post, or the person retires. There are also contingencies for 'mark-time' payments and interaction between short-term and long-term protection.

The conditions of service that can be protected include annual leave allowances while the basic pay is fully protected, period of notice appropriate to the former post, and subsistence rates applicable to the former post until the protected period expires.

The current protection agreement is due to be reviewed by the GWC not later than 31 March 1993 when it is open to the GWC either to extend the prescribed period or to negotiate alternative protection provisions.

Employees who feel aggrieved at employing authorities' decisions under Section 47 are entitled to take the matter to appeal by means of Sections 34 and 32.

It was noted that the GWC constructed a framework for local consultation in 1979 which became Section 39 of the GWC Handbook and, in 1980, a local disputes procedure was agreed (Section 33).

Section 39 recognizes that in many places joint consultative machinery already exists and where management and representatives of recognized staff organizations agree that existing arrangements are satisfactory, then these should not be changed. Because of the great variety in sizes, types and location of units, the GWC did not consider it practicable to prescribe any standard pattern for joint consultative machinery, but drew attention to the general principles that were outlined in recommendations 46 and 47 in Chapter 11 of McCarthy's report.

Section 33 points out that the GWC attaches great importance to the establishment of clear procedures for settling disputes which cannot be resolved through the existing Whitley appeals machinery. It is designed to deal with the local application of national Whitley agreements. In determining the content of local procedures, Section 33 provides the following guidance.

- The levels to which a dispute should be referred should be spelled out clearly in agreements.
- Disputes should be settled at the lowest possible operational level and the GWC recommend four stages of referral.
- If these procedures fail to resolve the dispute, then either party should be able to refer the dispute to a locally convened panel.
- This panel should consist of an independent chair (acceptable to both sides) and two members on each side appointed by the employing authority and the recognized staff organization(s) concerned.
- The role of chair would be that of a conciliator.

If the panel is unable to resolve the dispute, it may be referred to ACAS.

Status quo ante should operate until the agreed disputes procedures have been exhausted. If the dispute arises from the suspension or dismissal of an employee, the disciplinary procedures should apply.

The GWC contends that a dispute should be resolved within two months of the date when it was first brought to the attention of the employee's immediate local manager.

It is the case that the vast majority of disputes procedures that have been established throughout the NHS follow the GWC's recommended procedures.

Section 38 of the GWC Handbook is the facilities agreement for staff organizations in the NHS and establishes the minimum provisions to which accredited representatives of recognized staff organizations are entitled.

Finally, Sections 32 and 40 are the appeals procedures that apply for staff who (a) wish to appeal against decisions that affect their conditions of service – which includes grading – and (b) wish to appeal against disciplinary action that has resulted in a formal written warning or dismissal.

a)   Section 32

This enables any employee aggrieved in any matter that affects his or her conditions of service (other than dismissal or any disciplinary action) to appeal to the employing authority. If, following such an appeal, they are still aggrieved, then it is open to their recognized staff side organization to appeal to the GWC Regional Appeals secretariat for the matter to be heard at a Regional Appeal. If such an appeal is granted, a panel of not more than six members (eight members when the matter is within the purview of the Ancillary Staffs Council) are appointed in equal numbers by the management side and staff side. The management side members are selected from a panel representative of the Regional Health Authority, District Health Authority in the area of the RHA, Boards of Governors, Special Health Authorities and Departmental representatives.

The staff side members are selected from representatives of the recognized professional association or trade union. Clearly when grading issues are involved, most of the professional associations call upon experienced practitioners to sit on these panels in order that their specialist knowledge of the profession be put to positive use.

An appeal to the Regional Appeals committee has to be lodged with the management side secretary of the committee within three months of the receipt by the employee of notice of the decision on the appeal made to the employing authority. Written submissions have to be submitted by both sides and when the management side secretary receives these, a copy of each statement is sent to each member of the committee and to the staff side secretary of the appropriate Whitley council. Three copies of each statement are then sent to the two parties to the dispute together with a notification of the date and place of the hearing. This has to be as soon as possible, and in any event should be within a period of two months from the application.

The procedure that must be followed at each hearing is enshrined under paragraph 14 of GWC Section 32 and if, after considering both side's submissions, the committee fails to reach a decision, then it is open to either party to the dispute to refer the matter to the appropriate Whitley council within a three months' timescale. If the joint secretaries of the council agree to hear this appeal, it has to be heard as soon as possible – again a period of two months is recommended as being the maximum time scale – and the matter can either be heard by the full council, or a committee of that council. If this committee fails to agree, then paragraph 17 of Section 32 contains the following:

> it shall be open to either party to the dispute to refer the matter to arbitration in accordance with the terms of any arbitration agreement which may be made by the GWC (Section 32, paragraph 17).

It is, therefore, the case that any NHS employee who is aggrieved over a decision made by the employing authority over conditions of service, provided that employee is a member of a recognized staff side organization, is able to have his or her case considered from local level up to national. However, although recommended time limits are set out in the appeal procedures, as the nurses and midwives found following the 1988 grading review, in a service with over a million employees, if more than 20 000 of them wish to pursue a case through the proper appeals machinery, it can take several years before the matter reaches a regional, let alone national level. Equally, if the Whitley Council appeal panel fails to agree – a majority decision has to be a majority of both sides – then, such an inconclusive end to a long drawn out case can be the cause of great frustration.

b)   Section 40

This establishes the appeals procedure that employees of an authority are entitled to pursue if they are aggrieved by disciplinary action which either results in their receiving either a reprimand and formal written warning, or in their being dismissed. It is the employing authority which has to set up appeals committees which must consist of not less than three members of the authority, with preferably at least one member having a special knowledge of the field of work of the appellant. Failing this, at the appellant, or their representative's request, an assessor can advise the committee on professional matters. Employees may appear personally before the committee, either alone or represented by their trade union or professional organization. Alternatively, they may elect to be legally represented, but if they make such a choice they have to bear the costs, and in this situation, the employing authority may also elect to employ legal representation.

A speedy hearing is also recommended, with a three week time limit, for the appellant to lodge the appeal after receipt of the notice in writing of the disciplinary action. The hearing of the appeal by the committee should then take place within five weeks, and the employee be given at least 14 days' notice of the date of the hearing. Paragraph 8 of Section 40 details the procedure that the appeal committee must follow in order properly to hear both sides of the case, which includes its discretion to adjourn the appeal in order to obtain further evidence from either party, or for any other reason. The committee, with the officer appointed as secretary to the committee (usually a member of the personnel department) and, where appropriate, the assessor, then reach their decision.

If this decision still leaves the employee aggrieved, then he or she can appeal to a higher authority, namely the appropriate Secretary of State or, in the case of employees of the DHAs in England, the Regional Health Authority. It is at their discretion what action is subsequently taken. If the RHA decide that the case merits a further hearing, then the same procedures that applied at the district hearing apply for the regional hearing.

This is the limit to which an appeal against a disciplinary matter can be referred within the NHS. In the case of dismissal, of course, the appellant has the statutory right of referral to an Industrial Tribunal.

It is the case that within the NHS there are some who seek to see the appeals system radically changed. The National Association of Health Service Personnel Officers (NAHSPO) complained to the Social Services Committee in January 1989 that the Appeal arrangements were 'anachronistic, cumbersome and burdensome'.[69] The thousands of appeals that were lodged by the nurses and midwives following the 1988 regrading exercise probably had a large part to play in their contention that regional and national grading appeals machinery is but an extension of the bargaining process and even its reopening. NAHSPO further claimed that:

> It is a nonsense that an authority with 3000, let alone up to 15 500 staff should be obliged to hear directly appeals not only on dismissal, but also even on final written warnings from ANY member of its staff against such disciplinary action. It should be possible for the health Authority as employer, to determine and agree their own appropriate arrangements for appeals machinery. Appeals need to be aligned with those responsible for handling the consequences (particularly cost) and of their succeeding.[70]

The terms and conditions of service that apply generally throughout the NHS are established by the GWC and published within the GWC Handbook, an up-to-date copy of which has to be readily available within each employing authority. By the end of the 1980s the vast majority of employing authorities, in accordance with their statutory requirement, have negotiated with their JCCs their own written grievance as well as disciplinary and disputes procedures, but when these local procedures have been exhausted, it is open to all NHS employees, through their recognized trade union or professional association, to take their case beyond the local boundaries and have the matter ultimately decided at Whitley Council or Secretary of State level.

One reason for summarizing the GWC Handbook in such detail is to illustrate the extreme difficulties SGT managers will face when they seek to determine terms and conditions of employment for thousands of health staff at the level of the employer.

PAY DETERMINATION REVISITED

The conditions of service established by the GWC and the procedures by which grievances and disputes that arise over terms and conditions for all NHS staff can be resolved were described above. However, it is at the functional Whitley councils that the salary levels of specific groups of staff are established, whether this is by means of collective bargaining or a system of pay review. It is the functional councils where negotiations take place over the grading definitions and qualification requirements for the particular staff groups, as well as conditions of service in respect of, for instance, hours of work, annual leave, overtime and emergency duty payments and sick leave arrangements. Some councils also have various miscellaneous agreements which may include agreements over the payment of fees for lectures, study leave arrangements and incentive bonus schemes.

In 1979 the government introduced cash limits into the health service and the 1987 Health Services Act imposed a statutory duty upon health authorities not to exceed them.[71] This imposition of cash limits upon the NHS marked the reality of the Conservative Party's 1979 manifesto declaration that public sector pay should not be decided on the basis of comparability but by affordability, which represented a radical departure from one of the essential principles of pay determination that had long operated in the public sector.[72] Traditionally, the pay of NHS employees had been linked, with varying degrees of formality, with both internal and external comparators.

Since the NHS employs a wide range of occupational groups, the comparisons that were employed were necessarily diverse. For example, ancillary workers had links with local authority manual workers, and A&C staff with administrative grades in the Civil Service. NHS craftsmen had the only comparison with the private sector by being linked with electricians' pay rates in the electrical contracting industry[73] and ambulance staff, when they moved into the NHS in 1974, continued their links with local authority manual workers.

Following the 1979 dispute, the government broke the link between local authority manual workers and NHS ancillaries by bringing them into line through a common settlement date, rather than the local authority settlement date which preceded that of the NHS. They then pressed for a common pay settlement date of 1 April for all NHS employees which was achieved in 1980 and this assisted in breaking the various Civil Service analogues.[74] In 1981 the government set a pay 'norm' for the public sector and the government pay allowance within cash limits was set at 6% (nurses received 6% that year, while ancillary staff settled for between 6.1 and 8.4%). In 1982 the pay provision within cash limits was set at 4%, and this was the offer made to ancillary and clerical staffs in the NHS (although nurses and PAMs were offered 6.4%) against an 'across the board' claim by NHS staff for a 12% increase.

At the end of the 1982 dispute the final two-year agreement included pay increases of 7.5% for nurses, midwives and PAMs, 6.5% for ambulance staff and hospital pharmacists and 6.0% for other health workers. For the nurses and midwives and PAMs this package included an offer to establish an independent Review Body for their pay. In January 1983 the Secretary of State for Health announced to the House of Commons that such a system was to be established for these two groups of staff, but at the same time he made it clear that there was no possibility of similar bodies being established for other NHS staff. He informed the House:

> It has been clear from the beginning that there will be no question of the Review Body covering, for example, ancillary workers, administrative workers and clerical workers. We have made our position clear.[75]

The imposition of cash limits upon health authorities poses several problems for Whitley Council negotiations. First, it restricts the ability of management side representatives to negotiate according to the merits of the case and it means that the level of awards for non-PRB groups tends to be similar across the functional councils. However, the imposition of cash limits is not uniformly applied because the 60% of staff who have their pay adjudicated by a PRB have a means of overcoming these limitations. Although the Department, in its evidence to the Review Bodies, always presses the 'affordability' case, the Review Body has publicly emphasized that 'affordability is one of a number of important factors that we take into account in arriving at our recommendations, but it is not the overriding consideration'.[76] Thus, whenever the Review Body has recommended salaries over and above the established cash limits, the government has been able to make additional funds available in addition to the amounts already allowed for in financial allocations. The fact that cash limits have been waived for these groups of staff has led many in NHS management who were not enthusiastic about the creation of the Review Bodies to criticize the fact that there are two systems of pay determination operating in the NHS.

While the Minister of Health informed the Social Services Committee that pay gaps caused by the two-tier system were 'unavoidable', one district general manager expressed a different view of the situation, with which the Social Services Committee concurred. This was that it was not the machinery that was necessarily the cause of the problem, but rather 'the affordability limit given to the parties. ... The problem now arising is that there is not the sense of fairness perceived in the way the Review Body staff are treated and the way non-Review Body staff are treated.'[77]

Chapter 6 describes the manner in which the management and staff sides make their annual submissions to the Pay Review Body with written and oral presentations offering both sides ample opportunities to press home their claims. The Review Body's remit is only related to pay issues; other conditions of service are still collectively negotiated at the Nurses and Midwives and PAM(PT'A') Councils.

For the remaining 40% of NHS staff, each of the staff side organizations' views on a pay claim is considered by the staff side as a whole and a single staff side claim is then formulated and agreed. On some functional councils and committees, one union may predominate in membership or number of seats and will effectively determine the claim for the whole staff side. In other functional councils, organizations with numerically small representation may play an important role in agreeing the staff side claim.

The staff side claim is normally presented formally to the management side at a meeting of the full functional council or committee. On some councils the claim is referred to a joint negotiating committee of members from both sides, while on others, negotiations are conducted by the full council.

The date on which staff sides submit their claims varies, but in the 1970s and 1980s it has been during November or December. The management side usually responds formally to the presentation of the claim, with arrangements to reply in detail at a future meeting. In practice, no serious negotiations begin until the government announcement of the increase that will be made, from 1 April that year, to the Pay Review Body groups. The month that the government makes this announcement, together with the publication of the pay review reports, was brought forward in 1989 from May to February and this may well improve the general pay-round timetable. It is generally the case that the focus of pay negotiations in the NHS then shifts to the Ancillary Staffs Council and the percentage increase in pay for this group of workers is usually the 'going rate' for the remaining non-pay review groups within the NHS.

Pay negotiations have regularly been extremely protracted and often it has been September before a conclusion has been reached. Although many meetings may have occurred, it is seldom that the variation from the original management side offer exceeds 1%. The staff side may respond to the management side's first offer with proposals for ways in which the claim could be met, and it is rare for the management side to respond. The proposals are generally referred to consultation with regional chairs, and on some occasions go to wider discussion within the service. At the same time, regular discussions are assumed to be held between the Department civil servants and their counterparts in the Treasury. In some years possible pay offers have been referred to subcommittees of the Cabinet.[78] By the time that agreements have been concluded, and the Secretary of State has authorized the new payments, it is unlikely that staff will receive the pay increase due to them in April or the following months.

Once the new salary scales have been approved at national level, whether by means of pay review or through collective bargaining, employing authorities must, by statute, ensure that they are implemented. Any local variation to a nationally agreed salary level requires the prior approval of the Secretary of State who, after obtaining the approval of the joint secretaries of the relevant council, has to issue the appropriate variation order. There is, therefore, no local collective pay bargaining in the NHS although, as will be discussed below, moves towards some form of flexibility in these central arrangements have already begun and the proposals for SGTs include the option for them to establish their own non-Whitley terms and conditions for staff.

McCarthy raised the question of the inflexibility of the various grading structures that existed within the NHS[79] and over a decade later this same view was voiced to the Social Services

Committee by NAHA, who claimed that 'national agreements are generally thought to be too inflexible for the needs of local managers'.[80] Each functional council negotiates the grading structure for those groups of staff within its purview. The range of work that is performed within the NHS is clearly diverse and the grading structures that have evolved throughout the service necessarily have reflected such diversity. Medical, nursing, scientific and professional staff must be 'state registered' to work in the NHS and throughout all of the functional councils, in order to reach a given grade, defined tasks and/or qualifications and/or skill levels have to be met. It is the high level of 'prescription' that the Whitley grading structures have traditionally contained that has led to increasing complaints by employing authorities and their representatives that the grading system meant there was 'too much fitting jobs to Whitley rather than Whitley to jobs'.[81]

The alternative view to this argument, of course, is that without such clear instruction contained in the grading structure, many employers, particularly when faced with revenue difficulties, would be tempted to use a totally 'flexible' grading structure, not to reward staff for their expertise or skill, but, as one general manager informed a gathering of Whitley negotiators, 'to pay them as little as they could possibly get away with'.

For each grade of staff in the NHS (with the notable exception of the new 'General' and Senior Manager grades) there are a range of incremental points attached to each grade which the employee annually ascends until the top increment is reached. Thus, for example, a radiographer who 'is working under the direct clinical supervision of a senior or superintendent radiographer'[82] would be accorded the grade of 'Radiographer' and from 1 April 1989 to 31 March 1990 would have received an annual salary of £8620 which rose in four increments to £10 250 per annum. Similarly, a radiographer who is:

> responsible for one other qualified officer or assistant OR working single-handed: or carrying responsibilities greater than those of a Radiographer OR mainly undertaking duties requiring the exercise of a particular expertise or ability ... [83]

would be entitled to the grade of Senior II and a salary that from 1 April 1989 to 31 March 1990 ranged in four increments from £10 250 to £12 270 per annum.

Definitions as specific as these were, until the late 1980s, commonplace throughout the NHS, and while most staff sides wished to see changes that would reflect new working practices and skills, they were less inclined to believe that the degree of 'flexibility' that both the government and many of the management sides sought would be in the best interest of their members. However, between 1986 and 1989 the majority of functional councils renegotiated their job definitions.

The definition of work that is regarded as 'highly skilled and specialized' or 'requiring the exercise of a particular expertise of ability' is specified for each of the different professions with a particular grading structure. The most publicized and, for the government, costly (both in terms of finance and publicity) was the 1988 nurses, midwives and health visitors clinical grading review which, both sides claimed, sought to provide a grading structure that would reward clinical specialists. Although the Nurses and Midwives Council jointly agreed the new structure and an assimilation procedure, when the health authorities began to transfer their nursing staff into the new grades, it became clear that in assimilating staff, all too often it was financial criteria that were being primarily considered, rather than the work that had been, and continued to be performed by each individual. More than three years later, countless appeals by nurses and midwives against regrading decisions have still to be heard at all the Whitley levels.

New grading agreements were reached for ancillary staff in 1986, for ambulance staff in 1986 and for speech therapists in 1988 (although in January 1989 NAHSPO reported that there were currently 1500 plus claims from speech therapists awaiting resolution[84]). It was in 1988 that a new grading agreement was approved for MLSOs and in 1989 that the A&C Council agreed a grading structure that not only reduced the number of grades but which introduced for the first time the facility for employing authorities to pay local pay supplements. The Pharmaceutical Council agreed a new structure in 1989 and the negotiating forum for maintenance staff introduced multi-skilling for electrical, plumbing and engineering staff.

The group of staff who share the same Pay Review Body with the nurses, midwives and health visitors, the PAMs, also entered into negotiations for a new grading structure in 1988. However, the very public difficulties caused by the nurses' regrading exercise led the management side to withdraw from the negotiations, after more than 20 meetings of the two sides had taken place in a three month period. Despite public and private ministerial statements of the government's commitment to a new grading structure for PAMs, despite similar public requests from the Pay Review Body and despite the PAM(PT'A') staff side's willingness to reopen negotiations, it appears unlikely that such a review will occur until well into the 1990s, if at all.

Both McCarthy and the Social Services Select Committee received a good deal of comment on the inconsistencies in the relative pay and conditions of different NHS occupational groups. As the previous sections described, the manner in which pay is negotiated and the wide variety of work that is performed by the million or so employees of the NHS, necessarily leads to such variety. However, it is perhaps somewhat more surprising that conditions of service such as the normal working week, holiday entitlements and early retirement arrangements vary, not only across functional councils, but sometimes among the groups of staff whose conditions are considered by the same council.

Thus, while the nurses and midwives have (since 1981) had a normal working week of 37.5 hours, and ancillary staff hours were reduced in 1988 from 40 to 39 hours, on the PAM(PT'A') Council the range of hours classed as a normal working week varies from 35 for radiographers to 36.5 hours for groups such as chiropodists. Attempts in 1979 by the Clegg Commission to equalize these working hours was met with industrial action by members of most of these groups. It is the case, however, that despite management side resistance, all groups have, for several years, sought to reduce their hours to bring them into line with those of the radiographers.

Equally, among PAM and related grades, while the helpers and foot care assistants are only entitled to four weeks' annual leave, all other grades of staff receive five weeks' annual leave.

A further major difference in conditions of service amongst staff is the provision of, and payment for, emergency duty cover. While for the majority of health service staff their commitment to provide emergency duty cover is voluntary, whether this is 'oncall' at home or on 'standby' at their place of work, for radiographers there is no such option. Since 1958 radiographers have had a contractual obligation – following government regulation – to undertake emergency duties.[85] Because the provision of emergency duty is a condition of service, the radiographers receive a higher rate of payment for 'calls' than any of the other PAM staff.

Other conditions that are nationally negotiated (although these are not necessarily applicable to all functional councils) include: 'acting-up' allowances, additional leave for long service, annual leave entitlements, fees for locum tenems, incentive bonus scheme, minimum periods of notice, overtime payments and payments for lectures, sick leave and sick pay, student training allowances, transfer and promotion arrangements.

In evidence to the Social Services Committee, NUPE pressed the case for common conditions throughout the NHS. NUPE believed that it was no longer appropriate that manual workers, with less security and poorer status, should work longer standard hours, and they called for an end to the discrimination between white- and blue-collar workers.

One of the most significant government initiatives during the 1980s was the appointment of general managers as chief executives of health authorities which followed from the Griffiths Report.[86] Not only did this lead to the end of the 'consensus management' ethos upon which the health service had long been dependent, but it saw pay developments, for the first time, taking place outside the Whitley bargaining arena.

In the first instance, the salaries of the new general managers were determined (in the face of constant opposition from the staff side of the GWC) by the Secretary of State without reference to Whitley. Following this, a differentiated salary structure was introduced which was based on a complex formula attaching weight to 'restructuring' and development activities to be carried out within the manager's region, district or unit. Lastly a system of 'merit' payments was introduced which awarded pay enhancements to general managers dependent upon their performance. Both these schemes were constructed and implemented independently of Whitley.

The 'general management' principle was further extended when in 1987 the pay for senior managers at regional and district level (e.g. regional or district directors of nursing or personnel) was also established by the Secretary of State, despite previous Departmental commitments to the GWC that consultation on these salaries would take place. However, unlike the general managers, the latter group of staff retain their Whitley conditions of service. Proposals for an extension of senior managers' pay arrangements were made in 1989 which have resulted in some 7000 'functional' managers in regions, district and units being offered pay and conditions of service similar to senior managers at regional and district level.

The appointment of district and general managers appears to have had only a superficial effect on collective bargaining in the NHS. Locally, general managers have become the personification of management sides, and while some have spoken of the need to seize the initiative in communicating with, and involving the workforce in decision-making without reference to local trade union reorganization, there is little evidence to suggest that consultative machinery has been dismantled. It seems more likely that, in circumstances where local union organization has been significantly weakened by national initiatives, such as competitive tendering, general managers have found it easier to re-draw the local agendas for consultation.[87]

CONCLUDING COMMENTS

It has been government, rather than management, which has played the principal role in attempts to disestablish and destabilize the longstanding collective bargaining machinery in the NHS. Since 1979 it has been the Conservative government which has taken all the initiatives with only very limited reference to NHS management. The introduction of general management, while it fostered considerable uncertainty within health authorities, encountered little national or local opposition from weakened multi-occupation trade unions, although many of the professional associations conducted both local and national campaigns on behalf of their members. It was the RCN's expensive publicity campaign against the new managerialism that led many of the newly appointed general managers to ensure that their own management structures 'placated' nursing opinion, and within the PAM group, district-wide functional management posts continued to be established in spite of Griffiths's clearly defined 'unitization' of the service.

The ancillary staff unions throughout the 1980s were concerned to defend jobs, while simultaneously attempting to resist privatization. Of the four unions on the Ancillary Staffs functional council, it is COHSE and NUPE who have by far the largest membership and NUPE was particularly active in its opposition to competitive tendering. Although the TUC national policy called for resistance at every stage against privatization, once the health authorities had agreed a timetable for competitive tendering, local trade union representatives had little choice but to be closely involved in negotiating in-house tenders. The practical alternative to this was large-scale redundancies on unfavourable terms. Thus, many local union representatives, with the increasing involvement of full-time officials, agreed, against their personal principles, to negotiate or consult on the form of the in-house tender and for many the campaign became a 'damage limitation' exercise. Many NHS ancillary staff have obtained jobs with private contractors, where their terms and conditions are generally far inferior to those prevailing in the NHS.

For many other groups the major problem is the recruitment and retention of staff. Such difficulties are currently being faced in nursing (particularly in the recruitment of hospital midwives), physiotherapy, occupational therapy, radiography, pharmacy, medical laboratory scientific staff, medical physics and dental technicians, although it is not only amongst nursing, scientific and professional staffs that there are problems. Administrative and clerical staff, particularly medical secretaries, computing and accountancy staff, have become increasingly difficult to recruit and the 'flexibility' of the new A&C grading structure was agreed nationally in an attempt to resolve such problems locally.

The government put the blame for these significant staff shortages in some areas of the country entirely upon the Whitley system. The then Minister of Health informed the Social Services Committee in 1989, 'the monument to Whitleyism is the fact that we cannot fill vacancies in a number of key grades in a number of key parts of the country'.[88] Government perceived the introduced of 'regional pay' and greater 'flexibility' at local levels as the way in which such problems would be resolved. As the Secretary of State informed the House of Commons in November 1988:

> We all know that the costs incurred for staff vary from place to place, as do difficulties in recruitment. ... I believe that ... we should start to reflect local variations in conditions in future pay negotiations for a giant service such as this.[89]

And later that same month:

> We feel that [regional pay] is the only way in which the differing problems about pay that affect the recruitment and retention of essential staff in various part of the country can be resolved.[90]

However, both the staff sides of the Nurses and Midwives and PAM(PT'A') Councils and the NAHSPO drew attention to the fact that rather than resolve problems in recruitment and retention, regional pay would simply 'shift' the shortage from one area to another as staff in short supply chased the higher salaries. NAHSPO informed the Social Services Committee that 'the case for regionalisation of pay has not been made out ... and the starting base in any case would have to be in a far healthier state than it is presently'.[91] NAHA was equally concerned that local premium payments should be offered to groups of staff where the NHS is a monopolistic employer and believed that for non-Review Body staff there should continue to be nationally negotiated rates which should be the rate paid to most staff 'supplemented by local discretion where shown to be necessary in the light of the local market'.[92]

Thus, despite government attempts to undermine the role of many of the functional Whitley councils, through such initiatives as the introduction of Pay Review and the setting of general manager salaries by the Secretary of State, the system still survives. This is because many organizations on both sides of these councils have agreed to some form of 'local' flexibility being allowed to meet changing needs and new staff require- ments within the central bargaining role of the functional Whitley councils.

However, despite the fact that in March 1989 the Social Services Committee was generally supportive of the Whitley Council system of collective bargaining, the question posed by the then Minister of Health in February 1989 as to whether an 'unalloyed central bargaining system [was] really relevant to the 1990s as perhaps it was to the 1940s'[93] cannot be ignored. He went on to point out that:

> We have been trying to create a cadre of managers throughout the system, capable of and willing to take responsibility for a whole host of decisions which in previous times were pushed up the line. ... We want local managers to have ... an ability to determine their own recruitment and retention policies. A key element in that will be the questions of pay and conditions.[94]

NOTES

1   Merrison, A. (1979) *Royal Commission on the National Health Service*, HMSO, London.

2 Elwell, H. (1986) *NHS: The Road to Recovery*, Policy Study No. 78, Centre for Policy Studies, London, p. 27. Peet, J. (1987) *Healthy Competition*, Policy Study No. 86, Centre for Policy Studies London.

3 Social Services Committee of the House of Commons (1989) Third Report, p. xxv.

4 Ibid., p. xxi.

5 Social Services Committee of the House of Commons (1989) Third Report, Minutes of Evidence, 22/2/89, p. 146.

6 Third Report Social Services Committee of the House of Commons (1989) Third Report, p. xxiv.

7 NAHA and King's Fund (1985) *NHS Pay: A Time for Change*, NAHA and King Edward's Hospital Fund for London, London. NAHA and King's Fund (1987) *NHS Pay: Achieving Greater Flexibility*, NAHA and King Edward's Hospital Fund for London, London. NAHA and King's Fund (1988) *Flexible Pay Systems*, NAHA and King Edward's Hospital Fund for London, London.

8 Mailly, R., Dimmock, S. and Sethi, A. (1989) 'Industrial Relations in the National Health Service since 1979', in Mailly, R., Dimmock, S. and Sethi, A. (eds), *Industrial Relations in the Public Services*, Routledge, London, p. 130.

9 Metcalf, D. (1989) 'When Water Notes Dry Up: the Impact of the Donovan Reform Proposals and Thatcherism at Work on Labour Productivity in British Manufacturing Industry', *British Journal of Industrial Relations*, XXVII(1), pp. 1–32. Hayek, F. (1984) *1980s Unemployment and the Unions*, Institute for Economic Affairs, London.

10 Mailly *et al.*, op. cit., pp. 121–2.

11 Morris, G. (1986) *Strikes in Essential Services*, Mansell Publishing, London, pp. 159–161, 166–7.

12 Third Report Social Services Committee of the House of Commons (1989) Third Report, COHSE Minutes of Evidence, 1/2/89, p. 118.

13 Brown, W. and Rowthorn, R. (1990) *A Public Services Pay Policy*, Fabian Tract No. 542, The Fabian Society, London, p. 10.

14 Cleminson, J. (1989) *Review Body ...: Sixth Report on Professions Allied to Medicine*, Cm 578, HMSO, London, p. 17.

15 Social Services Committee of the House of Commons (1989) Third Report, p. xiii.

16 Ibid., NAHA Evidence, p. xiii.

17 Ibid., p. xiv.

18 Ibid., p. xv.

19 Brown and Rowthorn, op. cit., p. 7.

20 *Working for Patients* (1989) Cm 555, HMSO, London.

21 National Audit Office (1987) *Competitive Tendering for Support Services in the NHS*, HMSO, London.

22 Treasury, HM (1986) *Using Private Enterprise in Government*, HMSO, London.

23 Social Services Committee of the House of Commons (1989) Third Report, p. xxii.

24 Labour Research Department (1984) *Defending the NHS*, LRD, London, p. 30.

25 Privatisation Research Unit (1991) *Tender Tactics*, London.

26 Privatisation Research Unit (1990) *The NHS Privatisation Experience*, London.
27 Clay, H. (1929) *The Problem of Industrial Relations*, Macmillan, London, p. 153.
28 Ibid., p. 177.
29 Trades Union Congress Health Services Committee (1981) *Improving Industrial Relations in the National Health Service*, TUC, London, p. 22.
30 General Whitley Council Handbook, Appendix A5.
31 Clegg, H. and Chester, (1957) *Wage Policy and the Health Service*, Blackwell, Oxford, p. 1.
32 Ibid., p. 16.
33 Ibid.
34 Walton, R. and McKersie, R. (1965) *A Behavioral Theory of Labor Negotiations*, McGraw Hill, New York.
35 Clegg and Chester, op. cit., p. 19.
36 Ibid., p. 21.
37 Ibid., p. 93.
38 Loveridge, R. (1971) *Collective Bargaining by National Employees in the UK*, Institute of Labor and Industrial Relations, University of Michigan, Wayne State, p. 148.
39 Guillebaud, C. (1956) *Report of the Committee of Enquiry into the Cost of the National Health Service*, HMSO, London.
40 Loveridge, op. cit., p. 151.
41 Ibid., p. 159.
42 McCarthy, W. (1976) *Making Whitley Work*, HMSO, London, p. 2.
43 Ibid., p. 11.
44 Ibid., p. 51.
45 Ibid., p. 110.
46 Ibid., p. 74.
47 Ibid., p. 85.
48 Ibid., p. 89.
49 Ibid., p. 103.
50 Dimmock, S. and Farnham, D. (1975) 'Working with Whitley in Today's NHS', *Personnel Management*, 7(1), p. 35.
51 Pethyridge, F. (1977) 'The McCarthy Report', *Health Services Manpower Review*, special series 1, pp. 6–7.
52 Fisher, A. (1977) 'A Trade Union View of the McCarthy Report', *Health Services Manpower Review*, special series 1, pp. 8–10.
53 Williams, D. (1977) 'Making Whitley Work', *Health Services Manpower Review*, special series 1, pp. 13–14.
54 Cowie, V. (1977) 'Making Whitley Work', *Health Services Manpower Review*, special series 1, pp. 11–12.
55 Edwards, B. (1979) 'Managers and Industrial Relations', in Bosanquet, N.(ed.), *Industrial Relations in the NHS – the Search for a System*, King Edward's Hospital Fund for London, London, p. 125.
56 Winchester, D. (1983) 'Industrial Relations in the Public Sector', in Bain, G. (ed.), *Industrial Relations in Britain*, Basil Blackwell, Oxford, p. 155.
57 TUC, op. cit., p. 132.
58 Dyson, R. (1982) 'The Future of Whitley and Pay Bargaining', *Hospital and Health Services Review*, September, pp. 237–241.

59 Dyson, R. (1985) 'Making Whitley Work: Is It Time to Stop Trying?', *Health Services Manpower Review*, 11(1), pp. 4–6.
60 Leopold, J. (1985) 'Whitley II: Prizes and Penalties', *Health and Social Service Journal*, January, pp. 128–9.
61 Leopold, J. and Beaumont, P. (1986) 'Pay Bargaining and Management Strategy in the National Health Service', *Industrial Relations Journal*, 17(1) pp. 32–44.
62 Third Report Social Services Committee of the House of Commons (1989) Third Report, NALGO Minutes of Evidence, 1/2/89, p. 93.
63 Ibid., p. 94.
64 Social Services Committee of the House of Commons (1989) Third Report, p. viii.
65 Mailly *et al.*, op. cit., p. 125.
66 Social Services Committee of the House of the Commons (1989) Third Report, p. ix.
67 Ibid., NALGO Minutes of Evidence, 1/2/89, p. 95.
68 Ibid., NAHSPO Minutes of Evidence, p. x.
69 Ibid., NAHSPO Minutes of Evidence, 18/1/89, p. 36.
70 Ibid.
71 Ibid., p. xi.
72 Mailly *et al.*, op. cit., p. 120.
73 Dyson (1982) op. cit.
74 Mailly *et al.*, op. cit., p. 120.
75 Hansard 18/1/83.
76 Cleminson, J. (1989) *Review Body ...: Sixth Report on Professions Allied to Medicine*, Cm 578, HMSO, London, p. 41.
77 Third Report Social Services Committee of the House of Commons (1989) Third Report, p. xiii.
78 Ibid., NUPE Minutes of Evidence, 1/2/89, p. 112.
79 McCarthy (1976), op. cit., p. 69.
80 Social Services Committee of the House of the Commons (1989) Third Report, NAHA Minutes of Evidence, 18/1/89, p. 55.
81 Ibid., NAHSPO Minutes of Evidence, 18/1/89, p. 37.
82 PTA Handbook, paragraph 2067.
83 Ibid., paragraph 2066.
84 Social Services Committee of the House of the Commons (1989) Third Report, NAHSPO Minutes of Evidence, 18/1/89, p. 37.
85 Health Circular (58)44: Radiographer, emergency duty, 5/6/58, Ministry of Health.
86 Griffiths, R. (1983) *NHS Management Inquiry*,
87 Mailly *et al.* op. cit., p. 147.
88 Third Report Social Services Committee of the House of Commons (1989) Third Report, p. xxi.
89 Hansard 1/11/88, vol. 142, col. 806.
90 Hansard 22/11/88, vol. 142, col. 108.
91 Social Services Committee of the House of Commons (1989) Third Report, NAHSPO Minutes of Evidence, 18/1/89, p. 37.
92 Ibid., NAHA Minutes of Evidence, p. 57.
93 Ibid., Minister of Health Minutes of Evidence, 22/2/89, p. 146.
94 Ibid., p. 147.

Chapter 6

Deadlocked: arbitration, industrial action and pay review

INTRODUCTION

When negotiations become deadlocked for whatever reason then the parties either resort to a stoppage of work – a strike or a lockout – or seek outside help (third party intervention, which in extreme cases means arbitration). Industrial action or arbitration normally are used in cases of disputes of interest when new conditions of employment are sought. They are rarely used for disputes of right over the interpretation of existing agreements. The Pay Review Body initiative can be viewed as a form of arbitration to prevent, rather than to settle, disputes of interest.

The development of Pay Review Bodies in the 1980s to determine the pay of over half the NHS staff raises many important issues. These include the very nature of pay review. One argument is that the Pay Review Bodies are standing versions of previous short-lived pay inquiries such as those for doctors with Pilkington, and for nurses with Halsbury and later Clegg. Another view is that they are simply the creatures of government designed to make a public sector pay policy appear independent. Alternatively they can be seen as a device to prevent industrial action and/or quitting of individuals through mutually accepted arbitration. Whatever their true purpose and function these bodies have become a major plank of pay control for certain types of public sector worker. Their worth is such that other groups are demanding forms of pay review such as schoolteachers,[1] and others in the NHS such as ambulance staff.

This chapter examines the use of arbitration in the NHS, and then considers the general issues of industrial action in the NHS with brief summary references to the disputes in 1972, 1974, 1975, 1979, 1982 and 1989. Finally, the chapter examines pay review itself within the NHS in light of the discussion on arbitration and industrial action.

The argument is that pay review represents a form of permanent and compulsory arbitration which operates within cash limits imposed by the government and which is specifically designed to prevent industrial action through commonly accepted notions of being fair and, importantly, of being seen to be fair. If this suggests that there is some government pay strategy then it is not intended to also suggest that it is other than short-term and limited to the professionals in the NHS. Brown and Rowthorn suggest that Pay Review Bodies further illustrate their contention that 'Britain has entered the 1990s with a public service pay structure in disarray. This will breed short-run problems'.[2]

The point at issue is the continuation and desirability of collective bargaining as the most favoured mechanism for pay determination for any group of workers in our form of society. As the Webbs understood, and as Clay and later Clegg elaborated, collective bargaining depends on recognized trade unions:

> Moreover, it is the trade union alone which can supply the machinery for the automatic interpretation and the peaceful revision of the general agreement. To collective bargaining, the machinery of trade unionism may bring, in fact, both continuity and elasticity.[3]

The logic of collective bargaining is that mechanisms must exist to deal with disputes. These are different as between the machinery required for making new agreements (disputes of interest) and that for interpreting existing agreements (disputes of right). The importance of such mutually acceptable means of settlement was made clear by the Webbs:

> it is impossible to deny that the perpetual liability to end in a strike or a lockout is a grave drawback to the method of collective bargaining.[4]

The prime objective of the current NHS reforms is to prepare the way for selling off large sections of the service. The vital industrial relations aim must be to raise labour productivity and to do so through greater managerial flexibility over the labour process and the costs of employing staff. Collective bargaining may present one way of achieving these objectives, but it has attendant risks for the employer associated with strong unions and industrial action. These risks are great for managers but greater for the government. Arbitration was one of the favoured methods to reduce this risk even at the cost of some loss of managerial control. Pay review also reduces the risk at the cost to managers of losing control over their pay budgets.

It remains unclear how pay review will slot into the new pay determination models for SGTs and DMUs. NAHA and many of the unions want a mix between national pay determination, in any form, and local discretion. This, however, denies the financial logic of the NHS reform programme by allowing too high a level of total costs to be decided outside of the business. If pay review is then replaced by a complete pay determination system at the level of the single employer then either arbitration or industrial action is likely to become an increasingly important element within the new industrial relations. This will be the case whether trade unions are recognized or not. And will be more likely, rather than less likely, with the extensive use of job evaluation structures and performance related pay schemes.

ARBITRATION

Arbitration is best defined by the Webbs:

> The essential feature of arbitration as a means of determining the conditions of employment is that the decision is not the will of either party, or the outcome of negotiation between them, but the fiat of an umpire or arbitrator.[5]

The usual process of events is that negotiations become deadlocked and that neither party wishes a stoppage, they agree, therefore, to abide by the decision of an impartial outsider sometimes acting with representative assessors. Each party prepares a case, often rather elaborate, and this is laid before the tribunal. A key element in any decision will be the terms of reference, and these may themselves be subject to some form of conciliation or even mediation. The umpire's judgement is given in precise terms, but the relevant and deciding facts behind the decision are not revealed to the parties. Where arbitration is like collective bargaining is that the decision usually applies to all those involved and therefore there is no room for individual bargaining within the settlement. In other words, it establishes a standard rate for the represented workgroup.

The Webbs considered that this form of arbitration supplemented rather than supplanted collective bargaining and therefore was really a form of conciliation, and while acknowledging its high value in resolving wages disputes, it remains a 'temporary expedient' as the 1896 Act recognized.[6] Today's guardians of these mechanisms, ACAS, commented on the public sector in the 1980s thus:

> The most notable feature of our arbitration and mediation activities in 1989 were an increase, for the first time for some years, in the number of requests received by the Service and the significant contribution made by this type of third-party assistance to the resolution of several complex and long-running disputes in the public sector. In the early years of the decade recourse to arbitration had declined, reflecting the changing climate of industrial relations and changes in procedural agreements in the public sector. Many of these had previously provided that either party had the right to refer unresolved issues to arbitration, binding the other party to the process and its outcome.[7]

These points about government policy changing the nature of disputes resolution and therefore deliberately opening the way for industrial action applied with considerable force to the NHS. In 1956 Clegg and Chester noted:

> Of the 53 'major' settlements in the health service from 1948 to 1955, twenty-six were the result of decisions of the Industrial Court, the National Arbitration Tribunal, or the Industrial Disputes Tribunal. If anything these figures underrate the importance of arbitration.[8]

They argued that this happened because the 'staff side frequently seek arbitration because it pays them to do so'.[9] The reasons for the management side to allow cases to go to arbitration when they could prevent it by increasing their offer lie not in the industrial relations of the NHS but, then as now, with 'the need of the Ministry of Health, and of the Treasury, for political protection'.[10] When government urges wage restraint on others it cannot be seen to award state employees higher rates unless it is the decision of the independent arbitrator or Pay Review Body.

From what Clegg and Chester said it should be apparent that there was no internal industry arbitration system. As Loveridge claimed:

> As a result of this management stand taken in the early days of the Health Service a special board of arbitration has never been appointed. On the suggestion of management the Industrial Court has become the chief arbitration body for the NHS.[11]

In 1959 the Terms and Conditions of Employment Act effectively blocked traditional NHS staff side applications for arbitration. The main use of arbitration in the NHS before 1964 was by the ancillary and A&C staff, the professions preferred the *ad hoc* review. The delays and frustrations of Whitley tied with the prevailing economic conditions and the lack of conciliation and arbitration machinery put pressure on government and employers to adopt new pay determination mechanisms. This started with an increase in the number of one-off reviews such as for A&C staff in 1956 under Noel Hall.[12] As a result of Hall's recommendations, the Minister vetoed the Whitley agreement and this led 'on to one of the few nationally led actions taken by union members against the NHS. For five weeks staff side led by NALGO banned all overtime work by clerical and administrative workers'.[13]

The extent to which, until the late 1960s, the government enforced the postwar settlement between Labour and Capital embodied in the trade-off of pay arbitration for industrial peace is stated by Winchester:

> The final feature of collective bargaining to be noted here – the extensive provision of arbitration machinery throughout the public sector – provided further support for the peaceful settlement of conflicts that characterised so much of the first two decades following World War II.[14]

By the mid-1970s Donovan for all, and then McCarthy for the NHS, showed how rapid was government realization and public awareness of the changed reality of trade union influence and worker power at the point of production. If the postwar settlement could not hold in the public services, then what could be expected from the low paid and neglected staff in the NHS?

In 1976 McCarthy found little interest from the management in third party intervention. The staff side, in contrast, were unhappy with the prevailing muddle 'of the present arrangements which might involve approaches to Ministers, senior officials in the Health Departments, MPs or ACAS'.[15] McCarthy found little common ground among any of those involved on the need, type and method of invocation of the third party. McCarthy himself favoured the approach common in other industries of recourse to conciliation and arbitration supplied by ACAS when and if the need arose. This general proposition, he argued, should be enacted in practice at the discretion of functional Whitley Councils. In other words some move towards a more coherent system, but nothing that might outrage current malfunctioning arrangements.

In 1979 some of the national disputes were settled by reference to the Clegg Commission. In 1980 an authority-level disputes procedure was introduced which allowed either party to go to conciliation, and arbitration, if, and only if, both parties supported the application.

In 1981 the TUC wanted an independent NHS arbitration tribunal. The TUC favoured the Donovan approach which 'recommended its use ...., where workers are traditionally reluctant to use industrial action and thus unable "to bring their collective strength to bear" on the employer'.[16] The TUC opposed automatic arbitration, but supported voluntary arbitration arrangements in the form noted above. The Tribunal of three would have one person from each side and an independent chair. ACAS would service it, and references would be by joint agreement and only as a last resort.[17]

The 1980s have seen the government move away from both the use of arbitration in the public sector and the removal of some of the machinery. This was an explicit policy most favoured by Sir Keith Joseph, as the chief strategist in this area, on the basis that arbitrators did not have to pay for their awards. This approach explicitly took on board the likely consequence of more industrial action as the only way of remedying unacceptable employer offers. This certainly happened amongst schoolteachers who embarked on their largest and longest strike in 1985/6,[18] and other affected groups included civil servants, lecturers and local government workers. Arbitration ended in the 1980s for public service workers, but such are the pressures of political life that it resurfaced in another guise. In the NHS this took the form of the DHA disputes procedure, and of pay review.

The thesis presented here is straightforward: among many public service workers arbitration and one-off reviews and/or inquiries and/or commissions have been the acknowledged mechanisms to prevent industrial action and ensure elements of fairness in their pay. When, in the 1980s, these were politically eschewed then the consequence was industrial action. When that occurred in a major way in the NHS amongst groups with strong public support, such as the nurses, then government compromised with pay review. When it occurred with groups that the government felt able to defeat in a public battle, such as schoolteachers, then it ended with the abolition of their pay determination system and its replacement with imposed settlements via a pseudo-pay review (the Interim Advisory Committee), and in the case of the ambulance staff, with straight defeat.

This discussion of arbitration in the NHS, and the view that the Pay Review Bodies are a form of permanent but not very independent arbitration, now moves to examine the type of industrial action that forced arbitration, in any form, on the employers and the government.

INDUSTRIAL ACTION

This chapter comments on national disputes as they impinge on deadlocked negotiations while the next chapter examines local disputes and their resolution. The first major concern is the reluctance of NHS staff to take action which might affect patient care. Just as with schoolteachers, however, there comes a time when most sections of health workers will take some form of industrial action, including strike action.[19]

For many years industrial action in the NHS was virtually unknown. This was due partly to a low level of union membership and partly because 'militancy' was discouraged in case it affected patients. The 1970s witnessed a radical change in the conduct of industrial relations as ancillary workers, followed by nurses, ambulancemen, PAMs and other groups, embarked on major campaigns of disruptive action. In all official disputes the organizers were concerned to protect patients who required urgent treatment or continuous care, with any departures from such advice being blamed upon 'provocative' management action.

The doctors, through the BMA, have been willing, in certain circumstances, to threaten mass resignations of members from the NHS as a form of industrial action. In 1964, for example, the award of the newly formed Review Body 'sparked off a volcanic eruption ... the BMA ... collected undated resignations of general practitioners from the NHS'.[20] This was undoubtedly industrial action aimed at changing the decision of a Review Body influenced by the ultimate employer, the government. It was used as a bargaining counter in order to change the offer of the other party, the employer. There was also a five week overtime ban called by NALGO of its A&C members in 1964. But it was not until 1972 that the first strike in the NHS took place. Morris explains:

> widespread industrial action ... was taken by ancillary workers in support of a claim outside the limits of the Conservative Government's counter-inflation policy. A ballot following a one-day strike, during which cover for emergency operations was maintained, produced a majority in favour of an indefinite strike, but the unions concerned (NUPE, COHSE, TGWU and GMBATU) decided instead on a campaign of selective strikes, overtime bans, working-to-rule and withdrawing cooperation.[21]

In general, neither the unions nor the management knew how to handle the situation, but the government wanted it kept within acceptable limits, given their problems on other industrial fronts, and chose not to use strikebreakers. The action lasted over six weeks and affected about 300 hospitals, but the government was unmoved and the unions settled within pay policy. Most commentators agree that although the unions lost the dispute they won, along with their members, a real victory in terms of altering the balance of power within hospitals. After the dispute ancillary staffs were able to develop more successful local steward networks, local union activists were able to persuade national officials of the importance of their case, and hospital administrators were forced to bargain with ancillary staffs over more issues and with greater concessions. In addition the strike changed the relationship of ancillary staffs with other hospital workers as the latter realized the consequences for everyone of a stoppage of work by this group of low paid and frequently disregarded staff.

This 1972 strike followed the one in 1970 among local government manual workers, with three of the same unions being involved (NUPE, TGWU and GMB). It can be argued that the 1972 strike in hospitals prompted NUPE to examine its internal organization as with the 1975 Warwick study,[22] and helped Albert Spanswick to win the top job in COHSE in 1974.[23] The strike was the result of five years of rapid development in the collective organization of ancillary workers, and the massing together of staff into large district general hospitals. As Carpenter noted about these developments:

> Two things were happening: first, the work was often becoming more remote from the point of patient-contact, and second, those doing it were becoming subject to a more impersonal and 'functional' style of management.[24]

The cause of the 1972/3 dispute was low pay, but as with most strikes there were other important sources of discontent. These included the introduction and operation of the local incentive bonus schemes and the increasing development of managerial policies which tended to alienate and isolate groups of staff. The origins of the action went back to the Labour government's incomes policies and its broken promises with regard to making a special case for the low paid. It is clear that the strike was demanded by the workers and that several of the unions at national level were forced to back their members. It is important to remember that the strike was part and parcel of a wider campaign of wage militancy that brought strike action within the consciousness of white-collar workers, professional staffs and increasingly large numbers of women workers and trade unionists. As Carpenter reports, 'The battle lines were therefore drawn in hospitals up and down the country, and the face of hospital industrial relations was permanently changed'.[25]

This dispute, and the surrounding activity of industrial action and union growth within the public sector, fed into the nurses action of 1974. Taylor points out that as health service unions became more militant so they recruited more members.

> There is clear evidence of a correlation between COHSE militancy and the improved recruitment into the union during the early 1970s. The 1973 ancillary workers' dispute, which was a fiasco, and the 1974 agitation among the nurses, both contributed to an improvement in COHSE's strength. In June 1974 at the height of industrial action over nurses' pay the association received as many as 14,882 members.[26]

Nurses first took industrial action on a national scale in 1974 in support of their demand for an independent inquiry into their pay and conditions, which had failed to keep pace with inflation.

The government initially rejected this demand and the RCN, rather than call for industrial action, threatened that nurses would resign from the NHS and offer their services on an agency basis unless the inquiry was granted. The Labour government agreed and the subsequent inquiry, chaired by Lord Halsbury into nurses' and PAMs' salaries, gave nurses an average increase of 30%. A decade later, the Halsbury salary levels were used as the 'benchmark' for both nurses and PAMs when they first began presenting claims to their Pay Review Bodies.

The 1974 action by nurses was the result of years of neglect and frustration. With further NHS cutbacks under the Conservative government in 1973 and the election of a Labour government in the summer of 1974, the nurses, as with the schoolteachers, pushed hard for an interim pay rise. COHSE led this battle, which started when 'eleven nurses at Storthes Hall Hospital in Huddersfield took unofficial action by striking for an hour and closing three wards'.[27] Again, one consequence of the action was to force COHSE to modernize its activities and democratize its decision-making processes.

The 1974 dispute was based on the fact that nurses pay had fallen in real terms by 11% between 1970 and 1973 as a result of government pay policy. The RCN took the first steps in the 1974 campaign, although it was forced into action by its student section, and was soon backed up by NALGO and COHSE. The form of action was to campaign with mass demonstrations all over the country. COHSE, as was noted, was the spearhead of the activities while NUPE and the GMB stood aloof in order not to embarrass the newly elected Labour government.

As was mentioned in Chapter 2, the RCN under its Rule 12 forbids strike action by its members, and the same applies for the RCM. What does happen, as with doctors, is that the RCN threatens the government with mass resignations from the NHS, as in 1974. This must be counted as a form of industrial action, and so must another tactic used by the RCN and RCM of working to contract, as in the regradings' dispute in the late 1980s.

In 1975 hospital doctors applied sanctions. The consultants' action was in opposition to new proposed contracts which the Labour government wanted following the abolition of private beds from NHS hospitals. The BMA backed a work-to-rule and held the resignations of nearly 7000 consultants. The more important dispute of that year, however, was that involving junior hospital doctors. The junior doctors took action prior to

BMA support. By October over 8000 doctors were involved, and the BMA narrowly decided to back the Hospital Junior Staffs Committee to work a 40 hour week. The official action began in November. The action was unpopular among politicians and senior members of the medical profession alike, but its effects were marked. The ones on patients were hard to measure,[28] but the impact on the BMA and on hospital management was great. The BMA had been forced to sanction a traditional form of industrial action by its members, and hospital managers again were made aware of their lack of expertise in dealing with disputes that impinged on the operation of the hospital. A summary of the dispute argues that:

> The Junior hospital doctors' dispute did not only articulate an argument about overtime pay and hours of work, but contained within itself elements of the deep discontent felt by doctors in this country. And the very persistence and doggedness of the junior doctors encouraged the generally demoralised consultants to renew their industrial action in defence of their private practice privileges inside the NHS.[29]

Again the dispute must be put into the context of the mid-1970s: years of pay restraint and public sector neglect by the Conservatives followed by high hopes of Labour, which were soon met by further disillusion and pay pacts. From 1972 to 1975 the NHS was one of the most strike-prone industries in the UK, and indeed in 1973 the number of days lost through stoppages per 1000 of employees was greater in the NHS (353) then for the whole of Great Britain (324) for the first and only time (see Table 6.1).

The upsurge in trade union membership and action in the NHS, as has been seen in Chapters 2 and 3, had its origin in a range of factors. But a significant one was the operation of incomes policies and the need in the public services to avoid industrial action. This led to the use of one-off pay inquiries to restore pay differences between pay restraint phases. So in 1974 there was Halsbury for nurses and PAMs, in 1971 the NBPI had reported on ancillary staffs, in 1973 there was the Davison inquiry into electricians' pay, and in 1979, Clegg.[30]

What happened in 1979? The first point is that the Labour government, by and large, failed to meet the expectations of its supporters and failed to tackle low pay in the public sector. Indeed it embarked on a series of cutbacks in the NHS from 1976

Table 6.1 Strike data for NHS 1966–1977

Year	No. of NHS staff	No. of stoppages	No. of staff involved	No. of days lost	Average no. of days lost per 1000 NHS staff	Average no. of days lost per 1000 employees in Great Britain
1966	728 838	2	500	500	0.69	100.0
1967	753 486	1	78	200	0.27	124.7
1968	761 747	1	80	80	0.11	211.4
1969	778 998	8	2500	7000	8.99	309.1
1970	792 307	5	1300	6700	8.46	499.2
1971	799 673	6	2900	4700	5.88	625.9
1972	831 753	4	97 000	98 000	117.8	1104.3
1973	843 119	18	59 000	298 000	353.5	324.4
1974	859 468	18	4070	23 000	26.84	661.5
1975	914 068	19	6000	20 000	21.88	270.6
1976	945 877	15	4440	15 000	15.86	149.3
1977	970 900	21	2970	8200	8.44	448.0

Source: Royal Commission into NHS 1979, p. 163.

which led to large numbers of local disputes. This was at a time of wage restraint, mass influx into trade unions, professional and white-collar workers embracing trade union tactics, all within a more left-wing and at times active trade union movement with recent experience of the success of industrial action. In addition there were important changes in the composition of the health workers and their place and type of work. A union such as COHSE experienced an important shift in its membership base away from the dominance of white, male psychiatric nurses towards more women, more black members and more general nurses. In addition favourable employment legislation, the increased use of bonus schemes, fierce union rivalry, and inflation all fuelled the movement to more local union power, the spread of shop stewards, and the willingness to use industrial action.

The 1979 Royal Commission came too late to save the Labour government's NHS policies. In January 1979 COHSE with other NHS unions took industrial action in the so-called 'winter of discontent', highlighting the low pay and unfavourable conditions of ancillary workers in the public sector. This famous and damaging dispute ended when the Labour government set up the Clegg Commission to look into the pay of the relevant groups. It was not the start of a new era of fair comparability in the public services, but rather the end of the social democratic consensus started with Priestley's statement of the state as a fair employer in the mid-1950s. As Morris recounts:

> The 1979 ancillary workers' and ambulancemen's dispute arose when both groups sought increases well beyond the Labour Government's 5 per cent pay limit. A one day strike on January 22 was followed by selective action and various forms of restrictive working. The action had a rapid impact; by January 30, between a third and half of all hospitals were admitting only emergency cases, and over most of the country ambulancemen were handling only emergency calls.[31]

The government offered 9% and the Clegg inquiry, and all the unions bar NUPE accepted. NUPE continued and intensified its action. The government response, which earlier had been cautious as to the use of strikebreakers and management action, now become tougher. This released local managers to act at their discretion, and the dispute ended on the same terms as the other unions by March.

In April 1979, immediately prior to the General Election, the Comparability Commission (chaired by Professor Clegg) was appointed. The groups of NHS employees for which the Commission had a remit were ambulance and ancillary staff (in accordance with the terms of the settlement mentioned above), PAMs and nurses. The Commission produced its first report in August 1979 and although the other reports that followed recommended pay increases on average above the 5% norm set by the previous Labour government, only the ambulance staff's claim was met in full. Increases for NHS ancillaries ranged from 3.8% to 16.9%, while ambulancemen ranged from 12.8% to 25.8%.

The Clegg proposals for the PAMs gave an average 15.3% increase conditional upon staff changing their working hours to 36.5 per week. This resulted in many PAMs taking part in 'days of action' in March 1980, when the report was received. Clegg also recommended increases to nurses – the average was 19.6% to be paid in two equal stages – although this did not restore the salaries to their 1974 level as the nurses had requested.

It was mentioned in Chapter 4 that one consequence of this dispute was the production, by the newly elected Conservative government, of the Health Circular HC(79)20 'If Industrial

Relations Break Down'.[32] It placed the responsibility for handling industrial action at local level firmly with the health
authorities, pointing out that henceforth Ministers would hope
not to intervene in their decisions. Despite strong protestations
from NHS unions that the circular was intimidating, provocative
and damaging to industrial relations, the Secretary of State
refused to withdraw it. It remains in force.

The demand for clarity came from hospital based managers
and the response was mainly drafted by regional personnel
officers. The circular and its implementation was based on three
underlying assumptions:

> firstly that, in spite of a possible initial escalation, the policy will
> prevent, shorten, or reduce the intensity or effect of industrial
> action; secondly that future disputes will tend to be of the kind
> capable of settlement only at national level; and thirdly that the
> form taken by future industrial action will parallel that of past
> action.[33]

On this view the document was deemed to be 'ill-judged'. In
contrast, a leading proponent of the policy thought that 'the
circular will surely be welcomed and endorsed by most health
authorities'.[34] The argument was that clarity of management
action, and steps taken to improve communications and safeguard patients by the use of the so-called 'volunteers', would
help line managers at hospital level take the initiative away from
the over-powerful unions. This is a good example of managers
accepting at face value the work of politicians. The politics
behind the circular were not aimed at restoring managerial
prerogatives nor indeed at ending disputes, but at making the
disputes worse by driving the unions down the path of more
and more action and therefore into the real dangers of loss of
public support and division among themselves, thus allowing
the government to lay blame on the unions. Line managers do
not see these issues, and are vulnerable to snatching at any
proffered help in the short-run even if it makes matters worse.

The 1979 dispute is more famous as part of the cause of the
downfall of the Labour government than for its industrial relations aspects. Its significance is that it led again to a one-off
inquiry: arbitration to end conflict. It altered the balance of forces
within and between the unions, and enabled management at
local level, and advisers to the Conservative Party, to further test
their theories in the heat of battle. So the use of strikebreakers,

the so-called 'volunteers', and the role of the TUC code of conduct became important issues in the conduct of disputes. The key public issue was the definition of 'essential'; this would vary as between doctors, the media, government, hospital managers, unions and those in dispute. The balance between alienating community support and hurting the employer without hurting the patients is difficult to attain and yet must be attempted in any NHS industrial action.

In 1982 the pattern was repeated. This dispute has been referred to already; it started with a 12% common pay claim from the staff side. The government responded with a differential offer: 6.4% to nurses and 4% to ancillary and A&C staffs. The TUC health service committee coordinated the union action and enforced its code of conduct. The RCN backed some of the actions by the TUC-affiliated unions. The government stood more or less firm, and the divisions within and between the unions on industrial tactics meant a settlement of 7.5% for nurses and 6.4% for the others. For example, NUPE passed a motion at its annual conference for all-out action, but the GMB attacked this at its conference, accusing NUPE of using the dispute to recruit members. But as Mailly *et al.* note: 'A principal outcome of the 1982 dispute was the decision to determine a system for settling questions of pay in the longer term for certain staff groups.'[35] This was the setting up of a Review Body for nurses, midwives and health visitors and for the PAMs. The government argued that to become part of this system staff must not indulge in industrial action in the future, as, it was implied, they had not in the past. This was pure cant. All the groups had participated in industrial action in the past. The unions representing those still excluded from Pay Review felt that they lost the dispute, and in part attributed that to the TUC code of conduct which prevented certain tactical actions.

The thesis so far is that industrial action breaks the deadlock, and that when arbitration is removed then industrial action is the only course left to staff. It is now apparent that arbitration in the NHS saved it from disputes in the 1950s and 1960s even when trade union membership and activity was low, and that pay inquiries and Review Bodies have saved it from worse disruption in the 1970s and 1980s. The causes of the unrest lie primarily with government and its decisions on pay, and increasingly with managers in their determination of conditions of service. The workforce and the unions have shown genuine restraint, and the question really is why has there been so little major action in a service with such consistent ill-treatment of large numbers of staff, and with all staff suffering from pay policies, poor quality of management and Civil Service indifference.

The 1982 dispute, in which the vast majority of health service groups were involved, was conducted in accordance with a code of practice drafted the previous year by TUC-affiliated unions which had members in the NHS (see Chapter 4). In response, the Conservative government left health authorities to deal with the disruption themselves in line with the guidelines contained in HC(79)20. However, NAHA pointed out that employing authority management sides were as little involved in the conduct of negotiations during the 1982 dispute as they had been in 1979:

> For most of the protracted period of negotiation, they did not meet together at all, and there were widespread accounts of how representatives heard of fresh offers, made in their name, through the medium of the press or radio.[36]

A common pay settlement date for NHS staff was introduced in 1982 and an unwished for consequence of this decision for the government was that it increased the scope for union coordination over a common core claim of 12%. The divisiveness of the government's offer of a larger increase for nurses and PAMs was because of their 'direct treatment of patients'.[37] The government refused to allow the claim to go to arbitration and widespread action took place with a 24-hour strike on 19 May and designated days of industrial action in the following five months that were combined with locally applied sanctions of various kinds. A minority of nurses played some role in the early national stoppages, but this tended to diminish as the dispute developed, a critical factor being the position of the RCN.

The days of action attracted sympathetic action from other workers and members of the public; however, by the first week in December most staff were working normally. In mid-December the staff sides of the various functional Whitley councils accepted a revised government offer of a two-year settlement.

The dispute cost the service the loss of 610 150 worker-days, half of them in the Northern, Yorkshire, Mersey and North-Western regions, compared with 149 000 lost in this way in 1976 and 448 000 in 1977.

Morris claims that in 1982 'the health service unions won the moral argument in the eyes of the public, but lost the dispute'.[38]

Some trade unions attributed defeat to the TUC's code of conduct which, as the General Secretary of NUPE stated, meant that the unions were not prepared to lift emergency cover and let people die. 'This meant we were fighting with one hand tied behind our back.'[39] None the less, this was still the policy that was adopted by the trade unions during the 1989 ambulance staff's dispute.

It is claimed that the 1982 dispute significantly weakened the multi-occupation trade unions with major NHS interests. By comparison, the professional associations fared much better, especially the RCN, in achieving their longer run objectives for 'independent' methods of determining their members' pay, which in turn, relieved the pressure upon them to abolish Rule 12 of their constitution forbidding any withdrawal of service in furtherance of a dispute.

Although the employers' response to the 1982 dispute was more determined than in 1979, following the dispute, a survey of 31 districts in the southeast of England[40] discovered that responses to the industrial action varied between health authorities. All managers followed the only mandatory provision of HC(79)20 – that staff on strike should not be paid or receive payments. However, the new 'freedom' provided by the circular did not appear to produce a comprehensive harder line among health authorities. Of the 15 districts that experienced restricted working during the dispute, in only three cases were deductions made from pay, and in only five were staff actually sent home. In general, there seemed to be a tacit agreement between management and staff that, if management agreed to give exaggerated reports to the press of the impact of the dispute, then unions would not hit them so hard.

Morris and Rydzkowski found that in those authorities in which there had been close cooperation between management and unions over the effect of industrial action upon patients and relations with the press, industrial relations did not tend to suffer greatly as a consequence of the dispute. However, where authorities took such action as sending home staff who refused to work normally, or using internal volunteers (the minority), industrial relations tended to be adversely affected. Many local managers felt intensely frustrated by a dispute that was not within their remit to settle and in which they felt a degree of sympathy for the staff side's case. This situation occurred again during the 1989 ambulance staff dispute where several of the employing authorities added their voices to the staff side's plea to refer the matter to independent arbitration.

There is an arbitration enabling clause already in existence in NHS procedures, as noted above. Paragraph 17 of the GWC agreement on appeals procedures (Section 32) states that:

> In the event of a failure to reach a decision on the appeal, it shall be open to either party to the dispute to refer the matter to arbitration in accordance with the terms of any arbitration agreement which may be made by the General Council of the Whitley Councils for the Health Services (Great Britain).

However, there seems very little likelihood of such an arbitration system being established, despite this jointly agreed clause and despite a recommendation from the Social Services Committee in March 1989 that:

> the Government should take the initiative in getting discussions started between the Management and Staff Sides with the purpose of developing a mutually agreed arbitration procedure. We suggest that arbitration should be a last resort and that a strict timetable should be established and adhered to for issues referred to arbitration.[41]

The Conservative government's view of arbitration was spelled out in February 1989 by the then Minister of Health: 'We certainly do not agree with unilateral recourse to arbitration … because it removes the incentive to settle'.[42]

In view of the fact that 60% of the NHS workforce have their pay determined by a Review Body, it seems increasingly unjust that there is no right of access to independent adjudication for the remaining staff. As NUPE reported in 1989, 'If the DoH's case is so good then it ought to stand up to the scrutiny of independent investigation'.[43]

In view of the uncertainties for collective bargaining within the NHS, it is perhaps appropriate to summarize this section with the concluding paragraph of the March 1989 Report by the Social Services Committee on the Whitley Councils.

> We remain concerned about the level of pay for some groups of staff in the health service and the effects which that may have on recruitment and retention of staff, and ultimately on the quality of patient care. The Whitley system may not have helped their situation, but neither can it be entirely blamed for the dissatisfaction amongst health service staff about their terms and conditions of employment. But we do not see local flexibility as a magic bullet

that will solve the industrial relations problems of the health service or necessarily raise the pay of the lowest paid. Local flexibility may enable managers to respond to specific local manpower issues but there must be an adequate pay floor to safeguard the pay of health service staff in those areas where there are no staff shortages. The majority of health service staff are highly committed to their work and to the National Health Service. But their commitment is not bottomless: it should not be taken for granted. The pay of NHS staff is not merely a cost to the service. Any future arrangements for determining the pay of health service staff, whether national or local, negotiated, independently reviewed or ministerially determined, must take into account not only the balance of numbers which the service needs to employ, but the morale of its staff.[44]

Arbitration, through its current form of pay review, is the main mechanism to prevent and end industrial action, and the refusal to allow arbitration in any form to those groups outside the PRB system indicates a policy based on three factors. Firstly, the determination to bring into line health workers whose pay and conditions might be comparable with outside groups and therefore subject to market forces. Secondly, the wish to maintain divisions within the workforce and their representative bodies in terms of TUC affiliation, conduct and policies, and thirdly, the expedient that hospital based managers cannot ultimately be trusted to deal effectively with the professions and that central government control over doctors, nurses and PAMs, even at the cost of higher than average NHS pay rises, is politically essential.

The 1989/90 ambulance dispute illustrates these points and others. The ambulance dispute lasted for six months and won massive public support. The unions' wanted pay parity with the fire service and a pay formula as for other emergency services. The chosen means to secure their demands were carefully selected with strong evidence that the unions wished to avoid some of the problems associated with the 1984/5 miners' strike.

As with most disputes, the origins of the ambulance staff's action can be traced back to previous botched deals. In 1979 Clegg found that the service was low paid and felt undervalued. As mentioned above, Clegg awarded ambulance staff between 21.8% and 25.8% with inflation at the time running at 16%. The swift erosion of the Clegg settlement led to further action in 1981 and 1982, and this in turn led to a new salary structure in 1985.

This absorbed shift, weekend and bonus payments into an all-in salary. As a result of this deal, ambulance staff came into line with the pay of firefighters. By 1989, however, there had opened up a gap of more than 11% against the ambulance personnel. The key argument was that as essential service workers they required a pay formula as applied to the police and fire services. This view was deeply held by most ambulance staff as the felt-fair option for their pay determination.

The government opposed the claim because it did not like the inflationary potential of indexing, and it argued that the ambulance service was an essential, not emergency, service. The union pay claim for just over 11% was met be a counter-claim of 6.5%. During the dispute, which the unions saw clearly as one with the government and not with their employers, the unions took great care over the presentation of their case and tactics. All the unions agreed from the start for the need for the closest possible coordination of action and statement. At first the union leadership recommended acceptance of the offer but the membership twice rejected it in a ballot. The action started with a ban on overtime and rest day working, which was agreed by a large majority in the relevant ballot.

In September officers and controllers also voted to join in the industrial action which meant further unions involved in coordinated activity. In October the dispute escalated with a ban on non-urgent clerical work, rigid adherence to the 39 hour week, and a refusal to transfer non-urgent patients from hospitals. These actions were largely ineffective. So from mid-November 1989 all qualified ambulance crews on fully equipped A&E vehicles agreed to ban non-emergency work. The government's response was to threaten to dock their pay and to suspend them from normal duties. The unions made much of the point that non-working crews were suspended by the employer and not on strike. By December troops in army ambulances were deployed on the streets of London and also in South Yorkshire, Hertfordshire, Derbyshire and Lincolnshire.

There is not space to comment further on the details of this important action, but as the months dragged on the unions were faced with increasing problems. These included financial ones associated with strike pay, control over restless staff resorting to unofficial action, some media stories of suffering patients, and a government not interested in settling. Pay formula and/or pay review and/or arbitration was not on the government's settlement agenda. However skilfully Roger Poole of NUPE presented the case, however unified the unions, however strong public support, however much some local managers lost their nerve or agreed with their staff – none of this mattered. The action did not escalate to its logical finale and therefore the government could always ride it out.

By March 1990 the ambulance staff accepted the government's offer by a large majority. The deal included 9% from March to September 1990 with 7.9% from October to March 1991, some allowances for staff with paramedic skills, and some local flexibility money. But there was no pay mechanism and no pay formula.[45]

The lessons of this dispute are complex, but it shows the extent to which the government took complete control of the dispute with little reference to employers or managers. It also shows that the unions needed more than public support and a well-organized campaign to win. Afterwards several union activists felt that the TUC code had been too restrictive, and at the GMB annual conference their ambulance members accused NUPE of too close adherence to the letter of the TUC code, thereby limiting the effectiveness of action. The main point of interest is the extent to which government dug in to refuse the request for some form of pay formula and/or arbitration for this group of staff. Part of the explanation for this must be that government intends to sell off major parts of the ambulance service and does not wish to be hamstrung by some pay agreement unacceptable to future private owners.

PAY REVIEW

Pay Review Bodies run counter to most notions of collective bargaining. The main NHS trade unions have mainly taken the position that the best way to defend and progress their members' interests is through negotiations based on trade union representatives bargaining with their managers and/or employers. Whitley never worked quite like that, as has been argued above, but it still maintained the principal elements of a national collective bargaining schema through, albeit imperfect, systems of representatives of collective organizations exchanging offers across a table.

The move away from this created a qualitatively different pay determination mechanism in which both parties, employees and employers, made representations through their chosen representative bodies to a panel for a form of arbitrated decision. If Whitley was criticized for being remote and incomprehensible to ordinary health workers, so pay review is worse. If Whitley was criticized for the muddled role of government, so pay review is worse. It is anyway extraordinary that managers and employers who have clamoured for so long for greater freedom to manage should participate in such a system which removes from the employer any vestige of control or authority over pay.

The strangest element of the whole PRB system seems to be its acceptance on face value of the rationality of pay systems and arguments. In most public sector pay rounds the staff side present a set of interlocking arguments based on cost of living, comparability and some aspect of labour supply (see Wootton in Chapter 1). The management side prefers concepts of affordability, value for money and reward for 'good' performance. While these arguments are important, particularly in convincing the health workers themselves and that section of the public that may matter, the arguments do not determine the pay outcome. What determines that is the complex power relationships between the Ministers, their Cabinet colleagues, the Department's chiefs, the employers and the staff side, with some public opinion randomly thrown in from time to time.

Pay Review Bodies must be seen, therefore, as aping some aspects of the previous bargaining structures and methods, and appear to be based on taking account of rational pay arguments. In practice they are more under the control of central government than Whitley, and are best seen as a staging post in the abolition of a national collective bargaining system for the NHS.

The Pay Review Bodies were established in the NHS as a direct response to lengthy disputes over pay with doctors and dentists in the early 1960s, and with nurses, midwives, health visitors and PAMs in the early 1980s. The Doctors and Dentists Review Body (DDRB) arose from the recommendations of the Pilkington Commission. It was appointed in March 1962 to advise the Prime Minister on the remuneration of doctors and dentists taking any part in the NHS. Pilkington was set up following pay disputes which went back to the establishment of national grades for doctors and dentists with the creation of the NHS in 1948. In 1970 all the members of the DDRB resigned after the Secretary of State refused to implement the recommendations in its Twelfth Report. It was subsequently reconstituted with the same terms of reference on 5 July 1971 and has reported annually since then.

The creation in 1983 of an independent Pay Review Body for nurses, midwives, health visitors and PAMs followed the major dispute in 1982. The establishment of pay review for these groups was described by the government as a 'reward' for those not participating in industrial action. This was mere rhetoric since many of these staff had played a part in the action. The main reason for the setting up of the Pay Review Body was to enable the government simultaneously to distance itself politically from any future pay disputes with a popular group of health workers and to tighten its control over the whole pay process.

When the government introduced the Pay Review Body it linked it to future industrial action with the threat that if staff took action, they would be excluded from the review process. (The same proposition was put to schoolteachers in April 1991.) This threat has not been tested. Again the real reason for this line of argument was to try to split the trade unions away from the professional associations, and to encourage the latter to revert to their more traditional pressure group activities as opposed to their more recent industrial relations activities.[46]

The Review Bodies operate on a similar basis to those for the armed forces and the Civil Service (the so-called Top Salaries Review Body). They are serviced by the Office of Manpower Economics which provides a secretariat and research facility. The review body itself consists of eight members who are appointed by the Prime Minister for limited, but extendable, time periods. Several members sit on more than one body.

Each year both sides submit written evidence to their allocated Review Body. In addition RHA chairs, the Health Departments and some staff organizations provide 'supplementary' evidence to the main submissions. Two meetings then take place between the Review Body members and the respective staff and management sides of each of these councils, the latter is generally headed by the Minister for Health. The members of the Review Body then consider the evidence and submit their recommendations to the government. The government decides whether to implement the recommendations in full, in part, or in phases. Each of these alternatives has been used since 1983 for the Bodies set up in that year.

It should be clear from this account that the government has several bites at the pay cherry. It appoints the Review Body members, it presents the management side's case within in its own pay guidelines, and finally the government decides whether to implement and/or fund the Pay Bodies' recommendations.

The political benefits to the government from this system remain its ability to distance itself from pay bargaining and the responsibilities that go with that industrial relations strategy (including recognition of trade unions). The financial benefits, however, have been less certain. Since the pay review system was instituted for nurses and the other groups there have been significantly higher pay settlements than for those health workers whose pay is determined through Whitley. Despite this the staff side involved in pay review have rejected any argument from government that all settlements should be based on 'affordability', and that there is a need for 'regional' pay to resolve recruitment and retention problems in some regions for some groups of staff. The staff side did not block, however, the government use of pilot schemes on flexible pay supplements for nurses and midwives.

For pay review to succeed in averting industrial action and/or one-off pay inquiries it must fulfil certain functions. These include reasonable settlements, which are acceptable to the staff side. Since 1984 this has been achieved, more or less, but in order to do so notions of fairness and therefore comparability must be seen to be taken seriously by the Review Bodies. This might outrage the public utterances of the politicians, but they are probably happy that the reality of peace in the hospital service in times of major reform is better than the rhetoric of ideological commitment.

Pay review must also meet, more or less, the government's need to maintain pay within limits, which it does. Thus government can blame the Review Bodies for wrong-headed arguments, and the Review Bodies can blame government for inadequate funding, but both survive and there is no industrial action by nurses, doctors and PAMs. It is the new employers and the managers who are most frustrated by pay review since it goes against their demands for the freedom to manage and pay what they like. While they can now do this for Whitley staff, it is much harder for Review Body staff. The ways around this now being explored are new grading systems which provide greater local flexibility, new pay systems such as job evaluation which again allow payments within pay review but with some management control, and the increase in performance related pay. In other words, there is a move, at least for the moment, to combine national pay review pay determination with single-employer supplements.

The earlier chapters used the pay review reports to analyse pay arguments and examine the nature of pay levels for various staff. It is not necessary, therefore, to repeat all those points, although some summary across the PRBs might be useful. The view expressed here is that pay review is simply a version of previous *ad hoc* pay inquiries. Since 1970 the main ones were the NBPI in 1971 for ancillary workers, the 1973 Davison inquiry for electricians, Halsbury in 1974 for PAMs and nurses, and Clegg in 1979 for nurses, PAMs, ancillary staff and ambulance staff. There is not space here to examine the 1957 Hall report for administrative and clerical staff, and another one for A&C in 1963,[47] the 1967 NBPI for ancillary staff, or Pilkington for doctors in 1960.

The 1971 NBPI report concentrated on low paid (defined as full-time staff earning less than the bottom decile of average manual earnings) ancillary workers. At the time there were about 220 000 hospital based ancillary workers. Of these 28% were full-time men, and 35% full-time women with another 35% part-time women. They were employed in nearly 3000 NHS hospitals. In 1970 they represented 32% of the labour force and their labour costs were 30% of the total. The report recommended the use of job evaluation, better management and more incentive bonus schemes. The point is that the NBPI took evidence from all parties, took account of government policy and current economic and industrial relations thinking, and reached conclusions based on rational assumptions about ways of granting fair, felt-fair rewards, in exchange for meeting management needs. This in essence is the basis for all bargains whether achieved through collective bargaining or arbitration.

Davison did a similar job for the electricians. This time the two parties, the EETU/PTU and the employers in the guise of the Health Departments and Secretaries of State submitted cases. There were 2700 electricians at the time who formed part of the 20 000 maintenance force in hospitals. The employers wanted a common grading structure for all maintenance staff. Davison felt that the real issue was the internal relativities as between electricians and other maintenance staffs, and that a solution could only be achieved by a negotiated genuinely common pay system and not one imposed by the Departments. Once again outside help urged settlement through negotiated job evaluation if employers wanted workable solutions.

In 1974 there was Halsbury for nurses and midwives and the PAMs (with speech therapists). It is here that the clearest expression of the arbitrator's need to make their findings acceptable to staff through recognition of the major importance of pay differences can be found. Thus Halsbury concludes:

> In our deliberations and in reaching our conclusions, we have been particularly concerned to test the pay relationships between the individual professions supplementary to medicine and between them and the nursing profession. In the NHS the professions and the nursing profession share a common employer as well as a common place of work. They also have in common the fact that they are predominantly women's professions and that many of them work part-time only.[48]

This rather patronizing view reflects the judgement of civil servants and employers far more than that of the professions themselves. This reply came from the radiographers:

> The relating of radiographers to nurses is therefore not based on any soundly argued case, but has become merely an administrative expedient.[49]

None the less, the Halsbury awards were mainly a device to pay some staff more without appearing to give in to industrial action or to outrage pay policy. The arguments are just that: they are cobbled together to placate everyone and to allow each relevant group to find some comfort – the hallmark of the arbitrator.

Clegg in 1979 was no different despite great efforts to make pay more scientifically based and to address the question of comparators seriously. The importance of Clegg is the way in which the various reports outlined the pay arguments and enabled government again to make special awards. The Pay Review Bodies currently operating in the NHS, as was shown in Chapters 1–3, behave in similar ways to Clegg. They listen attentively, they weigh and judge evidence, they are sensitive to mood and pressure, and they conclude within government pay guidelines while sometimes granting that the unions have a case worth consideration by government next time.

Most of the arguments found in Halsbury and Clegg are familiar to everyone and have been discussed in reference to the work of Wootton in Chapter 1. The unions favour cost of living

and comparability as essential arguments for winning membership support and for fulfilling felt-fair settlements. Employers
prefer affordability and productivity/workload arguments to
meet the needs of the business and to retain flexible elements.
Both sides accept labour market realities on recruitment and
retention but do not agree how to resolve them – unions with
higher national rates, employers with more flexible local rates.
The point is that whatever the arguments, the Pay Review
system operates as an arbitration body but with government
fixing the global cash available.

The most common starting point for any wage claim is the
assumed rate of inflation for the period over which the pay rise
will run. This is based on a notion of equity: we, the workforce
and trade union do not cause inflation, therefore, there can be no
good reason why our pay should be worth less in 12 months
from now when compared with the present. On the contrary, we
expect a steady increase in our real standard of living irrespective of personal promotion. The strength of this case cannot
be overstated for many sections of health workers.

Even after 12 years of a government determined to deny this
principle, strong positive attitudes towards fairness remain. In
the Twentieth Report on doctors' and dentists' pay the authors
refer to this point with a world-weary comment: 'we have noted
the year on year increase in the retail price index',[50] and note
with equal enthusiasm that 'the BDA told us that the profession
should share in the general prosperity of the country'.[51] But they
base the use of this argument on the Department of Health's
comment that 'modest increases to take account of the expected
changes in the cost of living would seem appropriate this year'.[52]
Exactly the same points were made by the nurses, midwives and
health visitors report.[53] Importantly the Pay Review Body
thought that while these factors of economic indicators such as
inflation were important, 'they do not override all others'.[54]

The second main argument used by trade unions to advance
pay for public sector workers has been that of comparability.
Again union members feel strongly about the fairness of this and
are by and large wedded to customary views of pay differences.
As was argued in Chapter 1 for health service professionals, this
might be seen as the key argument, and the one in which pay
relates to professional worth, status and self-esteem.

In 1990 the government, through the Department of Health,
wanted pay comparison only to be used where it impinged on

labour market issues. The staff side argued strongly for increases in line with average earnings. COHSE, for example, quoted from its own survey of members that over half thought that their pay was neither fair nor adequate. The Review Body took the view that, 'we do not consider that external comparisons are the main factor that we should take into account in making our recommendations, but neither do we think that they can be ignored'.[55] A similar line was espoused for and about the doctors: 'The BMA said that there had been a progressive deterioration in the relative position of the profession compared with that of analogous occupations.'[56] On balance, the Review Body agreed without committing itself to the full importance of this point. In contrast, the PAMs were more belligerent towards the Pay Review Body, but made the same point in a strongly worded statement: 'the staff expect the Review Body system to produce relative fairness, especially between the groups directly under its consideration such as nurses and PAMs.'[57]

None of the comparability arguments adduced by the professional associations to the Review Bodies varies from the clear case made by the TUC for such a principle:

> the principle behind comparability is that people should be remunerated fairly for the work that they do … Comparability thus establishes relative fairness in pay and conditions.[58]

This is in direct agreement with the famous Priestley Commission view that 'the State is under a categorical obligation to remunerate its employees fairly'. This was not a statement of metaphysical assertion, but the restatement of Henry Clay's points about Whitley as a practical recognition of the balance of power and advantage as between public sector workers and their employers.

The importance of fair comparison underlies a great deal of NHS pay, and failure to take it on board fails to recognize its links with performance and morale. It also fails to recognize the way in which it enables agreements to be reached for very large numbers of staff at relatively low costs in time and effort of the negotiators.

The internal and external labour markets are an increasingly important part of the bargaining exchange. The ability to recruit and retain the right mix of staff is a major ingredient in the efficient operation of the health service. In recent years this has been the real battle ground as between the staff side, the management side and the Department of Health. A great deal has been made of these labour market constraints by government, and some elements of pay policy relating to the make-up of pay and the rights of the self-governing trusts to break away from Whitley, such as local pay and performance related pay, are based, at least in open argument, on labour market considerations.

In practice it is important to distinguish the recruitment from the retention argument, and to differentiate within the professions as well as between them. This is really quite difficult since the information required to make accurate comments is still somewhat unreliable despite claims to the contrary.

The government did not deny there was a recruitment problem for hospital doctors, but argued it could be offset by better retention in the service of doctors, especially women doctors. On the other hand, the BMA 'drew attention to the long term decline in applications to study medicine'.[59] The same point was made by the BDA. Overall, the Review Body was dismissive of the Department's complacency and urged them to pay more attention to the decline in student numbers. The government also admitted to a retention problem, but referred to its initiative 'Achieving a Balance: Plan for Action' which increased the number of consultant posts. The BMA emphasized the low morale amongst junior doctors. Overall, the Review Body took the view that once qualified and in the system, doctors had little choice but to work for the NHS and that as a consequence retention was not a serious issue.

The RCN's own survey of the nurse labour market, 'Grade Expectations', carried out by the Institute of Manpower Studies, showed that the new grades had encouraged nurses to stay in clinical grades, but provided no evidence that it encouraged nurses to stay in the NHS and to return to the NHS. COHSE's survey illustrated that half the respondents had considered leaving the profession in the previous 12 months owing to low morale, poor pay and stress.[60] The Department of Health disagreed and argued that there was no widespread shortage. If the parties are so at odds as to the real state of the labour market then any argument to adjust supply through pay, for example, only allows the parties to fall back to other arguments and threats of pressure. The RCM and HVA made similar points about recruitment and retention to those made by COHSE and the RCN.

The Review Body position was again less than clear. It was undecided on the labour market evidence, but argued that problems could and should be remedied largely by non-pay rewards rather than pay rises. As part of this the Review Body encouraged targeting of certain types of staff and the development of special local schemes. This type of advice may overcome short-term labour market shortfalls, but encourages labour hoarding and general beggar-my-neighbour labour policies by health authorities and leapfrogging by unions. The NHS Pay Review Bodies were a political escape route to allow a form of arbitration with elements of comparability and inflation-proofing in the short term in order to guarantee peace amongst the professional staff while other more profound reforms associated with privatization took place.

Under the heading 'workload and productivity', the DDRB argued that 'the separate contributions of individual categories of hospital staff to the overall rise in productivity could not be identified'.[61] In a statement which well illustrates that it is folly to be wise when ignorance is bliss, the Review Body is able to say in the same paragraph that,

> in the absence of information, we are unable to analyse the workloads and productivity of the various categories of hospital staff separately. There can be no doubt that hospital medical and dental practictioners have made a contribution to the increased activity.[62]

Let nobody doubt a claim based on no information!

This point is elaborated for hospital doctors and dentists as it is so important. The case rests on a total lack of serious research, but the political gloss remains important in times when appearance counts for more than reality, even new realism.

In 1989 a survey of the workload and responsibilities of consultants within the NHS was carried out by the OME. The BMA pointed out that one finding indicated that the mean weekly hours worked of 47.2 hours was far in excess of contracted hours of 38.5. The Review Body took the view that this represented no increase since a 1977 survey, and the significant issue was that the average consultant now spent 9–12% of their time on management duties, and that 'this underlines the need for appropriate remuneration for these duties'.[63] It is interesting to note that the Review Body likes the idea of consultants spending more time as managers and that this is in line with government intentions of drawing the profession into the management of the service. A contrary position, although not one presented by the BMA, might be that the most efficient use of doctor time was as doctors.

There was no parallel debate about the workload of nurses, midwives and health visitors other than under the heading of morale. The Review Body reminds its readers, the government Departments and Ministers, that 'we also commented last year on the continued stresses arising from increased workloads'.[64] As for the PAMs, the argument of the Departments was logically circular and empirically limited. They pointed out that the pay of staff in the professions 'had increased more rapidly than that of all other NHS groups (save nurses)'.[65]

The government's line is that we cannot measure productivity very well and we certainly cannot isolate the contribution of any given profession to global productivity increases, but if pay has risen relatively faster then this means so has productivity. No amount of reform will cure those responsible for that kind of contemptuously empty and incompetently researched argument.

The second prong of the productivity argument is that of profitability or affordability. In this case pay is linked solely to the business' ability to pay. For self-governing trusts, for example, the new executive boards can simply say to any group of workers we cannot pay what you require because the budget will not permit. This takes health workers, at least on the surface, to the position of large numbers of workers in the private sector.

In its submission to the 1990 PRB for PAMs, the Department of Health stated that since 1984 the pay of this group had increased more rapidly than that of all other NHS groups with the exception of nurses. This pay increase, it was argued, was higher than the average for both the private and public sectors. In real terms the salaries of PAMs had increased by 38% on average since 1979. In response to the Department's case, the PRB noted that:

> We do not consider that 1984 or any other single year is neces-
> sarily an appropriate starting point for comparisons. The appro-
> priate level of pay needs to be considered afresh each year in the
> light of changing circumstances.[66]

In the years from 1987 to 1990/1 the average pay increases that the PRBs have recommended for the three NHS groups of staff have been as shown in Table 6.2.

Table 6.2 Average pay increases under PRB 1987–1991 (%)

	1987/8	1988/9	1989/90	1990/1
Doctors/dentists	7.7	7.9	8.8	8.2
Nurses/midwives/health visitors	9.5	15.3*	6.8	9.6
PAMs	9.1	8.8	7.7	10.1

* The actual % increase varied widely throughout the UK because this was the year in which the new clinical grading structure was introduced to the NHS.
Source: PRB reports as average per cent increases.

In 1988 the PRBs for the nurses, midwives and health visitors and for the PAMs recommended that London 'supplements' to staff in the London weighting zones should be introduced. This decision established a much greater London weighting and led, in 1989, to the abolition of the London weighting consortium by the GWC management side.

The NHS London weighting allowances had, since 1979, been negotiated by a committee of the GWC, namely the London Weighting Consortium. This Consortium had been set up at the request of the GWC management side. In its brief life it had been unable to free itself from the financial restraints of the Treasury. All efforts by the staff side to gain significant increases were rejected and annual increases of 2–3% were the norm.

The range of London weighting allowances that had developed through agreements reached with functional councils prior to 1979 continued throughout the Consortium's existence. Thus, the largest group of staff (the nurses) and the doctors and dentists received a London zone allowance while groups, such as Professional and Scientific, Administrative and Clerical, and Ancillary, received Inner, Outer and 'fringe' allowances. Equally, the London allowance for Ambulance staff and officers was specifically defined, but happened to coincide with the London zone rate.

The evidence then indicates that the PRBs were able to increase allowances for those in and around London by amounts not ever reached by the bargaining forum of the Consortium. Before any judgements are made as to the reasons for this it must be noted that the structures cannot account for the differences, while the policy changes that created the new structures can.

While the PRBs are primarily about pay, none the less they make decisions on conditions of service which affect PRB staff and the whole NHS workforce. An example of this was when the staff side of the PT'A' Council presented the anomalous position of radiographic managers being the only PAM profession not to have established district posts through the PRB to the PT'A' management side, and reached an agreement which did away with this anomaly. This was in 1986.

The staff side representing staff covered by PRBs have been able to resist the government's insistence on 'affordability' as the sole criterion for pay settlements. The PRB argued that 'affordability' was one important factor among a number, but they did not accept that it should override all other considerations.[67]

Equally, the PRBs to date have rejected the government's case for 'regional' pay variations. Since the nurse group's grading changes in 1987/8 the PRB for PAMs has pressed the two sides to renegotiate a new grading structure for this group of staff. In their Seventh Report they stated that:

> We regret that no real progress has been made with the grading review. We continue to see a need for a new, coherent grading structure to accommodate more effectively the range of experience, skills and responsibilities of the staff ... It remains our view that some of the difficulties to which our attention has been drawn over a number of years can be effectively addressed only through a new grading structure: they are not susceptible to remedy by across the board pay increases. We therefore hope that the Sides will resume and carry through their negotiations this year.[68]

One must be very careful in deciphering this kind of comment. Is the PRB going it alone and showing their real 'independence', basing their logic on traditional managerial desires for cleaner and tighter grades? That is possible. Or, rather, are the PRB members floating ideas from civil servants unhappy with government policy and/or with managers seeking their independence from the Department? This seems more likely. Whatever drives the PRB on, there is a strong desire to please most of its audiences while placating government sufficiently to warrant another year in post!

The system of Review Bodies annually arbitrating over pay issues for the majority of 'front-line' staff has led to clear divisions between these and those groups not part of such a system. The majority of multi-occupation trade unions were initially opposed to giving up collective bargaining over pay – the speech therapists (represented then by ASTMS) withdrew from the PT'A' Council rather than become part of the review system.

The Review Bodies have shown themselves to be able to withstand strong government pressure over pay norms, they have gained the sometimes grudging respect of staff side organizations and through their regular visits in the service, have persuaded many that their knowledge and understanding of those for whom they establish pay levels, is greater than that of many management side members.

Thus, as speech therapists have discovered, in the first few years that review for nurses, midwives, health visitors and PAMs has been in existence, there is little doubt that the salary levels that have been achieved during this time would have been unlikely to have been achieved through Whitley without, at the very least, a great deal of industrial unrest. Whether this continues to be the case in the 1990s remains to be seen.

CONCLUDING COMMENTS

The whole question of deadlocked negotiations, whether settled through industrial action or through forms of arbitration, is riddled with contradictions based on government pay policy. It is worth taking a brief look at that with regard to future NHS developments.

Pay Review Bodies, as the current successors to the series of *ad hoc* pay inquiries, serve as a reminder of the varied use of arbitration as a method of resolving complex collective bargaining problems. Included in the advantages of pay review as arbitration is the incorporation of felt-fair comparability in wage determination without political embarrassment for the government, the avoidance of disputes, and the maintenance of the locus of power within the single-profession trade unions at national level through Whitehall influence rather than at local level through workplace bargaining. The importance of this for the NHS of the 1990s is immense since it leaves unresolved the contradictions at the heart of the policy reforms, namely greater managerial controls over labour costs and labour processes. Even if this is partially achieved for the majority of ancillary staff, ambulance personnel, A&C grades, and technical and maintenance staffs, the failure to tackle nurses' pay in the same manner leaves a gaping hole in the practice of the policy.

As Brown and Rowthorn remind us, the NHS has not been alone in inconsistent and damaging pay policy responses: 'For the past twenty years all public service workers have been subject to extremely erratic pay treatment.'[69]

Table 6.3 shows the extent to which customary pay differences as between groups within the NHS have been changed, with the relative position of nurses and doctors greatly enhanced over the decade, while that of the ambulance staff deteriorated until the 1989 dispute. The ancillary workers' position has sharply worsened, both within the NHS and by outside comparison. As Brown and Rowthorn conclude: 'There has thus been a substantial increase in the inequality of payment among those involved with the health service in the 1980s.'[70]

Table 6.3 Earnings charges for specific groups, 1979–1990

	% change relative to all employees' earnings		% change in real weekly earnings	
	1979–89	81–9	1979–89	81–9
Medical practitioners (M)	25	1	55	26
NHS nurses etc. (F)	26	14	57	38
Ambulancemen	1	–11	25	11
NHS ancillaries (F)	–11	–14	11	8
Hospital porters (M)	–17	–17	4	4
Hospital orderlies (F)	–19	–16	0	3
University teachers (M)	7	–16	33	5
FE teachers (M)	0	–15	25	6
Secondary teachers	10	–6	36	16
Primary teachers	10	–7	36	17
National govt admin. (M)	–4	–11	20	11
Local govt admin. (M)	–2	–13	21	9
Roadsweepers (M)	–8	–9	14	14
Refuse collectors (M)	–11	–16	10	5
Police constables (M)	8	1	34	26
Low paid private sector males	–13	–9	8	14
Accountants (M)	18	10	47	38
Finance specialists (M)	35	23	68	54
All male employees	0	0	24	25
All female employees	6	3	31	29
All employees	0	0	24	25

Note: Index for private sector males based on NHS data on male cleaners, general farmworkers, repetitive assemblers, packers and bottlers and building labourers.
Source: Brown and Rowthorn (1990), *A Public Services Pay Policy*, Fabian Tract No. 542.

The key point in all this is that Pay Review Bodies have allowed government to tighten its control, through the Treasury, of national pay settlements in the NHS even while discussing and enforcing in some cases decentralized pay bargaining. That issue will be dealt with in the final two chapters. In addition, the Review Bodies have, more or less, kept the pay criteria of felt-fair comparability as the main argument in their decisions and have dismissed, more or less, the government's urging of alternative criteria such as productivity and affordability. So 60% of the NHS staff, and in general the best paid staff as well, have been granted a form of permanent arbitration in exchange for industrial peace and tight central control over pay, and the rest of what has happened is mainly political window dressing.

NOTES

1 NASUWT (1990) *Pay Review Body For Teachers*, NASUWT, Birmingham. See April 1991 offer by the government to the teacher trade unions of a Pay Review Body in exchange for a promise not to strike.
2 Brown, W. and Rowthorn, R. (1990) *A Public Services Pay Policy*, Fabian Tract No. 542, The Fabian Society, London, p. 8.
3 Webb, S. and Webb, B. (1897) *Industrial Democracy*, 1920 edn, Longmans, Green & Co., London, p. 179.
4 Ibid., p. 221.
5 Ibid., p. 221.
6 Ibid., p. 243.
7 ACAS (1989) *Annual Report*, ACAS, London, p. 25.
8 Clegg, H. and Chester, T. (1957) *Wage Policy and the Health Service*, Basil Blackwell, Oxford, p. 91.
9 Ibid., p. 93.
10 Ibid., p. 94.
11 Loveridge, R. (1971) *Collective Bargaining by National Employees in the United Kingdom*, University of Michigan, Wayne State, p. 170.
12 Hall, N. (1957) *Report on the Grading Structure of the Administrative and Clerical Staff in the Hospital Service*, HMSO, London.
13 Loveridge, op. cit., p. 172.
14 Winchester, D. (1983) 'Industrial Relations in the Public Sector', in Bain, G. *Industrial Relations in Britain*, Basil Blackwell, Oxford, p. 163.
15 McCarthy, W. (1976) *Making Whitley Work*, HMSO, London, p. 84.
16 Trades Union Congress Health Services Committee (1981) *Improving Industrial Relations in the National Health Service*, TUC, London, p. 67.
17 Ibid., p. 77.
18 Seifert, R. (1987) *Teacher Militancy: a History of Teacher Strikes 1896–1986*, Falmer Press, Brighton.

19   Bain, G., Coates, D. and Ellis, V. (1973) *Social Stratification and Trade Unionism*, Heinemann, London.
20   Grey-Turner, E. and Sutherland, F. (1982) *History of the British Medical Association*, Volume 2, 1932–1981, BMA, London, p. 155.
21   Morris, G. (1986) *Strikes in Essential Services*, Mansell Publishing, London, pp. 154–5.
22   Fryer, R., Fairclough, A. and Manson, T. (1974) *Organisation and Change in the National Union of Public Employees*, Department of Sociology, Warwick University.
23   Carpenter, M. (1988) *Working for Health: The History of COHSE*, Lawrence and Wishart, London, p. 333.
24   Ibid., p. 339.
25   Ibid., p. 349.
26   Taylor, R. (1978) *The Fifth Estate: Britain's Unions in the Seventies*, Routledge and Kegan Paul, London, p. 243.
27   Ibid., p. 254.
28   Treloar, S. (1981) 'The Junior Hospital Doctors' Pay Dispute 1975–1976: An Analysis of Events, Issues and Conflicts', *Journal of Social Policy*, 10, pp. 1–30.
29   Gordon, H. and Iliffe, S. (1977) *Pickets in White: The Junior Doctors' Dispute of 1975*, MPU Publications, London, p. 6.
30   NBPI (National Board for Prices and Incomes). (1971) *The Pay and Conditions of Service of Ancillary Workers in the NHS*, Cmnd 4644, HMSO, London. Davison, W. (1973) *Report of an Inquiry into the Remuneration of Electricians Employed in the NHS*, HMSO, London. Halsbury (1974) *Report of the Committee of Inquiry into the Pay and Related Conditions of Service of the Professions Supplementary to Medicine and Speech Therapists*, HMSO, London. Halsbury (1974) *Report of the committee of Inquiry into the Pay and Related Conditions of Service of Nurses and Midwives*, DHSS, London. Clegg, H. (1979) *Local Authority and University Manual Workers; NHS Ancillary Staffs; and Ambulancemen: Standing Commission on Pay Comparability, Report No.1*, Cmnd 7641, HMSO, London. Clegg, H. (1980) *Nurses and Midwives: Standing Commission on Pay Comparability, Report No. 3*, Cmnd 7795, HMSO, London. Clegg, H. (1980) *Professions Supplementary to Medicine: Standing Commission on Pay Comparability, Report No. 4*, Cmnd 7850, HMSO, London.
31   Morris, op. cit., p. 156.
32   Health Circular HC(79)20 (1979) *If Industrial Relations Break Down*, DHSS, London.
33   Harrison, S. (1980) 'Responses to Industrial Action: Assumptions and Evidence', *Health Services Manpower Review*, 6(1), p. 15.
34   Button, J. (1980) 'Responses to Industrial Action', *Health Services Manpower Review*, 6(1), p. 19.
35   Mailly, R., Dimmock, S. and Sethi, A. (1989) ' Industrial Relations in the NHS since 1979', in Mailly, R., Dimmock, S. and Sethi, A. (eds), *Industrial Relations in the Public Services*, Routledge, London, p. 121.
36   Social Services Committee of the House of Commons (1989) Third Report, NAHA Minutes of Evidence, 18/1/89, p. 52.

37   Morris, op. cit., p. 159.
38   Ibid., p. 161.
39   NUPE *Journal* (1983), No.1.
40   Morris, G. and Rydzkowski, S. (1984) 'Anatomy of a Dispute', *Health and Social Service Journal,* 12th April.
41   Social Services Committee of the House of Commons (1989) Third Report, March 1989, p. xxxiv.
42   Ibid., p. 151.
43   Social Services Committee of the House of Commons (1989) Third Report, NUPE Minutes of Evidence, 1/2/89, pp. 23–4.
44   Social Services Committee of the House of Commons (1989) Third Report, p. xxxii.
45   Kerr, A. and Sachdev, S. (1991) *Third Among Equals: An Analysis of the 1989 Ambulance Dispute,* unpublished draft.
46   Thomason, G. (1985) 'The Pay Review Bodies', *Health Services Manpower Review,* 11(3), pp. 3 – 6.
47   Hall (1957) op. cit., and Green, L. (1963) *Report of the Committee of Inquiry into the Recruitment, Training and Promotion of Administrative and Clerical Staff in the Hospital Service,* HMSO, London.
48   Halsbury (1974), N&M op. cit., p. 32.
49   Society of Radiographers (1974) *Submission of Evidence by The Society of Radiographers to the Halsbury Committee of Inquiry,* SoR, London, p. 16.
50   Wilkins, G. (1990) *Review Body on Doctors' and Dentists' Remuneration, Twentieth Report,* Cm 937, HMSO, London, p. 4.
51   Ibid.
52   Ibid., p. 3.
53   Cleminson, J. (1990) *Review Body ...: Seventh Report on Nursing Staff, Midwives and Health Visitors,* Cm 934, HMSO, London, p. 6.
54   Ibid.
55   Ibid., p. 7.
56   Wilkins, op. cit., p. 5.
57   PTA evidence, paper 1, p. 14.
58   TUC, op. cit., p. 47.
59   Wilkins, op. cit., p. 4.
60   Bett, M. (1991) *Review Body ...: Eighth Report on Nursing Staff, Midwives and Health Visitors 1991,* Cm 1410, HMSO, London, p. 5.
61   Wilkins, op. cit., p. 6.
62   Ibid.
63   Ibid., p. 9.
64   Cleminson, op. cit., p. 8.
65   Cleminson, J. (1990) *Review Body ...: Seventh Report on Professions Allied to Medicine 1990,* Cm 935, HMSO, London, p. 7.
66   Ibid., p. 8.
67   Ibid., p. 7.
68   Ibid., p. 1.
69   Brown and Rowthorn, op. cit., p. 7.
70   Ibid.

Chapter 7

Workplace collective bargaining

INTRODUCTION

In 1979, in a memorandum to the Royal Commission on the Health Service, ACAS drew attention to problems in the development of appropriate local collective bargaining machinery in the NHS. It said: 'the most troublesome IR problems occur because of the absence of machinery at District level'.[1] This condemnation went to the very heart of the Whitley system. The whole point of the Whitley Council machinery was to establish uniform terms and conditions of service at national level but applied locally through joint consultative committees (JCCs).

A substantial element of the 1991 reforms of the health service is concerned with allowing single employers control over staff and services. The establishment of employer level and/or hospital level industrial relations is of vital interest at the present time. The history and current situation is one of piecemeal arrangements overlaid with some sporadic national policy initiatives and topped off with muddle and widespread inexperience on all sides about the basics of workplace bargaining.

The impetus for what workplace activity there is comes from influences outside the NHS as well as pressures from within. Those from outside include some employment legislation, incomes policies, variable labour market conditions, and the partial implementation of a series of *ad hoc* inquiries seeking expedient remedies for immediate consumption. Pressures from within for local bargaining include the demands of staff for improved pay and conditions, the increase in size of employing unit, the introduction of new technologies and techniques, and the impact locally of national strikes.

One example of legislation is the effect of the 1974 Health and Safety at Work etc. Act with its provision for health and safety representatives and health and safety committees.[2] Health, safety and welfare issues should be dealt with through health and safety representatives acting as workplace bargainers. In other words, they are just a special form of grievance, and, if treated as such, health and safety representatives can secure genuine improvements in conditions as well as establish a proper basis for workplace union activity. The legislation of the 1970s and the further regulations and practices of the 1980s have placed a requirement upon management to enter into local arrangements with staff side representatives. Other examples of the impact of outside influences on the development of local industrial relations include disciplinary procedures, time off provisions and disclosure of information rights as recommended by the ACAS codes, and bonus schemes from various NBPI reports.[3]

In all these cases there were real benefits for the stewards of certificated independent trade unions and so most professional associations become certificated. This helped the development of stewards amongst the professional unions, and their increased role in JCCs.

By the beginning of the 1980s most of the professional associations had established networks of industrial relations and health and safety representatives at local, district and regional levels. The arrival of the union steward in such numbers undoubtedly had an effect upon the increased recruitment that all of the trade unions enjoyed at this time.

Part and parcel of union growth and the attentions of government and outside experts on the NHS industrial relations systems was to force on the service the prescriptions of the Donovan report. This is what McCarthy wanted in 1976:[4] more joint regulation and the institutionalization of conflict through the rapid introduction of formal procedures along with the concomitant rise of the personnel function. The thrust of policy was to agree and use such formal agreements at the level of the employer. By 1990, however, the presence of procedures in the NHS was still not comprehensive, and the implementation of the national disputes procedure remained patchy.

The reasons for the lack of enthusiastic use of formal consultative and negotiating procedures at local level to resolve conflicts of right and of interest included the lack of experience and training of both sides, remnants of paternalistic management, and the recourse to informal methods of conflict resolution. For most NHS managers their experience of local level industrial relations has been confined to the local application of national agreements; negotiating and operating health authority-wide disciplinary, grievance and disputes procedures; and dealing with any aspects of local industrial action. This lack of experience has suddenly become very worrying for the implementation of the current reform programme, and an increasing number of managers are urging a slow-down in the pace of change to allow management training and development to catch up.

The late introduction of a formal disputes procedure and its reluctant use once introduced is in part due to the lack of need. Throughout the 1950s and 1960s industrial action over pay issues in the NHS was virtually unknown. The relatively few local disputes were referred to external third party arbitration. In the 1950s the Industrial Disputes Tribunal, operating under statutory machinery, dealt with more local references from NHS Management Committees than from any other employer. Most references concerned individual gradings and salary levels. This free and easy availability of arbitration meant that local disputes remained low key, and that the role of trade unions as primary bargainers was marginal. It also implied that when arbitration on pay issues became less acceptable to government, so the function of trade unions would become more relevant to many staff and the likelihood of disputes escalating become far greater.

By the late 1960s much of the assumed postwar acceptance of partnership and consensus was being questioned. Government attention to public expenditure and the spotlight of public scrutiny on the trade unions were among the first signs of change. These were followed by managerial reappraisals and the assertion of rights by groups of health workers and patients previously ignored. Throughout the public sector the years since 1967 have seen dramatic changes in industrial relations. These were characterized in the late 1960s and throughout most of the 1970s by growth in union membership, especially among the professional and white-collar workers, greater collective bargaining activities, more professional personnel management, and more industrial action. To argue, as some have, that this added up to some once and for all radicalization of those workers and their unions is doubtful, but what did happen was a major adjustment of the perception that such public sector employees had to their work, their trade unions and above all to their employers. It also significantly altered their view of the state as an employer, and of the traditional practices of managerial control.[5]

For health service workers these adjustments to the realities of a bad employer entrenched in paternalistic employment practices were made through a set of complex and contradictory experiences. The application of incomes policies, and the impact of bonus payment schemes for ancillary staff in 1967 and 1971 played a major role in these uneven awakenings. The TUC, which supported the development of district level Joint Shop Steward Committees (JSSC) and the Joint Consultative Committees (JCC), reported that 'the advent of bonus schemes meant that, for the first time, important aspects of pay and conditions would be negotiated locally'.[6] As a result, stewards become increasingly widespread, their status was enhanced and union membership grew rapidly. These developments were, however, limited. For by 1971 only 11% of ancillary workers were covered by bonus schemes. As the NBPI explained:

> The main reason for the slow introduction of interim schemes has been the time taken to reach agreement on their introduction. Even after this agreement had been reached there was little in the way of purposeful effort to expedite the installation of schemes.[7]

This was partly because of the lack of experienced union activists and coherent union organization, and partly due to the lack of management expertise. By 1973 less than half of the DHAs had personnel managers in post.

The development of local bargaining cannot be attributed solely to the changes in the late 1960s. There had always been strong local traditions in mental hospitals and some of the old local authority hospitals. None the less, the bonus schemes did cause an increase in union activity, although their introduction can be seen as a consequence of pressures from below for better pay and more control over the effort–pay bargain. Another cause of this move to local bargaining was the implementation of incomes policies. As Dimmock argued: 'The third effect of incomes policy lies in its impact on trade union growth and the emergence of hospital level trade union organization.'[8] This related to the embarrassment and scandal of low pay in the NHS for a Labour government at a time of tight incomes policy controls. The only political way to reconcile these competing policy demands was through the NBPI's line on linking the low paid ancillary workers to some local incentive schemes. This gave them pay rises with the public justification of more pay in return for higher productivity.

In addition to these factors the concentration of staff into large general hospitals and the hierarchical division of labour among managers within a context of union growth and legislative support for collective bargaining delivered industrial relations issues to a wider audience. This increase in size of the main unit of employment had important consequences, which included,

> changes in social relationships, as staff were massed together in the much larger district general hospitals that were being built in the 1960s. The policy of the day was centralisation, which was magically expected to achieve efficiency.[9]

In 1972 some ancillary staff took strike action without undue disasters for themselves or the patients. This signalled a major change in attitude, and in the absence of any coherent management strategy on this issue, the lessons from the strike were beneficial to those workers and trade unionists most concerned to pursue their claims through industrial action. As the TUC noted:

> In the 1972 ancillary workers dispute, shop stewards negotiated with local management over the organization of emergency services in individual hospitals all over the country. The nurses dispute in 1974, the junior hospital doctors dispute in 1975, and the disputes of the winter of 1979, were all characterised by militant local action. Even organisations which had previously distanced themselves from trade union methods began to move towards the development of workplace representatives.[10]

The importance of this impact on local industrial relations of national disputes applied equally to the 1982 disputes. The research done by Morris and Rydykowski[11] after the 1982 strikes showed that 'in those authorities which took action, such as sending home staff who refused to work normally or who used internal volunteers (the minority), industrial relations tended to be adversely affected'.[12] More and more groups became involved with local bargaining throughout the 1970s, such as ambulance and maintenance staff as well as the A&C grades.

This change in the 1970s based on higher levels of union membership, favourable legislation, the breakthrough of industrial action without guilt, and the impact on NHS staff of the actions and attitudes of workers in other industries coincided with larger employment units as hospital workers went to work in larger district general hospitals. While such patterns emerged in general terms, as for most industries, workplace industrial relations is as varied as the large number of workplaces in the NHS. These are mainly composed of the 1700 hospitals in England ranging in size from more than 600 with less than 50 beds, to ten with more than 1000 beds. The majority of hospitals have less than 250 beds. Since most health service workers work in hospitals, the issues covered in this chapter apply to about nine out of every ten members of staff (Table 7.1).

Even from the outset, hospitals were the core of the NHS, and subject to different traditions of operation and management. In 1948,

> Hospitals which had previously been voluntary or local authority were brought together into the same groups. In total, 1145 voluntary hospitals with some 90,000 beds were taken over, and 1545 municipal hospitals with about 390,000 beds.[13]

Power resided with hospital management committees operating at group level with some tendency to delegate to matrons and lay-clerks. These two shared responsibilities with the chair of the medical staff committee. As Abel-Smith summarizes:

> Such were the traditions – one almost strictly hierarchical, the other multilateral, with the actual power relationships varying according to the hospital and the personalities of those holding particular posts.[14]

The important point is that today's local bargaining cannot escape from the customs and traditions of the large variety of hospitals throughout the NHS, and that the events of the late 1960s that triggered off the now familiar industrial relations in the NHS, were deeply rooted in older practices and relationships which provided the seeds for the developments of the 1970s and 1980s.

Workplaces are subject to some further subdivisions such as departments and units and clinical directorates, which may in themselves be in the same or in separate buildings and even separate locations. It is also the case that several workplaces form together into the employing unit of a health authority, and that some of the points that are made apply not to workplace industrial relations but to the industrial relations at the level of the employer. These preliminary points need to be appreciated

Table 7.1 Distribution[1] of hospitals and hospital beds by size of hospital and broad type (England)

	1978	1982	1983	1984	1985	1986	1987/8[2]	1988/9
Hospitals								
All hospitals: total	2063	1917	1923	1891	1862	1870	1737	1730
with under 50 beds	754	706	722	720	723	753	655	692
50–249 beds	845	766	762	738	709	690	669	637
250–499 beds	238	239	234	230	236	244	244	245
500–999 beds	181	182	184	182	176	168	159	150
1000–1999 beds	45	24	21	21	18	15	10	6
Non-psychiatric hospitals: total	1653	1471	1465	1413	1351	1328	1282	1242
with under 50 beds	617	531	536	509	470	467	455	446
50–249 beds	731	650	642	618	594	575	544	516
250–499 beds	187	174	166	163	167	171	170	174
500–999 beds	109	110	115	117	114	108	107	101
1000–1999 beds	9	6	6	6	6	7	6	5
Psychiatric hospitals: total	410	446	458	478	511	542	455	488
with under 50 beds	137	175	186	211	253	286	200	246
50–249 beds	114	116	120	120	115	115	125	121
250–499 beds	51	65	68	67	69	73	74	71
500–999 beds	72	72	69	65	62	60	52	49
1000–1999 beds	36	18	15	15	12	8	4	1

[1] Figures are based on a count of hospitals which provided residential facilities. Day hospitals and clinics are therefore not included. Also not included are some isolation hospitals and hospitals which were temporarily closed.
[2] From 1988 collection of data changed from years ended 31 December to years ended 31 March. Mental handicap community units are excluded.
Source: Health and Personal Social Services Statistics.

Table 7.1 (*continued*) Distribution[1] of hospitals and hospital beds by size of hospital and broad type (England)

	1978	1982	1983	1984	1985	1986	1987/8[2]	1988/9
Available beds[3]								
All hospitals: total	377 554	348 104	343 091	334 513	325 487	315 706	297 342	282 937
with under 50 beds	19 714	18 976	18 949	18 219	17 980	17 889	16 045	16 017
50–249 beds	95 429	87 344	86 700	84 412	80 333	76 874	74 563	70 806
250–499 beds	85 079	87 214	85 140	83 482	86 748	89 648	89 254	84 490
500–999 beds	121 412	125 576	127 226	124 185	119 853	114 388	106 412	99 906
1000–1999 beds	55 920	28 994	25 676	24 216	20 572	16 908	11 066	6718
Non-psychiatric hospitals: total	245 730	231 355	229 850	226 040	222 631	212 019	212 019	205 309
with under 50 beds	16 166	14 797	14 630	13 433	12 636	12 373	11 866	11 329
50–249 beds	81 953	73 853	72 880	70 094	66 629	63 733	60 695	57 106
250–499 beds	65 858	62 488	59 086	57 769	60 252	62 489	62 209	63 966
500–999 beds	71 343	73 236	76 363	77 851	76 010	72 058	70 349	67 232
1000–1999 beds	10 410	6981	6891	6894	7104	7989	6900	5675
Psychiatric hospitals: total	131 824	116 749	113 241	108 473	102 855	97 064	85 321	77 628
with under 50 beds	3548	4179	4318	4876	5344	5515	4179	4688
50–249 beds	13 476	13 491	13 820	14 318	13 704	13 141	13 869	13 700
250–499 beds	19 221	24 726	26 054	25 713	26 496	27 159	27 045	25 524
500–999 beds	50 069	52 340	50 863	46 334	43 843	42 330	36 063	32 674
1000–1999 beds	45 510	22 013	18 186	17 322	13 468	8919	4166	1043

[1] Figures are based on a count of hospitals which provided residential facilities. Day hospitals and clinics are therefore not included. Also not included are some isolation hospitals and hospitals which were temporarily closed.

[2] From 1988 collection of data changed from years ended 31 December to years ended 31 March. Mental handicap community units are excluded.

[3] Figures are based on the average daily number of available beds during the year and may not add to totals because of rounding.

Source: Health and Personal Social Services Statistics.

since a great deal of the literature of workplace bargaining and the role of stewards is sensitive to the size of the workplace and the size of the employer.

This chapter is a general account of local industrial relations and thus fails to represent the richness of practice and the complexity of prevailing relationships as between the parties, health workers, unions, line managers, personnel managers and other interested groups and individuals. In reality, there is an endless stream of force and counter-force combining into a bewildering web of formal and informal practices as subtle and as difficult to untangle as any political phenomena based on power relations hidden by layer on layer of work, social and industrial relations appearances.

The rest of the chapter examines current practices at hospital and health authority levels, including the closed shop, union organization at local level, joint consultative arrangements, disciplinary and grievance procedures, industrial action and the disputes procedure, and the role of management. The empirical evidence for much of this is neither systematic nor comprehensive, and therefore much of the material is by example. The main objective is to examine some features of the local systems and bring out some traditional areas of difficulty and conflict. There are also comparisons made with general findings based on the industrial relations surveys in the 1980s.[15]

THE ORGANIZATION OF THE TRADE UNIONS AND PROFESSIONAL ASSOCIATIONS AT WORKPLACE AND AUTHORITY LEVEL

Local industrial relations in the NHS up until the 1960s were very quiet and by the end of that decade only the craft unions, TGWU and GMB, had shop stewards in NHS establishments. The major NHS unions operated exclusively through branch officers. Prior to 1974, a hospital group was considered unusual for having as many as 30 recognized stewards. By 1978, figures indicated that it was not unusual for a district to have more than 100 recognized stewards, and some had more than 150. This figure remained unchanged in 1990.

Until 1977 five categories of staff were able to claim representation on the JCCs. These were administrative and clerical, nursing and midwifery, technical and professional, domestic, and farm, garden and artisan. In 1977 hospital medical and dental staff were included as a sixth category of staff. Membership of the staff side of JCCs was limited to people who were members of recognized national staff side organizations. The seating allocation on the staff side of these committees is generally based on the principle of 'proportional' representation, which usually means that it is necessary for the smaller professional associations to 'share' seats.

These local union bodies became more important with the legislation of the 1970s, such as the Trade Union and Labour Relations Act (1974) and the Employment Protection Act (1975). As a consequence ACAS published codes of practice on disciplinary and dismissal procedures (ACAS Code 1), disclosure of information (ACAS Code 2) and time off for trade union activities (ACAS Code 3). These codes of practice all recommend formal procedures and encourage employers to enter into negotiations with their staff representatives to ensure that their practices and procedures are in line with the recommendations of the codes. As a result, between 1976 and 1977 most health authorities negotiated their own disciplinary procedures and many agreed grievance procedures. A few, led by Newcastle, negtiated agreements on facilities and time off for shop stewards.

These influences strengthened, and were strengthened by, the increasingly unionized health workers. In other words, most hospital and most non-hospital workers do belong to trade unions/professional associations, and before the coming of self-governing trusts in April 1991 employers recognized all the original Whitley based trade unions. So for the NHS recognition was not a live issue, and non-members were covered by collective agreements and customary practices along with union members.

As union membership rose and as the number of local issues for negotiation increased so, since the mid-1970s, there has been a huge increase in shop steward numbers and level of activity, and this has tended to be true for all groups and for most trade unions. The slowest in this respect was the BMA with their POWAR system. This reflects the paucity of workplace issues associated with doctors, and their reliance on a strong cadre of full-time officials.

The rise in shop steward numbers and influence was matched by the development of joint union committees over the past 15 years. In many hospitals they have proved very successful. The major weaknesses have been the lack of support from some health workers such as the doctors, and the division between TUC and non-TUC unions. This became very intense in the late 1970s and early 1980s, and still persists in some areas such as Oxford and Merseyside.

When hospitals are compared with other workplaces then, by the early 1980s, the extent and density of union membership was high for the size of workplace. Thus the average figure in the private sector for establishments with between 100 and 199 employees was 39%.[16] In the NHS this figure would be estimated at 65%. The NHS was more in line with other industries in the case of the prevalence of multi-unionism. As the workplace survey showed:

> Multi-unionism remains a notable feature of the British industrial relations scene and is especially common for manual employees in large manufacturing plants and for non-manual workers in the public sector.[17]

The larger the establishment, the higher the proportional numbers of stewards, with the largest establishments having stewards in 97% of cases.[18] Estimates of the numbers of stewards in the NHS are difficult to make, but assuming that each major union has at least two stewards in each hospital, and that the smaller professions have unit stewards in about one in three hospitals then the number is about 40 000 stewards, which would be about 4% of the workforce. Given the number of part-time workers this represents about 4.5% of the full-time work-force. In 1984 there was one steward for every 23 manual workers and one for every 21 non-manual, which is about 4%.

In terms of training, however, some NHS stewards appear better trained than is generally the case. The stewards from the large TUC-affiliated manual workers' unions either attend the ten day TUC courses, and/or receive training from their own unions such as at the GMB college in Manchester. Most of the professions, including the RCN, have used either their own trainers or, like the NUM, have utilized universities.

The extent of union representation can be judged by the varied nature of NHS employees and by the large number of part-time workers in certain occupations.[19] So in the case of ancillary workers there remains a high level of labour turnover which affects union recruitment and the stability needed for shop steward organization. In addition, while large numbers belong to unions, there remains widespread indifference to trade union activity and, partly as a consequence of sharp union rivalries, some dissatisfaction with the unions. The unions' local activities are often hit and miss, and this is due to a combination of union insensitivity to the needs of many of their members and the lack of management interest in worker complaints.

An important part of any steward's effectiveness is the facilities available to them, including time off. These are covered in general by national agreements and in the case of time off by ACAS Code 3 (as updated in 1991). In addition there are regional agreements often topped up by district and unit agreements. Facilities might include time off for training, office facilities, time off for industrial relations duties, meetings in working hours, and the right to receive visits from full-time officials. The main clash of interests is over time off. Line managers may feel that a member of their staff has too much time off to fulfil industrial relations functions elsewhere, while the personnel and/or senior managers may wish a known and experienced individual to deal with issues wherever they arise in the unit or district. Another practice which is currently under attack is that of the check-off system by which union members pay their subscriptions directly through the employer – the government has announced its intention to change the rules on this in its next Employment Act. The government believes that the abolition of DOCAS will reduce union funds and membership, but several NHS unions have already reverted to more traditional systems of dues collection.

Few NHS unions have workplace branches. The professional associations tend to have branches based on geographical areas with a minimum of trade union activity. The large multi-occupational unions may have workplace branches, but as with other union experience, their meetings tend to be badly attended unless there is a crisis. Branch secretaries and presidents may have powers which overlap with stewards and this can cause tensions, as experienced with other parts of the trade union movement and which led to the major internal reforms of unions such as the TGWU and NUPE.[20]

Among manual workers the most common form of branch organization remains the multi-employer one with a geographical basis. There has been a growth in single-employer branches, which are used in the NHS, with workplace branches the least popular form of organization.[21] The GMB and the TGWU are moving towards single-employer branches away from geographical ones, which means a fall in the average size of the branch. In contrast NUPE has been moving in the opposite direction, with larger geographical branches.

The manner in which union stewards are selected has always been of great concern. By election or appointment? If elected, by show of hands or by secret ballot? The smaller the workplace the more informal the arrangements for appointing stewards, although non-manual workers tend to prefer more formal electoral contests. The evidence from the NHS is that in many cases there is no competition for the post, but had there been formal elections would take place for non-manual workers, while a show of hands still existed for manual stewards.[22]

The functions and activities of stewards are more important than their method of selection. Again the NHS manual workers' experience corresponds with that of those outside the NHS. This is as expected since the majority belong to unions with large memberships in other industries, such as NUPE, GMB and TGWU. Again the behaviour of MSF stewards mimics that of their colleagues in other industries. It is the nurses and other professions who exhibit special features of activity. Nearly all NHS groups do organize a hierarchy of stewards or their equivalent. There are unit, district and regional stewards for the CSP and the RCN, and these last equate with senior stewards among the manual workers. Most of the more senior stewards reported that they met their full-time officials two or three times in the previous year.[23]

This is partly a function of union organization, regional and/or national bargaining, support from other stewards, habits of advice-seeking, and specific workplace issues. All the full-time officials approached for this study from nearly all the NHS unions indicated, as would be expected, a large increase in contacts with stewards in the past two years.

The NHS in 1991 has a set of stewards and steward networks which are well established, relatively well trained but inexperienced in terms of bargaining. The stewards representing ancillary staff, ambulance staff and technical staff have more relevant experience than most of the others but are still short of the levels of expertise found in much of British industry. While there are variations in the quality and quantity of stewards as between districts and regions and as between unions and occupations, none the less a health worker from the 1960s would not recognize the workplace trade union situation found 30 years later, nor would any manager!

THE CLOSED SHOP

The closed shop has not been a major issue in the NHS and hospital system owing to the nature of the industry and the type of workers involved. But the issue has been raised from time to time in various forms. The only serious research into the subject was by Harrison in the late 1970s. He argued that while the closed shop was spreading rapidly in some parts of British industry at the time, yet very few had resulted in the NHS despite the fact that 'trade unionists made frequent demands for the closed shop and where managers were apparently not unwilling to concede it'.[24]

By 1979 only four agreements covering a handful of workers had been reached, despite the existence of five factors which might be expected to encourage closed shops. Firstly, it was at a time of very rapid increases in trade union membership and density in the NHS – density rose from 32% in 1966 to 55% in 1974 and to 76% by 1978. Secondly, local industrial relations had become more intense due in part to policies adopted by NUPE and the TGWU to bargain over incentive schemes introduced at this time and with the new procedures in operation. Thirdly, joint consultation had revived and there was a marked increase in industrial action. Fourthly, manual workers in the NHS still laboured under poor conditions of employment, and fifthly they were subject to greater managerial controls then their counterparts in other industries or indeed as compared with the professions in the NHS.

In 1976 the staff side of Ancillary Whitley wanted to open negotiations on a national closed shop.[25] The DHSS and the management side took a neutral view on this, and the health authorities themselves varied in reaction. Most agreed that it should be up to local managers to decide, and that they should not be bound by a national agreement. In 1977 a similar demand came from the ambulance staff. By 1979 there had been 93 claims for a closed shop in 63 health authorities. All originated from the trade unions, and most from lay activists at branch level. NUPE led this campaign, while COHSE played a minor role. NALGO was the only white-collar union involved, but on a limited basis.

All authorities took these demands seriously. Forty-six had specific policies of which nine were opposed, and only 27 were written documents with notions of how to deal with claims and the likely content of any agreement. This reflected a pragmatic approach, based often on local traditions. Prior to 1972 there were 24 workgroups covered by a 'semi-closed shop' where 100% membership was the norm, but non-members would not be dismissed. The majority of these covered maintenance and ambulance staff. By 1980 just over 2000 staff were in a closed shop, of whom about half were NUPE members in the ambulance service.[26] Overall, therefore, the limitations of local bargaining and a workforce often divided into competing unions meant that the closed shop was an issue that flickered briefly but never caught on in the NHS. In the 1980s it became increasingly unimportant.

In 1984 30% of manual and 8% of non-manual employees in British industry were covered by a closed shop agreement.[27] This includes the two types of closed shop: the pre-entry where you have to be a union member to get the job, as with merchant seamen and actors; and the post-entry closed shop, which means you have to join the union as soon as you get the job, as in the mining industry and many sections of engineering. Legislation and changes in employers' policies have meant a decline in the closed shop throughout industry in the UK in the 1980s,[28] and the NHS, which was never vitally affected by this arrangement, is unlikely to witness its revival in the 1990s.

JOINT CONSULTATIVE AND NEGOTIATING ARRANGEMENTS

The TUC pointed out in 1981 that there is no single model for the conduct of industrial relations at local level in the NHS.[29] As far as joint union involvement is concerned there are two broad sets of bargaining arrangements: the Joint Staff Consultative Committee (JSCC or JCC) and the Joint Shop Stewards Committee (JSSC). In most health authorities some form of each exists, but there are a number of variations of constitution, scope and power of both types of committee.

In 1950 the GWC introduced a national model constitution for JCCs to be formed in hospitals. It required all consultative committees to conform to the model constitution and expressed the view that such committees were desirable in all hospitals except those where numbers of staff were small. As Dyson pointed out these joint consultative committees had limited functions –

mainly to promote cooperation between management and staff – and their opportunity to consider hospital rules was limited by the strict requirement that local arrangements should not cut across any national or regional provisions.[30]

The model agreement included the functions of these local consultative committees. These embraced cooperation between staff and their employer, 'to prevent friction and misunderstanding', and to deal with matters such as the distribution of working hours, holiday arrangements, and matters of physical welfare such as heating and cloakrooms. As McCarthy pointed out, between the start of this agreement in 1950 and 1974 'the experience of joint consultation was not happy'.[31]

In many places there were no committees and in many others they enjoyed a brief life. There is no proper evidence of the working of joint consultation in the NHS,[32] and the view of McCarthy was that it was muddled and varied. McCarthy discovered the main reasons for failure:

1. Lack of suitable subject matter – in general, managers felt that the committees discussed trivia and that many trade union representatives were incapable of 'realistically' discussing wider issues. In some DHAs, however, there were flourishing committees which consulted over major items of concern such as early retirement schemes.

2. Non-participation by doctors – everyone agreed that without the doctors many important issues could not be discussed with an adequate sense of relevance.

3. Lack of commitment – most managers took a paternalistic approach which disconcerted the trade union representatives, and this was particularly the case with senior nurses.

4. The composition of the staff side – the first issue was the method of selection, and in practice staff side representatives tended to be shop stewards despite the model agreement's emphasis on elections of representatives of all relevant staff groups. The second issue was the refusal of some TUC unions to sit alongside non-TUC unions. It was ASTMS which took the lead in this with a strong advocacy for local negotiations, and the exclusion of the professional associations from this process. The result was an increasing tendency in the late 1970s for there to be two joint consultative committees in some health authorities.

In the end McCarthy preferred formal consultative arrangements at national, regional and local level. At local level the staff side was to be based on nomination by recognized staff organizations. By the end of the 1970s these points were being fiercely debated as the importance of workplace bargaining dawned on civil servants at the DHSS and political leaders alike. The essential message sent by McCarthy was to formalize joint procedures at all levels in order to maintain control and guarantee the orderly conduct of industrial relations.

In 1978 ACAS had criticized the trade unions for their lack of coordination at local level (through the JSSCs) and inter-union rivalry, particularly between NUPE and COHSE.[33] They found that the practice of JCCs varied between flourishing examples to none at all. In addition some were influential in wider DHA decisions and others had the barest impact. ACAS disliked the regional tier proposed by McCarthy, and favoured building JCCs at unit and district levels.[34]

One barrier to this was the considerable unwillingness in some health authorities among those trade unions affiliated to the TUC (particularly ASTMS and NUPE) to sit alongside non-TUC affiliates (such as the RCN) on joint negotiation and consultative committees. This issue had largely diminished by the mid 1980s,[35] although there were still a few isolated examples of management negotiating with both TUC-affiliated and non-affiliated unions at separate joint negotiating committees, as at Oxford.

This discussion of the structural issues in JCCs should not cloud the true purpose of such committees. First, as was noted in Chapter 1, the distinction between consultation and negotiation is clear in theory but blurred in practice. The name of a committee and/or process should not allow any misunderstanding as to its potential. Secondly, consultation in the form discussed here is about ways in which staff can exert pressure on management to change decisions. This can occur either before the final option by management has been decided, or after the decision has been made and the discussion applies to its implementation. The TUC voiced the union position clearly enough:

> We have identified the main trends in local industrial relations in the NHS in recent years as the development of workplace representatives, notably shop stewards and safety representatives.[36]

Therefore, district level JCCs free to negotiate and consult, and based on shop steward representation on the union side, is the favoured TUC formulation. From this flows the setting up of JSSCs at district level with less formal arrangements at unit level. It is here that the TUC is reduced to special pleading on behalf of its affiliated members. This takes the form of urging staff in non-TUC organizations to seek representation through affiliated unions – a rehash of the COHSE dual membership idea. This view was then short-sighted, but is now irrelevant. Large industrial unions such as the EEPTU are no longer in the TUC while small professional associations such as the Society of Radiographers are. In addition, the artificial divisions built on prejudice rather than good trade union principles have damaged the effectiveness of joint staff action in years when such action was essential to prevent cutbacks, subcontracting and opting out.

The TUC did recognize that the underlying hostility to the non-affiliates among some of the TUC unions was based on membership competition. Inter-union hostilities still exist between the TUC unions: for example, at the 1990 GMB annual conference a GMB ambulanceman attacked NUPE colleagues and the TUC for the failure of the 1989/90 dispute. Membership is falling among the large TUC unions and still rising among most of the professional associations. This means both a shift in the balance of power and a reassessment of inter-union cooperation/competition.

None the less, the pressures from below, management reorganizations and outside influences kept up the relentless pace for more local industrial relations. This was given a further shove with the negotiation of 'enabling agreements' by the GWC – for example, one on career breaks and women returners.[37] In particular, the GWC agreed a framework for consultation in 1979 and for a local disputes procedure in 1980. These became Sections 39 and 33 of the GWC handbook.

Thus the most important feature of local collective bargaining by the late 1970s was its formalization. This was manifested by the introduction of local joint negotiation/consultation committees, largely at district level. The nature of these committees varied between health authorities. Mailly *et al.* point out that:

> in some, perhaps a minority, they were fora for genuine negotiation of issues of concern to management and staff: in others, they were a channel of communication whereby management passed information on to the trade unions.[38]

The subject matter of local negotiations/consultation includes such issues as local bonus schemes, staff rotas, health and safety, statutory holidays, discipline, grievance and other procedures. However, it is the case that local decisions must not contradict or override the provisions agreed nationally by the Whitley councils. This has limited their impact and created the demand for greater local freedom in the operation of self-governing trusts and directly managed units.

Throughout the lifetime of the NHS, the Whitley system of national collective bargaining over terms and conditions of service has remained intact. Local JCCs have gradually been established, although their scope and procedures are far from uniform and their degree of influence upon local decisions remains varied. As NHS employees enter the last decade of the century, the government's radical proposals to fragment the service undermine and threaten both the Whitley system and local collective bargaining arrangements. The situation in 1991 is that joint consultative committees between the employers and the unions are widespread in the NHS, and these operate at the level of the employer with lesser committees at the workplace. Most are fairly formal, with agenda and regular meetings, although few have a written constitution or set of rules. The normal pattern is that regular attenders from the union side dominate the joint union committee and deal with those matters of general concern to all health workers in the authority such as the disciplinary procedure and grievance handling. Specific issues for particular groups, such as overtime and skill mix, are dealt with by the groups outside of the joint union forum. A source of political activity within the organization is the relative strengths of joint committees and meetings as opposed to single-union and/or single occupation bargaining arrangements. Up until now there have been few regular issues of great moment and therefore the system has either fallen into disrepair or operates through a handful of individuals from both sides. In contrast, serious issues and crises such as ward closures, industrial action and safety matters may bring to life moribund institutional arrangements and intensify political antagonisms between and within the unions. As Sethi *et al.* claim:

> Hospital-based trade unionism has generally been concerned with the improvement of local circumstances in terms of earnings increases (where possible) and more favourable working conditions.[39]

This local level strength, which developed in random fashion, has been utilized to combat the cuts and privatizations of the 1980s. The level of success in outright terms has been very limited, but in terms of altering both the extent of the changes and the resultant terms of employment then their activities are more worthwhile. In addition, they have fuelled the movement at local level to greater concern with low pay, issues associated with part-time women workers, and those from ethnic minorities. So race and gender issues have become more important at local level through the struggles of trade unionists based in JSSCs and JCCs, and this means that more members' interests and concerns are being addressed at local and national level. This may help explain the survival of union organization at a time when the manual unions are experiencing deep crises from loss of members and reduced influence.

In a multi-union establishment the links between stewards are very important. In general in 1984 about 30% of manual and non-manual stewards reported meetings with other stewards from their union.[40] This was more frequent the larger the place of work. In the NHS this is probably higher due to the proximity of the working situation and the common cause of the industry, but on the best estimate there is not significantly more contact.

JSSC's are widespread in NHS hospitals, even when they are seldom used to the full. Again the overall pattern in the NHS formally would be higher than the national picture.[41] The extent of contact between stewards from different unions is dependent on the stewards involved, the traditions in the area, and the issues. But in the NHS, with several unions representing the same type of staff, then meetings are more frequent. NUPE, COHSE and the GMB have overlaps in several areas of hospital and ambulance recruitment, and although there are often sharp rivalries there are also sufficient pressures to force them together in some circumstances. Equally the unions representing PAMs have common cause and common conditions of service. So some meetings between their stewards would be expected. This applies to nurses and midwives, and nurses from the different nursing unions. Whether all this adds up to systematic joint union activity is doubtful owing to the lack of workplace organization among some groups, traditional rivalries and the lack of workplace and employer level issues. How this will change in 1991 with SGTs is unsure but the first guess must be more frequent meetings among the staff side than before.

Of greater interest for the future is the development of single-employer combine committees. This will depend on management strategies in terms of union recognition, bargaining arrangements and on the unions' ability to hold together under labour market and government pressures to fragment.

When there is joint consultation then the composition of each side is important, as is the method by which they are selected. Is it proportional? Is it by right of each recognized group? Is there a larger joint union committee which sends representatives to a negotiating committee? And, if so, how are they selected and how accountable are they to the larger committee? In 1984 such committees in the UK with manual workers tended to negotiate with management the most, then came those with non-manual only, while those committees with both manual and non-manual did the least negotiating.[42]

The union approach is increasingly typical of industrial relations throughout British companies, and is explained by COHSE: 'The very fact that there are trade unions, employers and/or managements means, by definition, that there will be conflict.'[43]

The pattern of joint negotiating/consultation committees is one that is now formally entrenched in most hospitals and authorities. The management, in the main, use them to communicate and consult with staff over a range of issues, while the unions normally act together in a loose federation on issues that effect all the staff. But with limited scope to negotiate over terms and conditions of employment the committees have tended to deal with other issues including a range of procedural matters such as discipline, grievance, disputes and equal opportunities policies.

An example of the work of such committees can help bring alive the issues. In 1989 a health authority announced the transfer of geriatric and medical services from a small local hospital to the larger district hospital. There was a formal meeting between the managers and the staff representatives at which there were two unit general managers, three unit personnel officers, the district personnel officer and two other managers. The staff side had representatives from the AEU, COHSE, NUPE, NALGO, HPA, BAOT, CSP and the Society of Radiographers. The meeting was there to discuss the application of the authority's redeployment, retraining and redundancy policies. About 300 staff would be involved in the transfer and all would receive counselling interviews.

The key negotiating areas were the 'ring fencing' of posts arising from the new developments for 'at risk' staff. The staff side wanted an immediate freeze on all outside recruitment, but the management rejected this. The staff listed by the management to be transferred included A&C grades, maintenance staff, nurses (the majority), some PAMs and some managers. In addition, ancillary staff would be moved from the catering, domestic, laundry and porter departments.

This meeting followed on from a meeting of the Joint Management and Trades Union Committee of the Community Services Unit on personnel issues for the staff involved. So formal meetings of both sides were held to negotiate over the application of policies on moving staff. The move itself was not negotiable. This is one example of a formal and well-functioning JCC activated for a serious but one-off purpose.

PROCEDURES IN GENERAL

In 1984 the British workplace survey claimed that:

> Since the publication of the Donovan Commission's report almost twenty years ago, the development of rules and procedures about employment matters has been widely seen as being central to the promotion of fairness and consistency in the treatment of individuals and in the conduct of industrial relations.[44]

The NHS has formal procedures at the level of all employing authorities on discipline and grievance, and they share a common disputes procedure. By 1984 virtually all establishments in the public sector had such procedures, and about 90% in the private sector. In almost every case a recognized union was involved. In general procedures represent the culmination of the social democratic consensus on the handling of industrial relations through joint job regulation as espoused by Whitley and Donovan and embraced by the trade unions, most large employers and, until recently, throughout the public sector. On this perspective procedures are mechanisms to prevent conflict through the forced orderly conduct of bargaining with, in some cases, the right to utilize third party arrangements. This is, in the classic sense, the institutionalization of conflict and the removal of collective bargaining from the point of production.

In cases of discipline and grievance it allows employers and managers to isolate individual workers and so to minimize collective considerations of the issues. At the same time the joint regulation of such issues does allow for some union activity, but the balance of advantage and disadvantage for workplace bargainers as between the existence of formal procedures and resolving differences in other ways is indeterminate. Thus the existence and operation of procedures forms a major part of workplace and employer level industrial relations, and this has been the situation in the NHS.

Every health authority has a written disciplinary procedure, and in almost every case one that has been agreed with the unions through the joint consultative committee. In most cases such agreements cover all staff bar the doctors and dentists, and nowadays senior managers. Similarly every health authority has a grievance procedure to 'settle differences with regard to conditions of service' and an associated appeals system.

DISCIPLINE

Elsewhere in the UK, disciplinary procedures do cover most employees, and are now written agreements. Again in most cases there is provision for some outside intervention as a final stage. The link with dismissal is so close that the two topics will be handled together. But redundancy will not be covered here.

The basis of discipline is that the employer claims the right to discipline and dismiss employees on the grounds of incapacity (incompetence, illness or inefficiency) or misconduct (disobedience). Most cases fall into one of these categories, although in some cases the two overlap. Misconduct would include being drunk on duty and lateness, while incompetence would relate to the carrying out of duties badly such as administering the wrong drug. Discipline is mainly a tool for management to maintain control over the workforce, and should be seen as part of a total relationship at work involving managers, employees and trade unions. In the late 1970s the NHS began to use written disciplinary procedures as part of the response by management to the increased unionization of the workforce with its concomitant increase in knowledge of, and willingness to challenge, management defined cases of misconduct and/or incompetence.

This response was based on McCarthy's summary of the prevailing wisdom as to the need to institutionalize conflict through orderly employer level procedures and the extension of collective bargaining to include these managerial relations. Once established the procedures operated in a variety of ways which in part reflected the procedure itself, in part the traditions of the authority and/or hospital, and in part the relationships between groups of staff.

Most NHS disciplinary procedures follow a similar pattern. The preamble, often referred to as the 'general policy', is essential as the expression of its 'spirit and intention', and it lays out the compromise as between the employer's desire for discipline to be applied to help achieve operational needs such as efficiency, and the workforce's collective need for fairness and consistency. This mix of rights is glossed over by ACAS in their Code of Practice, and their recommended form of words emphasizes this:

> This procedure is designed to help and encourage all employees to achieve and maintain standards of conduct, attendance and job performance ... The aim is to ensure consistent and fair treatment for all.[45]

The inclusion of counselling and informal warnings in most NHS disciplinary procedures is misconceived. The reason is that counselling requires consent and assumes a relationship which is based on trust. Any suggestion of potential discipline following on from counselling and/or its presence in a disciplinary document may well, and in fact tends to, undermine its purpose. In the case of informal warnings they are what they say they are, namely, the provision to tell someone off without recording it and without any blemish on the worker's record. Informal means just that, and therefore reference to informal warnings should not occur in the formal procedure. The failure to understand this has meant that, in the NHS, procedures have been wrongly applied and clumsily implemented. This failure to deal adequately with disciplinary cases has several serious consequences: other workers may resent the failure to punish a wrongdoer, other workers may resent the unfair punishment of a colleague, managers may be inconsistent which creates uncertainty and feelings of favouritism, and management authority may be undermined by inconsistent and at times incomprehensible disciplinary punishments.

Once into the formal procedure there are two major points: the first is the application of the rules of natural justice in terms of the right of representation, of a fair hearing, of appeal and so on. These need to be followed in order to prevent, from the employers' point of view, individuals going to industrial tribunals and winning unfair dismissal cases, and in order to prevent the trade unions from exploiting unfair treatment of individual workers. The second main point is that the punishments are ordered in severity from oral warnings through written warnings to suspensions and dismissal. In cases of incompetence the norm is to work through the levels in order to provide the individual with every chance to improve, but in cases of misconduct any level of punishment can be used as long as it is proportional to the offence.

To understand the importance of discipline in NHS industrial relations at local level reference can be made to one of the few systematic studies of the topic. Fewtrell, in 1983, looked at 13 health authorities over a one year period and found that five out of every six industrial relations 'incidents' were about discipline, where this meant a case resulting in a written warning or worse.[46]

This can be illustrated by reference to some typical disciplinary cases and the industrial relations aspects of them. The legal aspects will be kept to a minimum. In most cases in the NHS, for manual and technical staff stewards represented their members. For nurses and professional staff the practice was more varied, although stewards always represented when asked to do so. There are cases, however, where either the individual refused representation and/or there was no steward available from the relevant union. If the worker is not in a union then both the ACAS code and the agreed procedures allow for a 'friend' or 'fellow employee' to represent.

McCarthy found that stewards participated in three ways in discipline cases:

(1) they communicated to their members management concern over breach of rules and orders and warned of intentions to 'tighten up' on discipline. (2) They provided information as to the extent of breaches of rules and orders. (3) They acted as spokesmen for those of their members who were disciplined.[47]

This participation often took place with or without procedures or formal agreements. In other words, in most medium to large workplaces the managers understood the need for intermediaries as between themselves and the workforce, and that discipline, although applied to individuals, was essentially a collective act of control. This last point means that the law and legal accounts of discipline overstate the individual nature of cases and fail to see the wider power relations at work.

One area in which local union activists can become involved is during the negotiations on the procedure itself. In 1988 Portsmouth and South East Hampshire Health Authority decided to negotiate a new disciplinary procedure. The meeting to discuss Draft Nine was attended by trade unionists from the RCN, NUPE, CSP, UCATT, COHSE and NALGO. The management team was composed of the district personnel officer and two other personnel managers. The document distinguished between conduct, capability and ill health.

It lays out the nature and scope of disciplinary hearings to establish the facts and the procedures for the disciplinary interview. The union representatives have a role at all stages. It provides an appeal system, and importantly lays out considerations in special cases of alcohol-related work problems, for the positive control of absence, and for long-term illness. This example illustrates the importance of joint regulation in the establishment of procedures, the inconsistent attendance by the unions during such negotiations, and the relationship of formal discipline to other employment matters.

The main legal concerns in dismissals are that the employer has a 'good reason' and 'acts fairly'.[48] On this view a great deal hinges on the contract of employment itself. For example, the General Nursing Council advised that there were four aspects of a nurse's life subject to employer discipline: on-duty work affecting patients, on-duty work not affecting patients, off-duty activities on the premises, and off-duty activities off the premises.

Misconduct and/or disobedience cover a multitude of sins. A nursing auxiliary was threatened with dismissal if she refused to transfer from her work in the maternity ward to the geriatric ward, and the industrial tribunal (IT) upheld the employer's right to transfer in this case. A hospital porter refused one day to empty bins which he usually did because he claimed they now contained obnoxious substances. He was dismissed. One aspect of this case was that the porter was not informed of his right of appeal and that the alternative punishment of suspension was not considered – the IT felt these were important breaches by the management. In fact most NHS cases are characterized by poor management understanding of the issues and the law. Personnel managers have insufficient training in this area, and may be persuaded to act in breach of natural justice by powerful line managers anxious to rid themselves of incompetent, disobedient or troublesome staff.

There are many straightforward cases of misconduct relating to time keeping, theft and fraud, assault and drunkenness while on duty. These tend to be dealt with on their merits. The more intriguing cases relate to the problems of short-term contracts and non-renewal, redundancy, when a steward and/or some trade union activist is involved, and off-duty offences.

The main concern for now relates to discipline as used or related to trade union cases, since these may be an expression of wider industrial relations issues at the workplace.

> Two COHSE activists were both deputy charge nurses in a large mental hospital. One day both left their nursing duties on union business without permission. The authority called them to a hearing which they refused to attend. They were then suspended on full pay. They again refused to attend a hearing and their full-time official also refused to attend. They were dismissed. Both men took the case to an industrial tribunal but had not used their right of appeal within the NHS. They claimed they had been dismissed on grounds of union activity, which is unfair, but the tribunal decided that they had been dismissed for breach of contract, namely the refusal to attend the meetings and not for union activity.[49]

> Two electrical maintenance tradesmen and members of the AUEW were on a work-to-rule and refused to change air filters. They were ordered to change the filters and refused. The men were dismissed. The tribunal found that the work-to-rule was in breach of a Whitley agreement and a collective agreement, and that it was within the men's job description (although through custom and practice and not written down) to carry out the duties asked of them. Their dismissal was upheld.

> Ms X, a unit administrator and COHSE branch chair, was arrested on a picket line while protesting at a hospital closure. She received a final written warning and appealed to an IT on the basis that she was carrying out her trade union duties. She lost on the grounds that the picket was unlawful and that her industrial action was not covered under trade union duties. Mr Y, a porter in NUPE, issued a press statement about events in his hospital. He was sacked. The IT dismissed his appeal which had been based on his action being part of his trade union activities.

> Mr W, a senior shop steward in the GMB, was denied time off to attend a union conference on a Whitley Council matter. The IT

decided that the employer was not obliged to grant time off since there was no direct industrial relations issue in which the employer was involved. Mr Z, deputy head porter and NUPE branch chairman, was dismissed summarily for both incompetence and disloyalty when he led a strike of porters. His defence rested on two points: he was at a union meeting, and at worst he should receive a final warning. The IT upheld his dismissal on the grounds that his behaviour struck at the heart of the relationship of trust between employer and employee. The IT also criticized the management for its failure to control time off and for its handling of the case.[50]

These are examples taken from hundreds of cases and illustrate the importance of distinguishing between claiming rights as a local trade unionist such as time off and the practice of those rights in all and any circumstances. It also indicates how management can utilize the disciplinary procedures to rid itself of union activists, and therefore of the great importance to all parties of using the procedures in line with the intention of the ACAS code.

The NHS procedures in practice are variable, as already noted. In Fewtrell's survey of discipline in the NHS he found that policies as between health authorities varied on both the nature of the agreement and its implementation. In the first place procedures differed on definitions of categories of offence, number of stages, and length of time warnings stayed on the record.[51] He found in 1980/1 that there were on average 7.2 written warnings or worse given per 1000 staff in 13 authorities studied. But this ranged from more than 14 in one and less than 1 in another. He found it difficult to explain these variations, but felt that size of the health authority and the industrial environment in which it operated were more important than management style and control. This finding needs to be treated with great caution.

Of more interest is the breakdown as between categories of staff: proportionally to the numbers of staff there was more disciplinary action against ancillary workers, and proportionally less for nurses and professional staff. This is as expected in formal terms, although it hides a rich diversity of methods to rid the employer of unwanted professional workers through early retirement schemes and/or 'voluntary' quitting. In terms of offences, that most commonly attracting disciplinary action was unauthorized absence followed by poor timekeeping and

inadequate work. Others included theft, drunkenness, insubord-
ination, assault and drug misuse.

Taking just one example of these, theft, it can be seen that it is
not straightforward. If the theft was on the premises was it from
patients, other staff, or from the employer? Staff may view theft
from the employer as less important than from colleagues. What
was stolen? Was it cash or goods? To what value? If a £10 note is
stolen from a patient how does that compare with drugs valued
at £50 from the employer or a coat worth £30 from a colleague?
Are all instances treated as dismissal, or are warnings appropriate? These sets of questions are raised simply to indicate the
complexity of the issue and that managers need to be careful
about consistent implementation. There is also the case of theft
off premises, such as shoplifting.

> A registrar was accused of stealing a handbag from a shop and
> found guilty. Her employer then dismissed her. The GMC had
> taken no action. The IT found the dismissal fair in the reason and
> in the method. A similar decision was made when a mental
> hospital nurse stole a packet of cigarettes from a patient: she was
> dismissed and the tribunal upheld the decision. The final example
> was when a kitchen superintendent was charged with stealing
> 50p worth of cabbage and carrots from the health authority. The
> police did not proceed with the case but the employer dismissed.
> Again the tribunal upheld the dismissal. In all cases the good
> work record of the sacked workers was ignored and the special
> duties of health workers to patients cited as reason for the insis-
> tence on higher than usual standards.

The consequences of these cases on the individuals are clear,
but what of the impact on other workers and the unions? There
is no evidence about what happened in these cases, but in others
such decisions tend to strengthen the union and its reluctance to
go to tribunals. This may well encourage unions to adopt more
aggressive bargaining positions or to take industrial action.
Other workers may well take fright from such cases, but will be
less willing to cooperate with their employers in other matters.

Another important set of examples revolve around the issue
of discipline for revealing inadequate patient care and/or bad
management practices. These often find their way into the press
and cause genuine public concern. Some of these cases would
appear to be a misuse of the disciplinary procedures and rules to
enforce staff compliance with unacceptable work practices, and
are often linked with inadequate consultative machinery. In

early 1991 there were several such cases, including that of a doctor who told the local media that his hospital had refused an expensive drug to a cancer patient on the grounds of cost. He was disciplined. Several SGTs and DMUs have recently inserted new clauses to their disciplinary procedures about disclosure of information.

For example, South Derbyshire Health Authority issued a reminder to staff that they were forbidden to disclose 'any information, including details of salary, grade, performance related pay etc. to any unauthorised person'. Similar sentiments were being put into the contracts of doctors and other staff in SGTs. These moves may herald an era of commercially inspired confidentiality which outrages both professional ethics and public accountability.

The right of appeal within the NHS is of importance in this area. According to Fewtrell, appeals follow the ratchet principle: 'That is, like a ratchet, appeals tend to move only in one direction – that of reducing the severity of management action in respect of any employee.'[52] Employees have the right to appeal to their employers, but many authorities have a prior stage in which an appeal may be heard by the District Management Team. The appeal to the employing authority is to a committee with at least three members of the authority none of whom has been involved at an earlier stage.[53] These levels exist in recognition of the poor quality of junior management, to keep cases away from authority lay members, and because of the requirements of natural justice.

Disciplinary actions and incidents allow for a range of trade union and bargaining activities. These include negotiating the original agreements, being involved in issues relating to controls, representing members at all levels of hearings and interviews, and being involved in bargaining over the severity of the offence, the use of time limits on the record, and the conduct of cases by managers. In fact disciplinary cases have been an important element in turning high union membership levels into more participating union groups, and in bringing full-time officials into greater contact with their stewards.

In terms of the conduct of industrial relations at district/unit level discipline remains of great significance. It is an indicator of the method that management employ to control their staff in a wide range of circumstances. Even in cases of misconduct where the rest of the workforce supports action against an individual, the way in which the managers and the trade unionists behave puts down a series of markers for other tests of the application of managerial powers at work. When the case is contentious because of the issue, and/or the individual and/or the manager and/or its symbolic significance then the industrial relations consequences are harder to measure and more important to consider.

Neither the unions nor the managers have great experience in dealing with these issues. When they do go to third party intervention to be resolved, the experience of the arbitrators and/or tribunal chairs is of poor quality representation and inadequate understanding of the situation by the parties. Sandwell Health Authority has more than 4000 employees and all its managers receive relevant training in disciplinary matters, but none was given the ACAS handbook (IRS Employment Trends survey, August 1991). It is also the case that racial and gender overtones find their way into many cases which at first sight appear to concern other matters.

Overall, the use of discipline for reasons other than straight-forward correction of misconduct and/or inefficiency may be tempting for managers but is extremely risky. This applies with particular force when a trade union activist or steward is involved. COHSE is not alone among the unions in warning their stewards that

> It is sometimes the case that employing authorities may attempt to take exemplary action against representatives of the union. This may be done with the thought of discouraging recruitment, or of limiting the effectiveness of the union at local level.[54]

Discipline may be used in the future to enforce changes through flexibility policies, and it may also be tied to performance related pay systems. Such developments would endanger the fragile relationship that exists in many DHAs between management and the trade unions, and will undoubtedly sow the seeds for future breakdowns in industrial relations at district/unit levels.

GRIEVANCES

Grievances are, more or less, the opposite of discipline, for they allow workers to take a case against their employer. Grievances provide the bulk of bargaining opportunities for stewards at the

workplace. And, as McCarthy found, 'in most of the establishments studied the existence of incentive schemes represented a
major bargaining opportunity at shop floor level.'[55] This was
matched by a range of issues such as special payments,
allowances, grading, job evaluation and merit pay, conditions
and hours, staffing levels, sickness, discrimination and a host of
other matters. Within this list, McCarthy found that about two-
thirds of grievances arose from wage claims, wage mistakes and
wage drops.[56] Twenty years later the workplace survey found
that grievance procedures were universally present in establishments with more than 100 workers.[57]

The first point is that a grievance is not a complaint, and the
failure by most managers and many trade union activists and
officials to understand the exact nature of grievances remains a
major problem in the NHS. A grievance as defined by the
International Labour Organization is:

> The grounds for a grievance may be any measure or situation
> which concerns the relations between employer and worker or
> which affects the conditions of employment of one or several
> workers in the undertaking when that measure or situation
> appears contrary to provisions of an applicable collective agree-
> ment or of an individual contract of employment, to works rules,
> to laws or regulations or to the custom and usage or the
> occupation, branch of economic activity or country, regard being
> had to principles of good faith.[58]

In this context the grievances are about the implementation of
existing arrangements, that is they are about rights under an
existing agreement. When a steward is approached by members
the first requirement is that he or she decides whether or not
there is a grievance in this sense. The steward needs to decide
the source of the grievance: a straight violation of an agreement,
a disagreement over facts, interpretation of an agreement, or
differences over the 'fairness' or 'reasonableness' of the
employer's action.

A properly conducted interview will often be necessary to
establish the case and to distinguish between those union
members who feel aggrieved and those who have a grievance.
Much steward training is given over to this kind of practical
consideration.

Stewards will seek to discover the who, what, where and
when of the event and then decide whether it constitutes a
grievance. For example, if a member reports a case of sexual

harassment by another member of staff, then assuming it has happened, the grievance is against the employer for failing to provide a safe place of work. In all cases feeling aggrieved is not adequate, and a grievance means it is against the employer and that the employer has broken one of the types of rules listed by the ILO above. Another example would be when management withdraw a customary right, such as for a half-day off for Christmas shopping.

The latter is an interesting example for several reasons. In many departments this practice would arise in an unclear way, but current staff would enjoy their half-day off. The line manager concerned will present this as a favour and often suggest that the staff do not inform others since it is somewhat outside the realm of normal permission. Such a presentation by management allows the notion of a favour to dominate the views of staff. Favours can be returned and can be withdrawn. They also indicate the generosity of the giver. The secrecy adds to the 'favour' element and prevents staff discovering the possibility that other staff in other departments get a better deal and that there is nothing special about their arrangement. This example of custom and practice should be treated by staff as a local agreement, and any attempt to reverse it should be treated as a breach of the agreement and therefore subject to grievance or dispute. In addition, this illustrates the importance of being aware that the employer makes agreements and that managers only act as the employer's agent in these matters. Therefore, when managers act they can do so only with the authority of, and in the name of, the employer, and therefore it cannot be secret or a special favour.

If employees fail to define management actions in industrial relations terms then they will fail to respond in the appropriate manner if and when changes are made. This means that the lack of trade union awareness by many health workers has enabled their managers to pursue policies without any concomitant trade union response. This has been changing under the weight of better steward training and with recent reforms which exchanged fudged paternalism for more clear-cut managerialism. The new decisive chains of command may allow for improved managerial communications and clarity of purpose, but they may alter the traditional staff–management relationships since managerial authority can no longer hide behind notions of collegiate professionalism or paternalism.

If the issue is a grievance, then the next step is to decide how to handle it. This can be done informally or formally. The former requires a meeting with relevant managers to see if an early decision can be made: this route will depend on prior relationships and what else is going on at the place of work. In the NHS such informal resolutions of grievances are the norm. If the matter cannot be resolved then the formal grievance procedure will be invoked.

The main elements follow the 1971 Code of Practice which recommends speedy resolution, formal procedure, separate procedures for collective disputes and individual grievances, stages, time limits, and that no action be taken by either side while the procedure is in operation. There is also a *status quo* clause which means that no change takes place until after the grievance is settled. At present the GWC allows for an appeal to the employer, and then to the Regional Appeals Committee.[59]

As with discipline, stewards or relevant trade union negotiators have plenty to bargain over when the procedures are being drafted and implemented, and this in itself may increase their status and influence. Despite their widespread existence these procedures are rarely used in the NHS.[60] This is because both staff side representatives and managers prefer informal methods of resolution, and because both managers and stewards are largely ignorant as to their potential use and function.

In the NHS the profile of cases reflects the composition of the workforce and its concerns, and the extent to which manual workers and their unions are prepared to take up cases. Many cases are the classic stuff of workplace industrial relations: payment of expenses, workload and rota allocation, time off for training and union duties, discrimination on grounds of gender, race and union activity, and as McCarthy discovered anything to do with payment schemes and their application.

Grievance handling and sources of grievance again raise several areas of steward bargaining. Stewards typically utilize certain forms of bargaining methods: use of comparisons and precedent; use of sanctions such as withdrawal of cooperation, insistence on formal rights and customs, output limitations and restrictions on hours of work, flooding the grievance procedure and withdrawal of labour;[61] joint consultative committees; and informal arrangements based on a series of verbal understandings.

Grievances enable employees formally to bring to their employer's notice some breach of rule by managers. The scope for local bargaining is extensive and therefore the existence of grievance procedures may increase the influence of stewards and workplace trade union activity. On the other hand, as with discipline, the formalization of the processes and relationships may undermine independent work group interpretations of the situation they face, and thus prevent workers from actively pursuing their interests in the most effective ways. This, of course, is the main purpose of such procedures.

CONDITIONS OF SERVICE AND PAYMENT SYSTEMS: THE BARGAINING ISSUES

Even in a highly centralized system of bargaining with specific codified conditions of service and nationally graded staff there has always been scope for local variations. These stem from the realities of everyday life in the provision of health services where working practices must accord with patient workloads and availability of funds and staff. Most of the time such local variations would evolve through custom rather than be formally agreed and would tend to be marginal to the operations of the health authority, although not necessarily marginal to individual workers. Too much of the published work on the health service has been, like the service itself, top-down and insensitive to the daily richness of working life and to the needs of the health workers themselves.

The present concern is with the more important variations at local level from national agreements, and in particular, how such variations are agreed and implemented. Again research has been sadly limited in these areas, but some comments can still be made.

The full range of issues with some local element of discretion and variability includes expenses, leave, transport for staff, crèche and other child care facilities, meals and accommodation, long-service rewards, holidays, health and safety, sex and race discrimination, training and general matters of promotion and seniority. This book cannot cover such a wide range of points and so comment is limited to hours and shiftworking, equal opportunities policies, workforce reduction techniques such as redundancy and early retirement, gradings, job evaluation, incentive bonus schemes, and the complex web of negotiating arrangements that surround these issues.

Most NHS staff work under agreements which specify weekly hours ranging from 35 to 39 hours per week. Exceptions are the nurses who have a 75-hour fortnight, and medical and speech therapy staff who have unspecified hours. Additional hours come from either overtime or the use of oncall systems.

The 1990 New Earnings Survey (NES) lists the average amount of overtime for some of these groups. For higher professionals and managerial grades the measurement of overtime hours is unreliable although they still claim payment for it. Male nurse managers received on average 4.5% of their total earnings from overtime. In terms of hours worked, nurses and nursing auxiliaries averaged between 0.5 and 1.4 hours of overtime per week with men doing more than women. These levels correspond closely to the occupational averages for non-manual workers.

Manual workers do much more overtime throughout British industry than non-manual. On average men do 6.2 hours and women 1.8 hours. In the NHS, ambulancemen worked 4.3 hours and hospital porters 5.9 hours of overtime, while female hospital ward orderlies worked 1.3 hours.

In terms of this relationship with payment, remembering that some groups get paid with time off in lieu, then 15.7% of the porters' earnings came from overtime and nearly 10% for ambulancemen. These figures compare favourably with a national average for manual men of 16%. Male nurses earned 4.6% and female nurses 1.6% of total weekly earnings from overtime, which is about in line with non-manual rates elsewhere. The NHS reflects practice throughout British workplaces that men earn proportionally more overtime than women, and manual workers far more than most non-manual.

The local aspects of this arise over the distribution of overtime as between individuals and groups of workers, and the variable amounts for different parts of the year. If 15% of a worker's earnings depend on average on overtime, then the ability to work it becomes a major issue. It also means that overtime bans as a means of output restriction are bound to hurt employees as well as employers.

Shift work is widely used in the NHS among certain groups, especially nurses. In Britain as a whole over a third of all establishments use some form of shift system, and this rises to 90% for larger establishments.[62] In the NHS its extensive use amongst nurses is reflected in the proportion of total earnings from the shift premium: 9.1% for male nurses, 7.2% for female nurses and 9.7% for female auxiliary nurses. This applies with equal force to ancillary workers such as porters (8.8%) and ward orderlies (9.5%). Again the importance of the shift work money in earnings means its operation at hospital level and any rotation of shifts create important issues for staff. Shift work has notorious implications for the individual's home life and stress levels, and impinges in important ways on union organization within the hospital.

These are two examples of working practices with bargaining implications about their distribution and operation rather than about the overtime rates and shift allowances themselves. In the future these too may be subject to local employer variation.

Equal opportunities policies have been introduced after negotiation in many health authorities. The negotiations themselves as well as the monitoring and implementation of the policies have created additional issues over which workplace bargaining can take place. In East Yorkshire Health Authority, for example, in 1986 such a policy was introduced. Among its main elements were an introduction stating the employer's opposition to discrimination on grounds of sex, marital status and race. There is also reference to the employment of disabled people. As with most policies of this type, monitoring is very important, particularly of job applicants and current employees. Table 7.2 gives a breakdown of staff by sex and seniority.

The policy itself emphasizes the importance of the recruitment process and of promotion and disciplinary procedures. It also notes the importance of training for managers and of responsibilities on all employees. One further element associated with such policies is that of sexual harassment at work. Most health authorities have issued guidelines on this. Such advice often includes keeping full information of the facts and involving trade union representatives, and, in persistent and extreme cases, invoking the formal grievance procedure.

The gap between the introduction of policy and its implementation has been revealed in a recent survey by the Equal Opportunities Commission of women's employment in the NHS.[63] It notes that while the NHS is the largest employer of women in Western Europe it is 'far from being woman-friendly'. The general findings illustrate the overall point in this chapter, that the successful implementation of policy and procedures are dependent on a well-functioning set of union stewards and

Table 7.2 Monitoring of sex discrimination: numbers of male and female staff in post

	Males	Females	Total
Senior grades			
Salary equivalent to PAA and above			
All staff	972	2897	3869
All senior management	68	33	101
All staff	25%	75%	100%
All senior management	67%	33%	100%
Of all female staff 1.1% are senior managers			
Of all male staff 7% are senior managers			
Middle grades			
Salary equivalent to GAA and above			
All staff	972	2897	3869
All middle management	182	407	589
All staff	25%	75%	100%
All middle management	31%	69%	100%
Of all female staff 14% are middle managers			
Of all male staff 18% are middle managers			
Administrative and clerical			
All A&C staff	65	301	365
Senior managers	20	2	22
Middle managers	22	26	48
All A&C staff	25%	75%	100%
Senior managers	91%	9%	100%
Middle managers	45%	55%	100%

Of all female administrative and clerical staff 0.6% are senior managers and 8.6% middle management staff
Of all male administrative and clerical staff 31% are senior managers and 34% middle management staff

Source: East Yorkshire Health Authority

bargaining arrangements. Thus although 93% of health authorities had an Equal Opportunities Policy, only 70% have told their employees. Only 22% mention sexual harassment, 60% have no mechanism to plan or evaluate progress, 84% have no manager with specific equal opportunities responsibilities, and 75% do not monitor the policy. The picture in recruitment and retention is equally poor and shows that the gap between reality and managerial rhetoric is as great has this book has argued for a range of other issues (Table 7.3).

Table 7.3 The extent to which health authorities conform to the essential features of an EOP

Features which are essential to an EOP[1]	Health authority policies sent into the EOC (152 in total)	
	(No.)	(%)
Definitions of discrimination		
Direct Sex	152	100
Indirect Sex	139	91
Marital (direct and indirect)	151	99
Victimization	56	37
Sexual harassment	33	22
Equal Opportunities Policy	152	100
Name(s) of officer(s) responsible for equal opportunities	121	80
Details of structure for implementation	25	16
Obligation for employees to act in accordance	116	76
Procedures for dealing with discriminatory complaints	103	68
Examples of unlawful practices	26	17
Details of monitoring and review procedures	116	76
Commitment to remove barriers to equal opportunities	44	29

[1] 'Guidelines for Equal Opportunities Employers', EOC, pp. 2–6.
Source: Equal Opportunities Commission, *Equality Management*, EOC, London, p. 46.

Another major issue with important workplace implications is the reduction of the workforce. In 1984 the favoured method of reducing the level of staff was through natural wastage in the public services. Then, in order, came early retirement, redeployment, voluntary redundancy and compulsory redundancy.[64] In the NHS reduction of staff has been very much an occupational issue with most of the professions enjoying a continued expansion of their numbers in most workplaces. The ancillary staff have composed the bulk of the reductions, and this has been through sub-contracting more than any other means. None the less, there are always changes that require a given workplace to alter its workforce in terms of numbers and skill mix, and then these issues are relevant. Within three weeks of the start of SGTs in April 1991 large-scale redundancies had been announced.

In the case of natural wastage, the method is simply one of not replacing staff that leave, and this is indicated by the gap between staff in post and the agreed establishment size. Such vacancies are often cited by the staff side as labour market indicators of shortages needing higher pay to remedy, but they may be a consequence of the cash limits policies of the 1980s in which employers did not have the funds to employ extra staff at any salary. Whatever the reasons and methods, there is little for the unions to bargain over unless the fall in staff through natural wastage either is not met by a concomitant fall in workload or because it randomly rids the system of certain specialists. In the former case unions may object that staff run-down is faster than the fall in patient numbers and thus demand either replacements or more pay for those that remain. In the case of the randomness of natural wastage the unions might argue that it indicates a lack of staffing policy and that the consequences for those who remain may be changes in duties and responsibilities.

The other methods of staff reduction through early retirement, voluntary redundancy and redeployment are usually by agreed procedures operated jointly by staff side and management side representatives. In such cases the unions will want to be sure that their members have not been pushed into the decision, that selection procedures are fair, and that compensation is in line with national agreements or better. Typical redundancy and redeployment agreements will seek to safeguard jobs and individuals through specific references to retraining schemes, redeployment, freezing outside appointments, full counselling for those involved, full consultation with staff organizations, and fair selection procedures. These are set out by ACAS and might include 'last in, first out', attendance and/or disciplinary records, skills and/or qualifications, and standard of work performance and/or aptitude for the work.[65]

The employers may not want a particular category of staff to leave under these schemes and so may wish to retain a managerial veto over volunteers. This can be difficult, since if one volunteer is turned down then someone else may be selected in their place.

The hardest cases to deal with, and those with the greatest potential threat to orderly local level industrial relations, are those of compulsory redundancy. Here the union and its members are not given a choice. The employer in the NHS until April 1991 has only been able to justify compulsory redundancies by reference to cash limits imposed by a higher authority within the NHS and government. Unions will seek to reduce the impact by negotiating over numbers involved, the time period and the compensation. Employers, while relieved to reduce the labour force, recognize the serious knock-on effects that compulsory redundancies have on those that remain. These may include further loss of morale, industrial action, and a breakdown in trust relationships between staff and their line managers.

The most important local issue for manual workers remains that of pay. This applies even in times of lay-offs and cutbacks. For the non-manual staff and most professionals the pay argument at local level is based on allowances and gradings rather than on pay systems and structures.

As has been argued throughout this chapter, the introduction of bonus schemes for some ancillary workers as a result of demands both from the unions as a means of higher pay and from the managers as a means of greater control provided the impetus for the development of influential shop stewards and local bargaining arrangements at hospital level. The key report was the 1971 NBPI one which recommended job evaluation for all ancillary grades, better management of labour, incentive bonus schemes and measured day work, and an interim productivity deal.[66]

In general, the report blamed management for the prevailing low levels of pay and productivity, and in particular the unclear chain of command and lack of personnel expertise.[67] It is the bargaining aspects of the schemes that are of interest here rather than the schemes themselves. The NBPI suggested a staged approach, as follows. Stage 1 – an in-principle agreement at Ancillary Whitley Council on a work efficiency scheme. Stage 2 – a model scheme incorporating training for both managers and trade union representatives, O&M study to define and improve the work and supervision of the work, use of work study to agree staffing levels for a given level of performance, these schemes linked to bonus payments, and monitoring of the schemes. Stage 3 – negotiation of the findings at national Ancillary Whitley level with the inclusion of workforce reduction methods other than natural wastage. Stage 4 – rapid implementation of the scheme.[68]

The new model scheme was based on the view that the efficiency of a group of workers depends upon (1) working practices, equipment and departmental organization, (2) the effort of the workers measured as a rate of working, and (3) the percentage of attendance hours during which work is performed.[69] The bargaining areas in job evaluation and bonus schemes are well known and apply with equal certainty to the NHS.

As every survey of shop steward bargaining practices since McCarthy in 1966 has shown, the bulk of grievances and of workplace bargaining is derived from wage levels, pay systems and their operation. In the case of job evaluation this comes in various forms: the original agreement over the factors and their weight; the linking of pay grades to whatever points scores are achieved; the treatment of workers whose pay is above the new grading system (red circling); and the appeals system – a joint union/management system, a management only one, or the use of a permanent third party.[70]

Job evaluation is increasingly widespread throughout the private and public sectors as a favoured means by which to 'objectively' establish job rankings. Job evaluation does this through allocating scores to a variety of job characteristics such as experience, responsibility and educational attainment. The linking of such ranked jobs to grades and then to levels of pay is a separate activity. In addition to the bargaining points mentioned above, there is the very important issue of equal pay and equal value in job evaluation. As the EOC reminded those involved in such schemes:

> Job Evaluation is a system of comparing different jobs to provide a basis for a grading and pay structure. The aim is to evaluate the job, not the job holder, but it is recognized that to some extent any assessment of a job's total demands relative to another will always be subjective. Moreover, job evaluation is in large part a social mechanism which establishes agreed differentials within organizations.[71]

This last comment opens the way for the argument that traditional separation of men and women into different jobs will tend to mean that job evaluation schemes will discriminate against women.

In the NHS the use of job evaluation has been limited, but in line with other large organizations in the UK[72] many RHAs are considering the adoption of an all-embracing job evaluation scheme for staff ranging from ancillary workers to doctors. For example, the Manchester Central Hospitals and Community Care NHS Trust commissioned the consultants Peat Marwick McLintock to develop such a scheme. It includes such factors as operational knowledge, communication skills, resource management, working environment and cognition. This last factor includes elements associated with judgemental skills, innovation and freedom of action. The ways in which such a scheme will fit into other pay determination mechanisms is unclear, as is the extent to which each region will vary the scheme and therefore the pay grades allocated to the job ranks. The ancillary staff have agreed a new job evaluation scheme for national implementation in 1991 and the effects of this on SGTs and other health service employers in terms of their freedom to control the pay bill is uncertain.

The same story applies with measured day work and/or payment-by-results. Here the negotiations can start with the work study ground rules, then cover allowances and times themselves, then rates, and finally implementation and appeals. The Webbs noted over a hundred years ago that piecework was acceptable to trade unionists as long as there was an agreed rate for the job which formed the minimum for the occupation, trade, industry or region.[73] There is a large literature of research of the consequences for all parties of incentive schemes, but the main aspect remains the attempt by the employer to increase productivity at lowest cost and the effort by the unions to ensure fair rewards and proper controls over the schemes. The TUC, for example, warn trade union negotiators to ensure that the workforce get a 'fair share' from any productivity gains, that they seek non-wage benefits as well as higher wages, that they argue for job security, that there is no loss in safety, that there is no undermining of traditional collective bargaining, and that the schemes are carefully and continually monitored.[74]

In Chapter 1 it was argued that higher productivity was the major objective of the employers and managers in the reformed NHS. This could be achieved by greater labour flexibility including payment systems which linked performance and/or effort to rewards. The unions have recognized the inevitability of this and some, such as MSF and the EETPU, have welcomed it while others, such as NUPE and the Royal Colleges, are less enthusiastic.

The management of many NHS activities covered by bonus schemes fear that 'if incentive bonus payments are consolidated into basic pay and the scheme eventually scrapped, then output will drop and, in the absence of monitoring, management could lose control'.[75] The main features of payment-by-results schemes for bargaining purposes include that the work is measurable and directly attributable to the work group; that the pace of work needs to be controlled by the worker; and that management must supply a steady flow of work. The required tasks should remain consistent and not subject to sudden changes. The central relationship is between effort and reward and not between performance and reward. This has been widely accepted and applies with equal force to professional staff in the NHS. Until recently, therefore, such staff were subject to other pay adjustments for extra work and/or for special work.

Many staff, especially professionals, receive a series of allowances, including acting-up, training, and special payments if they work in London or in certain specialisms. The situation with allowances for professional and technical staffs is somewhat different, with these mostly strictly laid down at national level, and therefore the crucial bargaining point is over eligibility. This varies in terms of discretion. For example, the student training allowance recently granted to some grades of PAMs should be paid to anyone looking after students. In other words the payment of the allowance is based on fact. The same is true for London weighting. In contrast, the merit payment to doctors depend on a form of promotion or reward for special service and is decided traditionally by the doctor's peers. Overall the scope for local bargaining by stewards or through the JCC is limited.

Gradings have a similar aspect in so far as they are decided at national level. Their local application can raise major issues for grievance procedures, especially over the assimilation of old grades onto new ones. There is a separate procedure for appeals against gradings, and while this is in regular use it has been saturated in some districts and regions through the appalling confusion created by the very grave mistakes made by management in the recent nurses and midwives regrading.

Within this national pattern of grades and allowances is the spectre of more performance related pay and merit pay for professional and technical staffs including managerial grades. There has been an increase in this type of reward system in the

UK,[76] and there are important linkages with appraisal schemes and target setting. As will be argued in the final chapter, such developments are in part designed to remove groups of staff from collective bargaining and therefore reduce the influence of the unions and national rates.

The main concern of these schemes is to introduce greater flexibility into pay determination and to relate some of that flexibility to performance. Appraisal systems have been introduced into some parts of the NHS for managers and some professional staff. Appraisal may contain three elements: performance review is aimed at increasing the effective performance of the employee; review of development needs is aimed at identifying possible promotion and training; and reward reviews link pay and non-pay rewards to performance.[77]

This linking of pay to performance can take several forms. One possible one is its incorporation within an incremental pay system or spine with negotiated pay scales; another option is a low national minimum wage with large PRP incentives. Merit pay systems may take the form of cash bonuses on top of pay rates, accelerated or deferred increments, a salary range with a bar above which pay is determined by merit, spot salary ranges, merit-only pay rises, and any combination of these.[78] The most common system in current use in the public sector for white-collar and professional staff is the accelerated increments and policy line range.

This development fits well with the determination of managers to bring in more flexible pay systems. In 1985 NAHA believed that all the assumed advantages of local bargaining for the managers could be achieved through 'establishing a system of pay bands'.[79] Figure 7.1 shows how this was intended to work. Two years later NAHA attacked the government for allowing so many staff to opt out of collective bargaining and opt into pay review. They proposed a new system:

> The question of relativities is very much in the front of peoples' minds. There is a desire to create a 'spine' which is seen as a way of ironing out the gross distortions in pay between different groups of staff which are still apparent. We use the word 'spine' as a convenient shorthand for a system of job ranking in which, eventually, all occupations in the health service will be placed in an acceptable 'pecking' order.[80]

In 1989 the Department of Health proposed an experimental scheme for pay flexibility for nurses and midwives. The extra supplements would be used to tackle recruitment and retention

The proposed banding system (£)

Band	Range	Description
Band 1	21,500 / 21,000	General Managers, Senior Professional Advisers, Senior Scientific Advisers, Consultants
Band 2	9,000	Middle managers, Professional/Senior Professional officers
Band 3		Basic and training grades, Supervisory officers, First line managers

1984–5 pay structure (by Whitley Council)

£ scale	A & C	Medical & Dental	Nurses & Midwives	PT'A'	Ancillary Staffs	PT'B'	Maintenance Craftsmen	Ambulance Staff	Pharmacists & Opticians
35,000	DGM (non-Whitley)								
	RGM								
30,000	RGM (Whitley)	RMO	RGM (Whitley) / DGM						
	Scale A	DGM	RNO R1						
25,000	Scale F	Consultant	DNO DHA 1+	Regional Scientific Officer		Regional Works Officer / Regional Architect 1		Regional Ambulance Officer	
	Scale J								Regional Pharmaceutical Officer
	Scale 33			Top Grade		District Works Officer			
20,000		Associate Specialist	Regional Nurse						
	Scale 27		DNS DHA 1	Principal Grade		Asst Regional Architect		Chief Ambulance Officer	Principal Ophth Optician & Principal Pharmacist III
	Scale 23		Snr Nurse 1						
15,000		Snr Registrar		District II (Dist Snr Chief Chiropodist)		Works Officer 5 / Prn Asst Architect		Rank 2	
	Scale 18			Teacher (Principal)					
	Scale 14	Registrar	Snr Nurse 5	Superintendent 2		Snr Asst Architect / Tech Officer / Main Grade Eng			Snr Ophth Optician & Staff Pharmacist
	Scale 9					MPT 1			
10,000		Snr House Officer	Nursing Sister 1	Supt. Physiotherapist		Work Officer 1			
				Snr 1 Physiotherapist		District Engineer			Basic Grade Pharmacist
	Scale 1 (GAA)	House Officer	Staff Nurse	Technical Instructor		Asst Dist Eng	Rank 7		
			Enrolled Nurse	Physiotherapist	Group 18	Tech Asst 3 / MPT IV			
5,000	Clerical Officer		Nursing Auxiliary	OT Helper	Group 11	Junior Asst		Leading Ambulanceman	Graduate Student Pharmacist
					Baker Supervisor	Basic Grade ODA	Grade 5+PR / Grade 3+PR	Driver/Attdnt	Trainee Ophth Optician
					Group 1	Trainee ODA	Grade 1+PR / Grade 1	Control Asst Trainee Ambulanceman	

GLOSSARY

DGM	District General Manager	DNS	Director of Nursing Services
RGM	Regional General Manager	OT	Occupational Therapist
GAA	General Administrative Assistant		Ancillary Staffs
PR	Performance Related Bonus	Group 18	Garden Supervisor
RNO	Regional Nursing Officer	Group 11	Head Porter
DNO	District Nursing Officer	MPT	Medical Physics Technician
		ODA	Operating Department Assistant

Figure 7.1 1984–5 pay structure and proposed banding structure. (*Source*: NAHA.)

problems only. Here is a major problem for the policy-makers: pay flexibility to be used for labour market reasons and not to reward performance. For health employers to qualify for the extra money they would have to demonstrate the level of vacancies, labour turnover and exceptional local circumstances.[81] This ambiguity at the heart of policy with regard to flexible pay, as a reward for performance/effort or to respond to labour market shortages, reflects a confusion in both underlying economic theory of wages and wider government considerations of pay differences. The practical outcome of this major lack of clarity is that good performers may earn less than those in shortage areas, and those in short supply may be promoted above their ability to retain them. Both are a recipe for disaster on any view of the business.

A major issue for NHS staff in this debate is the measurement of their performance. In recent years this has been attempted through the development of Performance Indicators (PIs), now known as Health Service Indicators (HSIs). In the early days of their use they were intended to help regional reviews of DHA performance through a series of business ratios. More recently, thanks to some sophisticated computer programs, they have become measures of some detail as to hospital and even unit level activity. The current set are grouped into 42 'families' including, for example, ambulance, day care, hospital activity and regional finance. There are several thousand HSIs ranging from AM01 total cost ambulance service: patient journeys, to WL47 patients awaiting elective admission: resident population 75+.[82]

The main users appear to be 'those involved in strategic planning, such as district general managers, planners, health authority chairmen and information specialists.'[83] The industrial relations issues involved in these HSIs include: to help set targets for senior line managers which are then passed down to junior staff; possible deskilling as quantitative analyses of job tasks and performance become widely available and acceptable; a reduction in the numbers of senior posts as monitoring of performance is done by business ratios; and as an aid to flexible staffing levels as the week-by-week needs of departments are more quantitatively measured and judged.[84] The continued sophistication of the statistical treatment of HSIs along with the development of substantial computer-related projects[85] will mean that management will utilize these modern work study techniques to set targets and judge performance for bonus and PRP purposes.

The payment levels, schemes and structures aligned with certain key areas of conditions such as overtime, shift and lay-off policies provide the bulk of important local issues for JCCs to bargain over. The rest of local bargaining is associated with disciplinary and grievance matters dealt with either through the formal procedures or informal avenues of settlement. The other major issue, not dealt with here, is health and safety at work. The future holds out a situation with a rapid increase in local bargaining. The exact form, extent and scope of this move to more traditional workplace industrial relations will be discussed in the final chapter.

INDUSTRIAL ACTION AND THE DISPUTES PROCEDURE

The 1980 disputes procedure more than any other agreement embodies the concrete expression of an agreed balance of power frozen at a moment by the skills of negotiators and the powers of the interested parties. Its main purpose is to avoid conflict at the place of work. There are, however, limits to how far each party will go to avoid conflict and this may reflect either ideology or uncertainty as to the balance of bargaining advantage. The balance is defined within parameters set by the state through the Industrial Relations Code of Practice.[86] In the code 'good' industrial relations are based on several factors, including the orderly procedure for settling disputes. Disputes of interest, such as over new pay and conditions, are based on argument and power, and not on reference to any agreed set of rights.

The main point from other research is that bargaining continues before, during and after the operation of the disputes procedure. This is in contrast to the wishes of managers and some trade union officials that the procedure itself prevents unwanted bargaining by turning the process into a quasi-judicial form of fact-finding and blame allocation. Kuhn shrugged off the judicial and/or administrative version and concluded that 'bargaining is an intimate part of the grievance process'.[87] Hyman took up this theme in his study of disputes procedures in the engineering industry in Coventry.[88] He argued that trade unionists use the procedures because they are under pressure to exhaust all avenues before taking industrial action, and it might achieve a better offer from the management than at the start of negotiations. In this setting managers will prefer the use of procedures since they remove bargaining from the point of production, that is the point at which management control over the labour process is at its weakest. The fundamental point is that the use of the disputes procedure is part of the wider bargaining process at the place of work, and its use and useful-ness will depend on industry and workplace industrial relations traditions and issues rather than on any academic and/or political view of what is necessary to resolve issues.

The test of the procedures and the management's reaction to industrial action can be seen in the NHS throughout the 1970s. All parties, the civil servants, managers, politicians, some union leaders and outside commentators, were caught out by the extent of industrial action by a wide variety of health workers in the 1970s (Chapter 6). This was the result of the explosive mixture of complacent ignorance and arrogant neglect.

As with all industries, incidents of industrial action in hos-pitals go back a hundred years or more. For example, the first strike by schoolteachers was in 1896 in Portsmouth.[89] Carpenter is one of several historians of health unions that report a regular eruption of local action, as at the Bodmin Asylum in 1918 when nurses took strike action over the management's refusal to allow them to wear union badges,[90] and the 1921 Brentford dispute of nurses over management's disciplining of night nurses for skip-ping breakfast to prepare the hospital for the Easter dance.[91] The disputes in the 1970s took various forms, had a variety of causes, involved a wide range of hospital and community staffs, and created major changes in the industrial relations of many health authorities.

In the mid-1970s there was an upsurge in local disputes in the NHS. The lower paid manual workers were becoming caught up in the wage militancy of the coal miners and other industrial groups. In 1974 nurses and radiographers took industrial action over pay, reflecting their concern with levels of pay compa-rability and with the successes of other white-collar workers involved in action, such as schoolteachers. Most local action remained the product of national decisions, but in 1974 some local groups of trade unionists took purely local action over the issue of beds for private patients.

The action by hospital consultants over the issue of private patients lasted just over three months and proved to be the watershed in the history of local industrial action in the NHS, partly because their action limited the intake of patients and hence the work flow to other hospital staff. The junior hospital doctors took their own action in 1975 in a dispute over pay and long hours. Edwards was one of many commentators to suggest that:

> once both consultants and junior doctors have been presented as putting their own interests before that of their patients, every other group could do so with impunity ... the trade unions quickly realised this and came to demand local concessions that were either at variances with or, on occasion completely outside the national agreements ... Local shop stewards began to assert their authority to negotiate with their own management.[92]

The managers backed down when faced with the choice between paying doctors more or closing accident departments, and also between paying radiographers more and the ending of their emergency duties. The deals with ancillary staff on productivity tended to favour these workers. Management had no strategy and no support, and therefore acted to keep the service going.

The response by management was confused and inconsistent. In some areas management recruited 'volunteers' to do the work of ancillary staff in dispute in the early 1970s. As action became more widespread and involved professional groups this option proved of limited value. A few managers wanted to allow patients to suffer as a result of staff action and therefore allow blame to be put on to the unions. At the time this was generally rejected, but it has much more powerful support today from the highest levels within the NHS and Department of Health.

Nobody argued that the choices for individual managers were easy, and that when to hold the policy line and when to duck and weave was appropriate. In these circumstances government policy is crucial and managers increasingly sought out political guidelines. During the famous disputes in 1978/9 two problems emerged for the NHS managers: there was enormous local variation in dealing with disputes and staff taking action, and secondly, employers had virtually no role to play. This prompted many managers through their organizations to renew the call for an Independent Management Secretariat to advise and help managers in negotiations. In the end it was a pay comparability study under the aegises of Clegg that ended the disputes.

As a result of these lessons the government issued HC(79)20 entitled 'If Industrial Relations Break Down'. The circular instructed management not to pay staff on strike, to send staff home, to deduct part of pay, and to use 'volunteers' (Chapter 6).

The 1982 dispute lasted nearly eight months, and many local managers used the circular. In a survey of 31 DHAs in the southeast of England Morris found that in practice managerial response still varied greatly. Only in five authorities were staff sent home, few deducted pay and none used 'volunteers'. In those authorities that did follow the circular and take a hard line the evidence is that after the dispute 'normal' industrial relations took some time to recover to a reasonable level.[93] Many managers remained frustrated and disillusioned either because they could not settle at local level and/or because they were sympathetic to the staff's cause. In other words, most managers ignored government advice.

The 1982 dispute further split managers from government instructions and helped renew their efforts for a more independent role. As NAHA made clear in its evidence to the Social Services Committee, the employing side authorities were again excluded from the conduct of negotiations during the dispute. Throughout the period of the dispute they did not meet together and representatives frequently heard of new offers made in their name through the press.

By the time of the 1989/90 ambulance dispute most of these problems remained. This was another sign of the lack of coherent management strategy. The government set its face against both the pay demand and the pay formula call from the ambulance staff. The dispute lasted six months, and again NHS managers had only a marginal role. The Whitley Council met only once early on in the dispute, and once more local managers showed a mixed variety of approaches. This included the use of army and police, but again resulted in a sharp deterioration in industrial relations after the action in those areas where the management took the hardest line.

In some cases the considerable public support for the ambulance staff aligned with managerial feelings of sympathy pushed some chief ambulance officers to secure local agreements based on local budgets. When this occurred, the NHS's chief executive, Duncan Nichol, put pressure on the health authorities to prevent local agreements.

Throughout the ambulance dispute the government played a major role, and developed political objectives at odds with managerial objectives within traditional industrial relations parameters. In addition, the government refused to allow the dispute to go to third party arbitration. In a letter to health authority chairs in January 1990, Kenneth Clarke, the Secretary of State, claimed that what was at issue was 'the integrity of the NHS pay bargaining structure and the authority of management'. He indicated that there would have to be changes in pay bargaining since there was now seen to be a clear need for 'local flexibility because national bargaining had become a nonsense in much of the NHS'.

There is considerable evidence that this approach is part of a wider government policy within the public sector. Ferner noted that,

> the present government has changed the rules of public sector management by making confrontation possible as a management strategy for getting change ... It has been implacable in its refusal to mediate once hostilities have broken out.[94]

It was not just the local consequences of national disputes that altered the local industrial relations power balance, but there were numerous local disputes throughout the 1970s and 1980s over cutbacks, closures, and subcontracting. One of the more famous was the struggle to keep open the Elizabeth Garrett Anderson Hospital for Women in London. Some of the union tactics included occupations of wards, as when St Benedict's Hospital in Tooting[95] was threatened with closure. An important impact of subcontracting on the unions has been to force them to work together, particularly the GMB, NUPE, COHSE and the TGWU. COHSE and NUPE, along with NALGO, are in merger talks. In addition, some unions, such as COHSE, have decided to make all local disputes official as long as they fall within certain guidelines.

These examples of industrial action reveal only the cases which failed to be resolved before action was taken. There are hundreds of other examples of disputes which did not end in action. This is usually because they are resolved through informal or formal means before that stage is reached. The lack of a formal disputes procedure was seen by some as a major cause of the rise in local action in the 1970s. As a result, in 1980 the DHSS issued a national disputes procedure to be used at authority level.

The NHS-wide disputes procedure has similar features to the grievance procedures discussed above. It has four stages before reaching the employer. After that there is an appeals procedure which starts with a locally convened panel, and if no agreement is reached then either party can go to ACAS for conciliation or by joint agreement to arbitration. This is section 33 of GWC, and provides a major safeguard to the employment practices of an authority's managers through the use of outside scrutiny. In the new self-governing trusts such outside appeals will no longer be allowed. Some examples of the use of the disputes procedure follow.

> The works officer informed the gardening staff that their overtime was to be cut.[96] The gardeners through their unions, NUPE and COHSE, went into the disputes procedure. Senior management upheld the cut, and then an independent appeals panel was constituted composed of a COHSE official, a NUPE steward from local government, a personnel officer from outside the NHS, and a senior manager from another health authority. There was an independent chair. The panel's compromise solution was rejected by the health authority, and ACAS was then asked to conciliate. This also failed. After six months the authority imposed the cut in overtime and the gardeners and their unions accepted the decision unwillingly.

> There was acute understaffing at a large psychiatric hospital and the staff demanded the dismissal of a senior manager or they would strike. The case was taken through the disputes procedure to the highest level of internal management and was resolved there. The view was that involvement by full-time union officials and other senior managers indicated to staff that at last their views were being taken seriously. In addition, there had been a call for a public inquiry, which the management did not want, and therefore there was increased pressure for a settlement.[97]

> In another case management imposed changes to the bonus scheme for storekeepers. The men took strike action for 11 days, and every day union officials were in negotiations with management. The managers did the work of the men and other unions gave no support. As a result the men returned to work in defeat.[98]

These examples conform with the TUC view at the time that, 'most disputes in the NHS occur at local level over issues such as rotas, bonus arrangements and overtime schedules'.[99]

The overall impression is that managers resent the disputes procedure and see it as taking vital matters out of their hands either to senior managers or outside the employing authority altogether. This is in contrast to most union views, which were to support the procedure strongly. This difference in approach owes nothing to principled positions and everything to the current perceptions of the balance of power as between the parties. In the 1980s, in most places most of the time, managers felt they had the upper hand and therefore saw institutional procedures as hampering their right to management. Evidence for this comes from a study in 1986 of the use of the disputes procedure by Swabe. Six years after its introduction about one in five authorities had adopted the model procedure, and about one in three had a local version. So more than 40% of authorities had no agreed and permanent disputes procedure. The cases that went through procedure included breakdown of consultation (12%), ward closures (8%), local incentive schemes (7%), disputes over interpretation of agreements (17%), grading (5%) and discipline (3%).[100]

Swabe and his colleagues concluded that the disputes procedure was introduced 'to encourage employing authorities towards reform', but they felt that many employers and managers were not interested and that the new style of management introduced in the 1980s would further reduce the willingness of NHS managers to adopt a pluralist solution to disputes in favour of a tougher anti-union approach.[101] The TUC noted the difficulties in practice for the NHS:

> It is the lack of a developed, smooth-working local system of industrial relations which most starkly differentiates the NHS from most other large employers'.[102]

The TUC's evidence was that the disputes procedure had prevented industrial action. This was based on anecdotal accounts and conveniently fits the TUC wishes. The main areas of difficulty in the procedure have been identified as:

1. The scope of the procedure and the role of *status quo* clauses.
2. The role of health authority members on a panel – this must be seen as the final stage within the employing authority, and not, as some managers view it, as the decision of neutral outsiders.
3. The role of the local disputes panel – this is to conciliate and/or mediate between the parties.

The vast bulk of disputes are solved through informal channels, and this will tend to be the pattern for the future.

The avowed purpose of the industrial relations disputes procedures is to avoid disputes. Industrial action does take place at local level, and is usually disruptive as to the operational needs of the hospital or relevant unit of care. As with most other industries there are significant amounts of local industrial action in the NHS which are not recorded in the official statistics, and are difficult to assess. The task is to have some notion of the frequency of action by various groups, and to measure the impact of local and national action on the future conduct of industrial relations at local level. This has been discussed to some extent in Chapter 6 with reference to the DHSS circular on the handling of action and the consequences of various national disputes. Attitudes may change and they may harden. Trade unions as a whole may benefit, or they may lose. Individual unions may gain at the expense of other unions. The position is fluid and uncertain, but a lack of consistent strategy by employers and unions may create in the NHS of the 1990s the situation faced in other industries in the UK in the 1960s. Namely, unofficial and/or unconstitutional industrial action as the only means for the overworked staff to have their voices heard in a system which replaces negotiation/consultation through trade unions by a veneer of individual employee participation.

In 1984 it was estimated that about one in ten establishments in the UK were affected by some form of strike action, and about one in 20 by overtime bans. Smaller numbers were affected by work to rules, boycotting of work, lockouts and go-slows.[103] The major causes given for strikes and other action were pay-related. Other issues included working hours, redundancies, trade union matters, conditions, staffing, dismissal and other disciplinary matters.[104] In the public sector nearly 80% were official actions.

Twenty years earlier McCarthy had outlined the main types of local activity. Withdrawal of cooperation was considered to refer to situations where the stewards had developed a positive and useful role from management's point of view, and then decide to stop the extent of this helper function. It can apply to professional workers such as teachers outside the health service, and most professionals inside. Here the argument is that there are areas of work which are carried out as 'goodwill', that is although customary activities, they are not deemed contractual. In disputes this can mean their withdrawal. Teachers withdrew lunchtime supervision[105] in their disputes in the 1980s, and professionals in the NHS could do the same with, for example, refusing to treat the 'last' patient in the queue.

Stewards may swamp the grievance procedure as a form of action. The nurses and midwives did this with their regrading appeals. It takes up management time and dislocates many working practices. This may be linked with work to contract. As McCarthy found, 'Usually the deliberate use of procedure to this end is coupled with the insistence on certain other rights ... for example all forms of traditional job-demarcations.'[106] Restriction of output has always been a major form of action, taking various forms such as slow-downs or overtime bans. Finally there is the strike weapon. The length of strike action is of great importance, since many strikes last for a few hours or less in the form of walkouts or downers.

In 1983 Fewtrell found it difficult to establish the facts for NHS disputes. In his study of 13 authorities over a year there were 39 incidents of which ten were in the form of restricted work.[107] In addition, half of the incidents were related to national disputes. For example, one health authority had 34 staff on strike for the day in protest against Clegg's 1980 comparability award for PAMs. An interesting case was that of a NUPE steward and branch officer who was under disciplinary warnings for unauthorized time off. He then encouraged over 300 staff to join in a one-day strike at which time the authority dismissed him. This led to a three-day strike of nearly 400 staff. This interweaving of national and local disputes, and the management's use of discipline to control trade union activities, is a more sensitive account of the realities of workplace industrial relations then too many arid research findings.

The real size of the problem in the NHS is very difficult to estimate, but it is known that industrial action has diminished throughout the 1980s at local level, and that the incidence amongst medical and professional staffs is much less than among the manual and technical staff. This should not be seen as a comment in itself on the unions involved, although the RCN, BMA and other smaller groups do not like any form of industrial action in the traditional sense. They can often achieve their objectives through other means. This, of course, raises the issue of the extent to which action is caused by managers' refusal to bargain, and that that refusal is more likely the weaker the groups are in terms of power in the workplace. Doctors are unlikely to be dealt with by managers in the same way as they treat catering ancillaries, although it is also the case that ancillary workers are more likely to respond in a collective fashion to management actions. This again is a sign of the weakness of the individual worker. Whether in the future world of health provision more staff will feel vulnerable as individuals and therefore play more active roles in the collective organizations, or whether they will take an increasingly individualistic solution to their problems, remains to be seen.

THE MANAGEMENT OF LOCAL INDUSTRIAL RELATIONS

The story of the management of hospitals and of health authorities is a sad mix of well-intentioned effort, half-hearted professionalism and arrogant, narrow-minded paternalism. The fault lies not with badly trained individual managers but with the civil servants charged with running the NHS and with successive governments unwilling to invest in information technology, management techniques and the managers themselves. The picture by the middle of the 1970s was of a core of hard-pressed administrators with inadequate authority, confused lines of communication, unclear decision-making powers, and faulty information. In addition, the demand for the service they ran was greater than ever, the staff were better organized and more willing to defend their own interests, the patients' expectations had risen, and the 1974 Labour government had just inherited a reorganization of the NHS which it did not seek.

The main tradition of management was that of the Civil Service: non-specialists in charge for their apparent breadth of knowledge and critical faculties, rule-based and rule-bound systems, high levels of centralization, and a cautious conservatism which has so ill-served the country in the postwar world. In industrial relations terms this meant 'that since local management could only influence pay and conditions on the margin they could evade responsibility for dealing with industrial relations problems'.[108]

Of the unions, the GMB and ASTMS argued that this reduced union effectiveness at local level, and that full-time union officials had virtually no contact with senior management. As a result some managers tended either to hide behind higher echelons of the system or remain ignorant of the trade union position on most issues. The consequences of this were delays and escalation of local disputes, and both local managers and trade unionists felt that important decisions were taken out of their hands.

ACAS agreed with many others that the 1974 reorganization was a disaster from the point of view of industrial relations. It created wide gaps between staff and management and generated a sense of unease among lower managers. 'Consequently the credibility of managerial authority in general is diminishing.'[109]

The problems start with poor communications between staff and managers and are made worse by the lack of personnel expertise. ACAS found that even where there were DPOs they were excluded from the district management team and that 'in the absence of guidance from above and lack of professional expertise to assist their deliberations, the general opinion is that management has abdicated its authority to the trade unions by default'.[110] ACAS recommended that there should be clear lines of authority and the proper use of a fully worked out personnel policy. In particular, ACAS concluded its gloomy analysis:

> the personnel function is fragmented not only geographically but also organizationally so that nurses often have their own separate personnel functions, most ambulancemen are administered at Area level and some Districts have no personnel officer at all. The anomalies and disunity which this causes have been the root of many problems in which ACAS's assistance has been sought.[111]

ACAS was quite right in its assessment of the state of industrial relations management at local level, but the success of its recommendations depended not just on correct prognosis but on an understanding of the reasons for the mess. One reason was that until the 1972 ancillary workers strike most managers did not take industrial relations seriously. They remained either unaware or unmoved by the persistently shocking levels of low pay. In face of these underlying issues the failure of management to respond helped create the basis for rapid union growth in numbers and influence.

Management responded either by seeking to maintain the paternalistic order that had served for so long or to adjust to the shifting power relations. The latter was very much a minority position. As a result it took harsh realities to change their minds. As Edwards has pointed out:

> It was during this period that the first evidence began to emerge of the uncoordinated approach to the problems of industrial relations management. Even in one authority, district management teams would be negotiating separately with their local trade union officer

and were so concerned to dampen the fires raging all around them
that little, if any, effort was made to coordinate their settlements
with management in other districts or other areas. As a consequence, leap-frogging claims became common.[112]

That was more than ten years ago. Since then the Griffiths
proposals for a clear chain of command have been implemented
with another reorganization (Chapter 4), and the ancillary and
ambulance staff trade unions have been defending jobs and terms
of employment from government privatization and management
counter-attacks. But the root failure of the 1970s seems to have
been harder to be rid off than first thought. Certainly the professionalization of personnel and its enhanced status helped coordinate and control the response to local issues, but the most
recent changes under the new unilateral and unitarist systems
mean that industrial relations objectives have once again been
buried under corporate objectives and tightening Treasury
controls. The upshot is human resource management strategy
which seeks to reduce union influence through employee participation schemes and individual bargaining, and the imposition of
TQM (total quality management) as recommended by the plague
of management consultants paid handsomely for reinventing the
wheel.

At least one study of the increased personnel function in the
1980s took the view that personnel managers may make industrial action worse through encouragement of strong stewards
and a tendency to favour centralized management decision-
making. The influential work by Batstone concluded that 'on the
evidence of the survey at least, it seems possible to suggest that
personnel managers have not done much for industrial
relations'.[113]

In response to both this type of criticism and to the evidence
of NHS daily operations, senior NHS personnel managers
responded in familiar style. First and foremost, at least in public,
Len Peach (the head of personnel in the late 1980s) argued the
need for more and better communication. This theme, so
tirelessly repeated by managers throughout British industry,
hides more than it reveals and usually is a substitute for serious
policies. Of more importance was his view that 'linked with the
central theme of providing a more efficient management is the
need to increase productivity'.[114] This is the central issue for
the government. The 1990 reforms are another example of an

attempt to increase productivity through decentralization and financially driven incentives. But so was it the central theme in 1971 when the early productivity schemes were launched, and again in 1974 with reorganization, and again in 1982 and 1986. Why should it succeed now and not then? The answer lies partly in definitions of productivity, partly in what else happens to achieve it, and partly on the extent to which higher productivity is the true objective rather than just the stated objective of the controllers of the NHS's future.

General research in the 1980s into British industrial relations was concerned with the main personnel functions as defined by Brown:

> The ways in which labour is recruited and dismissed, trained and remunerated, are central to the employment relationship and have a powerful effect in moulding workplace institutions.[115]

The 1984 workplace survey found that most personnel managers spent most of their time in dealing with disciplinary cases, recruitment, training, grading and negotiating terms of employment.[116] In periods such as the 1980s, with frequent staff losses and a growing body of employment legislation, the thrust of the personnel function has been blunted. Its limited access to the highest decision-making bodies suggests that it is still of low rank when the major corporate decisions are made.

All of this will be familiar to NHS personnel managers. As Barnard and Harrison found:

> Most recently, and reflecting the quickening of political interest in applying the discipline of commercial enterprise management in the health sector, there has been concern to replace the resulting role-based culture with more results-oriented arrangements designed to facilitate policy execution and the implementation of decisions, all in the pursuit of efficiency and cost containment.[117]

The management function in general, and that of personnel management in particular, is subject to a complex power relationship as between professional staff with their clinical freedoms, other staff with their trade union organization, civil servants and governments with the purse strings and a marked reluctance to let go of central powers, and rival management groups themselves. In all this the patients and the community are external influences, and the reconciliation of contrasting and competing demands makes the system vulnerable to surges of uncertainty and blinkered management practices. The blinkers are there to protect line managers and personnel managers from the (too many) hard questions posed in such a difficult business. They are necessary to allow managers to muddle through and actually to manage the operation of the service. Local industrial relations is one of several additional elements of concern which can only be handled from day to day and never strategically or coherently.

Neither the unitarist desire to drive industrial relations underground through neglecting the rights of the unions and incorporating personnel functions and objectives within corporate policy, nor the pluralist quest for sound and formalized agreements, procedures and institutions as recommended by ACAS, McCarthy and some unions and managers, can overcome the serious issues that exist in hospitals and community services of low pay, discrimination against women and part-time workers, undemocratic decision-making, lack of funds, over-powerful consultants and poorly educated and badly trained managers.

CONCLUDING COMMENTS

This chapter has taken the history and themes of industrial relations in the NHS into the workplace and down to the level of the employing authority. It has therefore laid the basis for discussion of the 1990s reforms in terms of decentralization and the search for higher productivity.

The trends and arguments of the past few years have seen a strong head of steam building up for more managerial controls at local level to deal with both labour market and performance issues. The managers have been able to push their views successfully upwards to senior civil servants and Ministers. The professions have taken evasive action through pay review and the unions representing manual, technical and A&C grades have fought a rearguard action in defence of traditional agreements, negotiating rights and procedures. The pay determination systems and new selective conditions of service of the 1990s will have a major impact on workplace industrial relations in the NHS. The final chapter charts these developments and assesses their impact.

NOTES

1   ACAS (1978) *Royal Commission on the National Health Service: ACAS Evidence*, Report No. 12, ACAS, London, p. 19.
2   For example, see Caldwell, P., Croucher, R., Eva, D. and Oswald, R. (1980) *What's Happened to Safety?*, WEA, London.
3   ACAS (1977) *Disciplinary Practice and Procedures in Employment*, Code of Practice 1, HMSO, London. ACAS (1977) *Disclosure of Information to Trade Unions for Collective Bargaining Purposes*, Code of Practice 2, HMSO, London. ACAS (1977) *Time Off for Trade Union Duties and Activities*, Code of Practice 3, HMSO, London. NBPI (1971) *The Pay and Conditions of Service of Ancillary Workers in the National Health Service*, Report No. 166, Cmnd 4644, HMSO, London.
4   McCarthy, W. (1976) *Making Whitley Work*, HMSO, London.
5   Bellaby, P. and Oribabor, P. (1977) 'The Growth of Trade Union Consciousness among General Hospital Nurses Viewed as a Response to "Proletarianisation"', *Sociological Review*, 25(4); Parry, N. and Parry, J. (1977) 'Professionalism and Unionism: Aspects of Class Conflict in the NHS', *Sociological Review*, 25(4).
6   Trade Union Congress Health Services Committee (1981) *Improving Industrial Relations in the National Health Service*, TUC, London, p. 143.
7   NBPI, op. cit., p. 12.
8   Dimmock, S. (1982) 'Incomes Policy and Health Services in the UK' in Sethi, A. and Dimmock, S. (eds), *Industrial Relations and Health Services*, Croom Helm, London, p. 338.
9   Carpenter, M. (1988) *Working for Health: The History of COHSE*, Lawrence and Wishart, London, p. 339.
10 TUC, op. cit., p. 144.
11 Morris, G. and Rydzkowski, S. (1984) 'Approaches to Industrial Action in the National Health Service', *Industrial Law Journal*, 13, pp. 153–64.
12 Mailly, R., Dimmock, S. and Sethi, A. (1989) 'Industrial Relations in the NHS since 1979', in Mailly, R., Dimmock, S. and Sethi, A. (eds), *Industrial Relations in the Public Services*, Routledge, London, p. 147.
13 Abel-Smith, B. (1964) *The Hospitals 1800–1948*, Heinemann, London, p. 491.
14 Ibid., p. 493.
15 Daniel, W. and Millward, N. (1983) *Workplace Industrial Relations in Britain*, Heinemann, London. Millward, N. and Stevens, M. (1986) *British Workplace Industrial Relations 1980–1984*, Gower, Aldershot.
16 Millward and Stevens, op. cit., p. 58.
17 Ibid., p. 73.
18 Ibid., p. 80.
19 Stevens, M. and Wareing, A. (1990) 'Union Density and Workforce Composition', *Employment Gazette*, August, pp. 403–13.
20 Fryer, R., Fairclough, A. and Manson, T. (1974) *Organization and Change in the National Union of Public Employees*, Department of Sociology, Warwick University. England, J. (1981) 'Shop Stewards

in Transport House: a Comment upon the Incorporation of the Rank and File', *Industrial Relations Journal*, XII(5).
21 Millward and Stevens, op. cit., p. 115.
22 Ibid., p. 126.
23 Ibid., p. 126.
24 Harrison, S. (1988) 'The Closed Shop and the National Health Service: A Case Study in Public Sector Labour Relations', *Journal of Social Policy*, 17(1), p. 61.
25 Ibid., p. 68.
26 Ibid., p. 73.
27 Millward and Stevens, op. cit., p. 105.
28 Stevens, M., Millward, N. and Smart, D. (1989) 'Trade Union Membership and the Closed Shop in 1989', *Employment Gazette*, November.
29 TUC, op. cit., p. 154.
30 Dyson, R. (1979) 'Consultation and Negotiation', in Bosanquet, N. (ed.), *Industrial Relations in the NHS: the Search for a System*, King Edward's Hospital Fund for London, London, pp. 75–6.
31 McCarthy, op. cit., p. 89.
32 Miles, A. and Smith, D. (1969) *Joint Consultation – Defeat or Opportunity?*, King Edward's Hospital Fund for London, London. This is a rare but limited study of the subject.
33 ACAS (1978), op. cit., p. 16.
34 Ibid., p. 20.
35 Dimmock, S. and Mailly, R. (1982) 'Joint Consultation Arrangements in the NHS', *Industrial Relations Briefing Paper No.1*, Leeds University.
36 TUC, op. cit., p. 156.
37 Advance Letter (GC) 2/90 (1990) DHSS, Equal Opportunities Retainer Schemes.
38 Mailly *et al.* op. cit., p. 141.
39 Sethi, A., Stansel, R., Solomon, N. and Dimmock, S. (1982) 'Collective Bargaining among Nonprofessional and Allied Professional Employees in the Health Sector', in Sethi and Dimmock (eds), op. cit., p. 226.
40 Millward and Stevens, op. cit., p. 127.
41 Ibid., p. 128.
42 Ibid., p. 145.
43 COHSE (1976) *Union Stewards Handbook*, COHSE, London, p. 62.
44 Millward and Stevens, op. cit., p. 169.
45 ACAS (1989) *Discipline At Work*, ACAS Advisory Handbook, ACAS, London, p. 59.
46 Fewtrell, C. (1983) *The Management of Industrial Relations in the National Health Service*, IHSA, London, p. 31.
47 McCarthy, W. (1966) *The Role of Shop Stewards in British Industrial Relations*, Research Paper 1, Donovan Commission, HMSO, London, p. 12.
48 Whincup, M. (1979) 'Discipline and Dismissal: Legal Aspects', in Bosanquet (ed.), op. cit., p. 25.
49 Whincup, M. (1985) *Law and Practice of Dismissal in the Health Service*, Mercia Publications, Keele, pp. 147–8.

50 Examples taken from the NHS Industrial Relations Officers Working Group, *Employment Law Register*, West Midlands RHA, Birmingham.
51 Fewtrell, op. cit., p. 42.
52 Ibid., p. 53.
53 Gourlay, R. (1983) *Presenting and Hearing Appeals in the NHS*, Health Services Manpower Review, Keele University, p. 22.
54 COHSE, op. cit., p. 97.
55 McCarthy (1966), op. cit., p. 10.
56 Ibid., p. 15.
57 Millward and Stevens, op. cit., p. 171.
58 International Labour Office (1967) *Examination of Grievances Recommendation*, No. 130, ILO, Geneva.
59 Gourlay, op. cit., p. 15.
60 Fewtrell, op. cit., p. 63.
61 McCarthy (1966), op. cit., p. 19.
62 Millward and Stevens, op. cit., p. 212.
63 Equal Opportunities Commission (1991) *Equality Management: Women's Employment in the NHS*, EOC, Manchester.
64 Ibid., p. 220.
65 ACAS (1988) *Redundancy Handling*, Advisory Booklet No. 12, ACAS, London, pp. 16–17.
66 NBPI, op. cit., p. 8.
67 Ibid., p. 22.
68 Ibid., pp. 29–30.
69 Ibid., p. 132.
70 Armstrong, M. and Murlis, H. (1988) *Reward Management: A Handbook of Salary Administration*, Kogan Page, London. Trade Union Congress (1975) *Job Evaluation and Merit Rating*, TUC, London. ACAS (1989) *Job Evaluation: An Introduction*, Advisory Booklet No. 1, ACAS, London.
71 Equal Opportunities Commission (1985) *Job Evaluation Schemes Free of Sex Bias*, EOC, London, p. 1.
72 ACAS (1983) *Collective Bargaining in Britain: Its Extent and Level*, ACAS, London.
73 Webb, S. and Webb, B. (1920) *Industrial Democracy*, Longmans, Green & Co., London, pp. 280–310.
74 Trade Union Congress (1970) *Productivity Bargaining*, TUC, London, pp. 30–3.
75 Knight, C. (1985) 'Are Bonus Schemes on Borrowed Time?', *Health and Social Services Journal*, January, p. 132.
76 Labour Research Department (1990) *Performance Appraisal and Merit Pay*, LRD, London.
77 ACAS (1988) *Employee Appraisal*, Advisory Booklet No. 11, ACAS, London, p. 3.
78 LRD op. cit., p. 13.
79 NAHA and King's Fund (1985) *NHS Pay: A Time for Change*, NAHA and the King Edward's Hospital Fund for London, London, p. 13.
80 NAHA and King's Fund (1987) *NHS Pay: Achieving Greater Flexibility*, NAHA and the King Edward's Hospital Fund for London, London, p. 11.

81 Department of Health note to the 1990 Pay Review Body for Nursing Staff, *Pay Flexibility for Nurses and Midwives*.
82 Department of Health (1989) *Health Service Indicators Guidance Directory*, HMSO, London.
83 CASPE (1988) *How Did We Do? The Use of Performance Indicators in the NHS*, CASPE RESEARCH, London, p. 5.
84 Seifert, R. (1989) 'Performance Indicators in the NHS', *Radiography Today*, May, pp. 30–3.
85 Wagstaff, A. (1988) *Some Regression-Based Indicators of Hospital Performance*, University of York. National Audit Office (1990) *Managing Computer Projects in the NHS*, HMSO, London.
86 Industrial Relations Code of Practice 1972.
87 Kuhn, J. (1961) *Bargaining in Grievance Settlement*, Columbia University Press, New York, p. 77.
88 Hyman, R. (1972) *Disputes Procedure in Action*, Heinemann, London.
89 Seifert, R. (1987) *Teacher Militancy:* A History of Teacher Strikes 1896–1987, Falmer Press, Sussex, pp. 16–18.
90 Carpenter, op. cit., pp. 72–3.
91 Ibid., p. 175.
92 Edwards, B. (1979) 'Managers and Industrial Relations', in Bosanquet (ed.), op. cit., p. 129.
93 Morris, G. (1986) *Strikes in Essential Services*, Mansell Publishing, London.
94 Ferner, A. (1989) *Ten Years of Thatcherism: Changing Industrial Relations in British Public Enterprises*, Warwick Papers in Industrial Relations No. 27, University of Warwick, p. 17.
95 Carpenter, op. cit., p. 373.
96 Fewtrell, op. cit., pp. 64–5.
97 West, C. and Goodman, T. (1979) 'Disputes Procedures and Grievance Procedures' in Bosanquet (ed.), op. cit., p. 64.
98 Ibid., p. 66.
99 TUC (1981) op. cit., p. 153.
100 Swabe, A., Collins, P. and Walden, R. (1986) 'The Resolution of Disputes in the NHS', *Health Services Manpower Review*, 12(1), p. 3.
101 Ibid., p. 5.
102 TUC (1981), op. cit., p. 148.
103 Millward and Stevens, op. cit., p. 264.
104 Ibid., p. 271.
105 Seifert (1987), op. cit., pp. 234–5.
106 McCarthy (1966), op. cit., p. 20.
107 Fewtrell, op. cit., p. 69.
108 McCarthy (1976), op. cit., p. 70.
109 ACAS (1978), op. cit., p. 10.
110 Ibid., p. 11.
111 Ibid., p. 13.
112 Edwards, op. cit., pp. 129–30.
113 Batstone, E. (1980) 'What Have Personnel Managers Done for Industrial Relations?' *Personnel Management*, 12(6), p. 39.
114 Peach, L. (1986) 'A New Direction for Personnel in the NHS', *Health Services Manpower Review*, 12(1), p. 7.

115 Brown, W. (ed.) (1981) *The Changing Contours of British Industrial Relations*, Basil Blackwell, Oxford, p. 102.
116 Millward and Stevens, op. cit., p. 30.
117 Barnard, K. and Harrison, S. (1986) 'Labour Relations in Health Services Management', *Social Science and Medicine*, 22(11), p. 1216.

Chapter 8

The market, collective bargaining and the survival of custom

INTRODUCTION

The nature of the industry – health care – and the strong traditions associated with the delivery of that care suggest that the pattern of management of the staff at the point of service delivery will not alter dramatically as a result of changes in the financial and organizational systems. Customary elements in job task and hierarchies will remain more or less intact despite important changes in skill mix. The overwhelming impression is that whatever way the system is shaken up, the power of custom based on deeply held views on how to deliver health care will preserve the central structures and practices. It is likely, therefore, that the use of collective bargaining to determine pay and conditions of service will remain the dominant mechanism.

The market structures now in place will, however, influence the behaviour of managers, the power relationships within and between groups of staff and the management, the bargaining arrangements and industrial relations. They will establish a new set of tensions between national decisions and agreements and employer- and hospital-level decisions and agreements. The points at which settlements are made will vary across the country and this will influence bargaining outcomes and the relative remuneration packages available to staff.

A powerful, complex and fluid set of industrial relations issues has existed, on and off, for most of the period since 1950. The most harmful aspects of these issues from the government's and employers' point of view have been industrial action, uneven and uncertain labour markets, restrictive practices and the growth of trade unionism among all groups of staff. The solutions applied to control and contain such 'problems' have varied in detail since the 1960s, but until now have not been greatly different in substance.

The setting up of self-governing trusts and elements of market-type financial targets for directly managed units will mean a substantial change in the institutional arrangements for bargaining. To impose such reforms on an unwilling workforce, a sceptical public and a hostile group of representative organizations suggests a dangerous disregard for the management of the workforce and a disdain for the industrial relations consequences of change. Redefining the personnel function and incorporating it into higher-level decision-making centres as an afterthought will not be an adequate safeguard against troubles ahead.

This is, of course, a serious mistake. As was argued in Chapter 1, there are two interrelated areas of industrial relations practice which impinge directly on the success of the reform package. These are the need to increase labour productivity while holding down labour costs, and the requirement to exercise more managerial controls over all staff groups. The favoured mechanisms to achieve these objectives include flexibility through the increased powers of managers at local level, attacks on the trade union's traditional areas of bargaining, and important changes in skill mix in order to reduce the numbers and influence of the professions.

The earlier chapters have outlined the relevant industrial relations issues for the NHS since 1948. In the 1980s the government was caught between the desire to reduce public expenditure, including health service expenditure, and the growing and ever more public demand for patient care. Demand outstripped available supply. Waiting lists became, quite wrongly, the barometer of efficiency and government commitment to health services. The potential of ever-lengthening waiting lists for political damage remained, and therefore it became imperative that control over the demand for treatment passed from the medically based decisions of doctors and others able to refer patients to the system, including patients themselves, to budget holders forced to eliminate some forms of demand in order to keep within set limits. The consequences are that some patients cease to register on waiting lists altogether, their demand cancelled by lack of resources, while others are sent to a provider whose location is irrelevant but whose low cost bid is paramount. In this system some people simply will not be treated.

The alteration in the pattern of effective demand for treatment will alter the pattern for demand of the staff that provide the treatment, and those currently in strong markets may soon find themselves in weaker bargaining positions than they had anticipated. In other words, the long-term labour market issues will be contained in the cost-determined pattern of treatment as opposed to the traditional medically determined pattern. Payments systems geared to solving short-term local labour market difficulties will add to the burden on employers to provide services for 'paying customers' only. The new markets will distort the demand and supply of health worker labour and not, as claimed, eliminate imperfections and inefficiencies.

These changes are taking place at a time when the NHS is highly unionized across all staff groups, and when the unions and the professional associations enjoy greater support with more activists than at any other time in the NHS's history. While this remains uneven on a regional and occupational basis, none the less it is a major fact of life for managers, reformers and all staff.

The high levels of unionization are attributable to several different causes discussed in earlier chapters. Some were external to the health service, such as the imposition of incomes policies, the wider movement among women and low paid workers to join unions, and the increasing move by professional and white-collar workers to turn their defence organizations away from pressure group activity towards collective bargaining. The level of staffing, the mix of staff and their places of work changed and this created a new type of health worker – less subservient, more willing to act in their own interests, and more aware of their important role within the total operation of the hospital and community services.

This fuelled, along with the legislation of the 1970s and the public policy commitment to productivity bargaining and formalized industrial relations, a crisis in the management of the NHS at all levels. The old paternalistic system hidden by Civil Service centralism from the prying eyes of radical politicians and some unhappy employers and managers was giving way. Whitley was seen as too slow, too unrepresentative and finally too unresponsive to the operational needs of the service. Arbitration was abandoned on the doubtful grounds that it was inflationary, and the consequence was the start of industrial action by health workers.

The wave of strikes in the 1970s highlighted the poor quality of management in this area and the inadequacy of local bargaining arrangements. Throughout the 1970s, therefore, senior managers allied themselves with conservative academics and politicians to create a new reform strategy. McCarthy's 1976 report incorporated some of their demands, but essentially restated the old order with a more formal role for the unions and a more influential role for senior managers.

While this debate raged, and while the 1980s saw reorganizations of the service and the management systems, large numbers of health workers remained on low pay, and the nurses and allied professions remained frustrated by their lack of influence, career structure and reward system. The Pay Review Body for these groups went some way to mollify their pay crisis, but went counter to the other reforms which tried to allow for greater local flexibility.

This summary of the situation so far indicates that reforms of the 1990s were not designed to resolve the industrial relations issues as such, but rather to tackle the outstanding questions of reducing costs and increasing managerial powers within a staged programme of selling off large sections of the NHS to the private sector. The central industrial relations aspect of this remains the decentralization of decision-making and bargaining. The rest of this chapter examines this imperative from an institutional perspective and from a market- and performance-led perspective.

The decade of the 1990s will witness years of effort to relate the complex set of factors that determine the relevant markets and their imperfections to an uneasy state policy of health intervention. For industrial relations the ghosts of Whitley and Donovan will be laid. New spectres will come to haunt the NHS: performance related pay, local flexibility, single-employer bargaining and a mishmash of terms and conditions of employment for an ever more divided and alienated staff. The predictions for the future rest on two elements: the evidence from those areas of the NHS which have already experienced tomorrow, and the pursuit of interests which have already been seen elsewhere in public services.

REMUNERATION PACKAGES:
PERFORMANCE AND LABOUR MARKETS

The needs of any business require an optimal mix of staff and a highly motivated workforce. To achieve the first for any given firm may require a recruitment and retention strategy which rewards those whose skills are in short supply. Thus the advent of 'golden hellos' and 'golden handcuffs'. Since the demand for labour is derived from the demand for the product/service, then the higher the productivity (better the performance) of each unit of labour the better for the customer, worker and employer. In practice if the employer pays X because he is in short supply and Y because she is a strong performer then how does any pay structure work? And what is the purpose of any pay based on grades, job evaluation and promotion? If X is rewarded more than Y just because X is in short supply whatever X's performance, then Y becomes disillusioned. If Y is paid more than X then X can quit. If they are paid the same then what is the point of performance related pay and labour market flexibility? These questions and issues are not unique to the NHS and form the basis for the underlying debate in economic theory concerned with remuneration levels as between individual workers. They do, however, present serious decisions to managers in the NHS. The logic of the market, whether for supply or performance reasons, will result in a diverse set of pay levels which outrage customary felt-fair views of comparative remuneration packages and will probably result in providing neither the best skill mix nor a motivated workforce.

The 1990/1 round of pay settlements incorporated two main features: for those within Pay Review Bodies their pay rises have been in line with the pattern set for much of the public sector, and Secretary of State William Waldegrave has indicated his desire to keep this system in place, with most SGTs responding by accepting the dominant role of pay review in determining the pay of the professions. The second element is the use of minimum national agreements on pay for most other staff, including technical, ambulance, A&C and now ancillary. The tendency is for such national agreements to contain more room for local discretion than before (Whitley plus), and again most SGTs are currently falling into line on these issues. Conditions of service are more likely to vary at the new employer level than pay in the short term, although the increasing use of enabling agreements at national level may form the pattern of minimum bargaining.

This section summarizes the 1990/91 pay round and then examines the potential for performance related pay systems and structures.

The 1990/91 pay round

The most recent survey of pay developments comes from Incomes Data Service (IDS). They are aware that government policy in the NHS reflects its policies across the public sector and that

> The 56 self-governing trusts, due to start running in the NHS from 1 April 1991, are being strongly encouraged to withdraw from national agreements and introduce local pay arrangements.[1]

IDS warns that such moves may mean leapfrogging and, initially at least, higher wage bills. They favour national agreements with built-in local discretion. This appears to be one pattern emerging throughout the public sector, as with schoolteachers, local authority chief executives and in the NHS, groups such as MLSOs, technicians and works staff. In addition, local managers in the NHS can now extend pay scales by up to three incremental points for posts carrying responsibility or requiring specialist skills. Ambulance staff accepted a deal which incorporated another 2% for local productivity.

During 1990/1, therefore, the NHS continued its move towards adopting more flexible pay systems. The 1989 pay supplements for nursing and administrative staff were extended to some professional and technical staff. Of great importance was the introduction of the Health Care Assistant grade without any national bargaining arrangements. IDS noted that most of the pay flexibility schemes were aimed at solutions to labour market shortages. The problems associated with this policy are discussed below.

Apart from these developments, most NHS staff did not receive pay rises in 1990 in line with inflation. The Review Body groups received 7% from 1 April 1990. Most other NHS workers received between 7.7% and 8% – among the lowest in the public sector. The local variations mentioned above for technical staff, works staff and MLSOs include a supplement worth up to 30% of salary in the four Thames regions and 20% elsewhere. They are not performance related, which again raises the spectre of panic response to short-term market shortages.

The new pay structure for senior nurses and midwives in 1990 added two extra spine points above the maximum of each salary range. These can be used to recruit new staff, retain a 'valued' member of staff or to reward a postholder who can 'command a higher salary for similar responsibilities in the same locality outside the NHS'. All are market-related reasons. In exchange for this these senior nurses and midwives have lost their right of appeal against grading decisions to the Whitley Council. The appeals will now end at the level of the employer, and progression through incremental points will no longer be automatic but based on performance and/or labour markets.

Staff in the new 57 SGTs have been transferred on existing contracts, but in future the trusts will be able to set their own rates of pay and conditions of service. Most will move away from national bargaining as it is now constituted but may remain within a looser system for most items and/or form their own pay and conditions cartel. The development of a 'pick and mix' or 'cafeteria' approach in which staff are asked to select a range of conditions traded off against others is becoming fashionable. IDS among many others warn of the dangers: personnel managers will be overwhelmed by local bargaining, leapfrogging and, owing to immediate financial problems, there will be little money to pay supplements without savings elsewhere.

The 1990 settlements were poor throughout the NHS by national and public sector standards. The Pay Review Body settlements were staged, and extra increases at the top of the consultants' scale rejected. Senior nurses and midwives have been assimilated on to the pay spine for other senior managers. The Pay Review Body will play a less important role in setting their pay in the future. Tables 8.1 and 8.2 provide the details for all the agreements.

In January 1991 COHSE, GMB, NUPE and TGWU launched their pay campaign on behalf of 180 000 ancillary workers. The key elements are for a £20 a week flat rate increase, review of the job evaluation scheme to establish equal pay for work of equal value, increases in annual leave, the end of discrimination against part-time workers in the payment of shift allowances and overtime, and the right to go to arbitration. Roger Poole, the chief union negotiator, said,

Table 8.1 Public sector pay: settlements 1984–1990

April–March each year	1984/5	1985/6	1986/7	1987/8	1988/9	1989/90	1990/1
Inflation (at start of period)	5.2	6.9	3.0	4.2	3.9	8.0	9.4
Average earnings (underlying at start of period)	7.7	7.5	7.5	7.75	8.5	9.25	9.75
Central government							
Armed Forces (Review Body)	6.5–9	4–8.5	5.5–9.5	4.7	6.4	6.8	7 + 1.7–2.5 (staged)
Civil Service (staff)	4.55[1]	4.9[1]	6	4.25 (basic)	4.5 (admin. staff)	4 + new pay structure (admin. staff)	8 or 8.5
NHS							
Nurses (Review Body)	6–8	4–14.7	7.9–9.5	9.5	15.3[1]	6.8[1]	7 + 2–4.4 (staged)
Doctors (Review Body)	3 + 6.9	6.2 (average)	6.9–7.2	8.25	7.9	8	7 + 2.5–3.5 (staged)

The earnings increase is the DE estimated 'underlying increase' (whole economy).
[1] Paybill increase.
Note: The increase in settlements shown should be seen as a guide to the settlements in each period, rather than as an exact description.
Source: Incomes Data Service.

Table 8.1 (continued) Public sector pay: settlements 1984–1990

April–March each year	1984/5	1985/6	1986/7	1987/8	1988/9	1989/90	1990/1
Ancillaries	4.8–3.5	4.7[1]	6[1]	5[1]	6	7.7[1]	7.8[1]
Administrative & clerical	4.5	4.7	6	5	5	6.25+3.25 for restructuring	7.7
Local government							
Manuals	5.7–4.7	12.0–6.7	7.2–6.3	10.6[1]	5.6[1]	8.8[1]	9.4[1]
APT&C Staff	4.6–5.6	5.25	6.0	7.1–8.8 (staged)	5.4	8.8 (average)	9.4[1]
Police (Indexed)	5.4	7.5	7.5	7.75	8.5	9.25	9.75
Fire (Indexed)	7.2	7.2	7.3	7.3	8.6	8.6	9.5
Teachers (E&W)	5.1	6.9+1.6	5.5	16.4 (staged) (15 months)	4.2	6[2]	7.9[1]
Public Corporations							
British Coal (miners)	5.2	5.1–3.8	2.6–3.6	4.3	5–6.1	7.64	10[3]
Electricity (manuals)	5.2	4.8–6.7	6.5	5.6	7	9.2	10.2
British Rail (manuals)	4.9	4.8	5	4.5	5	8.8	9.3 (8.6[1])
Post Office (postmen)	5.2	5+0.5	5.3[1]	5[1]	5[1]	8.1[1]	10.9 (9.8[1])

The earnings increase is the DE estimated 'underlying increase' (whole economy).
[1] Paybill increase.
[2] Heads and deputies received 7.5%.
[3] 2-year deal: RPI for September in 1991.
Note: The increase in settlements shown should be seen as a guide to the settlements in each period, rather than as an exact description.
Source: Incomes Data Service.

Table 8.2 Pay settlements: the settlement levels for the various NHS bargaining groups in the 1990 pay round

	Date	Numbers	Increase	Comments
Review Body groups				
Nurses and Midwives	1.4.90	491 000	7% + 2%(1.1.91)	8% on pay bill
Professions Allied to Medicine	1.4.90	41 400	7% + 2.7% –3.8% (1.1.91)	7.8% on pay bill
Doctors and Dentists	1.4.90	100 000	7% + 2.5% –4.5% (1.1.91)	10.9% on pay bill
Whitley Council groups				
Administration and Clerical	1.4.90	141 000	7.7% or £8 p.w.	
Ambulance	1.3.90	22 500	9% +7.9% +2% prod.(1.10.90)	
Ancillary	1.4.90	156 000	£8.45 p.w.(£9.90 p.w. for supervisors)	7.8% on pay bill
Professional andTechnical				
MLSOs	1.4.90	18 000	7.9%	
Technicians	1.4.90	19 000	7.9%	
Works staff	1.4.90	6500	7.9%	New pay structure
Scientific and Professional				
Biochemists, etc	1.4.90	—	7.9%	
Clinical psychologists	1.4.90	2000	7.9%	
Hospital chaplains	1.4.90	—	7.9%	
Maintenance Staff Advisory Panel				
Building workers	1.4.90	8500	7.25%	+ £2 p.w. consol. (1.10.90)
Engineers and electricians		No settlement in 1990		
Managers				
General managers	1.9.90	800	8.5%	+ merit increase
Senior managers	1.9.90	—	8%	+ merit increase

Source: Incomes Data Service.

this year we will be giving NHS management notice that our members whose skills underpin the nation's health care are not prepared to settle for less than a decent deal after a decade of decline.[2]

The agreed outcome was a general settlement of between 7% and 8% with a new pay spine from December 1991. The most significant part of the deal was the introduction of locally bargained supplements as an early version of the 'Whitely plus' system favoured by some unions.

Performance related schemes

As will be argued below, most of these measures are labour-market-related rather than performance related, and this undermines the purpose of the reforms and will result in weakening rather than strengthening the power of local managers. Elements of pay related to productivity and performance, however, are being widely canvassed throughout the NHS. The main forms include traditional payment-by-results (pbr), forms of job evaluation, performance related pay (prp), merit pay linked to appraisal, and changes in the package of non-pay rewards and conditions.

The first task of any such scheme must be to provide an agreed method of measuring performance. For many tasks among the ancillary and ambulance staff, elements of traditional work study can be applied in principle, and have been in practice. Such schemes allow for well-organized stewards to bargain over the introduction of the schemes, their application and the resultant pay levels and pay composition. It provides an endless case load of grievances and possible industrial action over interpretation and change. Such were the consequences of the early productivity deals brought in with government support in the early 1970s (Chapter 7). The impact of these has been matched by the subcontracting of many of the affected services, a mechanism partly designed to break the power of the stewards.

For technical, clerical, administrative and some professional staff alternatives include job evaluation, appraisal-related pay and performance related pay. All exist and all have their supporters. Some regions are tinkering with the all-embracing job evaluation scheme to include ancillary workers through to consultants. Managers are already subject to performance related pay, while some professional staff may encounter appraisal-related pay. The SGTs certainly and the DMUs probably will be able to utilize some mix of these notions. As IDS discovered:

> Public sector organizations have continued to introduce performance-related pay schemes for their employees ... In most cases these arrangements started with managers or senior staff, but there are signs that they are 'cascading' down to cover other groups of staff.[3]

British Rail introduced such prp schemes for their managers in 1989; in 1990 this applied to electricity industry, Royal Mail letters, the BBC, local authorities, for schoolteachers, civil servants and HMSO. In 1986 NHS managers received it and this has now been extended to include senior nurses and midwives. The central issues include the measurement of performance. One system is through appraisal of individuals. The member of staff is asked to set agreed targets which if reached trigger payment. The payment may take the form of an increment or an additional element on top of any increment. Alternatively the payment could be linked to more 'objective' measures such as developed through Health Service Indicators (HSIs) (Chapter 7).

Most research and evidence about performance measures find that they are unable to provide usable business information, and that their use for target setting and reward allocation is doomed to failure. All internal NHS efforts to predict the future with these information systems in place alongside new management structures and markets have proved disastrous. Reference is made later to the document from the Trent RHA on industrial relations in SGTs, but an even worse analysis for the immediate future came from the East Anglia RHA's efforts to anticipate problem areas. This was through the use of a simulation management 'game' with senior managers as 'players' and based on best assumptions about the future of the service. The experiment, known as 'The Rubber Windmill', found managers and the new systems unable to escape the logical rigours of the market financial requirements. Quality of care and measurement of performance proved fragile guarantors of a better future.[4]

There are serious misgivings about the schemes based on performance and/or productivity. For some managers, such as unit general managers, they may be linked to short-term contracts.

The problems of this are that it may encourage short-term solutions and target-hitting may become more important than actual improvements. There is substantial evidence that such pay reward systems inhibit innovation rather than stimulating it. ACAS in particular found that such systems ended in chaos since as soon as some managers failed to receive increases they altered their view of their colleagues and withdrew effort. The chairman of ACAS, Douglas Smith, has made his view quite clear on numerous occasions that performance related pay does not work, and that appraisal methods in practice are full of pitfalls. The difficulties in making the system felt-fair are immense, and companies often regress back to a more collective approach to reward management.

The general managerial argument for flexible pay and conditions at unit and/or cost centre and/or district level has been based on a series of practical aims. The influence over pay and conditions was seen by line managers in particular as an important factor by which high levels of motivation among the staff can be best achieved. The practices require the managers to review incentives, rewards and sanctions in relation to their own staff, and to consider anew rewards for merit, and the redeployment and/or dismissal of poor performers.

This includes the payment of spot salaries on flexible pay spines. The extent of the flexibility is always limited in practice by ever tightening financial constraints. No manager, for example, can earn more than 85% of the maximum basic salary of the relevant general manager. This has created short-term anomalies. For example, there have been some cases of managers covered by Pay Review Bodies who have been offered salaries at a level below the new unilateral senior management contracts, and which are thus lower than their existing salaries! More recently, in April 1991, the Secretary of State has urged health authorities and SGTs to limit the pay of senior managers. This is yet another example, along with Pay Review and junior hospital doctors national protection, of the main thrust of policy being blunted by the policy-makers themselves. The pattern emerges of pragmatic deal-as-you-go arrangements so that weak or small groups of workers can have pay determined locally by managers, but strong and/or numerous groups are kept within tight Treasury control through Pay Review. Free market forces are applied where possible but formal national institutional arrangements are used when necessary.

Senior managers need to be able to move around the country and to plan careers without suffering from a series of worsening pay and conditions. Initial appointment and the decision on whether to award performance related pay are local decisions, but basic salaries and conditions are not. This government practice mirrors fears amongst professional staff in the NHS that significant pay differences as between geographical locations and specialisms (and after all, if they are not significant than why adopt them) will inhibit career planning and the free movement of staff from place to place which has been seen as an important part of the professional learning process as well as aiding a continuous cross-current of treatment methods throughout the NHS. Parallel arguments are being used for schoolteachers.

In addition to this problem, are the doubts that surround the effectiveness of performance related pay systems. Traditional payment by results and piecework systems among manual workers relate pay to effort and not to performance. For managers and professional workers the attempt to link pay with measurable performance is fraught with difficulties. In the NHS this has been attempted through the extensive use of HSIs, but the lessons from other such exercises seem lost. The two iron laws of HSIs are that they grow at an exponential rate and that the managers hit the indicators and do not change the real practices and outputs. There is no good evidence that performance related pay improves performance.[5] Moreover the prognosis for this form of local bargaining is poor:

> The carrot of local bargaining dangled before the management and staff of many large DGHs has rapidly gone mouldy. Performance-related pay for health care workers is much harder to implement in practice than it ever appears to be in theory. The recruitment and retention problems, allied with the abandonment of Whitley, will create a massed web of local agreements which will prove a nightmare to negotiate and implement.[6]

In addition, even generous allocations of funds to managerial pay irrespective of performance may not solve problems of managerial exodus and/or poor morale. In February 1990, Maureen Dixon, the director of the Institute of Health Service Managers, bitterly complained that the growing tendency to 'blame the Health Service's financial problems on managerial incompetence' was contributing to low morale and quitting by managers. She said that there was widespread acceptance of the clear evidence that the NHS was underfunded.

The overall impact of the pay and conditions of employment changes for many NHS managers has started the development of a more private sector approach to the management of the business. This has been achieved through devices such as regional review, remodelling of the planning process, the new management accounting framework, individual performance review and the related performance related pay, competitive tendering, income generation, estate rationalization (which is instructive given that the main business of the new appointees to the boards of SGTs is property development), resource management and information technology (which has made real improvements in technical areas although its managerial applications remain haphazard).

Merit pay is linked to these systems as well, but once again the difficulties of implementation are severe.[7] The prognosis is that performance related pay will remain for the current set of managers, but is unlikely to become widespread among other groups. It may create quite sharp differences in the performance of the managers, and make hospitals and SGTs more, not less, vulnerable to serious management error and cover-up.

Similar considerations apply to proposed changes in conditions of service. A recent management document coordinated by Warlow lays out some of the changes in conditions of service that some senior managers would wish to see. Astonishingly it starts with the statement that: 'This review of NHS conditions of employment is the only comprehensive review to have taken place since the inception of the NHS.'[8] The importance of this particular review is summarized on its opening page:

> Conditions of employment of NHS staff greatly influence how managers manage services and staff. They often determine what work staff do, when, where and how they do it, who does it, and they influence the cost of doing it. They affect not only operational requirements but also the recruitment, retention and return of staff and opportunities to develop staff potential and skills. Absence from work, discipline, grievance, appeals and disputes as well as redundancy and dismissals are largely governed by employment conditions.[9]

Some specific suggestions contained in this report include:

- more flexible hours of work including management's right to change working hours, rotas and shift arrangements;

- greater flexibility in determining staff grades;
- abolition of most pay allowances in order to permit greater flexibility in the use of manpower;
- reduction of oncall through extension of normal working hours;
- overtime to be paid at plain time rates;
- merit awards for doctors should be based on their performance in the NHS;
- urgent introduction of appraisal for all staff;
- incentive awards for performance for individuals using the award of an increment;
- removal or radical reduction in the power of the *status quo* clause in disputes procedures;
- reduction in the number of recognized trade unions;
- flexible pay to help recruitment;
- local employment package based on a 'starter kit' of choices, for example, creche facilities, meal provision and hours arrangement. This represents a 'menu' with individual health workers selecting between the different conditions.

In procedural matters the managers are equally obvious in the expression of their new found freedom. Namely, that the disciplinary procedure is too long, that decisions are made too high up the management hierarchy, and that the appeals system is too easily available to the staff. As usual such comments are made without reference to why the procedures have developed in the way they have and the possible consequences of adopting the changes.

The overall view of the report was that most managers want decisions devolved to district level for most pay and conditions of service. As the report concludes:

> Most see the desirable position as one where there is wide flexibility and local decision making within a general 'none too specific' national framework of conditions.[10]

Labour markets

There have been many attacks on the weaknesses of such reforms and in particular on the problems associated with market-led pay rewards. The government's policies in the 1990s are deeply flawed and will lead to severe practical difficulties for managers, staff and the users of health services. The government 'is relying heavily upon the fragmentation of public service bargaining as a means to control costs and improve labour utilization'.[11] The fallacies in policy have been magnified and distorted by an overreaction to labour shortages in the London region in the late 1980s and will undoubtedly mean leapfrogging and 'me-too' claims from all sections of staff. In addition, the public sector move to decentralization is based on geographical labour markets and makes no economic sense. In the private sector, which is the model, decentralization has been mainly used to relate pay more closely to local profit centres as an aspect of the strategies of multi-divisional companies.[12] This is not happening in the NHS. Geographical decentralization of pay, therefore, makes no economic sense for the NHS. It will tend to be badly managed and lead to a mishmash of pay differences which may create a hospital in which, as Christine Hancock of the RCN has frequently argued, the pay of doctors and nurses will fall and those of groups in short supply, such as accountants and IT specialists, will rise.

The only feasible use of decentralized bargaining in the public sector would operate where pay is linked to the performance of different functional groups of staff. This would be very difficult to implement in the NHS with its increasingly multi-disciplinary approach to treatment and its subtle cross-subsidization of costs and knowledge.

Brown and Rowthorn conclude that the fragmentation of pay desired by the government's reforms will lead to uneven delivery and quality of health services and in particular to leapfrogging, immobility and low morale.

The managers

The role of managers is central to a great deal of the analysis underpinning the reform programme. From the strong unitarist stance adopted by the NHS reformers, the managers will lead the new health service and captain the new missions. They cannot be relied on to do so by themselves and they require the carrot of performance related pay and the stick of short-term contracts.

The 800 senior managers discussed in Chapter 4 were the first to be put on performance related packages. These were imposed unilaterally by government with no consultation with the relevant recognized unions. It was the first step in the derecognition of trade unions for managers which was seen as a central strategy by government throughout the public services. In 1987 another 12 000 managers were put on performance related scales, and in 1988 another 7000 below UGM level. By the end of 1990 20 000 nurse/midwife managers were put on to this pay system with their salaries determined by the Secretary of State. A strange action for a government set on minimizing state intervention!

Most of the managers involved so far have reacted with muted acquiescence. The only points at issue have been the size of the bonus and the shortness of the short-term contracts. For important sections of the administrative staff the immediate pay rises have compensated them for the relative falls under the cash-limited A&C Whitley Council. There are no early signs of this group forming a new staff association. Whether the larger numbers of managers in more junior and specialist posts will respond in similar ways is doubtful, but remains to be seen.

There are over 20 000 nurse managers of various grades overseeing the work of the half million nurses working in the NHS. Nurses fought very hard for management autonomy even where they were denied clinical autonomy. The nurse managers were affected by the 1982 reorganization and lost a number of management posts at that time. However, the real change came with the implementation of the 1983 Griffiths report in which one major theme was that general management could and should be extended to run a wide range of services in the NHS, including nursing. It seemed that most nurse management posts would disappear. The RCN reacted with a £250 000 anti-general manager campaign which achieved a great deal of publicity with its question 'Why is Britain's nursing being run by people who don't know their coccyx from their humerus?'. Some general managers tried to incorporate nurse opinion through the invention of such posts as Patient Care Managers or Quality Assurance Managers. The RCN in general failed to prevent the Griffiths-inspired changes which broke the senior management structure for nurses.

Their pay is now linked to that of the general management pay spine with performance related additions. In addition, the Secretary of State has taken their pay levels into his domain of unilateral and centralized pay decision. This suggests *de facto* derecognition of the unions representing senior nurse managers, and in particular the RCN. This edges the industry towards a union-free NHS management with pay determined through a combination of central decision and local performance related pay.

The limited grasp of industrial relations practices shown by successive Secretaries of State and the inherent difficulties of payment systems for professional staff and managers within the NHS have combined to create an absurd situation. After Waldegrave's clumsy efforts to resolve some of the issues several health authorities turned, in hope rather than with a sense of real resolution of the problem, to the use of job evaluation structures devised by the management consultants Hay. The combination of the Hay scores (which take little account of clinical management responsibility) and the rule which states that a subordinate cannot be offered more than 85% in basic pay of the basic pay of the general manager to whom that individual is accountable has led to a number of health service employers offering both PAM and nursing managers general management pay scales that would have meant a reduction in salary of between £2000 and £3000 per year. Most made the offer only for it to be rejected – a poor reflection on an early excursion into local pay flexibility. In 1991 it is expected that PAM and nurse managers will formally move on to general management pay scales. This will serve to increase insecurity throughout these professions at a time of maximum uncertainty.

THE NEW BARGAINING: RESPONSES AND ARRANGEMENTS

The implementation of employer and sub-employer level pay and conditions agreements to achieve performance and labour market objectives requires changes in the bargaining arrangements. The ideas surrounding the move to more local level bargaining are not new. In 1976 McCarthy noted that,

> there is a widespread belief in the NHS that too many decisions are taken at too high a level, and this view is often expressed about the operation of Whitley. ... I prefer, in this report, to consider the case for *decentralisation* – i. e. the arguments that more decisions about terms and conditions ought to be taken below national level.[13]

Flexibility

At present, as indicated in Chapter 7, local variations to national conditions are very limited. The main exceptions are salary on appointment, some regradings, special cases agreed by the Secretary of State, and locally calculated bonus schemes for ancillary, ambulance and maintenance staff.

The four main problems that arose from the centralized system were: (1) inflexibility resulting in the inability of management to respond in pay terms to local labour market circumstances. This gave rise to operational problems which were a source of frustration to some unions as well as managers, and anomalies as, for example, between hospital based and community nurses in that the former could claim extra payment if they worked in psychiatry while the latter could not. (2) The lack of a proper role for local management was bemoaned by managers as well as unions such as ASTMS and the GMB. (3) Lack of local managerial powers might mean that local disputes escalated. (4) There was the temptation to 'grade-fix' where managers put staff on phoney grades in order to recruit and retain.

Most managers wanted greater local discretion over terms of employment, and in most cases they wanted these to be unilateral. McCarthy did not like that and advocated, instead, local bargaining. ASTMS pushed for this solution. It wanted bargaining at the level of the employer over a range of issues including allowances, overtime arrangements and special day working – quite tame requests by today's standards! The point was that ASTMS favoured 'minimum rate' national bargaining in the place of 'effective rate' bargaining. Most other unions at the time preferred more national rates with some limited local bargaining supplements.

The ASTMS position reflected three factors at the time: first the competition among the unions for members spurred ASTMS to take a strong and clear line to show up the vacillations of their competitors. Secondly, ASTMS represented groups of staff with labour market and job situations in which local bargaining would probably enhance pay and conditions. Thirdly, ASTMS may have felt that, as 'the new kid on the block', it had most to gain from a shift away from the entrenched representative position of national Whitley.

The most popular proposal put to McCarthy in 1976 was that of flexible national agreements. This entailed 'that at national level a general framework for different grades would be settled, but this would be capable of being applied in various ways at local level'.[14] Local managers would have more freedom to progress individuals through the looser grading structures. This broad banding approach was supported by most professional associations and many managers.

What irony then that the main opposition to decentralization 15 years ago came from the civil servants and senior management. Their main stated fear was that local bargaining and/or more flexible national agreements would highlight the lack of local expertise and that this would fuel the tendency for anomalies to be created through leapfrogging. As McCarthy pointed out, 'the ambulance service was cited as a good example of havoc wrought by local variation'.[15]

Before SGTs started there was a move to more flexibility in NHS national pay agreements. The main example of this was the 1989 agreement for A&C grades. The government and most managers favour the continued recognition of unions for pay bargaining purposes at local level for the moment. This is in part to allow the management side to develop the necessary expertise currently furnished through NAHSPO. The key to higher productivity in the SGTs will be the employment of fewer, even if better paid, professional staff, and with the rest substituted with generic helper and assistant grades.

ACAS in their survey of flexible working practices in UK industries found that the main impetus for their introduction included: economic recession, technological change and greater competition. The main areas of flexibility have been, firstly, numerical flexibility, adjusting staffing levels in line with demand which would mean part-time work, temporary contracts and outside contracts. Functional flexibility means the relaxation of traditional demarcations between skills and jobs, this is seen in the NHS with multi-skilling, deskilling and the concentration of skills. Flexible hours means shifts, annual hours, flexitime and overtime. Finally flexible labour costs entail integrated job evaluation (a single company-wide scheme to incorporate all the jobs), merit pay and performance related pay.[16]

Local government has also been involved in flexible pay. Some employers and managers in that industry want more flexible national agreements. Present experience is that there are severe problems in practice in achieving flexibility in terms of its link to efficient and effective use of staff. The most important lesson for the NHS is that if pay rates of certain groups of staff such as ancillary and technical workers rise above competitive rates then the employer will subcontract out the relevant services. A dire warning to the unions and the patients.[17]

Many NHS managers remain very keen on their freedom to be flexible. In Merseyside they have adopted a three-prong strategy – more flexibility within Whitley, new staff groups such as health care assistants subject to only local bargaining, and three of the SGTs are going it alone. The care assistants will replace nursing auxiliaries and other helpers and some duties of the qualified nurse as part of the process known as 'reprofiling the workforce'.[18]

This is the present consequence of policies which, in 1979, the government embarked on with the intention not of making Whitley work but of ridding the NHS of national bargaining and handing over unilateral determination of pay and conditions to local employers as one step in the preparation for selling off hospitals along with many of the other services already subcontracted. This meant that in the 1980s the ancillary unions spent much time and effort defending jobs and resisting privatization measures. In practice most union stewards ended up involved in negotiations over in-house tenders. This was due to ambivalence amongst members, confusion among many stewards and a realization that they had to live and work there whatever the TUC or national union had to say.

The fight was fierce and destructive, as Mailly *et al.* note:

> In general the union campaign became a 'damage limitation' exercise. There were areas where the local membership resisted. For example, at Addenbrookes Hospital in Cambridge, and at Barking in London, where cleaning staff went on strike in opposition respectively to the incoming contractor and to cuts in wages made by the private contractor.[19]

The industrial relations consequences of tendering out include fragmentation of the ancillary staff. As a weapon to weaken the unions, contracting out has been relatively successful in the short term. It does, however, raise important issues of the future method of pay determination for these and other groups.

Union responses to SGTs: the principles

Despite managements' preference for unilateral wage imposition the reality is that some form of negotiating system will have to emerge in the SGTs and DMUs. The starting point for this is the statement in *Working for Patients* that trusts will be able 'to set the rates of pay of their own staff'.[20] What follows from this? Each employing trust will have to set up machinery to determine pay and to negotiate with the unions. How do managers and the unions react to this?

The most famous of the first wave SGTs was Guy's Hospital in London. In its lengthy, 231-page, policy document one of the main points it makes about industrial relations is that it favours flexible pay. This is reported in the moralistic rhetoric with which most documents resound:

> We will need to strike a balance between pay, other benefits and the working environment to create the right culture for recruiting and retaining the right staff with the right skills.[21]

To set aside fears, the document then says that:

> our proposed NHS trust has made a clear statement of intent to recognize all nationally agreed Whitley Council rates of pay as the basic minimum under Trust status.[22]

It promises higher rewards linked to performance and to the labour-market situation. The funds for these better terms are to come from higher productivity based on a more 'satisfied' workforce and changes in the skill mix. In practice this has meant redundancies. Guy's recognize the need for better pay information through the Integrated Personnel System Recruitment and Payroll Modules, and will soon be paying for specialist pay bulletins from a private agency in order to compete in the bargaining round with other employers, the unions and some individuals.

The document continues:

> it is our intention to recognize all relevant trade unions where they are recognized nationally ... similarly we will continue to consult/negotiate with the relevant trade unions as appropriate.[23]

Current DHA policy is to operate a decentralized personnel management system within which UGMs, backed up by a small district team, control personnel matters. At unit level duties have covered all aspects of recruitment, selection and termination procedures. At more senior levels there is involvement in law, conditions of service, and industrial relations. At district level more strategic decisions are made on issues such as job evaluation, corporate strategy and management. The SGT will need to change much of this with 'a much higher level of input from the

Personnel function on strategic staffing issues'.[24] This means the adoption of human resource management, better employee relations, a coherent pay policy, job evaluation, performance appraisal and gradings. The director of human resource management will sit on the Trust Board. The new personnel function's mission statement is:

> to provide the facilities to enable the Trust to create the right environment and culture to attract, retain, motivate, develop and reward the required quantity and calibre of staff.[25]

The language is positive and managerial. Its substance suggests a move away from collective bargaining, and a reduction in the importance of recognizing unions. The theme is a move towards a Marks and Spencer style of strong personnel function to outflank the unions. This is unitarist and paternalist, and will be very difficult to implement in the NHS with its strong bargaining and union traditions.

The trade unions and professional associations reacted to these mission statements and to the principle of SGTs in similar ways. All were opposed. The RCN was clear:

> The Royal College of Nursing of the United Kingdom expresses the gravest concern that the proposals in the White Paper, 'Working for Patients', threaten the principles and effectiveness of the National Health Service.[26]

The case against SGTs continued in a robust style:

> the main risks posed by the proposal to establish self-governing hospitals are the threat to continuity of care, reduced consumer and community access to a comprehensive range of local health facilities, dislocation of the acute sector from primary health care facilities, disruption to long-term strategic planning, over-supply of facilities for high-volume cold surgery, under-supply of other facilities in acute care, escalation of wage, administrative and medical costs and the emergence of anti-competitive cartels, distortions to the labour market and the worsening of regional skill shortages.[27]

The BMA, RCM and most PAM groups expressed similar feelings in their official responses. MSF made similar points but more directed to industrial relations:

> Opted-out hospitals and services are likely to be used as a lever to weaken national pay bargaining for health service staff ... 'opted-

out' hospitals may also try to reduce the staffing levels and pay levels and worsen the conditions of other staff, leading to an additional strain on the remaining staff and risking poorer service to patients.[28]

But as John Chowcat, MSF National Officer, said in a statement to the author, 'MSF believes a national framework for all NHS staff should be maintained', but 'our experience of servicing local negotiations in other sectors of the UK economy means that MSF fulltime officers ... are already equipped to cope with local level bargaining'.

SGTs may increase the pay of some of their staff thus creating shortages elsewhere in the NHS, and they may cut pay to other staff thus reducing the morale of those who remain and making for a worse service.

NALGO voice the common frustrations of many unions:

> We have never been told why it is better for the ambulance service to opt-out, why a trading agency is better than a supplies department, why a private firm is better than a cheaper profit making estates division. Never has it been explained how such proposals improve the effectiveness of the service or how patient care is to benefit. What is clear is that such moves are an attempt to break up the integrated provision of health services and promote the private sector at the expense of the NHS. All such schemes undermine the system and its ability to deliver a comprehensive service.[29]

Most of the staff organizations neither believe nor accept the arguments for SGT status. Their fears are both for the NHS as a whole and for the pay and conditions of their members. The strength and depth of opposition is so great that it must be a major factor in the operation of SGTs and their success and/or failure. Alan Jinkinson, NALGO General Secretary, in a statement to the author in 1991, warned of problems ahead:

> The creation of NHS Trusts with powers to set their own condition of employment, central government's drive to dismantle what have been seen as the minimum guarantees of the Whitley System, and the notion that the package of pay and conditions will be increasingly determined locally and individually, rather than collectively, all serve to heighten apprehension among staff about the future shape and extent of the NHS. This in turn will feed through into staff having a lower sense of identity with the Service and growing problems of recruitment, retention and motivation.

The union concerns reflect their belief that market forces, supply and demand, will be used to reduce the pay and conditions of those workers tied into weak local labour markets. These will tend to be married women, part-time workers and the lower levels of the ancillary and clerical grades. The unions see a limited role for themselves in the protection of their most vulnerable members. The professions may do better through the protection of Pay Review and with stronger regional and national labour markets. Here the employers will assess their own strengths and weaknesses. Where the employer is in a weak position they will hide behind national agreements and deal with the unions locally as before about implementation, but where the employer is well placed then they will seek to pay some staff more and some less through local negotiations with individual staff. In all this employers will seek to reduce those areas for negotiation and therefore make union recognition and the bargaining arrangements less important.

SGTs and management wants

The managers and employers in SGTs, in contrast, are greatly in favour of the new freedoms and choices available to them in setting pay and conditions of service. While paying lip service to union recognition and the maintenance of national agreements, they are implementing far-reaching changes in staff profiles and skill mix. This will involve locally determined pay for the least skilled groups, an increase in the health care assistant as a replacement for all grades of unqualified staff involved in patient care and an extension of their tasks to the duties carried out by nurses and other professionals, and multi-skilling of some skilled craftsmen and professional groups. In this the changes to the internal labour market will be immense and there will be a rapid fall in the numbers of qualified professionals working throughout the NHS. Those that remain will increase their relative pay over the other ancillary and care assistant groups, but will receive increasingly lower relative pay than their colleagues working in the expanding private sector.

Many of these points and others on the treatment of unions and staff were explained in a document for senior managers in SGTs prepared in 1989 by senior personnel officers from the Trent RHA. It was called, 'Paper for General Managers of Self-governing Hospital Trusts. Personnel Policy and Practice', and

was marked 'strictly confidential'.[30] It was based on their best
guess of the future pattern of industrial relations in SGTs
although there is a strong suggestion that such a pattern may
have to be copied in DMUs. It is a most revealing account of the
thoughts of the men and women responsible for turning government policy into practice. The parallels with similar documents
issued for Civil Service agencies, local government and schools
indicated not so much a conspiracy, but that managers are
forced down a set path created by the logic of the new financial
systems in labour-intensive public services. Higher productivity
at lowest cost in the provision of management-defined 'core'
services and the selling off of the remainder.

The paper calls for 'an imaginative approach to human
resource management'. It assumes that in the short term the pay
determination methods will remain intact, but that in the
medium term there will be the need

> to create capacity to respond to increasing volatility; to create
> flexibility by minimizing open-ended commitments; to create
> elbow room by fixed-term contracts; contracting out; redundancy
> policies etc.[31]

Many of these points were made in Chapter 1 about flexibility
as the management panacea. The key concern is to allow local
managers greater control over 'manpower costs', because traditionally labour costs (80% of the total) have had to be treated by
local managers as a given cost of service operations. The document then provides a clear statement of the move away from
personnel management as part of a pluralist bargaining environment to a human resource management, unitarist and unilateral
form of decision-making. In this world the line managers control
industrial relations.

> Personnel policy has rarely been 'owned' by front-line managers
> and its perpetrators have generally been perceived as having
> rendered it an obstacle to operational effectiveness rather than a
> means to that end.[32]

Unit managers of the future will be given control over their
largest cost, labour costs. Local solutions can now be found to
local problems. The aim is to reduce costs, improve productivity
and reward incentive. Thus industrial relations becomes the
servant of corporate strategy. It is recognized that management
skills will need to be developed and more management time

devoted to these issues. Much of the Trent RHA document is a call to arms, a set of exhortations and homespun philosophy. Little or none is based on evidence.

The focus is that of a small business with the need to build identification with the business. This is seen as an important ingredient in winning over the staff against the wishes of their organizations. The answer, of course, is through 'satisfiers'. The document says,

> Given that SGTs will never be 'top payers' and are unlikely to lead any pay leagues; and given that in any case that pay generally tends to be a negative dissatisfier and only a very short-term satisfier and motivator – what do SGTs need to do to overcome this? How do they nevertheless identify people with the business and generate pride, ownership and commitment?[33]

The answer is a range of satisfiers. These include 'pride in a job well done', 'recognition and thanks' and 'social relevance in their work'. It is difficult to comment on this type of statement since it is so riddled with half-digested social science, the most phoney type of private sector experience and a total unwillingness to face the real experiences of health service staff. The rest of the document is a list, such as might be found in any elementary textbook on management, about improving communications, changing organizational culture and redefining the management relationship.

In industrial relations terms the issues are (1) the transfer of staff, and (2) trade union recognition – the recommendation is not to recognize any union and later pick and choose the favoured ones. A variety of models are put forward: single-union deals; multi-union recognition as now; and prime union recognition whereby one organization is recognized as the prime bargaining group for a functional group within the organization. The consequences of these alternatives are not explored, and the assumption is that the employer will make the running on these decisions.

It is also considered that the best form of consultation will be with the staff themselves and not the unions. The key point is the needs of the business. The view is that there might be a separation out of recognition of bargaining over substantive issues from those procedural activities such as discipline and grievance. The document suggests that SGTs have a choice as between no bargaining, the Whitley system or imposition of pay

rises. The tone of the argument takes no notice of the consequences of such behaviour, and importantly it ignores the fact
that if different SGTs adopt different strategies with different
results then the competition between them and the DMUs will
be dependent on a random set of industrial relations policies.

Again SGTs are given the choice between individual
performance related pay for everyone or a mixture of this for
some and national agreements for others. The staff and unions
are assumed passive in all this. It is inconceivable that any
complex business employing several thousand staff in a range of
occupations wanting to, let alone being able to, pay each individual on an individual basis. It is both unrealistic and massively
counterproductive.

The final irony is that a document based on management
freedom at local level and the choices founded in market economics wants 'to look at simplification and harmonization of
pay and terms and conditions of service'.[34] And worse is to
come. The people raging against the rigidity of Whitley and the
damage done by decisions being taken in far away places now
want, 'to develop into an "Employer's Federation" and may
wish this organization to take the lead on achieving a collective
bargaining framework for pay'.[35]

Having given away their powers on pay to a federation, they
also want to retain employer autonomy in respect of payments
to groups in scarce supply and those in common supply. The
idea is thus to keep Whitley when it benefits the employer and
abandon it when it does not. While this may be very sensible,
this pragmatic view hardly contains any of the high principles
expressed as the reason for reform. It does not understand the
severe problems that arise when employers respond too robustly
to short-term labour market forces.

In addition, performance related pay is strongly supported by
the Trent group. This is needed to reward performance and to
resolve the recruitment and retention issues. There is some
concern expressed about the need to keep such packages secret!

Union response to SGTs – the practice

Since the inauguration of the SGTs the unions have been preparing their members and local stewards for the changes in
bargaining arrangements and management attitudes. Their main
concern has been to establish SGT-based JCCs with the right to

negotiate over all relevant issues. In addition each union has been eager to win its place on the major JSSC and JCC while the horse-trading has been going on. The situation has been rife with rumour, kite-flying and the whiff of distant gunfire. It is difficult to distinguish belligerent attitudes from negotiating postures and between the will of individual senior managers and the hand of the Departments and government.

None the less, certain features are emerging along predicted lines. Most of the trade unions are seeking to establish collective bargaining rights and machinery, the professional associations are equally worried about these aspects of their activities but have been more internally divided as to the emphasis. The choice is between closer relations with the unions and the pursuit of collective bargaining, or closer links with other professional groups and the use of political influence and Pay Review Body protection.

NUPE issued advice on negotiating in an SGT which reflects their concerns.

> At present union recognition follows from the provisions of the General Whitley Council. If a hospital is given trust status, the Transfer of Undertakings Regulations provide for the transfer of collective agreements, including those covering trade union recognition. However, the Department of Health has said, 'It is for the Trust itself to consider whether it wishes to seek changes in existing recognition arrangements after the transfer. Trade union recognition may therefore be at risk.'[36]

NUPE supports joint union approaches to employers and insists on it with NALGO and COHSE. Recognition agreements should cover terms and conditions of employment, engagement and termination of employment, the allocation of work and duties, negotiating/consultation machinery, discipline and facilities for union officials. There should be joint consultation and negotiating committees with joint secretaries, alternate chair, regular meetings and the composition of the staff side should be in proportion with union membership. In addition, the management side should include Trust directors.

There must be a grievance, disputes and disciplinary procedure. These would be in line with ACAS guidelines and previous NHS agreements. For disputes there should still be an appeals procedure similar to the current Whitley Section 33, but NUPE want arbitration to ACAS if either party wants to go.

Other issues covered in the NUPE document include health and safety, equal opportunities and disclosure of information for collective bargaining purposes.

A similar document was also produced by NALGO for NALGO, NUPE and COHSE. This examines pay and conditions agreements. Under pay, protection must be sought for scales, annual uprating, appeal, allowances, new staff, increments, acting-up and protection on redeployment. Stewards are advised to watch out for changes in hours of work – normal, overtime, shifts, emergency cover and rotas – and further advice is given on annual leave, maternity leave, training, pensions and subsistence.[37]

COHSE is one of several unions issuing members in SGTs with advice as to how to bargain over pay. This is now part of most steward training. The main thrust is that the SGT should be forced to use all pay review and Whitley national agreements as the starting point and then negotiate additions on top. COHSE believe that:

> For the 110 000 staff employed in the Trusts and the trade unions that represent them, this change is the greatest challenge to their rights and achievements since the inception of the NHS.[38]

As Hector MacKenzie of COHSE said in a statement to the author,

> at national level through the Whitley Councils we are pursuing a strategy of 'Whitley plus'. An example of this is the 1991 ancillary pay deal where a national increase will be topped up by locally negotiated supplements and incentive schemes. We have made clear our determination to retain a full role for the Review Body and strongly opposed the pilot flexible pay scheme for nurses. We are also pressing for the new Health Care Assistant to be brought within a nationally negotiated framework.

The intentions of SGT personnel managers are to weaken the unions and reduce the pay and conditions of some staff. Problem Trusts, from the union perspective, include Northumbria Ambulance Service which is bypassing the unions, the Hillingdon Consortia and Epsom Health care are interested in 'prime' union recognition based on membership strength, and some, such as Freemans, are considering a single-union deal. For example, the Epsom Health Care Trust in its Employment Handbook dated April 1991 agrees only to minimum rights for trade union members under current legislation. There is no mention of trade unions/trade union representatives in either the grievance procedure or disciplinary procedure.

Whatever the bargaining arrangements, most SGTs have indicated their desire to negotiate with local union represen-tatives, their employees, rather than through union officials. Nearly three-quarters of the SGTs have said they will introduce performance related pay. This varies in form from group bonuses to individual payments. West Dorset Consortia intend to use salary bands with progress within each scale by a mixture of non-negotiable cost-of-living increases and merit payments. Many SGTs will use some form of local pay supplement for staff in short supply to combat labour market forces. Job evaluation and a single pay spine are finding favour among several Trusts.

Such are the uncertainties and difficulties in getting the system started in the best of times. These will be far worse in what is the worst of times. Management as well as unions express continual concern at the 'sunshine stories' of senior policy-makers. As one management report states, 'if badly organized, local bargaining arrangements could result in mutual distrust, a climate of conflict, a breakdown of communications and a very poor working environment'.[39] This management document, which was widely circulated just before SGTs were formally invested with their new powers, set out the varieties of bargaining arrangements open to managers with advantages and disadvantages listed. It is a straightforward document containing the most limited knowledge of the unions and expressing the conventional wisdom as espoused by managerial advisers and consultants. The options suggested include:

1. Recognize all Whitley unions; this avoids unrest and discontent among unions and their members, but it means too many unions, too many sets of negotiations, conflicts between trade unions and the professional associations, and too many small unions will still exist.
2. Recognize all but negotiate with a few – avoids unrest and unhappiness and central negotiations on some issues save time, but there remains the issue of representation for new staff organizations, there are still too many small unions, and it is not suitable for specific staff issues.
3. Recognize a few unions – few unions but wide coverage. This gives a more manageable number but deciding which to recognize is a problem, and there will be resentment among those not recognized.

4. JCCs for small numbers of unions which represent specific staff groups – deals with staff groups like Whitley, but ignores common problems. It can be time consuming and may encourage leapfrogging union claims.
5. Single union deal – not practical.
6. Use of staff council without unions – not sensible.
7. Individual only negotiations – too many negotiations.

The advice is to make sure that if there is collective bargaining then the structures are representative, practical and feasible. On this model the two front runners are recognizing all the unions but with only some 'invited to sit on negotiating committees', and balloting staff on the recognition of the organizations they want. This latter is a recipe for disaster if treated as genuine, or else it is an effort to remove collective bargaining by the back door. The quality of advice from senior management on these issues is very poor and presents line managers and staff with a serious shortfall in policy guidelines, direction and control.

The most recent survey to date of bargaining in SGTs was published in July 1991 by IRS[40] and provided the following summary: on recognition of trade unions the report concludes that 'with the exception of a maverick handful, derecognition of trade unions by the new trusts is uncommon'.[41] The normal practice is to do nothing new, that is to allow previous recognition agreements to stand. This means that by May 1991 there were only nine new formal recognition agreements. For example, First Community Health in Mid Staffordshire will recognize for consultation all organizations recognized by the Department of Health and working in the Trust. The membership of its Joint Staff Committee (JSC) is the managing director, assistant managing director (personnel), director of patient services and a locality manager. The basis of the staff side is that 'each organization recognized within the Trust for joint consultation and negotiation purposes will have an entitlement to one representative'.[42]

This is the main committee, but there is a sub-committee for health and safety and another one for policy, procedures, pay, and terms and conditions. The management side is composed as for the main committee but with the addition of a neighbourhood nurse manager and a professional head of service. The staff side has six representatives as determined by the recognized staff side organizations (see Figure 8.1). This is in line with general SGT practice following a Whitley type system. Most

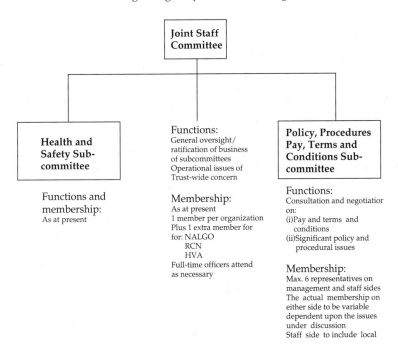

Figure 8.1 Consultation and negotiating machinery within one SGT – First Community Health: Mid-Staffordshire.
(*Source*: First Community Health (Mid-Staffordshire).)

SGTs are waiting before final decisions on recognition for collective bargaining purposes through new and/or revamped local JNCs/JCCs. Several Trusts are concerned about the nature of staff side representation, a concern going back to early Whitley and the McCarthy report. There is some limited evidence of a shift from trade union to functional representation. Many observers are watching developments at the Walsall Trust, which is seen as a model in terms of the maintenance of the collective bargaining tradition.

The recognition agreement between the Walsall Trust and the staff side JSC recognizes 15 unions: the big three nursing unions (RCN, NUPE and COHSE), the main white-collar unions of NALGO and MSF, three of the multi-occupational general unions (TGWU, UCATT and EETPU), the RCM, the ACB and five of the PAM unions (the CSP, BAOT, BOS, BDA and the Society of Radiographers). No GMB and no doctors'/dentists' representatives are recognized. The latter omission is due to their continued non-participation at this level of decision-making.

The document lays out the basic pluralist model of collective bargaining through general principles based on negotiation, consultation and information. It provides a list of the functions of the JSC, which include 'to establish and maintain regular methods of negotiation and consultation', 'to seek to prevent differences and resolve them should they arise', and 'to implement agreements entered into by the relevant National Joint Bodies'. In addition, time off for trade union/industrial relations duties and facilities for trade union representatives are detailed.[43]

Most Trusts have altered their grievance and disciplinary procedures to reflect new employer and management structures. The most important change has been the removal of an appeals stage beyond the employer. As IRS states:

> trusts tend to be creating their own internal panels to consider such issues at the final stage, a practice criticized by COHSE on the basis that the trusts will be performing the role of 'judge, jury and executioner in their own court.[44]

IRS concludes that,

> most trusts state that it is their intention to retain national pay rates for the majority of staff. However, the long-term objective of the majority is to move to local pay determination.[45]

The changes already taking place include new packages for new staff and special incentives to retain certain key staff – labour-market responses. Only the Northumbria Ambulance Service and the Lincolnshire Ambulance Service have radically departed from currently agreed national rates of pay. Many Trusts feel the new flexibility within Whitley agreements is enough and the move to local pay flexibility is viewed with much caution. However, some SGTs have changed terms and conditions for staff, mainly for the worse. The other movement is based on targeting specific groups with recruitment and retention problems, such as consultants and medical secretaries.

Most of this debate has excluded the doctors, and yet the history of the NHS illustrates the fundamental proposition that the doctors' fierce and powerful opposition to many of the elements within the original NHS put in place a political marker which later governments have been careful to circumnavigate.

Rows with doctors and the BMA are politically unsound, and to be avoided. Once within the NHS, largely on their own terms, the doctors have been able to cultivate a Department of Health which took its point of departure from the bargaining position of the doctors. Hospital consultants have dominated hospital based care and dominate the whole jobs hierarchy within hospitals. The traditional view of the NHS held by many senior consultants is that the service is a set of personal empires run by doctors with a quasi-ownership approach to management, and this tends to place the profession on the side of managers more often than on the side of other health workers. This attitude is now changing.

The power and influence of the medical profession stems in part from their central role as direct service providers and is in part due to the development of a deference culture by many groups in society towards doctors. In addition, doctors are often able to appeal directly to the public which makes both managers and civil servants wary of taking them on as a group.

In the new reformed NHS doctors in hospitals will face similar problems to other staff. Tighter budgets, tougher senior managers, commercial related patterns of patient treatment, and challenges to customary terms and conditions of service. There may well also be some dilution of the senior ranks. GPs may cope with the new systems in different ways – some delighted by the new pro-business ethos while others will continue to struggle under dwindling resources and discontented patients. The BMA is alarmed and antagonistic. It is particularly wary of the SGTs as employers of consultant labour. The BMA's campaign pack, under the slogan 'People lose out if our hospital opts out', provided detailed advice on the practicalities of opposing SGT status. It had no doubts as to the consequences of going Trust:

> The proposals promote profitability and cost-containment rather than improvements in the services and choices available to patients.[46]

As a leading official of the BMA said in a statement to the author,

> the major problem facing the BMA during the 1990s will be the devolution of negotiations as a consequence of the changes in the NHS management structure. There is every prospect that many – if not all – elements of doctors' terms of service will be subject to local negotiations.

In a document for internal use of its officials and lay representatives, the BMA makes its claim for collective bargaining:

> There is great urgency about establishing machinery to negotiate
> terms and conditions of service and contractual issues collectively
> at hospital, unit or trust level and about ensuring that this
> machinery is BMA driven ... it is imperative therefore that the
> BMA approach the staff of each hospital in the first wave and
> encourage them to elect a negotiating team to represent them in
> negotiations with trust management.[47]

The BMA having fought to reduce the collective nature of
bargaining in the NHS and of the NHS itself in 1948, is now
seeking to fight to keep alive the traditions of collective bargaining within the hospital system. Such is the transformation in the
health workers' perception of the state as a guardian of public
employees that even the doctors, the most powerful and conservative force within the industry, are happier with collective
bargaining than with other means of protecting their interests.

The common cause which the doctors increasingly accept is
shared with most health workers is the protection of a National
Health Service with, at least, minimum national agreements and
fully representative local bargaining. This acceptance of reality
has had the effect of bringing most of the 'labour partnerships' in
the NHS closer together. The PAMs are working through their
umbrella organization the FPO, the health visitors have merged
with MSF, the radiographers have joined the TUC, and the RCN
and RCM have flirted with joint activities with other unions. The
most important and tangible evidence of this move towards
common cause for health workers is the merger of NALGO,
NUPE and COHSE (discussed in earlier chapters). The firmness
of the timetable and the close cooperation of local union
activities makes the merger more likely.

CONCLUDING COMMENTS

The industrial relations in the NHS of the 1990s will be characterized by the pursuit of traditional issues by the unions and
staff at a time of increasing demand for their services – what Bill
Morris of the TGWU has called 'business as usual'. The changes
will be in the supply of services through control of budgets, a
private and public mix of provision, and new institutional
bargaining arrangements at employer level.

The national arrangements will bear witness to the continued relevance of a Whitley-type system and of the political convenience of the Pay Review Body solution. In both SGTs and DMUs the national elements of pay will continue to provide the minimum for most staff's basic pay. Terms and conditions agreements will be reached at national level through collective bargaining, although there will be an increase in the number of enabling agreements and ones with some local flexibility.

At employer and/or hospital level there will be more subcontracting out of some services, although this will be uneven and is less likely to be on the scale already achieved in the late 1980s. For the rest of the staff basic pay will fail to keep level with either inflation or the average earnings index. This means that they will be ever more dependent on local supplements in the form of performance related bonuses, job evaluated grades, overtime payments, shift premiums, and labour-market allowances. This will create uncertainty in the internal labour markets and make career moves for many staff harder to plan.

Competition for staff in short supply will be based mainly on conditions of service. The management grades will certainly receive benefits in kind in line with private sector practice and most of these will be negotiated on an individual package basis. The consequences for managers will be a wider range of remuneration packages, more mobility between the NHS and other employers, and an increase in the more 'professional' but less committed manager. This group will tend to fade away from trade union membership.

Most professional staff will find themselves better off in pay and conditions. But their daily delivery of the service will be under new and tighter management controls decided by managers who are not members of the profession and whose own pay will be based on performance targets derived from financial considerations outside patient care. Some will leave for the growing private sector, but most will stay under the pay protection umbrella of pay review and a strengthening labour market for most, exploited by their increasingly trade union-minded associations. There will be a reduction in the numbers of qualified nurses, midwives, health visitors and PAMs, and some dilution in the consultant grade.

There will grow up and expand a grade of unqualified professional: the therapy helper and the care assistant. This staff group will be composed largely of part-time women workers with no national collective bargaining protection who will be less union-ized than other staff. The potential for this group to help increase productivity at lowest cost may be considerable, and in practice they will substitute for qualified staff in politically less sensitive areas such as the care of the elderly, mentally handicapped and long-term sick. This group of staff, however, will be subsumed into the customs and practices of health service industrial relations and there is a strong potential for them to join unions, especially any merged version of NUPE/COHSE.

The ancillary staff are the most vulnerable to the changes. They are already under attack from subcontracting and the large number of low paid part-time women makes it difficult for unions to improve their lot at local level. The ambulance staff will also be deskilled on the whole and their position will become vulnerable to local labour market conditions. The tradi-tion of strong unionization and willingness to take action may prevent them from being exposed totally to the rigours of the market.

The A&C grades will increasingly dissolve into low paid clerical workers represented by NALGO and remaining the domain of low paid female staff. Their ability to act collectively will be curtailed by substitution and deskilling by information technology, although this will create new and better paid jobs as well. The more senior administrators in management grades will tend to drift away from NALGO and any form of collective bargaining.

The doctors in hospital service will be subject to a range of contradictory pressures based on their increasing numbers, more variation in their pay by specialism, and the dilution of the consultant grade. This will create very uneven and uncertain conditions for them throughout the NHS. The relationship with private practice may become even more blurred, but the BMA will tend to fight to maintain the bulk of doctors within a national framework agreement and as employees rather than as self-employed contractors of their own labour.

The unions will regroup and merge. Most will be recognized for bargaining purposes at local and national level, and union density will remain high among most groups. The main TUC-affiliated unions, NUPE, NALGO, COHSE and MSF, will work ever more closely together and will forge influential local bar-gaining groups. The smaller TUC groupings such as the TGWU, GMB and UCATT, might agree a transfer of members to the new larger groupings. The Royal Colleges and professional associations will remain steady in membership strength and financial stability. They will drift further towards trade union remedies pushed by local activists from below rather than embracing strategic policies from above. Their industrial relations departments will continue to grow in numbers and influence, and their training of stewards will have to become more intense as local bargaining and individual case loads increase.

The arrangements for bargaining at local level will formally allow for some functional negotiations as between the employer and traditional staff groupings. There will emerge the equivalent of the GWC at local level, already dubbed the Pay and Conditions Executive, and some bargains will be between individuals and individual unions and managers. In all this the personnel management function will be given more resources to treat with the unions, but will be more controlled by corporate management policies and the needs of the ever more powerful line managers – those set to deliver the contracts.

Whatever the arrangements, the issues will be familiar: low pay for large numbers of health workers, especially the ancillary staff and part-time women. Shortages of some types of staff in some areas met by a range of labour market pay adjustments. The fight to maintain traditional differentials as between different staff categories even in the face of changes in demand, technology and labour process. The allocation of overtime, shifts and extra payments will remain local issues. The operation of any PBR and job evaluation schemes will create more bargaining issues for local union representatives, as will disciplinary and grievance cases. There will be some local industrial action, and this will tend to be more damaging to managers locked into commercial contracts than in the past.

In fact most of these activities will increase at local level, and the unevenness of the pay and conditions as between different health employers will create great uncertainty and mean leap-frogging, labour poaching and hoarding, beggar-my-neighbour policies, and a real increase in inefficient management of labour. More power will devolve not just to local managers but to workplace trade union representatives as well. The 1990s for the NHS at workplace level may well resemble sections of British manufacturing industry in the 1960s. In this case expect wage drift, restrictive practices and unofficial industrial action to gain ground and in a few years hear senior managers and civil servants suggesting a radical reform programme of national bargaining arrangements to restore order, management's freedom to manage – and this in the name of an efficient system.

The real test of industrial relations in the NHS in the 1990s will be how the powerful influence of customary pay differences and job hierarchies survives the push for market solutions from employers and collective bargaining ones from the staff organizations. Health care more than any other service requires the cooperation and support of staff. Accepted private sector management attitudes to control and productivity, the cornerstones of the 1990 reforms, may prove disastrously wrongheaded for the traditions of NHS staff.

Statements from senior managers are not encouraging. One document on personnel management in SGTs ponders how to deal with 'renegades, subversives and opposers of what is being attempted'.[48] The recommendation is to get rid of them: that is, after all, how business operates. The NHS unions, professional associations, staff and users will find that very hard to swallow, especially when directed at health workers concerned to maintain traditional standards of care. The final word, however, must be given to the politician with the mission statement that forced through the NHS in the beginning, Nye Bevan:

> The field in which the claims of individual commercialism come into most immediate conflict with reputable notions of social values is that of health ... the collective principle asserts that the resources of medical skill and the apparatus of healing shall be placed at the disposal of the patient, without charge, when he or she needs them; that medical treatment and care should be a communal responsibility; that they should be made available to rich and poor alike in accordance with medical need and by no other criteria. It claims that financial anxiety in time of sickness is a serious hindrance to recovery, apart from its unnecessary cruelty. It insists that no society can legitimately call itself civilized if a sick person is denied medical aid because of lack of means.[49]

NOTES

1   Incomes Data Service (1991) *Pay in the Public Sector*, IDS, London, p. 11.
2   *Hospital Workers News*, issued by COHSE, GMB, NUPE and TGWU, 30/1/91.
3   IDS, op. cit., p. 13.

4   East Anglian Regional Health Authority (1990) *The Rubber Windmill*, East Anglian RHA, Cambridge.
5   Armstrong, M. and Murlis, H. (1988) *Reward Management: A Handbook of Salary Administration*, Kogan Page, London.
6   Seifert, R. (1990) 'Prognosis for Local Bargaining in Health and Education', *Personnel Management*, June, p. 56.
7   Labour Research Department (1990) *Performance Appraisal and Merit Pay*, LRD, London.
8   Warlow, D. (1989) Report of the conditions of employment of staff employed in the NHS, Department of Health, London, p. v.
9   Ibid., p. 1.
10   Ibid., p. 43.
11   Brown, W. and Rowthorn, B. (1990) *A Public Services Pay Policy*, Fabian Tract No. 542, The Fabian Society, London, p. 11.
12   Marginson, P., Edwards, P., Martin, R., Purcell, J. and Sisson, K. (1988) *Beyond the Workplace*, Basil Blackwell, Oxford.
13   McCarthy, W. (1976) *Making Whitley Work*, HMSO, London, p. 68.
14   Ibid., p. 73.
15   Ibid., p. 75.
16   ACAS (1987) *Labour Flexibility in Britain*, Occasional Paper 41, ACAS, London.
17   Local Authorities Conditions of Service Advisory Board (1991) *Pay in Local Government 1990*, LACSAB, London.
18   Fillingham, D. (1991) 'When Bargaining is a Life-or-Death Issue', *Personnel Management*, March.
19   Mailly, R., Dimmock, S. and Sethi, A. 'Industrial Relations in the NHS since 1979', in Mailly, R., Dimmock, S. and Sethi, A. (eds), *Industrial Relations in the Public Services*, Routledge, London, p. 139.
20   *Working for Patients* (1989), Cm 555, HMSO, London, p. 4.
21   Guy's Hospital, Lewisham Hospital and Mental Illness Services (1990), *Your Trust in the NHS: Consultation Document*, Guy's Hospital, London, p. 93.
22   Ibid.
23   Ibid., p. 94.
24   Ibid., p. 102.
25   Ibid.
26   Royal College of Nursing (1990) *RCN Response: Working for Patients*, RCN, London, p. 1.
27   Ibid., p. 6.
28   MSF (1990) *MSF Guide to the National Health Service and Community Care Bill*, MSF, London, p. 7.
29   NALGO (1990) *Patients before Profits: A Positive Agenda for the NHS*, NALGO, London, p. 16.
30   Trent RHA (1989) 'Paper for General Managers of Self-Governing Hospital Trusts: Personnel Policy and Practice – The Challenges of the SGTs', confidential document.
31   Ibid., p. 1.
32   Ibid., p. 2.
33   Ibid., p. 5.
34   Ibid., p. 11.

35 Ibid., p. 11.
36 NUPE (1990) *Negotiating in an NHS Trust*, NUPE, London, p. 3.
37 NALGO (1990) *Checklist for Negotiating in an NHS Trust*, NALGO, London.
38 COHSE (1990) *To Boldly Go? A COHSE Research Department Special Report on the Personnel Policies of the First Wave NHS Self Governing Trusts*, COHSE, London, p. 3.
39 North West Thames RHA (1989) *Preparing for Collective Bargaining in Directly Governed Hospitals and Self Governing Trusts: A Practical Guide*, Draft 1, circulated to other regions in 1990 and 1991, paragraph 1.4.
40 Industrial Relations Service (1991), 'NHS Trusts: Employment Terms and Bargaining Surveyed', *Employment Trends*, No. 491, 5 July, pp. 9–15.
41 Ibid., p. 9.
42 First Community Health: Mid-Staffordshire (1991) Constitution of Joint Staff Committee, p. 1.
43 Walsall Hospitals NHS Trust (1991) Recognition Agreement.
44 IRS, op. cit., p. 11.
45 Ibid., p. 9.
46 British Medical Association (1990) *Campaign Pack for Self-Governing Trusts*, BMA, London.
47 British Medical Association (1990) 'Conclusions on Representation of Doctors in Self-Governing Trusts', confidential internal document, BMA, London, p. 21.
48 Trent RHA, op. cit., p. 6.
49 Bevan, A. (1952) *In Place of Fear*, 1978 edn, Quartet Books, London, pp. 98–100.

Bibliography

Abel-Smith, B. (1960) *A History of the Nursing Profession*, Heinemann, London.

Abel-Smith, B. (1964) *The Hospitals 1800–1948*, Heinemann, London.

ACAS (1977) *Disciplinary Practice and Procedures in Employment*, Code of Practice 1, HMSO, London.

ACAS (1977) *Disclosure of Information to Trade Unions for Collective Bargaining Purposes*, Code of Practice 2, HMSO, London.

ACAS (1977) *Time Off for Trade Union Duties and Activities*, Code of Practice 3, HMSO, London.

ACAS (1978) *Royal Commission on the National Health Service: ACAS Evidence*, Report No. 12, ACAS, London.

ACAS (1983) *Collective Bargaining in Britain: Its Extent and Level*, Discussion Paper 2, ACAS, London.

ACAS (1987) *Labour Flexibility in Britain*, Occasional Paper 41, ACAS, London.

ACAS (1988) *Employee Appraisal*, Advisory Booklet No. 11, ACAS, London.

ACAS (1988) *Redundancy Handling*, Advisory Booklet No. 12, ACAS, London.

ACAS (1989) *Discipline at Work*, ACAS Advisory Handbook, ACAS, London.

ACAS (1989) *Job Evaluation: An Introduction*, Advisory Booklet No. 1, ACAS, London.

Armstrong, M. and Murlis, H. (1988) *Reward Management: A Handbook of Salary Administration*, Kogan Page, London.

Atkinson, J. (1984) 'Manpower Strategies for the Flexible Firm', *Personnel Management*, August, p. 28–31.

Bain, G. (1970) *The Growth of White-Collar Unionism*, Clarendon Press, Oxford.

Bain, G. (ed.) (1983) *Industrial Relations in Britain*, Blackwell, Oxford.

Bain, G., Coates, D. and Ellis, V. (1973) *Social Stratification and Trade Unionism*, Heinemann, London.

Bain, G. and Price, R. (1980) *Profiles of Union Growth*, Basil Blackwell, Oxford.

Barnard, K. and Harrison, S. (1986) 'Labour Relations in Health Services Management', *Social Science and Medicine*, 22(11), pp. 1213–28.

Batstone, E. (1980) 'What Have Personnel Managers Done for Industrial Relations?', *Personnel Management*, 12(6), p. 36–9.

Beardwell, M. (ed.) (1988) *The Directory of the NHS Whitley Council System 1988/0*, Mercia Publications, Keele.

Bellaby, P. and Oribabor, P. (1977) 'The Growth of Trade Union Consciousness among General Hospital Nurses Viewed as a Response to 'Proletarianisation'', *Sociological Review*, 25(4).

Bett, M. (1991) *Review Body for Nursing Staff, Midwives, Health Visitors and Professions Allied to Medicine: Eighth Report on Nursing Staff, Midwives and Health Visitors 1991*, Cm 1410, HMSO, London.

Bett, M. (1991) *Review Body for Nursing Staff, Midwives, Health Visitors and Professions Allied to Medicine: Eighth Report on Professions Allied to Medicine 1991*, Cm 1411, HMSO, London.

Bevan, A. (1952) *In Place of Fear*, Quartet Books, London.

Blackburn, R. (1967) *Union Character and Social Class*, B.T. Batsford, London.

Bosanquet, N. (ed.) (1979) *Industrial Relations in the NHS: the Search for a System*, King Edward's Hospital Fund for London, London.

Bosanquet, N. (1982) 'What is the Impact of Trade Unionism on the NHS?', *Health Services Manpower Review*, 8(2), pp. 11–13.

Bowman, G. (1967) *The Lamp and the Book: The Story of the RCN 1916–1966*, The Queen Anne Press, London.

Briggs, A. (1972) *Report of the Committee on Nursing*, Cmnd 5115, HMSO, London.

British Association of Occupational Therapists (1981) *The Way Ahead*, BAOT, London.

British Dietetic Association (1984) *Industrial Relations Code of Practice*, BDA, Birmingham.

British Medical Association (1981) *The BMA Division in the New Health Service*, BMA, London.

British Medical Association (1982) *Handbook for Hospital Junior Doctors*, BMA, London.

British Medical Association (1989) *The BMA: 'Friendly and Scientific'*, BMA, London.

British Medical Association *POWAR Handbook*, BMA, London.

British Medical Association (1990) *Campaign Pack for Self-Governing Trusts*, BMA, London.

British Medical Association (1990) *Conclusions on Representation of Doctors in Self-Governing Trusts*, confidential internal document, BMA, London, p. 21.

Brome, V. (1953) *Aneurin Bevan*, Longmans, Green & Co., London.

Brown, W. (ed.) (1981) *The Changing Contours of British Industrial Relations*, Basil Blackwell, Oxford.

Brown, W. and Rowthorn, R. (1990) *A Public Services Pay Policy*, Fabian Tract No. 542, The Fabian Society, London.

Buchan, J. and Pike, G. (1989) *PAMs into the 1990s – Professions Allied to Medicine: the Wider Labour Market Context*, Institute of Manpower Studies Report No. 175, Brighton.

Button, J. (1980) 'Responses to Industrial Action', *Health Services Manpower Review*, 6(1).

Caldwell, P., Croucher, R., Eva, D. and Oswald, R. (1980) *What's Happened to Safety?*, WEA, London.

Carpenter, M. (1982) 'The Labour Movement in the NHS: UK' in Sethi and Dimmock (eds), *Industrial Relations and Health Services*.

Carpenter, M. (1988) *Working for Health: the History of COHSE*, Lawrence and Wishart, London.

CASPE (1988) *How Did We Do? The Use of Performance Indicators in the NHS*, CASPE RESEARCH, London.

Chaplin, N. (1982) *Getting it Right?: the 1982 Reorganisation of the National Health Service*, IHSA, London.

Chartered Society of Physiotherapy (1982) *Fair Pay for Physiotherapists*, CSP, London.

Chartered Society of Physiotherapy (1987) *Source Book*, CSP, London.

Clay, H. (1929) *The Problem of Industrial Relations*, Macmillan, London.

Clay, T. (1987) *Nurses: Power and Politics*, Heinemann, London.

Clegg, H. (1979) *The Changing System of Industrial Relations in Great Britain*, Basil Blackwell, Oxford.

Clegg, H. (1979) *Local Authority and University Manual Workers; NHS Ancillary Staffs; and Ambulancemen: Standing Commission on Pay Comparability, Report No. 1*, Cmnd 7641, HMSO, London.

Clegg, H. (1980) *Nurses and Midwives: Standing Commission on Pay Comparability, Report No. 3*, Cmnd 7795, HMSO, London.

Clegg, H. (1980) *Professions Supplementary to Medicine: Standing Commission on Pay Comparability, Report No. 4*, Cmnd 7850, HMSO, London.

Clegg, H. and Chester, T. (1957) *Wage Policy and the Health Service*, Basil Blackwell, Oxford.

Cleminson, J. (1987) *Review Body for Nursing Staff, Midwives, Health Visitors and Professions Allied to Medicine: Fourth Report on Nursing Staff, Midwives and Health Visitors 1987*, Cm 129, HMSO, London.

Cleminson, J. (1987) *Review Body for Nursing Staff, Midwives, Health Visitors and Professions Allied to Medicine: Fourth Report on Professions Allied to Medicine 1987*, Cm 130, HMSO, London.

Cleminson, J. (1988) *Review Body for Nursing Staff, Midwives, Health Visitors and Professions Allied to Medicine: Fifth Report on Professions Allied to Medicine 1988*, Cm 361, HMSO, London.

Cleminson, J. (1989) *Review Body for Nursing Staff, Midwives, Health Visitors and Professions Allied to Medicine: Sixth Report on Nursing Staff, Midwives and Health Visitors 1989*, Cm 577, HMSO, London.

Cleminson, J. (1989) *Review Body for Nursing Staff, Midwives, Health Visitors and Professions Allied to Medicine: Sixth Report on Professions Allied to Medicine 1989*, Cm 578, HMSO, London.

Cleminson, J. (1990) *Review Body for Nursing Staff, Midwives, Health Visitors and Professions Allied to Medicine: Seventh Report on Nursing Staff, Midwives and Health Visitors 1987*, Cm 934, HMSO, London.

Cleminson, J. (1990) *Review Body for Nursing Staff, Midwives, Health Visitors and Professions Allied to Medicine: Seventh Report on Professions Allied to Medicine 1990*, Cm 935, HMSO, London.

COHSE (1976) *Union Steward's Handbook*, COHSE, London.

COHSE (1977) *Memorandum of Evidence to the Royal Commission on the National Health Service*, COHSE, London.

COHSE (1979) *Evidence to the Standing Commission on Pay Comparability: Nurses and Midwives*, COHSE, London.

COHSE (1990) *To Boldly Go? A COHSE Research Department Special Report on the Personnel Policies of the First Wave NHS Self-Governing Trusts*, COHSE, London.

Cowell, B. and Wainwright, D. (1981) *Behind the Blue Door: The History of the Royal College of Midwives 1881–1981*, Bailliere Tindall, London.

Cowie, V. (1977) 'Making Whitley Work', *Health Services Manpower Review*, special series 1, pp. 11–12.

Craik, W. (1955) *Bryn Roberts and the National Union of Public Employees*, George Allen and Unwin, London.

Craik, W. (1968) *Sydney Hill and the National Union of Public Employees*, George Allen and Unwin, London.

Crawshaw, R., Garland, M., Hines, B. and Anderson, B. (1990) 'Developing Principles for Prudent Health Care Allocation: The Continuing Oregon Experiment', *Western Journal of Medicine*, 152, pp. 441–6.

Daniel, W. and Millward, N. (1983) *Workplace Industrial Relations in Britain*, Heinemann, London.

Davison, W. (1973) *Report of an Inquiry into the Remuneration of Electricians Employed in the NHS*, Department of Employment, HMSO, London.

Department of Employment (1972) Industrial Relations Code of Practice, HMSO, London.

Department of Health (1989) *Health Service Indicators Guidance Directory*, HMSO, London.

Dimmock, S. (1982) 'Incomes Policy and Health Services in the UK' in Sethi and Dimmock (eds), op. cit.

Dimmock, S. and Farnham, D. (1975) 'Working with Whitley in Today's NHS', *Personnel Management*, 7(1), pp. 35–7.

Dimmock, S. and Mailly, R. (1982) 'Joint Consultation Arrangements in the NHS', *Industrial Relations Briefing Paper No.1*, Leeds University.

Dix, B. and Williams, S. (1987) *Serving the Public: Building the Union. The History of NUPE*, vol. I *1889–1928*, Lawrence and Wishart, London.

Donovan (1968) *Royal Commission on Trade Unions and Employers' Associations*, Cmnd 3623, HMSO, London.

Dyson, R. (1974) *The Ancillary Staff Industrial Action*, Leeds Regional Hospital Board.

Dyson, R. (1977) 'Can Whitley be Made to Work?', *Health Services Manpower Review*, special series 1, pp. 2–5.

Dyson, R. (1979) 'Consultation and Negotiation', in Bosanquet, N. (ed.), *Industrial Relations in the NHS: the Search for a System*.

Dyson, R. (1982) 'The Future of Whitley and Pay bargaining' in *Hospital and Health Services Review*, September, pp. 237–241.

Dyson, R. (1985) 'Making Whitley work: is it time to stop trying?', *Health Services Manpower Review*, (1), pp. 4–6.

Dyson, R. and Spary, K. (1979) 'Professional Associations', in Bosanquet N. (ed.) op. cit.

East Anglian Regional Health Authority (1990) *The Rubber Windmill*, East Anglian RHA, Cambridge.

Eckstein, H. (1964) *The English Health Service*, Harvard University Press, Cambridge, Mass.

Edwards, B. (1979) 'Managers and Industrial Relations', in Bosanquet, N. (ed.) op. cit.

Elwell, H. (1986) *NHS: The Road to Recovery*, Policy Study No. 78, Centre for Policy Studies, London.

England, J. (1981) 'Shop stewards in Transport House: a Comment upon the Incorporation of the Rank and File', *Industrial Relations Journal*, XII (5).

Epsom Health Care Trust (1991) *Employment Handbook*, Epsom Health Care NHS Trust.

Equal Opportunities Commission (1985) *Job Evaluation Schemes Free of Sex Bias*, EOC, London.

Equal Opportunities Commission (1991) *Equality Management: Women's Employment in the NHS*, EOC, Manchester.

Ferner, A. (1989) *Ten Years of Thatcherism: Changing Industrial Relations in British Public Enterprises*, Warwick Papers in Industrial Relations No. 27, University of Warwick.

Fewtrell, C. (1983) *The Management of Industrial Relations in the National Health Service*, IHSA, London.

Fillingham, D. (1991) 'When Bargaining is a Life-or-Death Issue', *Personnel Management*, March.

First Community Health: Mid-Staffordshire (1991) Constitution of Joint Staff Committee.

Fish, J. (1983) *The Guild of Hospital Pharmacists 1923–1983*, ICI.

Fisher, A. (1977) 'A Trade Union view of the McCarthy Report', *Health Services Manpower Review*, special series 1, pp. 8–10.

Flanders, A. (1970) 'Industrial Relations: What is Wrong with the System?', in *Management and Unions: The Theory and Reform of Industrial Relations*, Faber, London.

Foot, M. (1975) *Aneurin Bevan*, vol. 2, *1945–1960*, Paladin Books, London.

Fox, A. (1966) *Industrial Sociology and Industrial Relations*, Research Paper 3, Donovan Commission, HMSO, London.

Fredman, S. and Morris, G. (1989) 'The State as Employer: Setting a New Example', *Personnel Management*, August.

Fryer, R., Fairclough, A. and Manson, T. (1974) *Organisation and Change in the National Union of Public Employees*, Department of Sociology, University of Warwick.

Goldthorpe, J. (1974) 'Industrial Relations in Great Britain: A Critique of Reformism', *Politics and Society*, IV.

Goodrich, C. (1920) *The Frontier of Control*, G. Bell and Sons, London.

Gordan, H and Iliffe, S. (1977) *Pickets in White – the Junior Doctors Dispute of 1975*, MPU Publications, London.

Gourlay, R. (1983) *Presenting and Hearing Appeals in the NHS*, Health Services Manpower Review, Keele University.

Green, L. (1963) *Report of the Committee of Inquiry into the Recruitment, Training and Promotion of A&C Staff in the Hospital Service*, HMSO, London.

Greenborough, H. (1986) *Review Body for Nursing Staff, Midwives, Health Visitors and Professions Allied to Medicine: Third Report on Professions Allied to Medicine 1989*, Cmnd 9783, HMSO, London.

Grey-Turner, E. and Sutherland, F. (1982) *History of the British Medical Association*, vol. II, *1932–1982*, BMA, London.

Griffiths, R. (1983) *NHS Management Inquiry*, Letter to Secretary of State.

Guillebaud, C. (1956) *Report of the Committee of Enquiry into the Cost of the National Health Service*, Cmd 9663, HMSO, London.

Guy's Hospital, Lewisham Hospital and Mental Illness Services (1990) *Your Trust in the NHS: Consultation Document*.

Hall, N. (1957) *Report on the Grading Structure of the Administrative and Clerical Staff in the Hospital Service*, HMSO, London.

Halsbury (1974a) *Report of the Committee of Inquiry into the Pay and Related Conditions of Service of Nurses and Midwives*, DHSS, London.

Halsbury (1974b) *Report of the Committee of Inquiry into the Pay and Related Conditions of Service of the Professions Supplementary to Medicine and Speech Therapists*, DHSS, London.

Ham, C. (1982) *Health Policy in Britain*, Macmillan, London.

Hancock, C. (1991) 'Pay Flexibility and the NHS', *Health Services Management*, February.

Harrison, S. (1980) 'Responses to Industrial Action: Assumptions and Evidence', *Health Services Manpower Review*, 6(1), pp. 15–19.

Harrison, S. (1988) 'The Closed Shop and the National Health Service: A Case Study in Public Sector Labour Relations', *Journal of Social Policy*, 17(1), pp. 61–81.

Hayek, F. (1984) *1980s Unemployment and the Unions*, Institute of Economic Affairs, London.

Health Visitors Association (1985) *Local Representatives' Handbook*, HVA, London.

Holdsworth, T. (1991) *Review Body on Doctors' and Dentists' Remuneration*, Twenty-First Report 1991, Cm 1412, HMSO, London.

Hyman, R. (1972) *Disputes Procedure in Action*, Heinemann Educational, London.

Incomes Data Service (1991) *Pay in the Public Sector: Current Patterns and Trends*, IDS, London.

Industrial Relations Service (1991) 'NHS Trusts: Employment Terms and Bargaining Survey', *Employment Trends*, No. 491, 5 July, pp. 9–15.

Industrial Relations Service (1991) 'Discipline at Work 1: Practice', *Employment Trends*, No. 493, 2 August, pp. 6–14.

Industrial Relations Service (1991) 'Discipline at Work 2: Procedures', *Employment Trends*, No. 494, 16 August pp. 5–14.

Industrial Relations Service (1991) 'The New Green Paper', *Legal Bulletin* 431, 16 August, pp. 2–6.

International Labour Office (1967) *Examination of Grievances Recommendation*, No. 130, ILO, Geneva.

Kerr, A. and Sachdev, S. (1991) *Third Among Equals: An Analysis of the 1989 Ambulance Dispute*, forthcoming.

Knight, C. (1985) 'Are Bonus Schemes on Borrowed Time?', *Health and Social Service Journal*, January, p. 132.

Kuhn, J. (1961) *Bargaining in Grievance Settlement*, Columbia University Press, New York.

Labour Research Department (1984) *Defending the NHS*, LRD, London.

Labour Research Department (1990) *Performance Appraisal and Merit Pay*, LRD, London.

Local Authorities Conditions of Service Advisory Board (1991) *Pay in Local Government 1990*, LACSAB, London.

Lee, J. (1980) *My Life with Nye*, Jonathan Cape, London.

Leopold, J. (1985) 'Whitley II: Prizes and Penalties', *Health and Social Service Journal*, January, pp. 128–9.

Leopold, J. and Beaumont, P. (1986) 'Pay Bargaining and Management strategy in the National Health Service', *Industrial Relations Journal*, 17(1), pp. 32–45.

Levitt, R. and Wall, A. (1984) *The Reorganised National Health Service*, Croom Helm, London.

Little, E. (1932) *History of the British Medical Association*, vol. 1, *1832–1932*, BMA, London.

Loveridge, R. (1971) *Collective Bargaining by National Employees in the UK*, Institute of Labor and Industrial Relations, University of Michigan, Wayne State.

Mailly, R., Dimmock, S. and Sethi, A. (1989) (eds) *Industrial Relations in the Public Services*, Routledge, London.

Mailly, R., Dimmock, S. and Sethi, A. (1989) 'Industrial Relations in the NHS since 1979', in Mailly, Dimmock and Sethi (eds), *Industrial Relations in the Public Services*.

Marginson, P., Edwards, P., Martin, R., Purcell, J. and Sisson, K. (1988) *Beyond the Workplace*, Basil Blackwell, Oxford.

McCarthy, W. (1966) *The Role of Shop Stewards in British Industrial Relations*, Research Paper 1, Donovan Commission, HMSO, London.

McCarthy, W. (1976) *Making Whitley Work: A Review of the Operation of the NHS Whitley Council System*, HMSO, London.

Megaw, J. (1982) *Report of an Inquiry into Civil Service Pay*, Cmnd 8590, HMSO, London.

Merrison, A. (1979) *Royal Commission on the National Health Service*, Cmnd 7615, HMSO, London.

Metcalf, D. (1989) 'When Water Notes Dry Up: the Impact of the Donovan Reform Proposals and Thatcherism at Work on Labour Productivity in British Manufacturing Industry', *British Journal of Industrial Relations*, XXVII(1), pp. 1–32.

Miles, A. and Smith, D. (1969) *Joint Consultation – Defeat or Opportunity?*, King Edwards Hospital Fund for London, London.

Miliband, R. (1973) *The State in Capitalist Society*, Quartet Books, London.

Millward, N. and Stevens, M. (1986) *British Workplace Industrial Relations 1980–1984*, Gower, Aldershot.

Moodie, I. (1976) *The Society of Radiographers. Fifty Years of History*, Society of Radiographers, London.

Morris, G. (1986) *Strikes in Essential Services*, Mansell Publishing, London.

Morris, G. and Rydzkowski, S. (1984) 'Anatomy of a dispute', *Health and Social Services Journal*, 12th April.

Morris, G. and Rydzkowski, S. (1984) 'Approaches to Industrial Action in the National Health Service', *Industrial Law Journal*, 13, pp. 153–64 .

MSF (1990) *MSF Guide to the National Health Service, and Community Care Bill*, MSF, London.

NAHA and King's Fund (1985) *NHS Pay: A Time for Change*, NAHA and the King Edward's Hospital Fund for London, London.

NAHA and King's Fund (1987) *NHS Pay: Achieving Greater Flexibility*, NAHA and the King Edward's Hospital Fund for London.

NAHA and King's Fund (1988) *Flexible Pay Systems*, NAHA and the King Edward's Hospital Fund for London.

NALGO (1989) *Member's Handbook*, NALGO, London.

NALGO (1990) *Checklist for Negotiating in an NHS Trust*, NALGO, London.

NALGO (1990) *Patients before Profits: A Positive Agenda for the NHS*, NALGO, London.

National Audit Office (1987) *Competitive Tendering for Support Services in the NHS*, HMSO, London.

National Audit Office (1990) *Managing Computer Projects in the NHS*, HMSO, London.

NBPI (National Board for Prices and Incomes) (1967) *Pay and Conditions of Service of Manual Workers in Local Authorities, the National Health Service, Gas and Water Supply*, Report No. 29, Cmnd 3230, HMSO, London.

NBPI (National Board for Prices and Incomes) (1971) *The Pay and Conditions of Service of Ancillary Workers in the National Health Service*, Report No. 166, Cmnd 4644, HMSO, London.

Newman, G. (1982) *Path to Maturity: NALGO 1965–1980*, NALGO, London.

North West Thames RHA (1989) *Preparing for Collective Bargaining in Directly Governed Hospitals and Self Governing Trusts: A Practical Guide*, Draft 1.

NUPE (1972) *Union Steward: a Handbook for Health Service Ancillary Staffs*, NUPE, London.

NUPE (1990) *Negotiating in an NHS Trust*, NUPE, London.

Parry, N. and Parry, J. (1977) 'Professionalism and Unionism: Aspects of Class Conflict in the NHS', *Sociological Review*, 25(4).

Patients First: *Consultative Paper on the Structure and Management of the NHS in England and Wales* (1979) DHSS, London.

Peach, L. (1986) 'A New Direction for Personnel in the NHS', *Health Services Manpower Review*, 12(1), 6–8.

Peet, J. (1987) *Healthy Competition*, Policy Study No. 86, Centre for Policy Studies, London.

Pethyridge, F. (1977) 'The McCarthy Report', *Health Services Manpower Review*, special series 1, pp. 6–7.

Pilkington, H. (1960) *Report of the Royal Commission on Doctors' and Dentists' Remuneration 1957–1960*, Cmnd 939, HMSO, London.

Phelps Brown, H. (1979) *The Inequality of Pay*, Oxford University Press, Oxford.

Pollard, S. (1968) *The Genesis of Modern Management*, Penguin.

Priestley, R. (1955) *Royal Commission on the Civil Service*, Cmnd 9613, HMSO, London.

Privatisation Research Unit (1990) *The NHS Privatisation Experience*, COHSE, GMB, NALGO, NUPE and TGWU.

Privatisation Research Unit (1991) *Tender Tactics*, COHSE, GMB, NALGO, NUPE and TGWU.

Purcell, J. and Sisson, K. (1983) 'Strategies and Practice in the Management of Industrial Relations', in Bain (ed.), op. cit.

Report of the Resource Allocation Working Party (1976), HMSO, London.

Routh, G. (1980) *Occupation and Pay in Great Britain 1906–1979*, Macmillan, London.

Royal College of Midwives (1986/7) *Members' Handbook*, RCM, London.

Royal College of Midwives (1987) *Evidence to the Review Body for Nursing Staff, Midwives, Health Visitors and Professions Allied to Medicine for 1988*, RCM, London.

Royal College of Nursing (1981) *Members' Handbook*, RCN, London.

Royal College of Nursing (1986) *What the RCN Stands For*, RCN, London.

Royal College of Nursing (1986) Constitution for RCN Branches, RCN, London.

Royal College of Nursing (1990) *RCN Response: Working for Patients*, RCN, London.

Seifert, R. (1987) *Teacher Militancy: A History of Teacher Strikes 1896–1987*, Falmer Press, Sussex.

Seifert, R. (1989) 'Performance Indicators in the NHS' *Radiography Today*, May, pp. 30–3.

Seifert, R. (1990) 'Prognosis for Local Bargaining in Health and Education', *Personnel Management*, June.

Sethi, A. and Dimmock, S. (eds) (1982) *Industrial Relations and Health Services*, Croom Helm, London.

Sethi, A., Stansel, R., Solomon, N. and Dimmock, S. (1982) 'Collective Bargaining among Non-professional and Allied Professional Employees in the Health Sector' in Sethi and Dimmock (eds), *Industrial Relations and Health Services*.

Smith, A. (1776) *The Wealth of Nations*, Everyman 1910 edn, London.

Smith, C. (1987) *Technical Workers*, Macmillan, London.

Spens, W. (1948) *Report of the Interdepartmental Committee on the Remuneration of Consultants and Specialists*, Cmd 7420, HMSO, London.

Spoor, A. (1967) *White Collar Union: Sixty Years of NALGO*, Heinemann, London.

Social Services Committee of the House of Commons (1989) *Resourcing the NHS: Whitley Councils*, Third Report and Minutes of Evidence, HMSO, London.

Social Services Committee of the House of Commons (1989) *Resourcing the NHS: Midwives' Regrading 1988–89*, Fourth Report and Minutes of Evidence, HMSO, London.

Social Services Committee of the House of Commons (1989) *Resourcing the NHS: Working for Patients*, Fifth Report and Minutes of Evidence, HMSO, London.

Social Services Committee of the House of Commons (1989) *Resourcing the National Health Service: the Government's Plans for the Future of the NHS*, Eighth Report and Minutes of Evidence, HMSO, London.

Society of Radiographers (1974) *Submission of Evidence by The Society of Radiographers to the Halsbury Committee of Inquiry*, SoR, London.

Stevens, M., Millward, N. and Smart, D. (1989) 'Trade Union Membership and the Closed Shop in 1989', *Employment Gazette*, November.

Stevens, M. and Wareing, A. (1990) 'Union Density and Workforce Composition', *Employment Gazette*, August, pp. 403–13.

Swabe, A., Collins, P. and Walden, R. (1986) 'The Resolution of Disputes in the NHS', *Health Services Manpower Review*, 12(1), pp. 3–5.

Taylor, R. (1978) *The Fifth Estate: Britain's Unions in the Seventies*, Routledge and Kegan Paul, London.

Thomason, G. (1985) 'The Pay Review Bodies', *Health Services Manpower Review*, 11(3), pp. 3–6.

Thorold Rogers, J. (1923) *Six Centuries of Work and Wages*, T. Fisher Unwin Ltd, London.

Trades Union Congress (1970) *Productivity Bargaining*, TUC, London.

Trades Union Congress (1975) *Job Evaluation and Merit Rating*, TUC, London.

Trades Union Congress Health Services Committee (1981) *Improving Industrial Relations in the National Health Service*, TUC, London.

Trainor, R. (1987) *A Directory of the NHS Whitley Council System 1986–7*, Health Services Manpower Review, University of Keele.

Treasury HM (1986) *Using Private Enterprise in Government*, HMSO, London.

Treloar, S. (1981) 'The Junior Hospital Doctors' Pay Dispute 1975–1976: An Analysis of Events, Issues and Conflicts', *Journal of Social Policy*, 10, pp. 1–30.

Trent RHA (1989) 'Paper for General Managers of Self-Governing Hospital Trusts: Personnel Policy and Practice – the Challenges of the SGTs', confidential document.

Turner, H. (1962) *Trade Union Growth, Structure and Policy*, George Allen and Unwin, London.

Vulliamy, D. and Moore, R. (1979) *Whitleyism and Health*, Studies for Trade Unionists, 5, no. 19, WEA, London.

Wagstaff, A. (1988) *Some Regression-Based Indicators of Hospital Performance*, University of York.

Walsall Hospitals NHS Trust (1991) Recognition Agreement.

Walton, R. and McKersie, R. (1965) *A Behavioral Theory of Labour Negotiations*, McGraw Hill, New York.

Warlow, D. (1989) Report of the conditions of employment of staff employed in the NHS, Department of Health, London.

Watkin, B. (1978) *The National Health Service: the First Phase 1948–1974 and After*, George Allen and Unwin, London.

Webb, S. and Webb, B. (1920) *Industrial Democracy*, Longmans, Green & Co. Ltd, London.

Webster, C. (1988) *The Health Services since the War*, vol. 1, *Problems of Health Care: the National Health Service before 1957*, HMSO, London.

West, C. and Goodman, T. (1979) 'Disputes Procedures and Grievance Procedures', in Bosanquet, N. (ed.), *Industrial Relations in the NHS: the Search for a System*.

Whincup, M. (1979) 'Discipline and Dismissal: Legal Aspects', in Bosanquet, N. (ed.), *Industrial Relations in the NHS: the Search for a System*.

Whincup, M. (1985) *Law and Practice of Dismissal in the Health Service*, Mercia Publications, Keele.

Whitley, J. (1917) *Interim Report on Joint Standing Industrial Councils*, Cd 8606, HMSO, London.

Wilkins, G. (1989) *Review Body on Doctors' and Dentists' Remuneration*, Nineteenth Report 1989, Cm 580, HMSO, London.

Wilkins, G. (1990) *Review Body on Doctors' and Dentists' Remuneration*, Twentieth Report 1990, Cm 937, HMSO, London.

Williams, D. (1977) 'Making Whitley Work', *Health Services Manpower Review*, special series 1, pp. 13–14.

Winchester, D. (1983) 'Industrial Relations in the Public Sector' in Bain, G. (ed.) *Industrial Relations in Britain*.

Wootton, B. (1962) *The Social Foundations of Wage Policy*, Unwin University Books, London.

Working for Patients (1989), Cm 555, HMSO, London.

Names index

Subject index

Numbers in italic refer to tables, those in bold refer to figures